Kitchen Princess

8

Natsumi Ando

Story by Miyuki Kobayashi

Translated by Satsuki Yamashita

Adapted by Nunzio Defilippis and Christina Weir

Lettered by North Market Street Graphics

Ballantine Books · New York

A Del Rey Manga/Kodansha Trade Paperback Original

Kitchen Princess volume 8 copyright © 2007 by Natsumi Ando and Miyuki Kobayashi
English translation copyright © 2008 by Natsumi Ando and Miyuki Kobayashi

Published in the United States by Del Rey Books, an imprint of The Random House Publishing Group, a division of Random House, Inc., New York.

DEL REY is a registered trademark and the Del Rey colophon is a trademark of Random House, Inc.

Publication rights arranged through Kodansha Ltd.

First published in Japan in 2007 by Kodansha Ltd., Tokyo.

ISBN 978-0-345-50805-8

Printed in the United States of America

www.delreymanga.com

9 8 7 6 5 4 3 2 1

Translator: Satsuki Yamashita
Adaptors: Nunzio DeFilippis and Christina Weir
Lettering: North Market Street Graphics
Original cover design by Akiko Omo

Contents

This volume's featured menu is high tea. As I worked on this volume I tried out various high teas at different locations. Just seeing the tea set placed in front of me made me feel like a celebrity.

—Natsumi Ando

Honorifics Explained

Throughout the Del Rey Manga books, you will find Japanese honorifics left intact in the translations. For those not familiar with how the Japanese use honorifics and, more important, how they differ from American honorifics, we present this brief overview.

Politeness has always been a critical facet of Japanese culture. Ever since the feudal era, when Japan was a highly stratified society, use of honorifics—which can be defined as polite speech that indicates relationship or status—has played an essential role in the Japanese language. When addressing someone in Japanese, an honorific usually takes the form of a suffix attached to one's name (example: "Asuna-san"), is used as a title at the end of one's name, or appears in place of the name itself (example: "Negi-sensei," or simply "Sensei!").

Honorifics can be expressions of respect or endearment. In the context of manga and anime, honorifics give insight into the nature of the relationship between characters. Many English translations leave out these important honorifics and therefore distort the feel of the original Japanese. Because Japanese honorifics contain nuances that English honorifics lack, it is our policy at Del Rey not to translate them. Here, instead, is a guide to some of the honorifics you may encounter in Del Rey Manga.

-san: This is the most common honorific and is equivalent to Mr., Miss, Ms., or Mrs. It is the all-purpose honorific and can be used in any situation where politeness is required.

-sama: This is one level higher than "-san" and is used to confer great respect.

-dono: This comes from the word "tono," which means "lord." It is an even higher level than "-sama" and confers utmost respect.

-kun: This suffix is used at the end of boys' names to express familiarity or endearment. It is also sometimes used by men among friends, or when addressing someone younger or of a lower station.

-chan: This is used to express endearment, mostly toward girls. It is also used for little boys, pets, and even among lovers. It gives a sense of childish cuteness.

Bozu: This is an informal way to refer to a boy, similar to the English terms "kid" and "squirt."

Sempai/ Senpai: This title suggests that the addressee is one's senior in a group or organization. It is most often used in a school setting, where underclassmen refer to their upperclassmen as "sempai." It can also be used in the workplace, such as when a newer employee addresses an employee who has seniority in the company.

Kohai: This is the opposite of "sempai" and is used toward underclassmen in school or newcomers in the workplace. It connotes that the addressee is of a lower station.

Sensei: Literally meaning "one who has come before," this title is used for teachers, doctors, or masters of any profession or art.

-[blank]: This is usually forgotten in these lists, but it is perhaps the most significant difference between Japanese and English. The lack of honorific means that the speaker has permission to address the person in a very intimate way. Usually, only family, spouses, or very close friends have this kind of permission. Known as *yobisute,* it can be gratifying when someone who has earned the intimacy starts to call one by one's name without an honorific. But when that intimacy hasn't been earned, it can be very insulting.

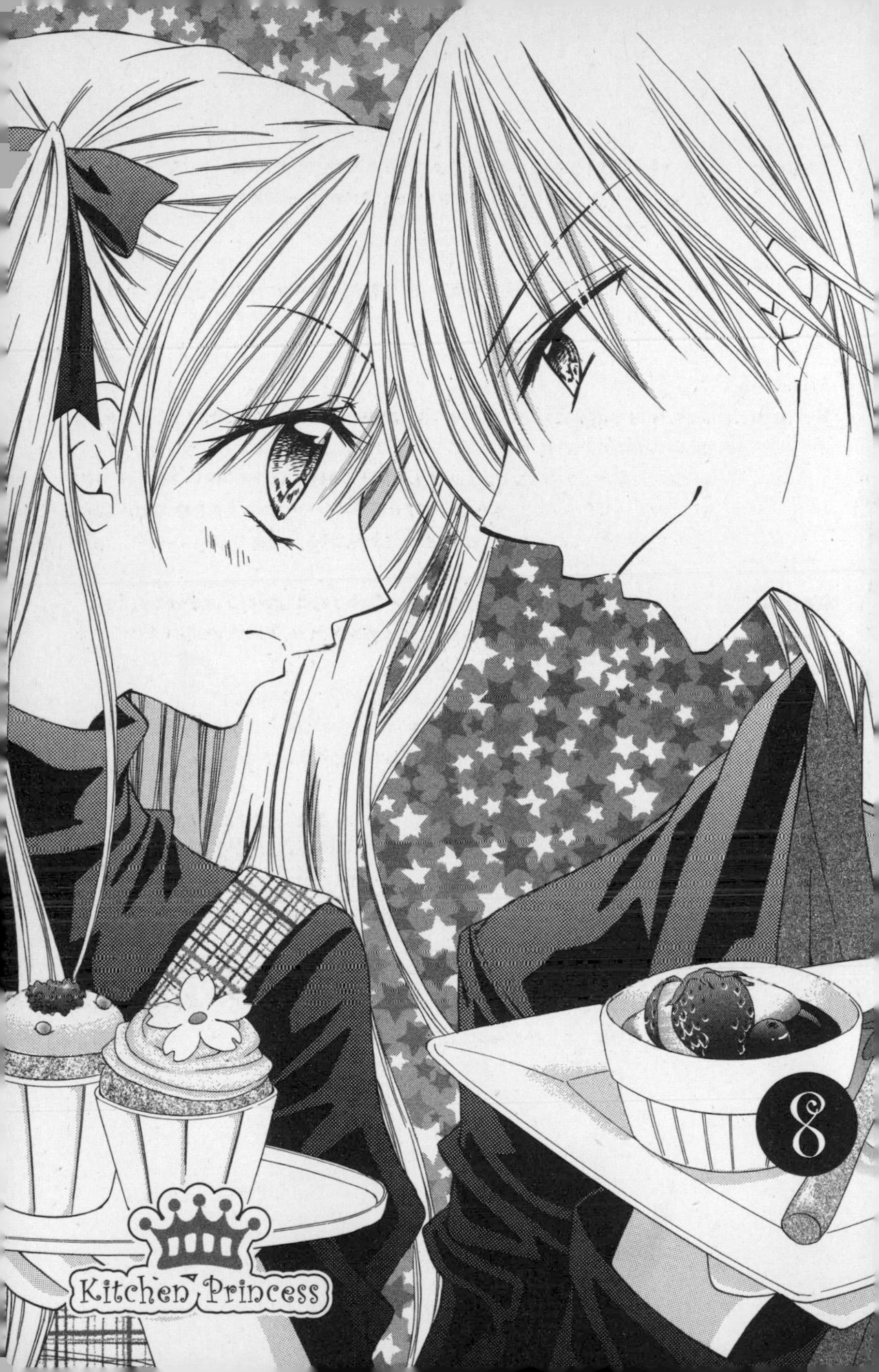
8
Kitchen Princess

Kitchen Princess

Table of Contents

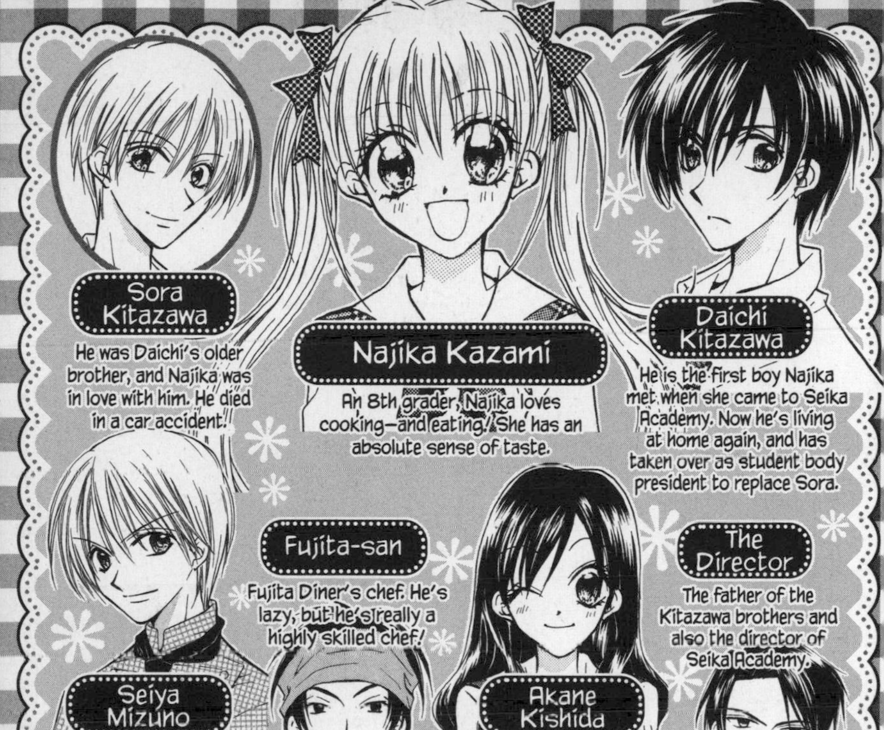
Sora Kitazawa
He was Daichi's older brother, and Najika was in love with him. He died in a car accident.
Najika Kazami
An 8th grader, Najika loves cooking—and eating! She has an absolute sense of taste.
Daichi Kitazawa
He is the first boy Najika met when she came to Seika Academy. Now he's living at home again, and has taken over as student body president to replace Sora.
Fujita-san
Fujita Diner's chef. He's lazy, but he's really a highly skilled chef!
The Director
The father of the Kitazawa brothers and also the director of Seika Academy.
Seiya Mizuno
An up-and-coming star pastry chef. He is the son of the head of the Mizuno Group.
Akane Kishida
A teen model who is popular in the fashion magazines. At first, she didn't like Najika, but now they've made up and are great friends.

The Story So Far...

Kitchen Princess

Najika lost her parents when she was young and lived in Lavender House, an orphanage in Hokkaido. She joined Seika Academy in Tokyo to find her Flan Prince, a boy who saved her from drowning when she was young. There she met Sora, Daichi, and Akane. Najika entered the National Confectionary Competition but lost in the finals, owing to her grief over the death of Sora. Najika was transferred into the regular class at the Academy—and the school welcomed a new special student to replace her. That student is Seiya Mizuno, who looks exactly like Sora. Furthermore, Najika was shocked to find out that *he* might be her "Flan Prince"!

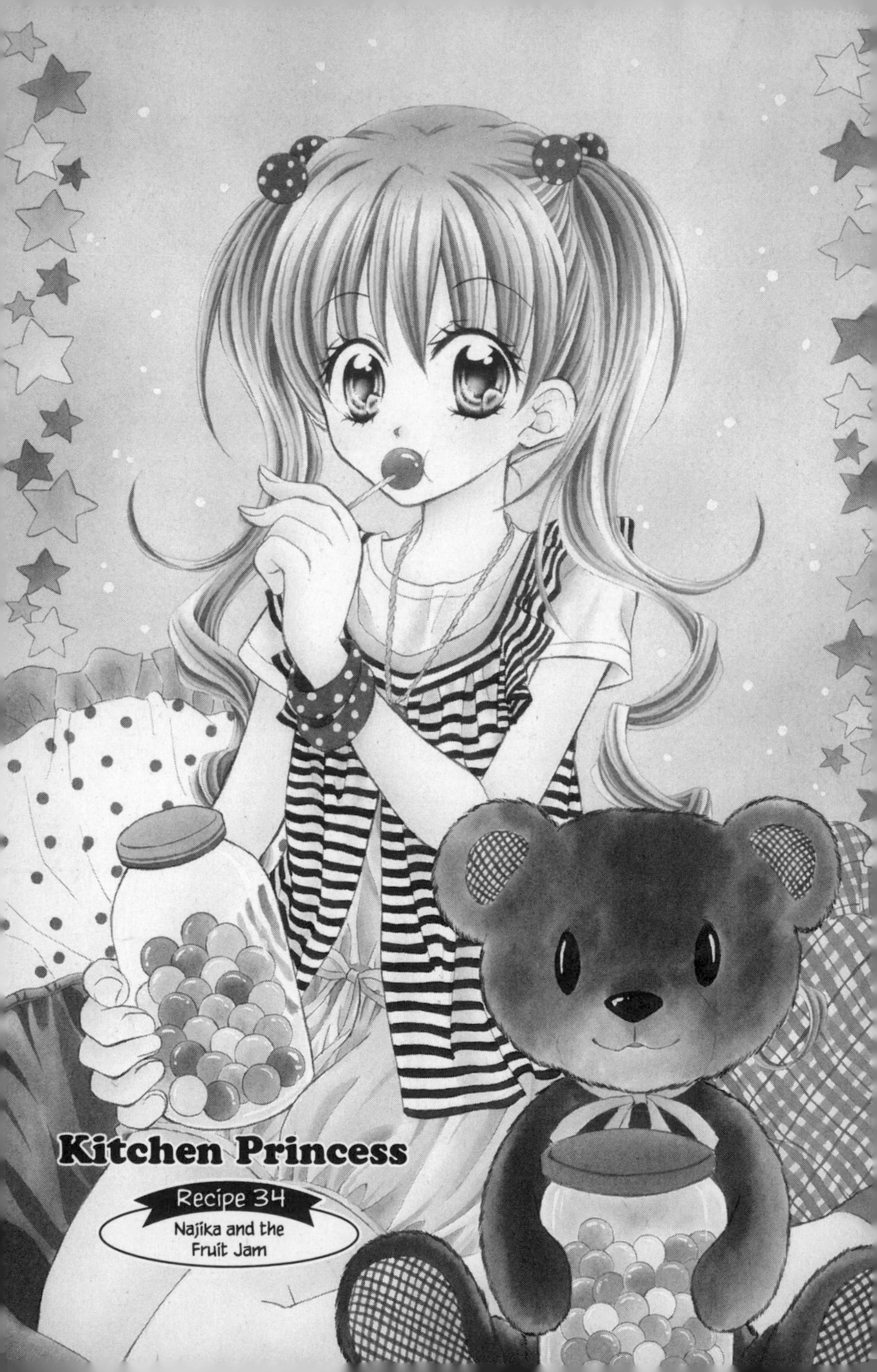
Kitchen Princess
Recipe 34
Najika and the Fruit Jam

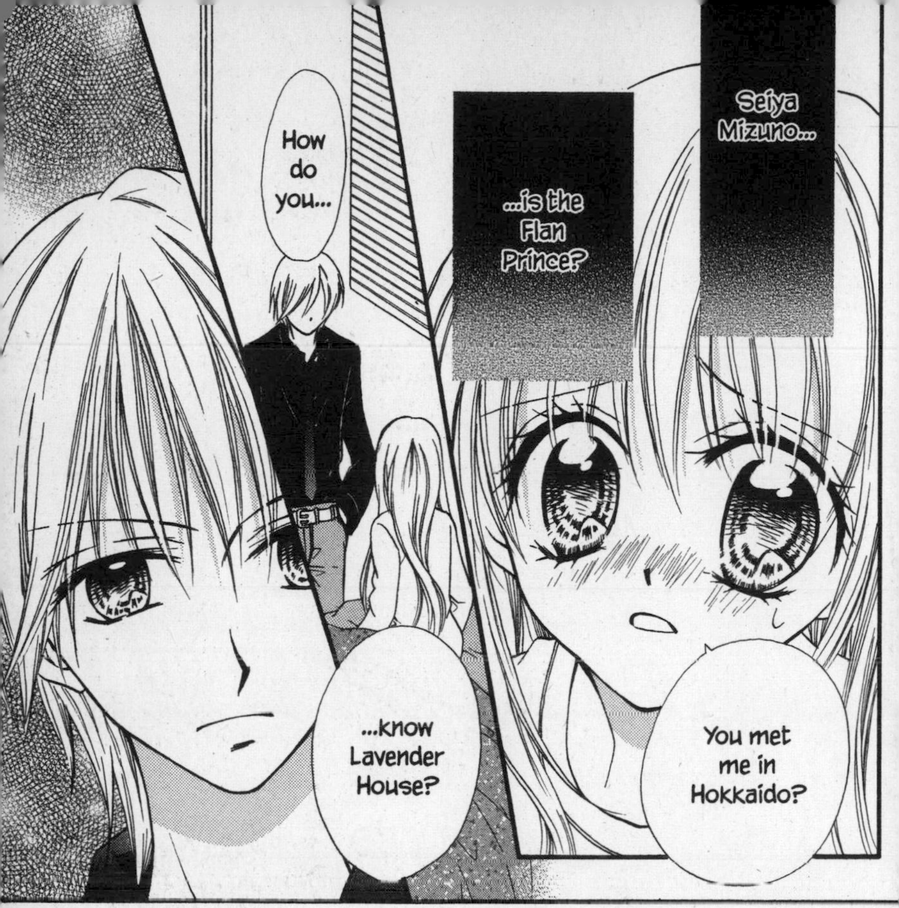
Seiya Mizuno...
...is the Flan Prince?
You met me in Hokkaido?
How do you...
...know Lavender House?

About Recipe 34's Splash Page

You can't tell in this black-and-white version, but I wanted to make this splash page look cheerful, so I used a lot of primary colors. But I didn't make the main lines thick enough, so it turned out a little fuzzy.

I tried making the jam in this chapter, but I had the heat on too high and the water evaporated and it came out too sweet.

But once I added yogurt instead of sugar, it was really delicious.

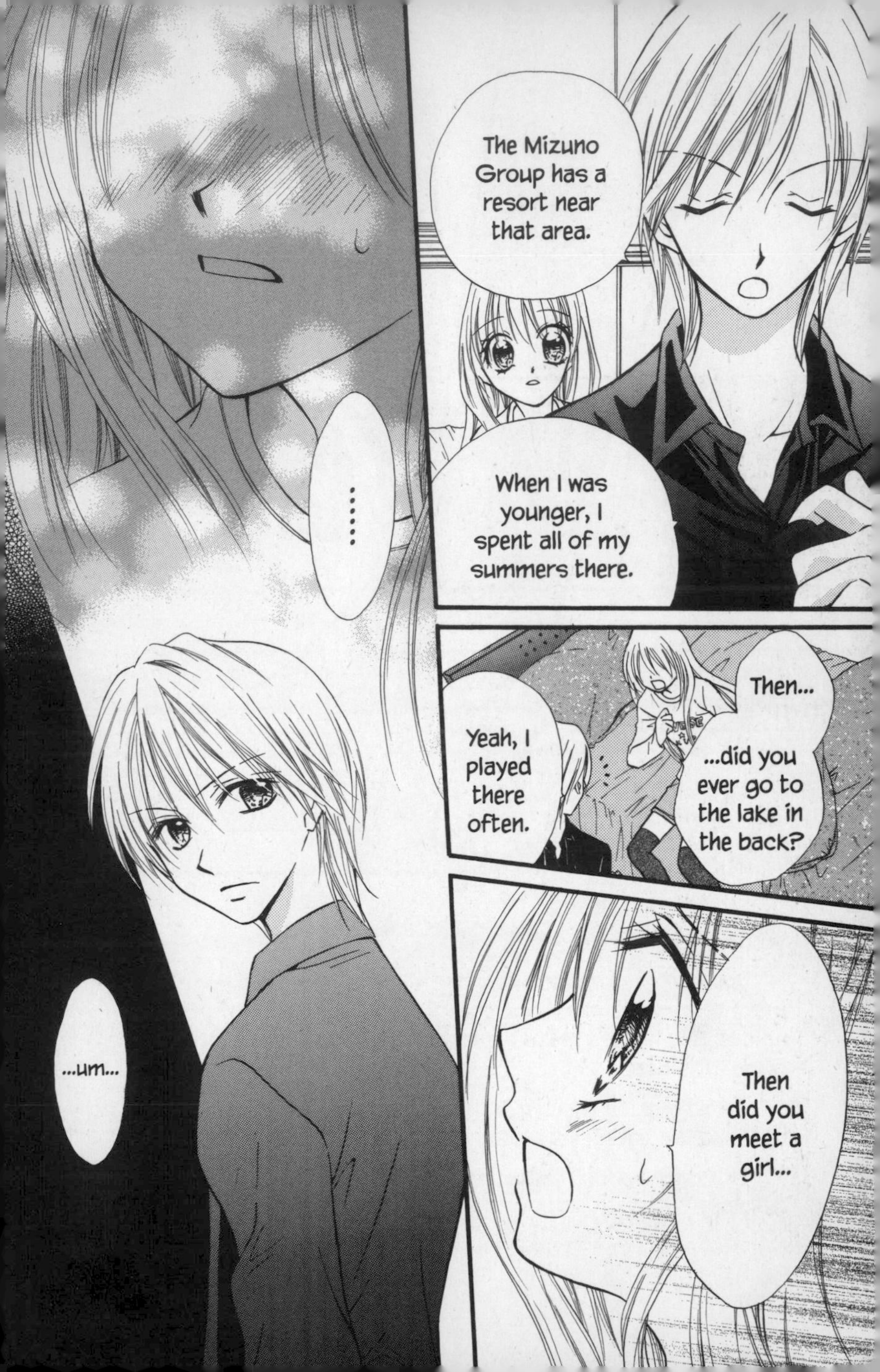
The Mizuno Group has a resort near that area.
When I was younger, I spent all of my summers there.
Then...
...did you ever go to the lake in the back?
Yeah, I played there often.
Then did you meet a girl...
......
...um...

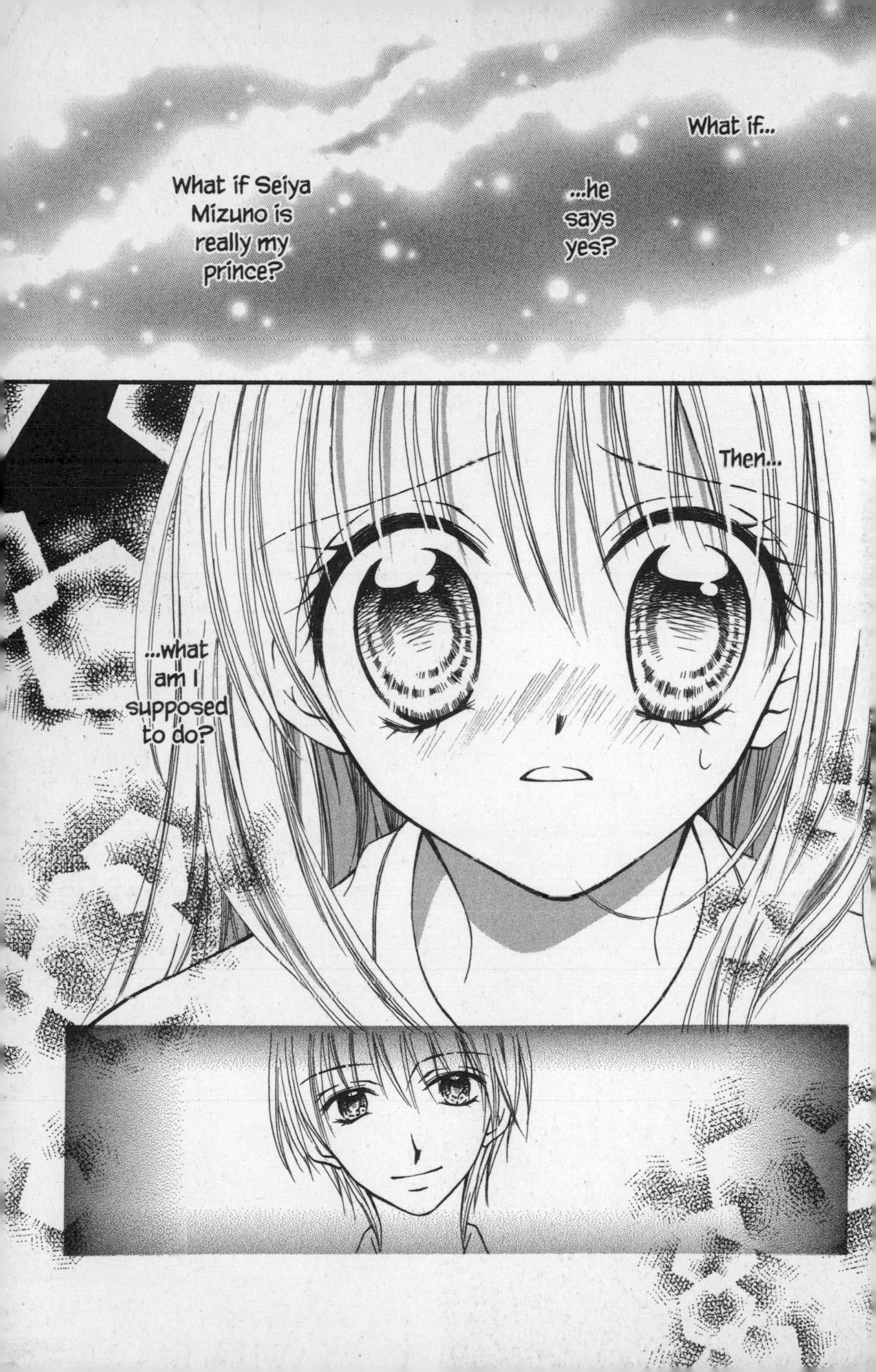
What if...
...he says yes?
What if Seiya Mizuno is really my prince?
Then...
...what am I supposed to do?

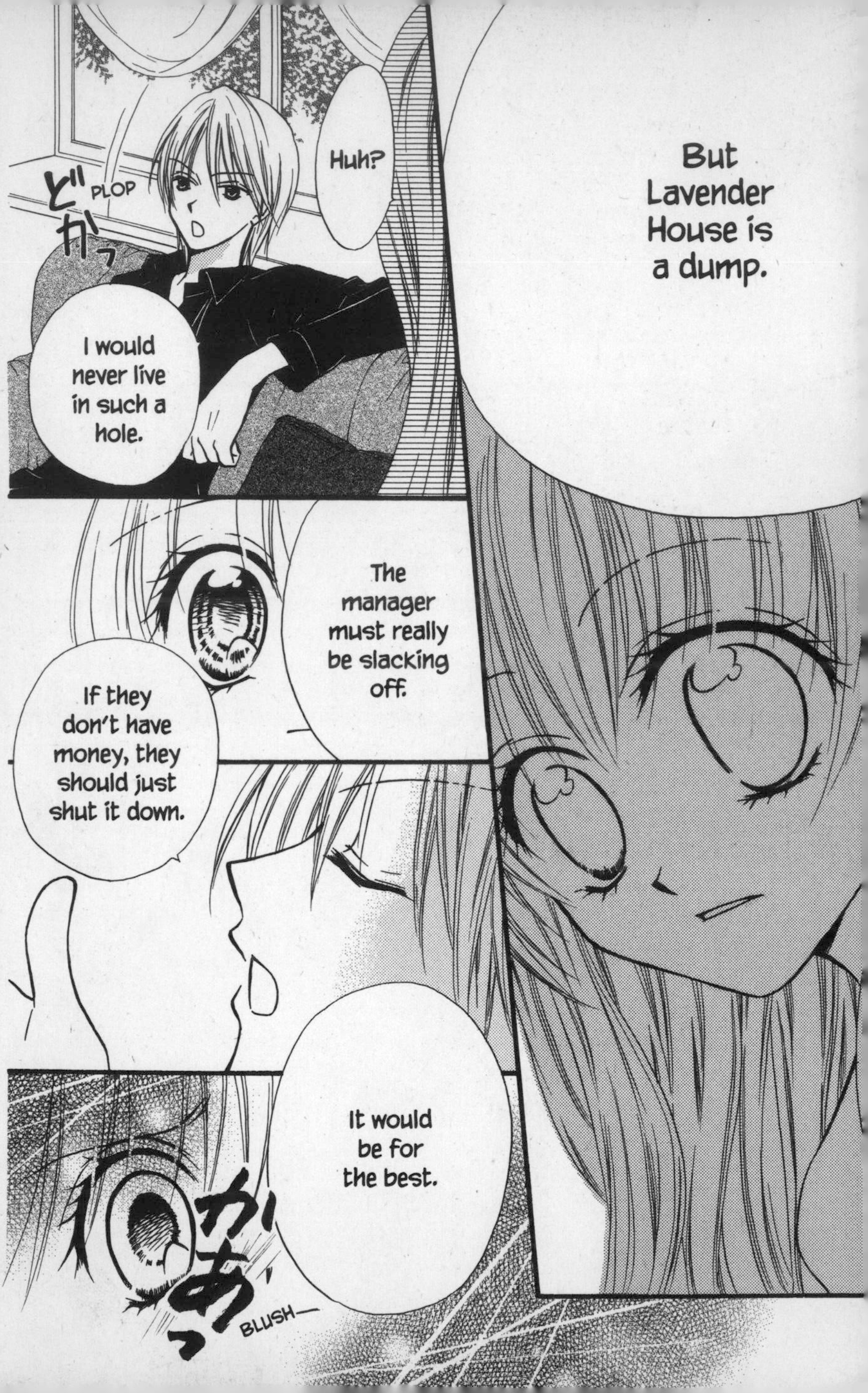
But Lavender House is a dump.
Huh?
どがっ
PLOP
I would never live in such a hole.
The manager must really be slacking off.
If they don't have money, they should just shut it down.
It would be for the best.
かあっ
BLUSH—

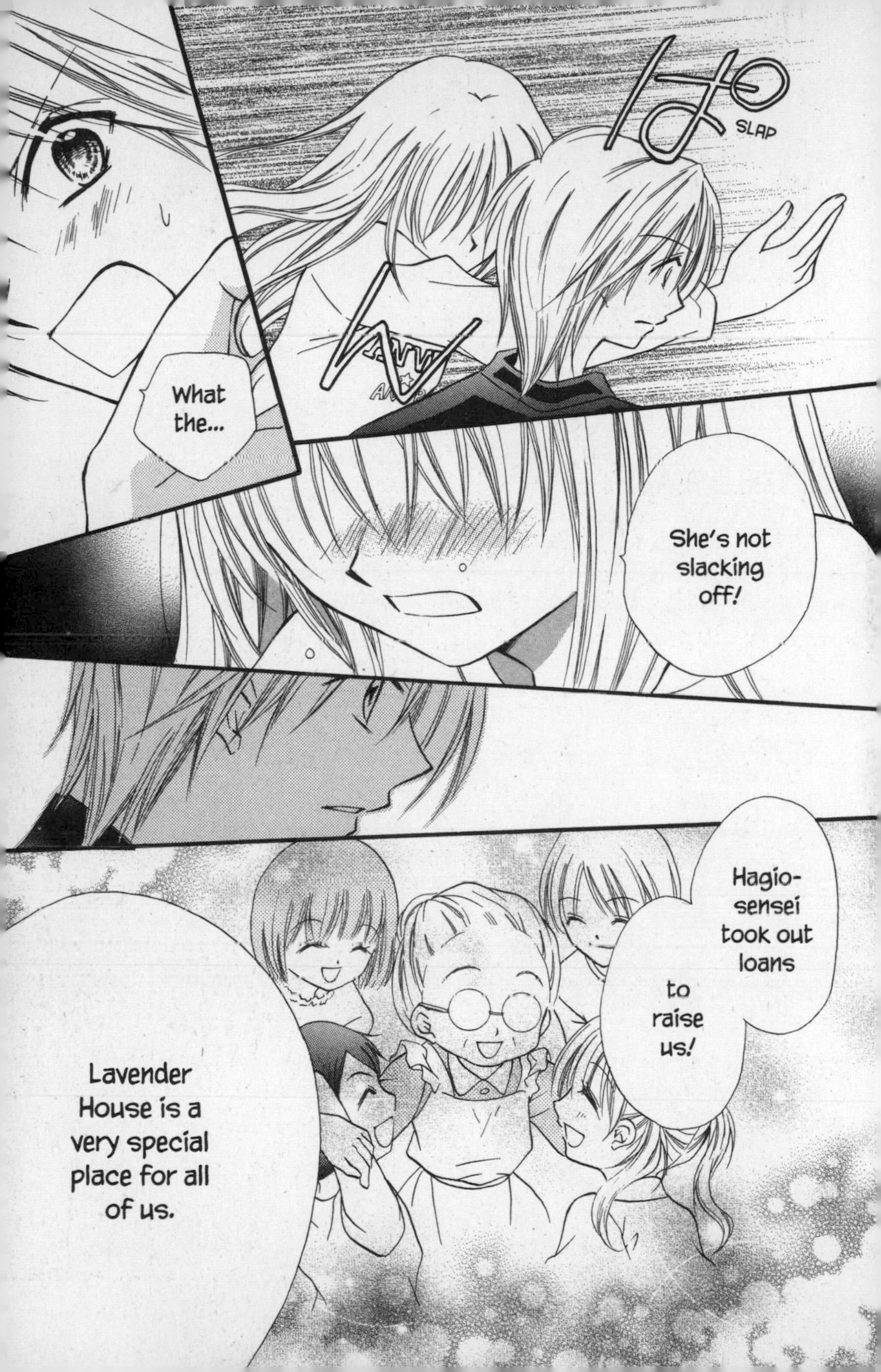
SLAP
What the...
She's not slacking off!
Hagio-sensei took out loans
to raise us!
Lavender House is a very special place for all of us.

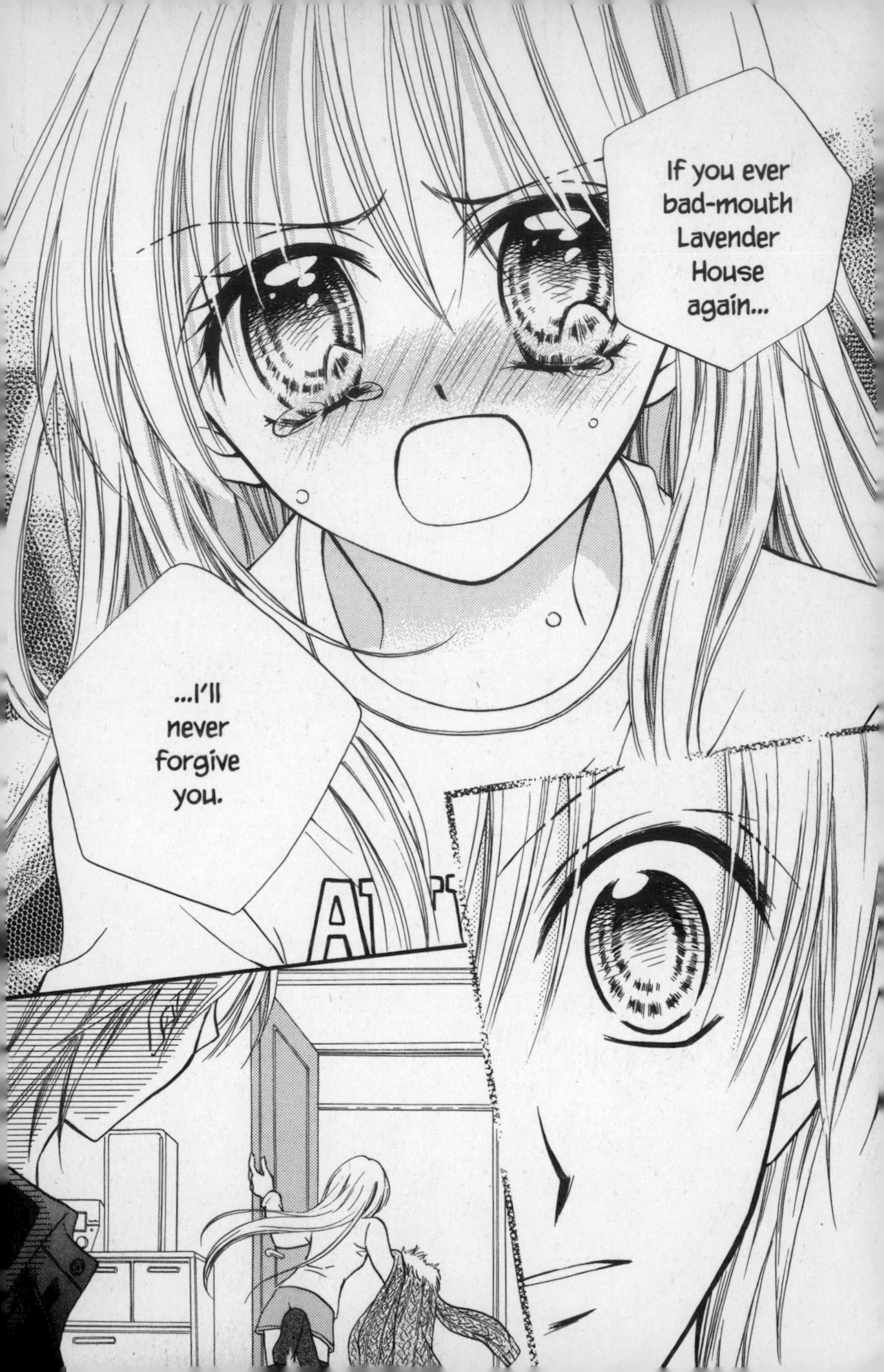
If you ever bad-mouth Lavender House again...
...I'll never forgive you.

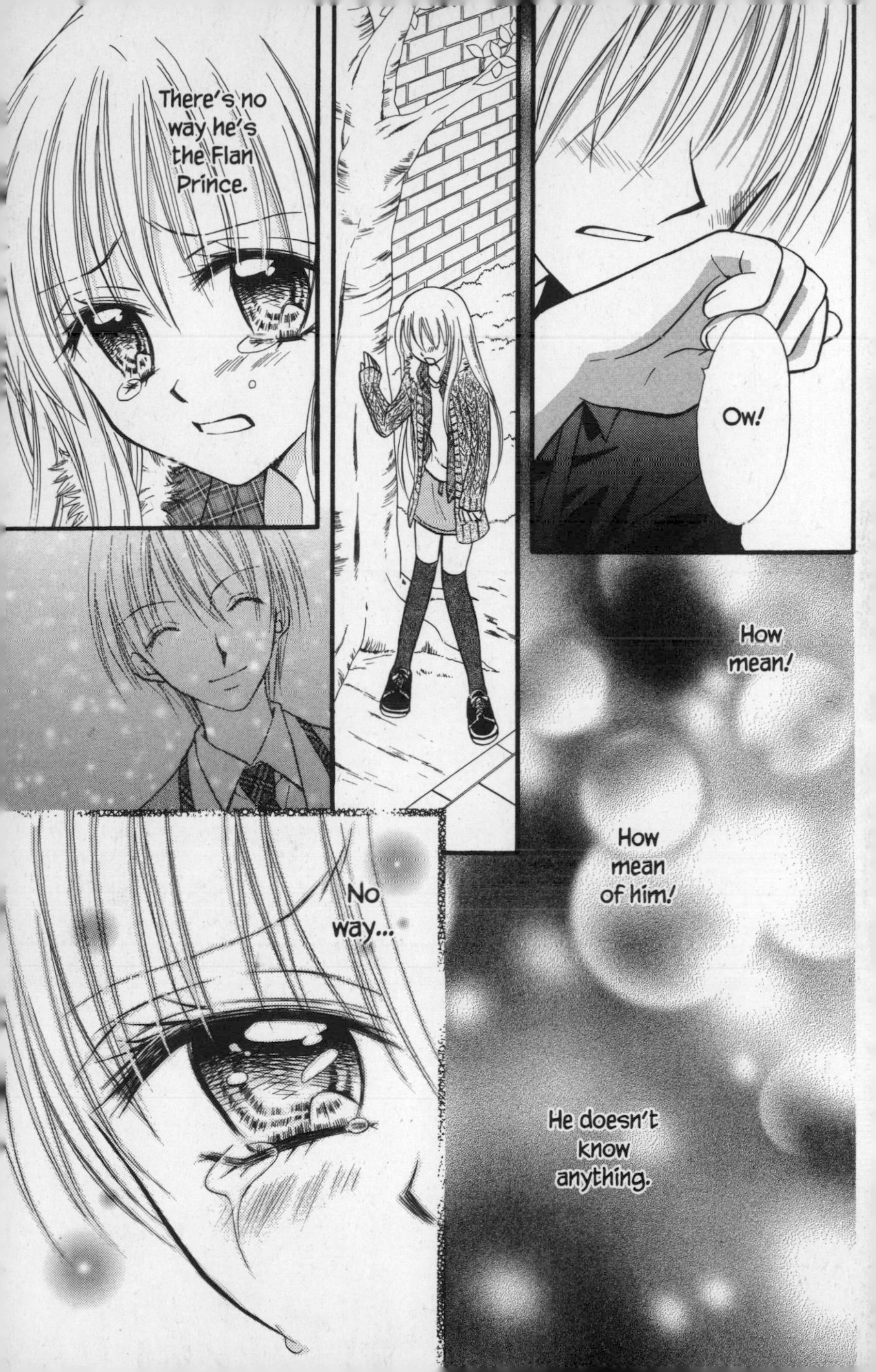
Ow!
There's no way he's the Flan Prince.
How mean!
How mean of him!
He doesn't know anything.
No way...

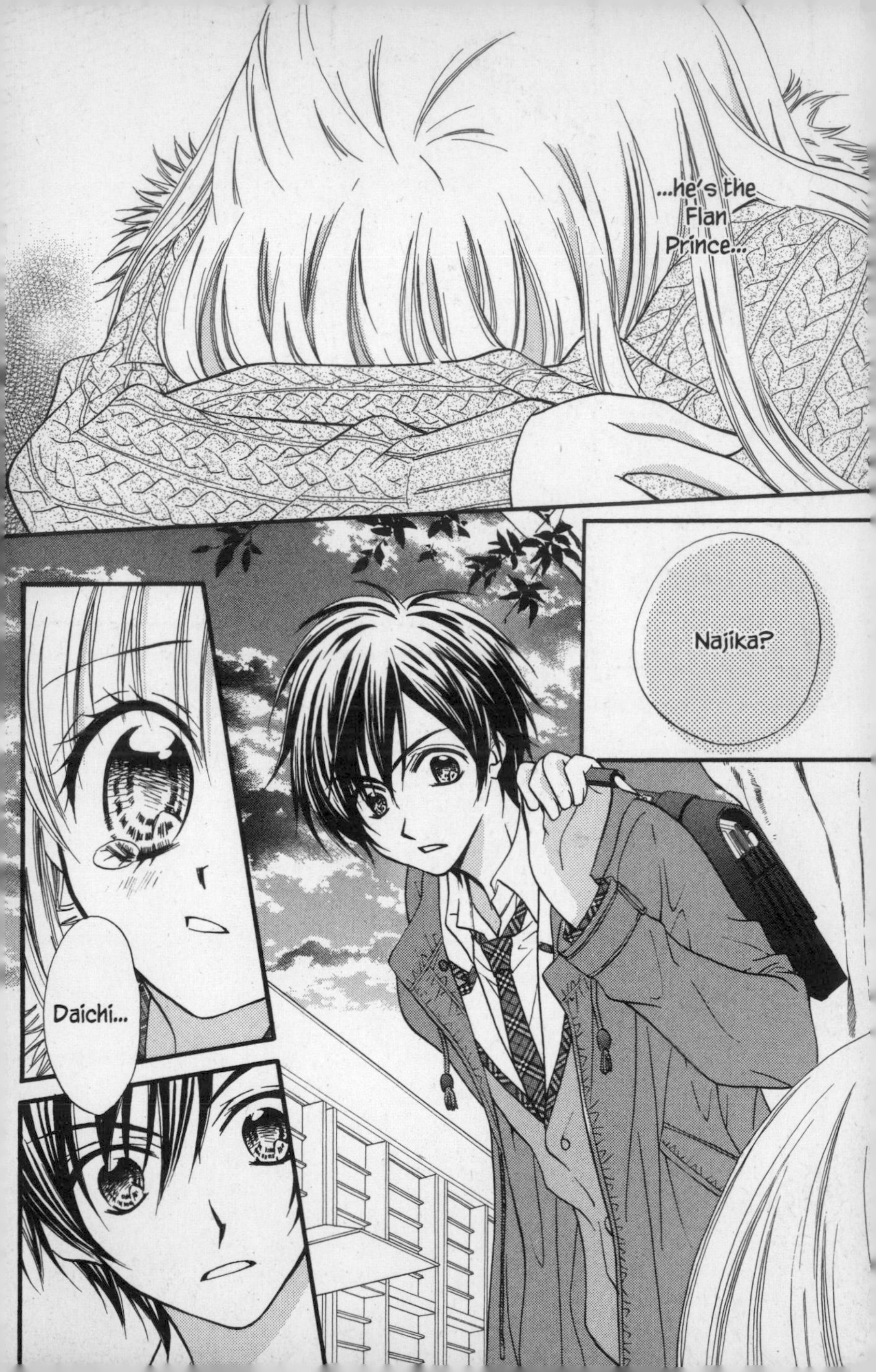
...he's the Flan Prince...
Najika?
Daichi...

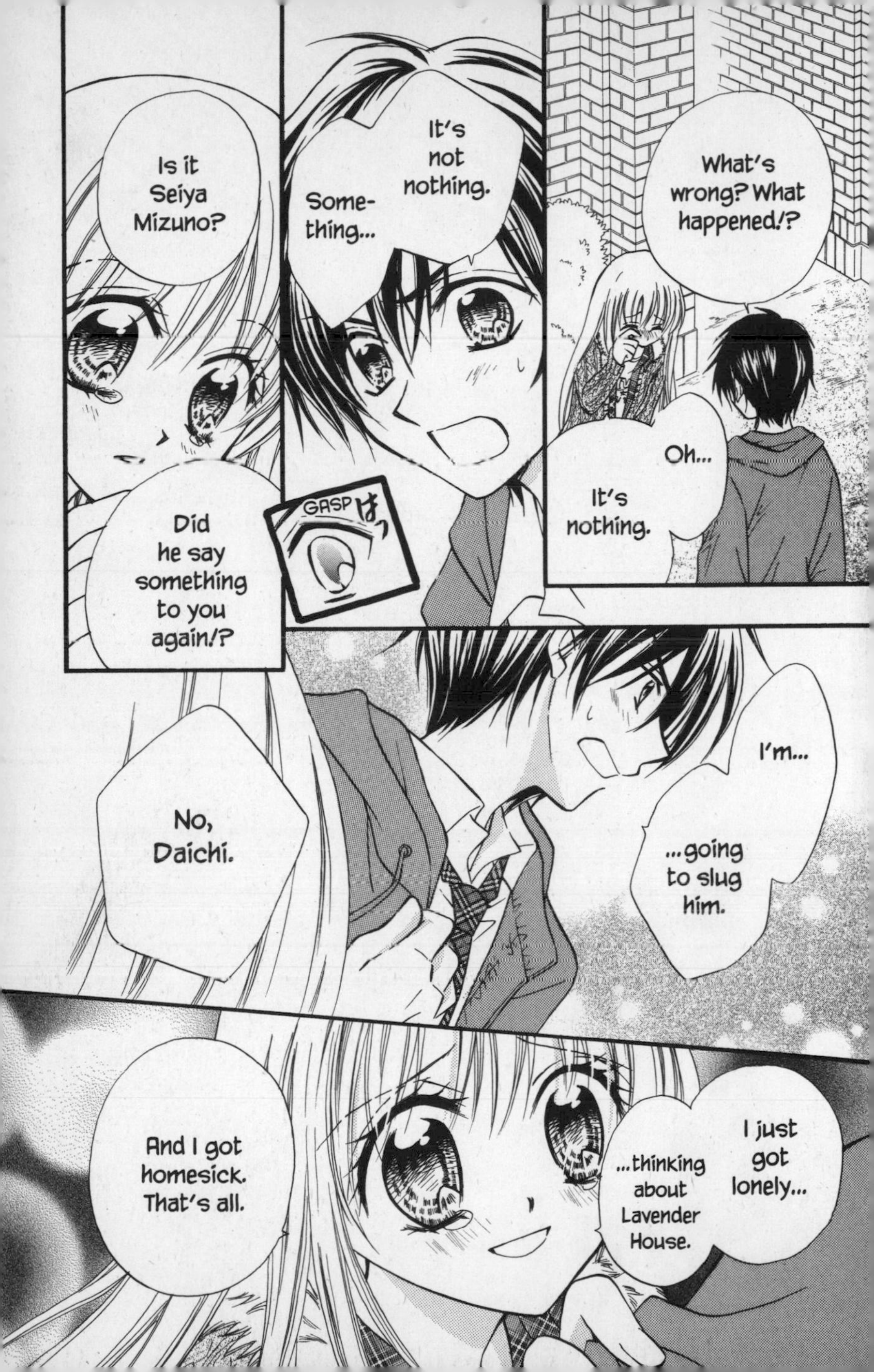
What's wrong? What happened!?
Oh...
It's nothing.
It's not nothing.
Some-thing...
GASP はっ
Is it Seiya Mizuno?
Did he say something to you again!?
I'm...
...going to slug him.
No, Daichi.
I just got lonely...
...thinking about Lavender House.
And I got homesick. That's all.

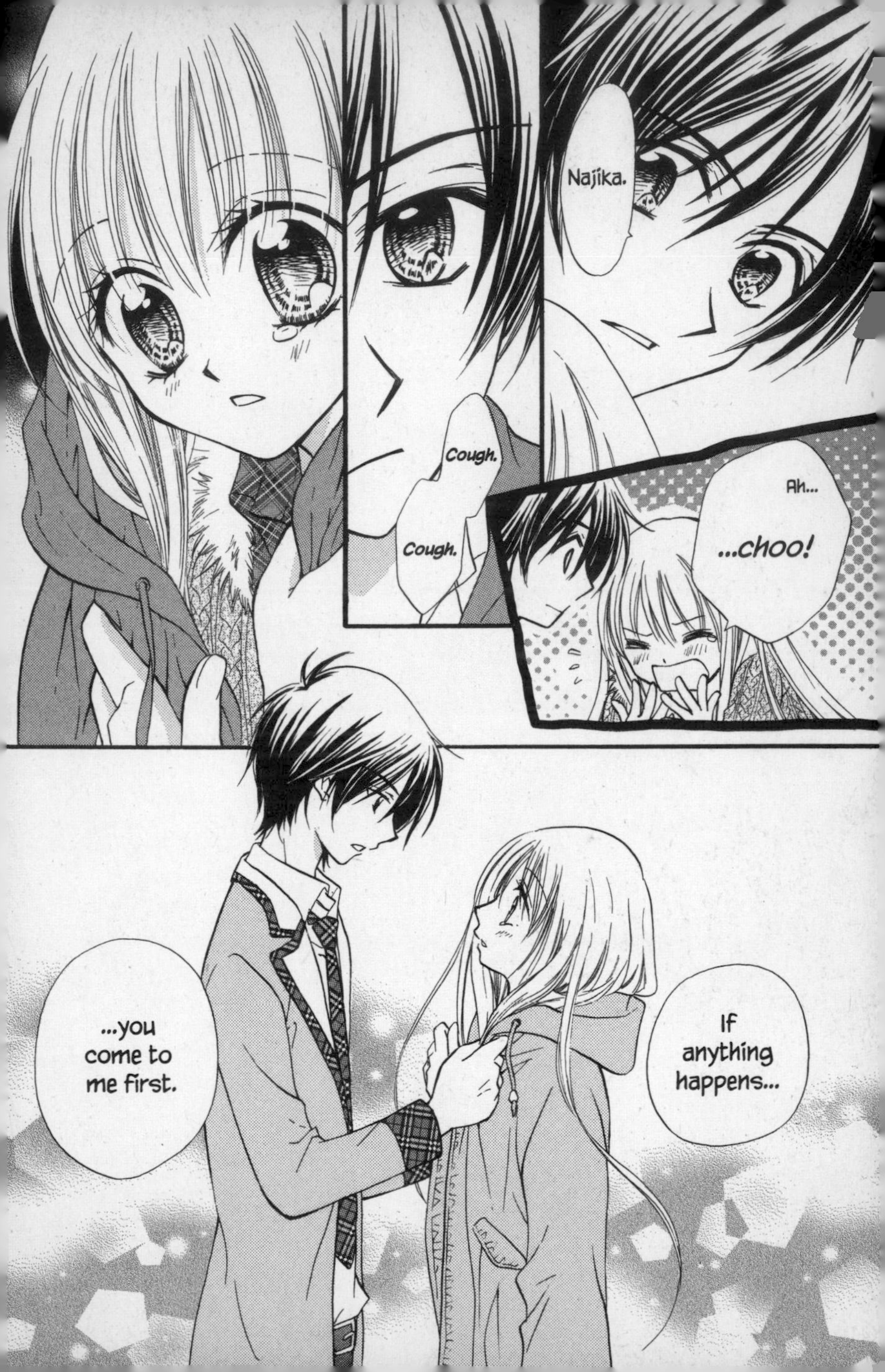
Najika.
Cough.
Cough.
Ah...
...choo!
If anything happens...
...you come to me first.

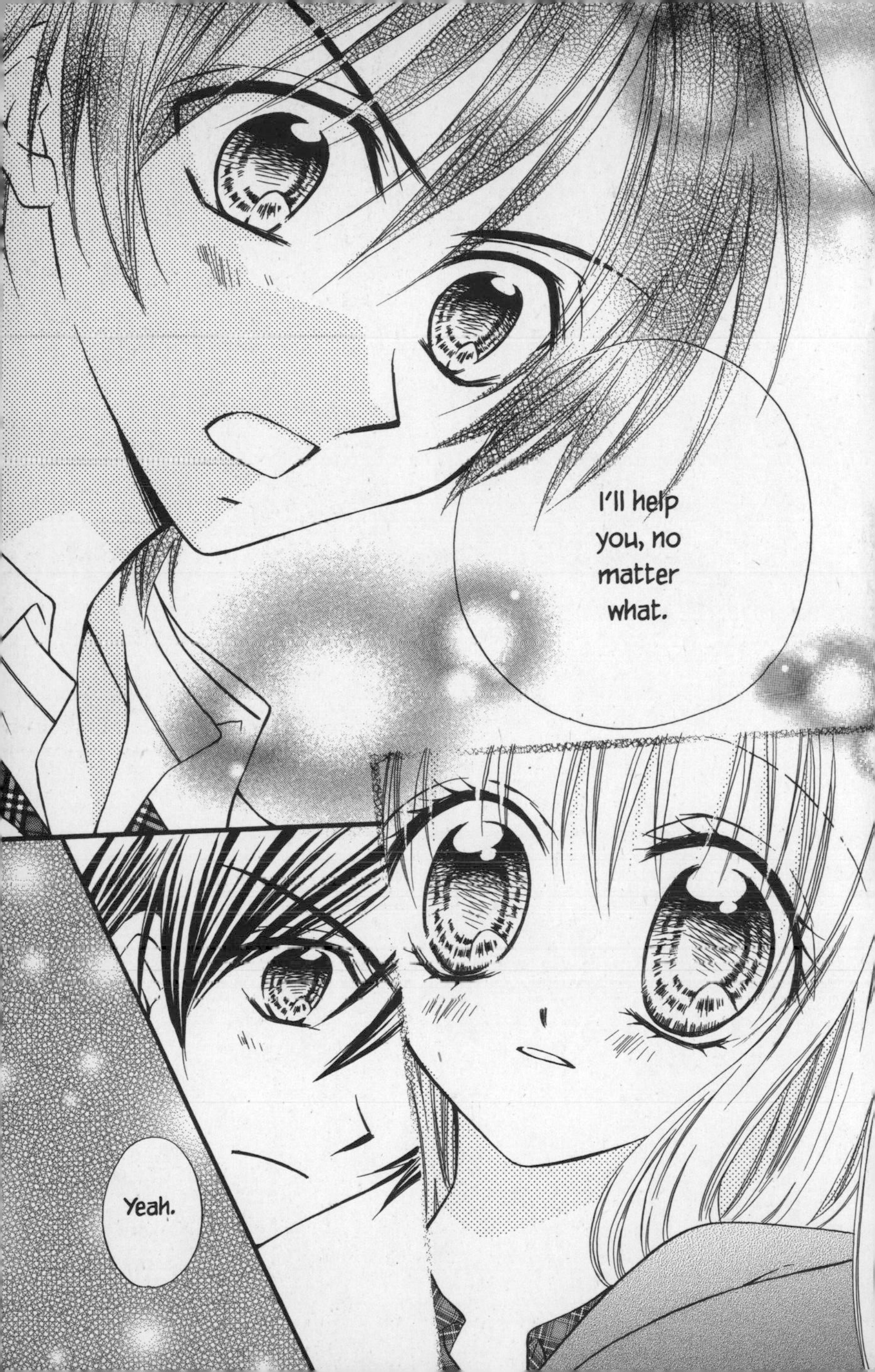
I'll help you, no matter what.
Yeah.

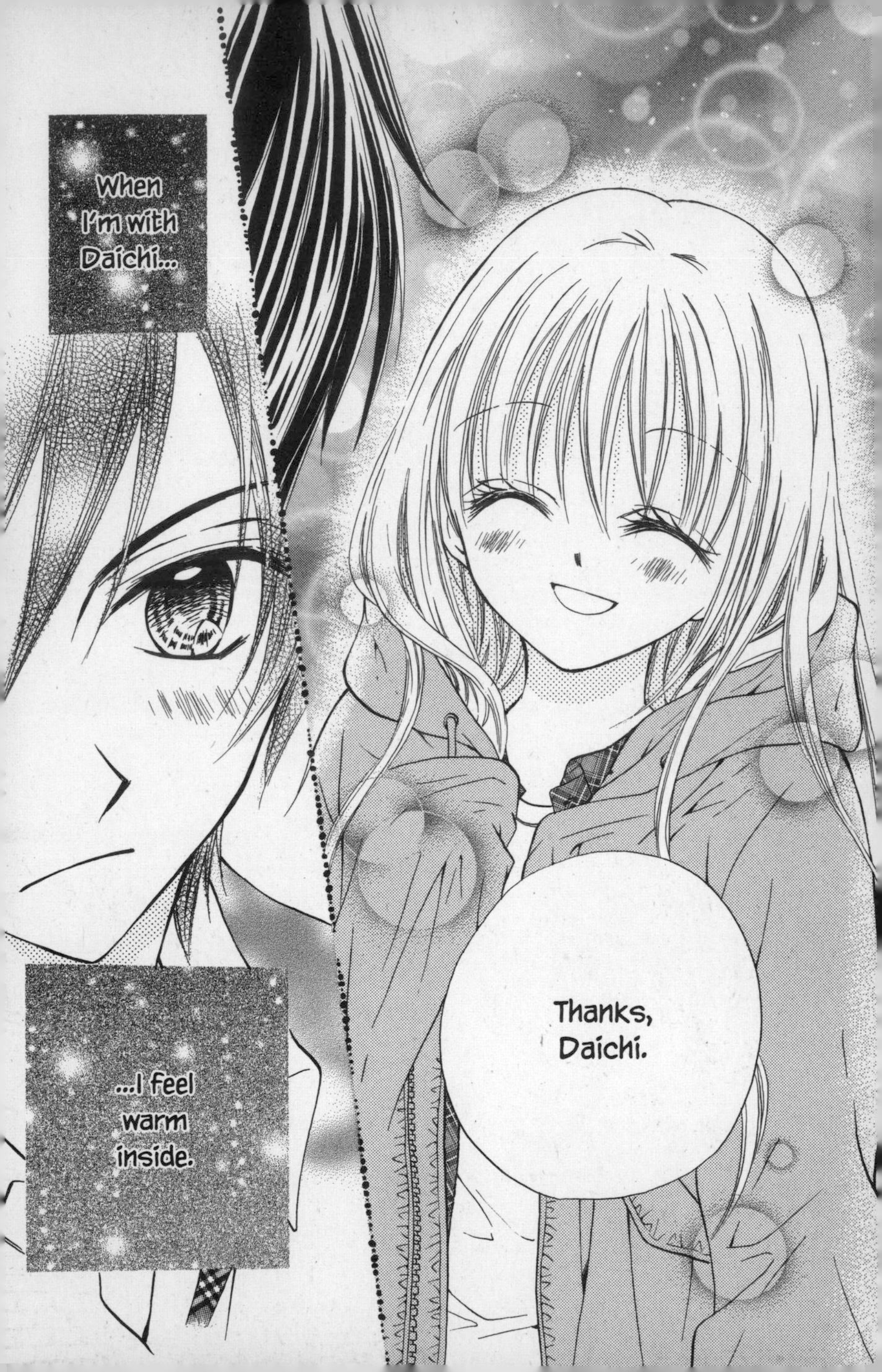
Thanks, Daichi.
When I'm with Daichi...
...I feel warm inside.

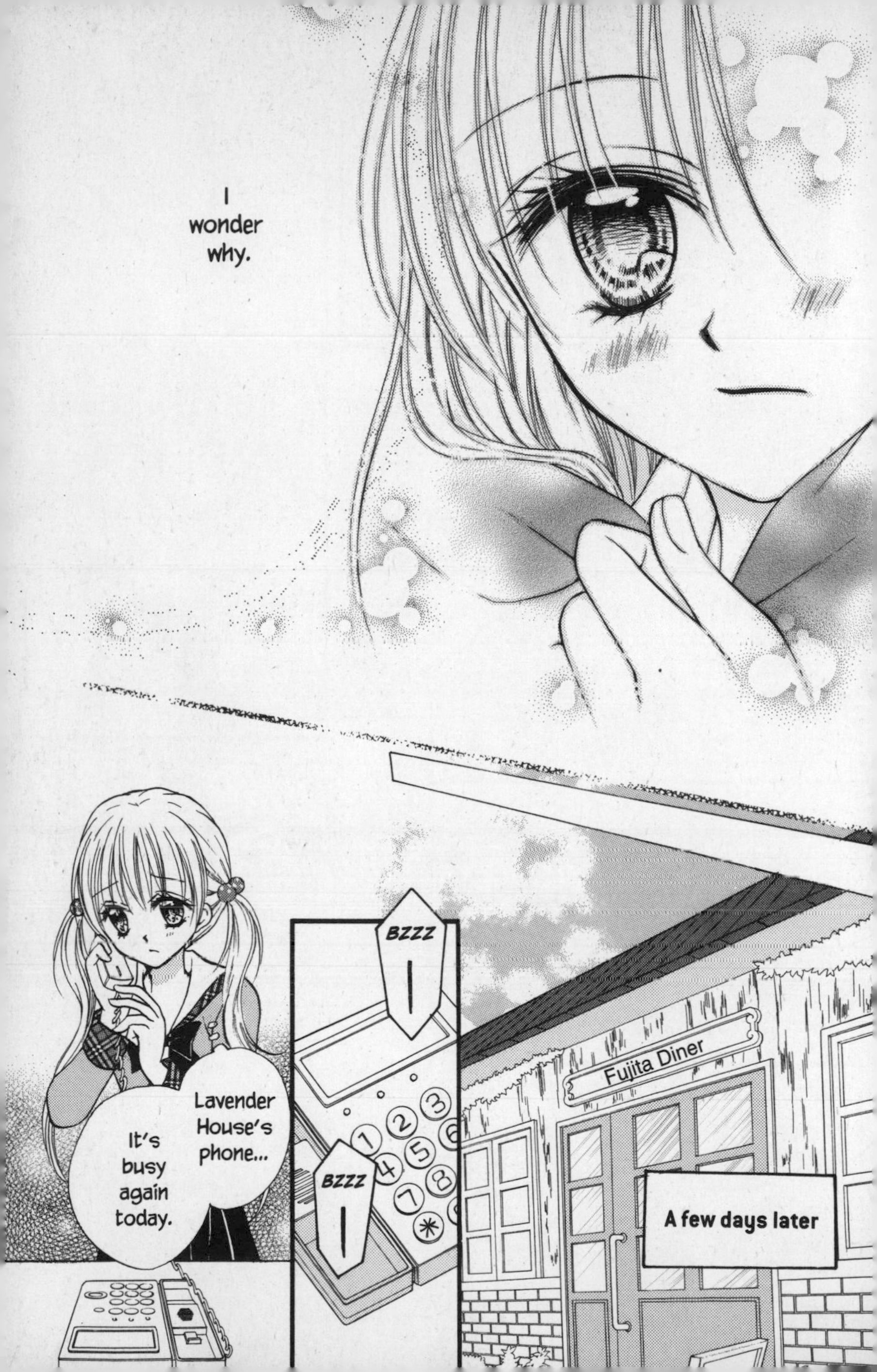
I wonder why.
Fujita Diner
A few days later
BZZZ
BZZZ
Lavender House's phone...
It's busy again today.

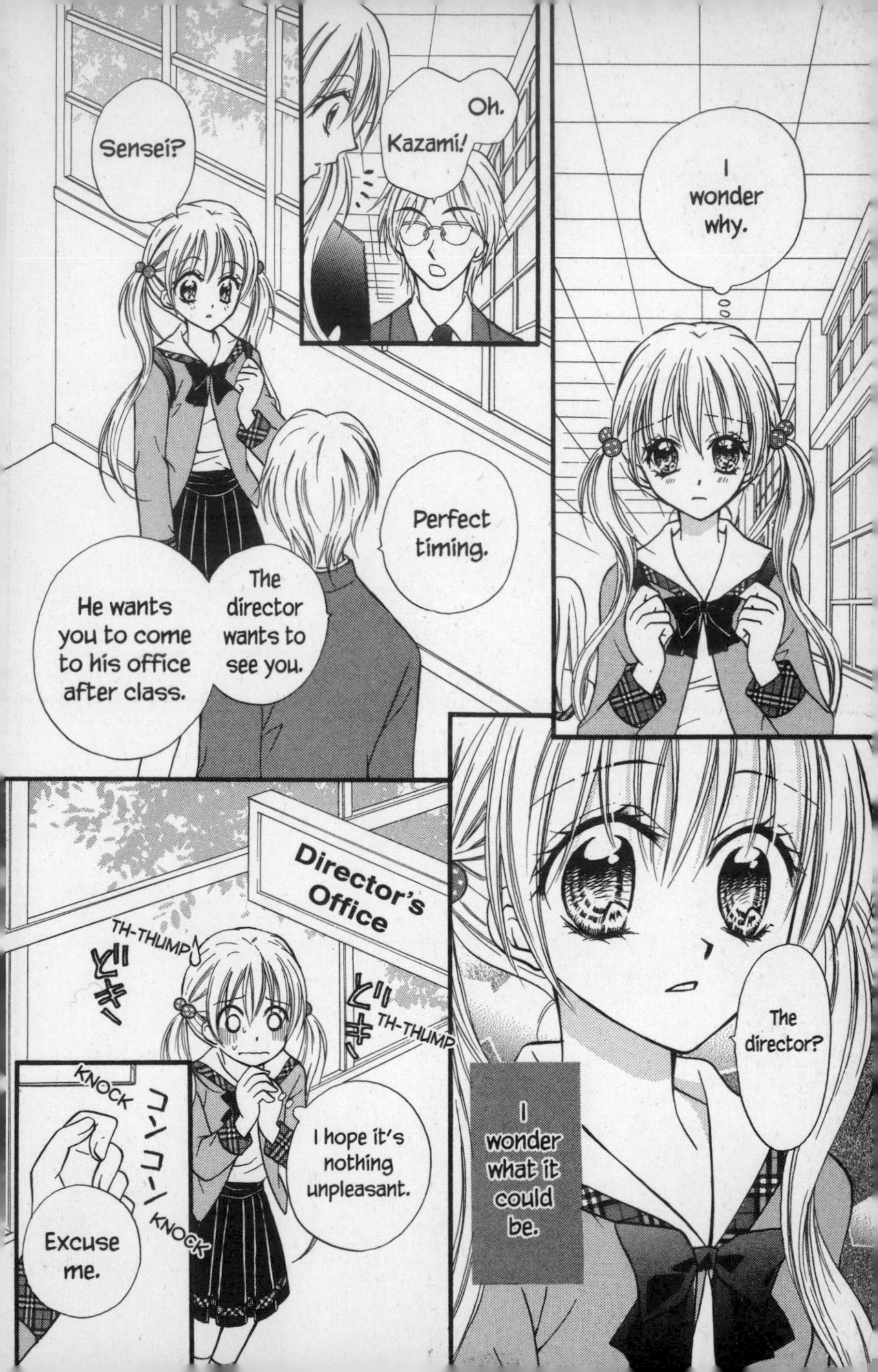
Sensei?
Oh.
Kazami!
Perfect timing.
The director wants to see you.
He wants you to come to his office after class.
I wonder why.
The director?
I wonder what it could be.
Director's Office
TH-THUMP
TH-THUMP
I hope it's nothing unpleasant.
KNOCK
KNOCK
Excuse me.

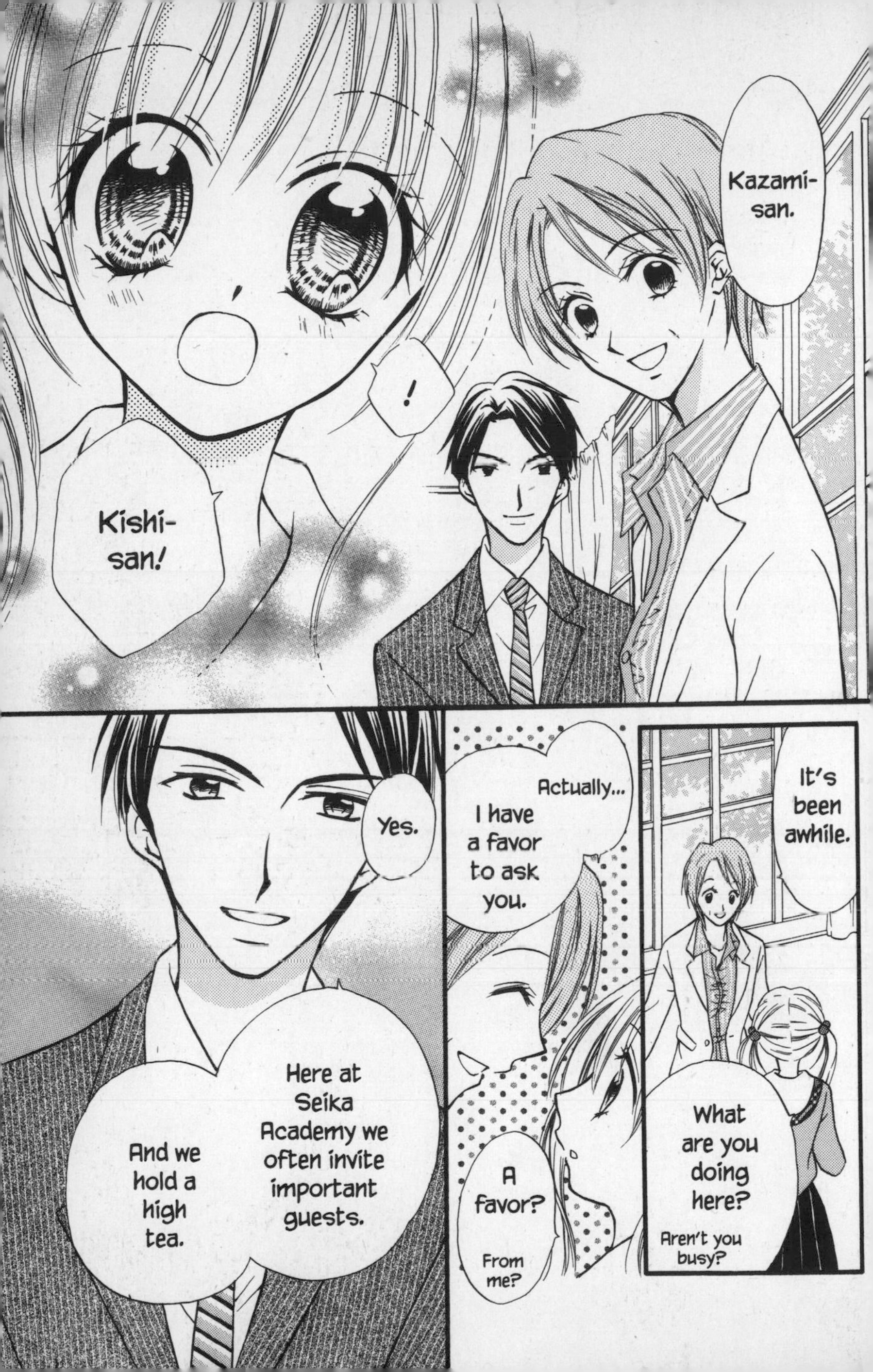
Kazami-san.
!
Kishi-san!
It's been awhile.
What are you doing here?
Aren't you busy?
Actually... I have a favor to ask you.
A favor?
From me?
Yes.
Here at Seika Academy we often invite important guests.
And we hold a high tea.

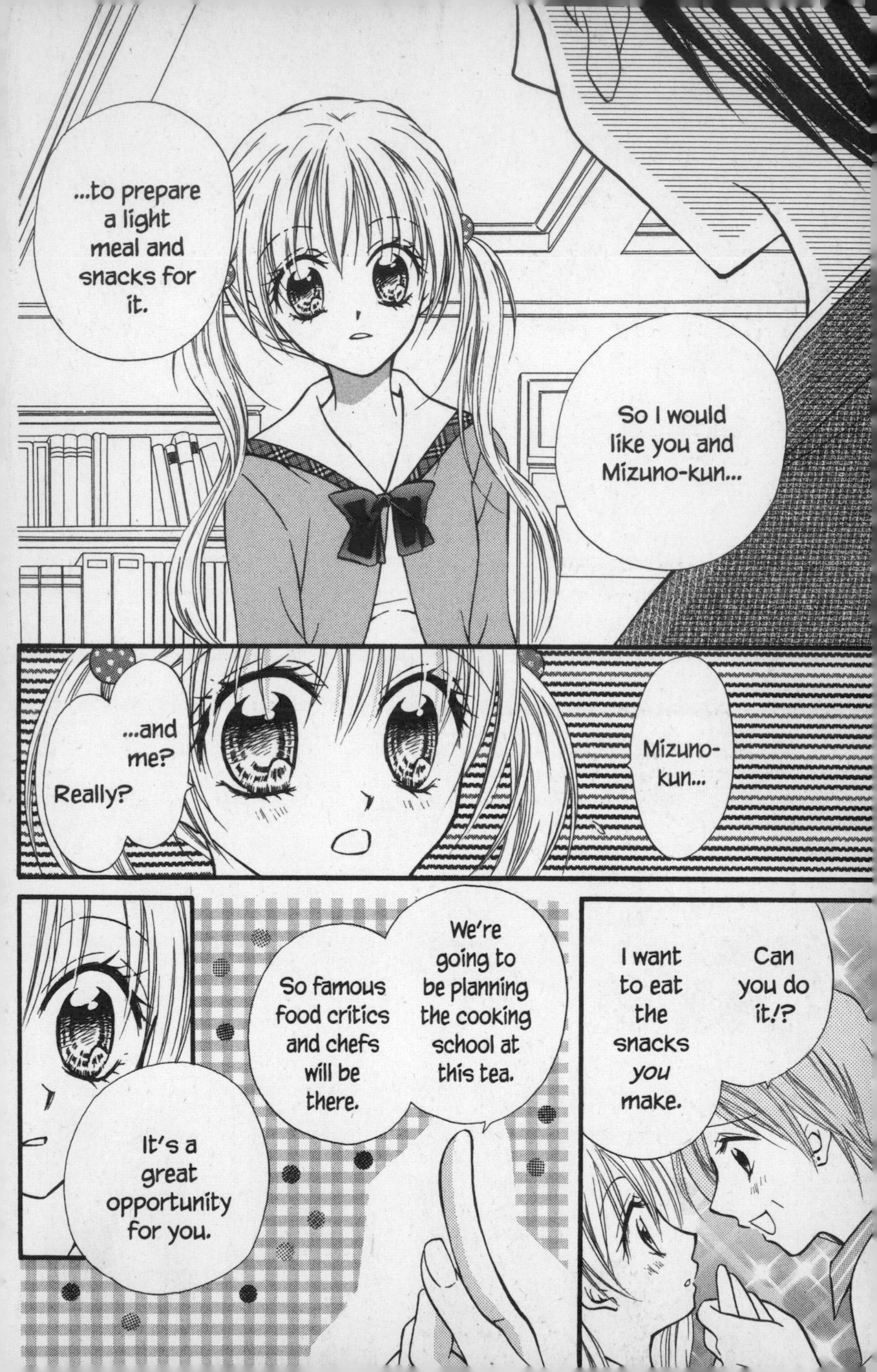
So I would like you and Mizuno-kun...
...to prepare a light meal and snacks for it.
Mizuno-kun...
...and me? Really?
Can you do it!?
I want to eat the snacks *you* make.
We're going to be planning the cooking school at this tea.
So famous food critics and chefs will be there.
It's a great opportunity for you.

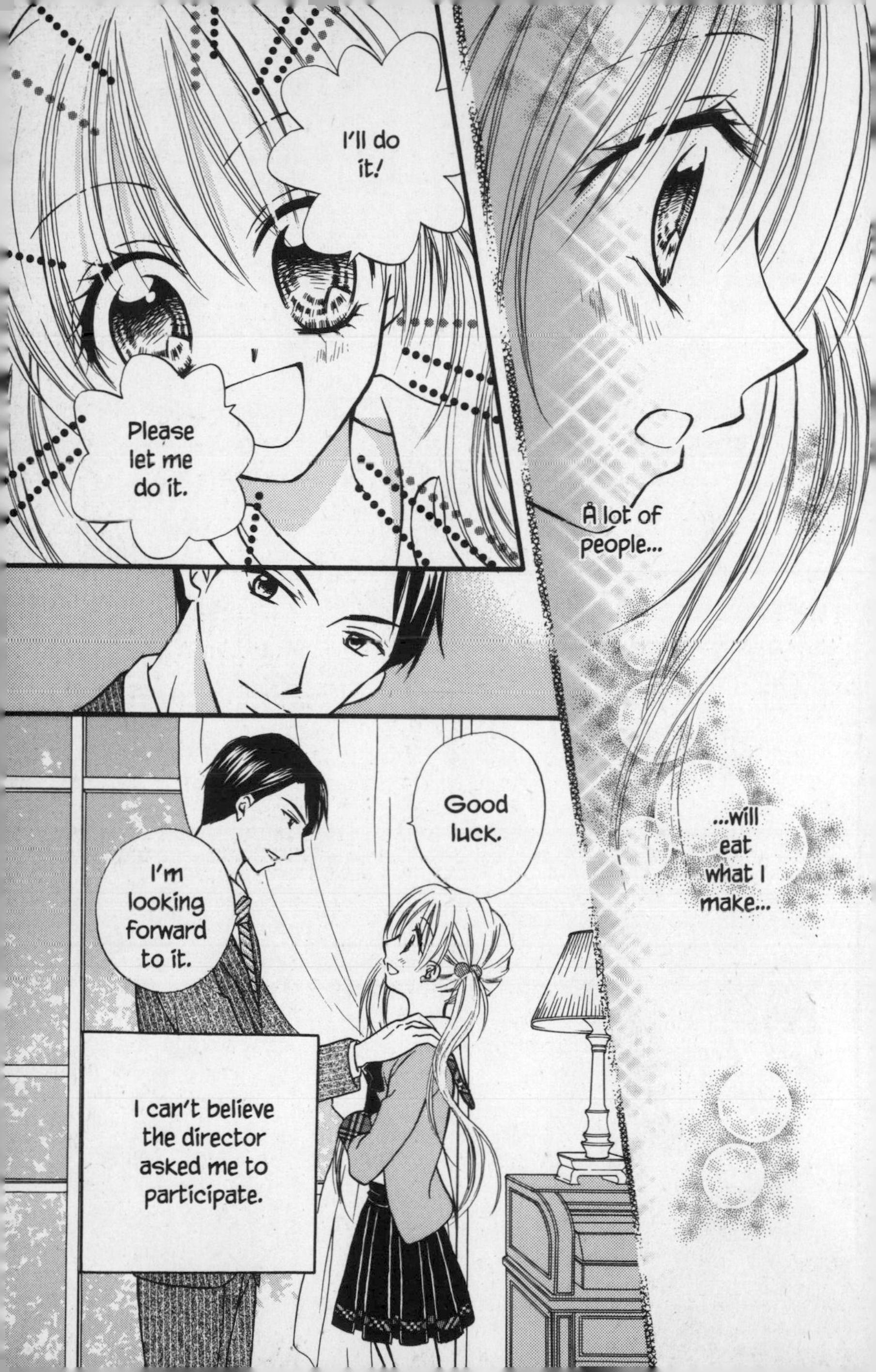
A lot of people...
...will eat what I make...
I'll do it!
Please let me do it.
Good luck.
I'm looking forward to it.
I can't believe the director asked me to participate.

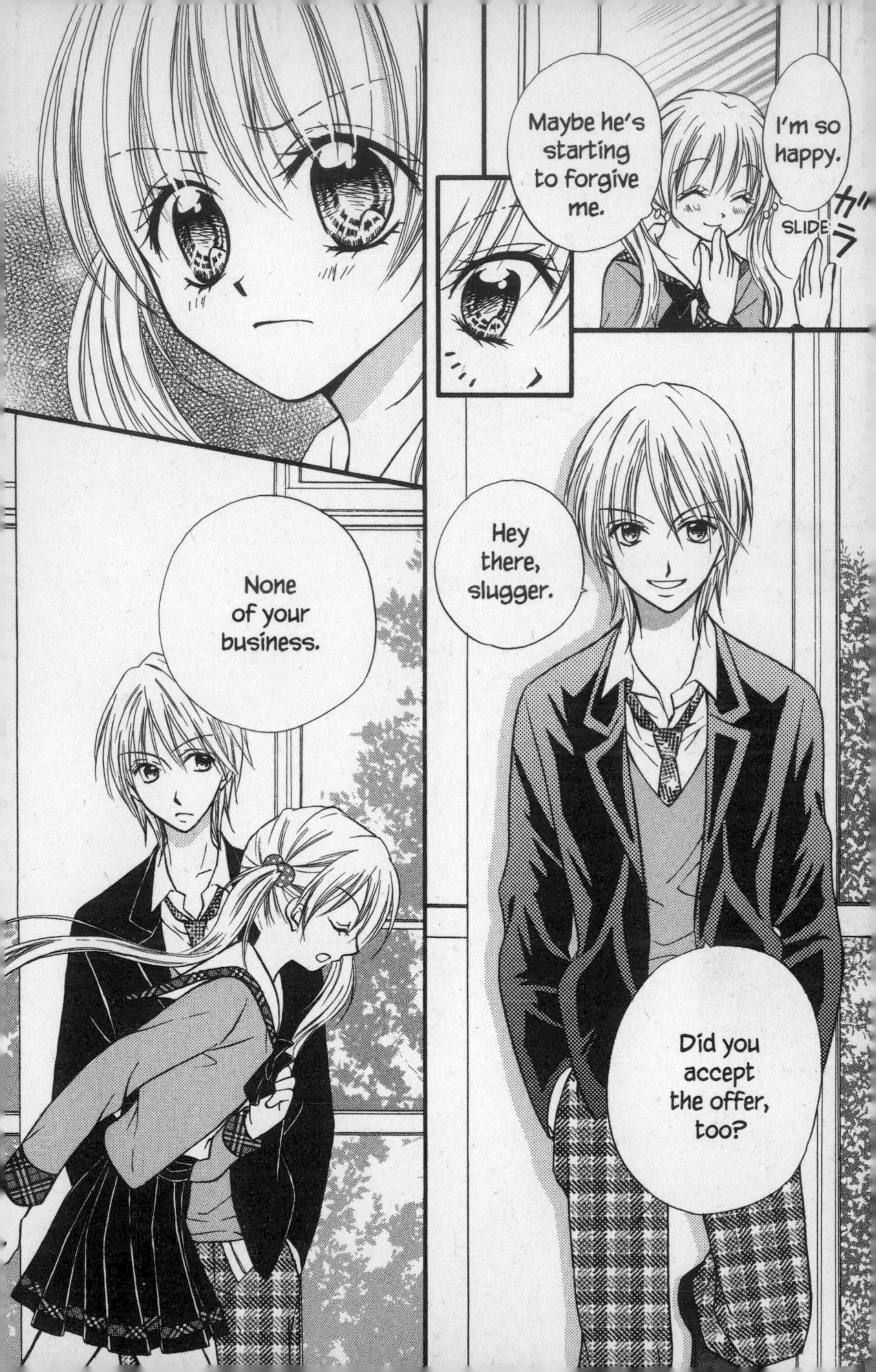
I'm so happy.
Maybe he's starting to forgive me.
ガラ
SLIDE
Hey there, slugger.
Did you accept the offer, too?
None of your business.

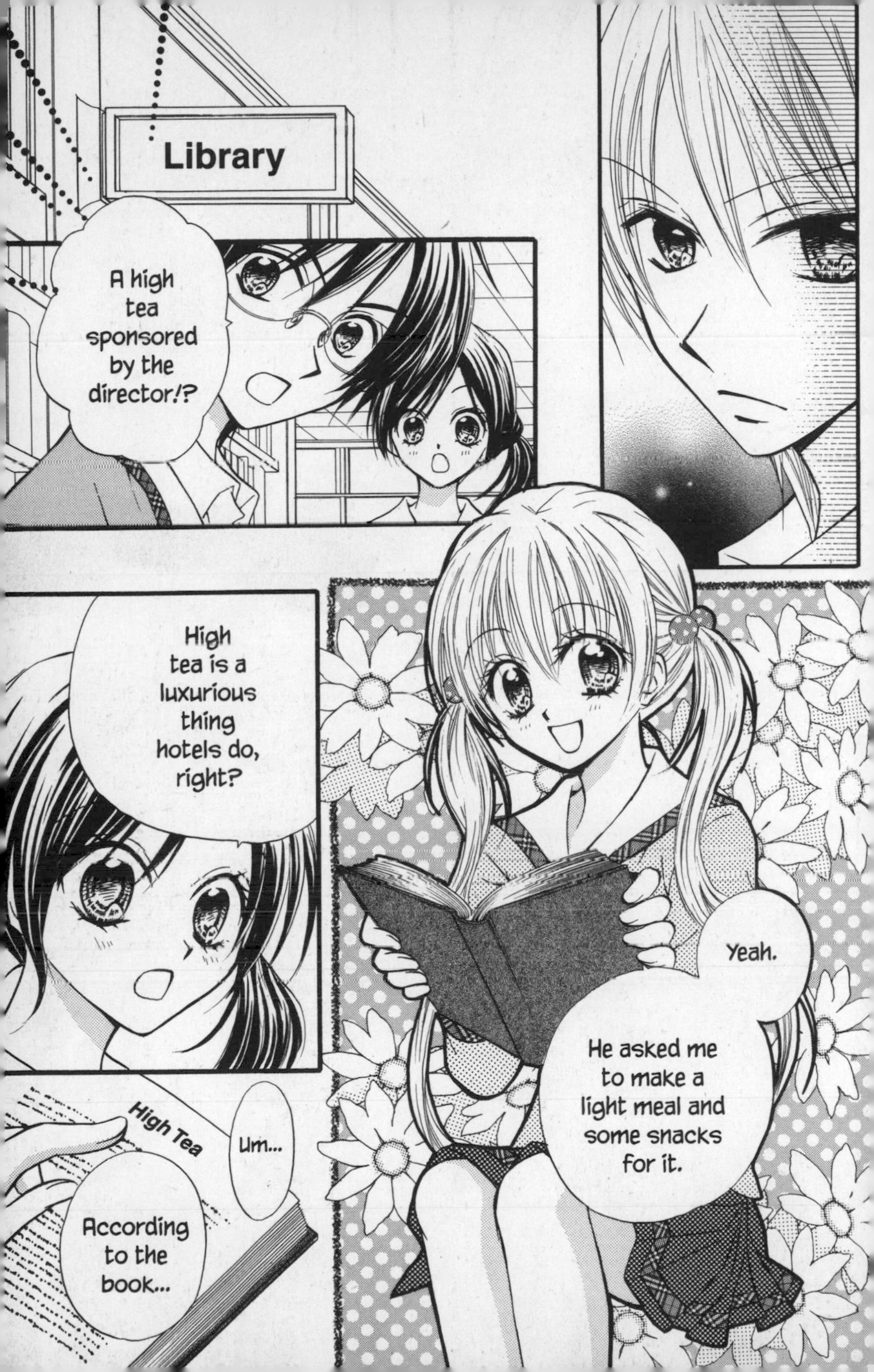
Library
A high tea sponsored by the director!?
Yeah.
He asked me to make a light meal and some snacks for it.
High tea is a luxurious thing hotels do, right?
High Tea
Um...
According to the book...

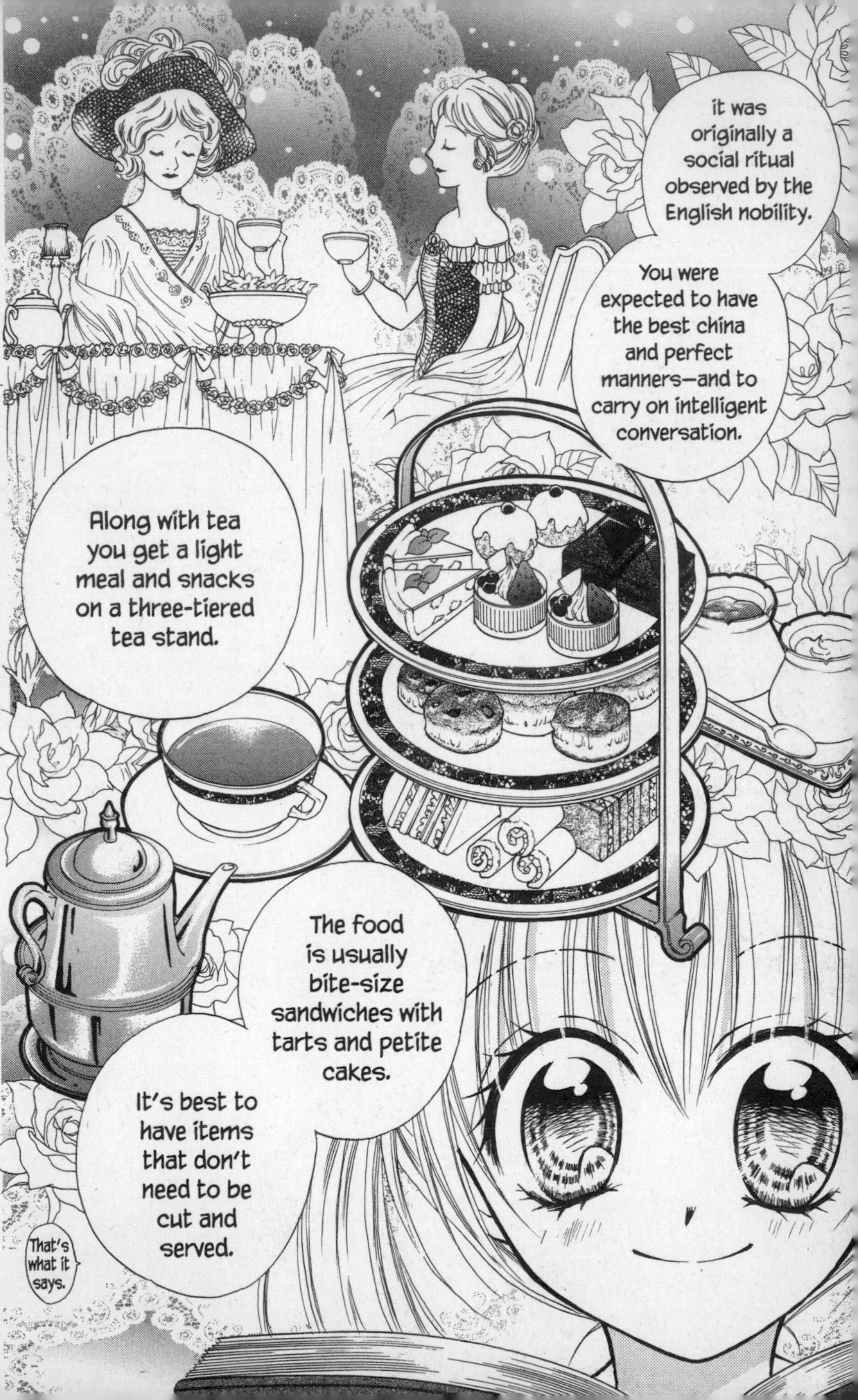
it was originally a social ritual observed by the English nobility.
You were expected to have the best china and perfect manners—and to carry on intelligent conversation.
Along with tea you get a light meal and snacks on a three-tiered tea stand.
The food is usually bite-size sandwiches with tarts and petite cakes.
It's best to have items that don't need to be cut and served.
That's what it says.

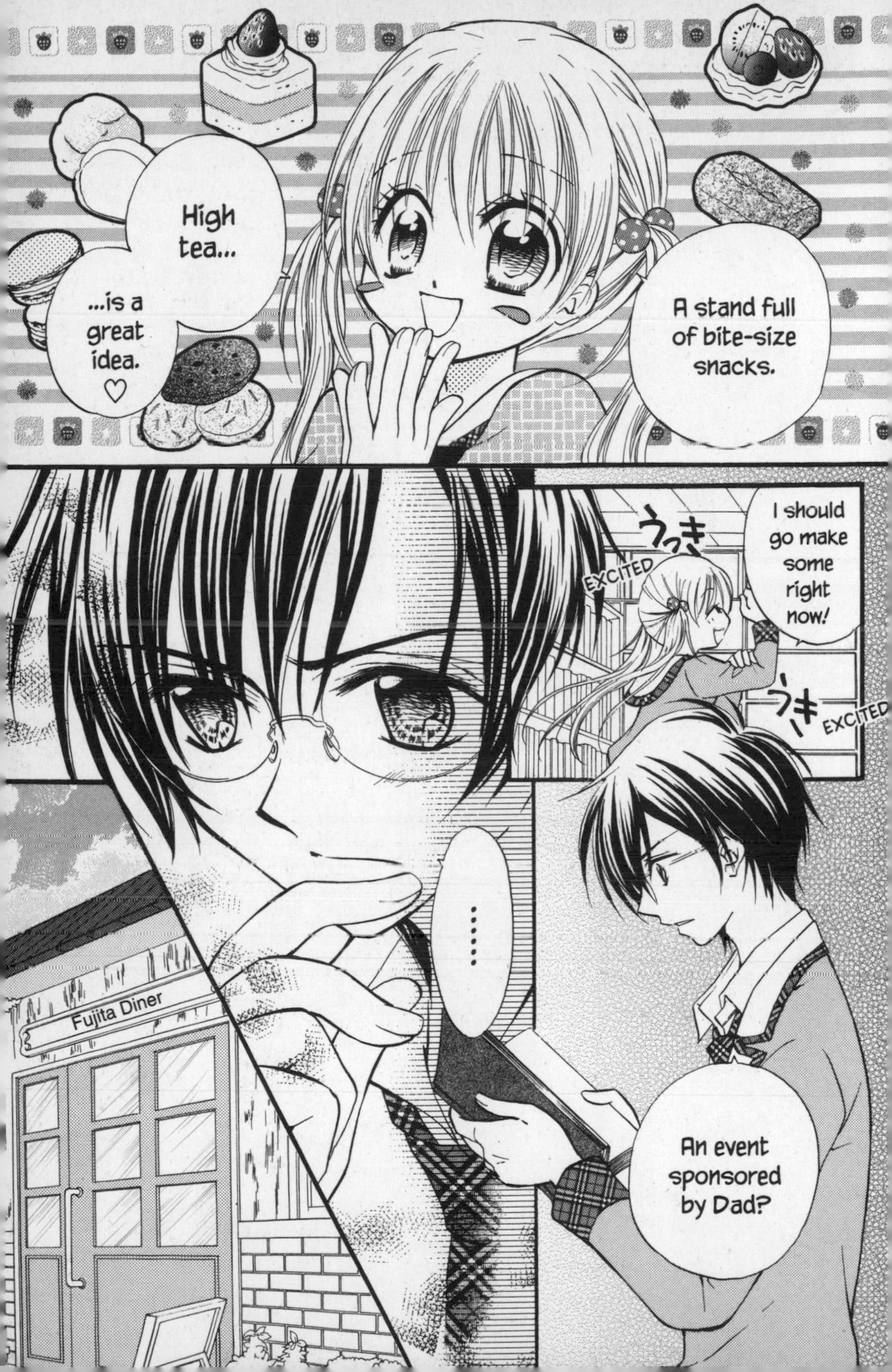
A stand full of bite-size snacks.
High tea...
...is a great idea. ♡
うっき
EXCITED
I should go make some right now!
うき
EXCITED
......
An event sponsored by Dad?
Fujita Diner

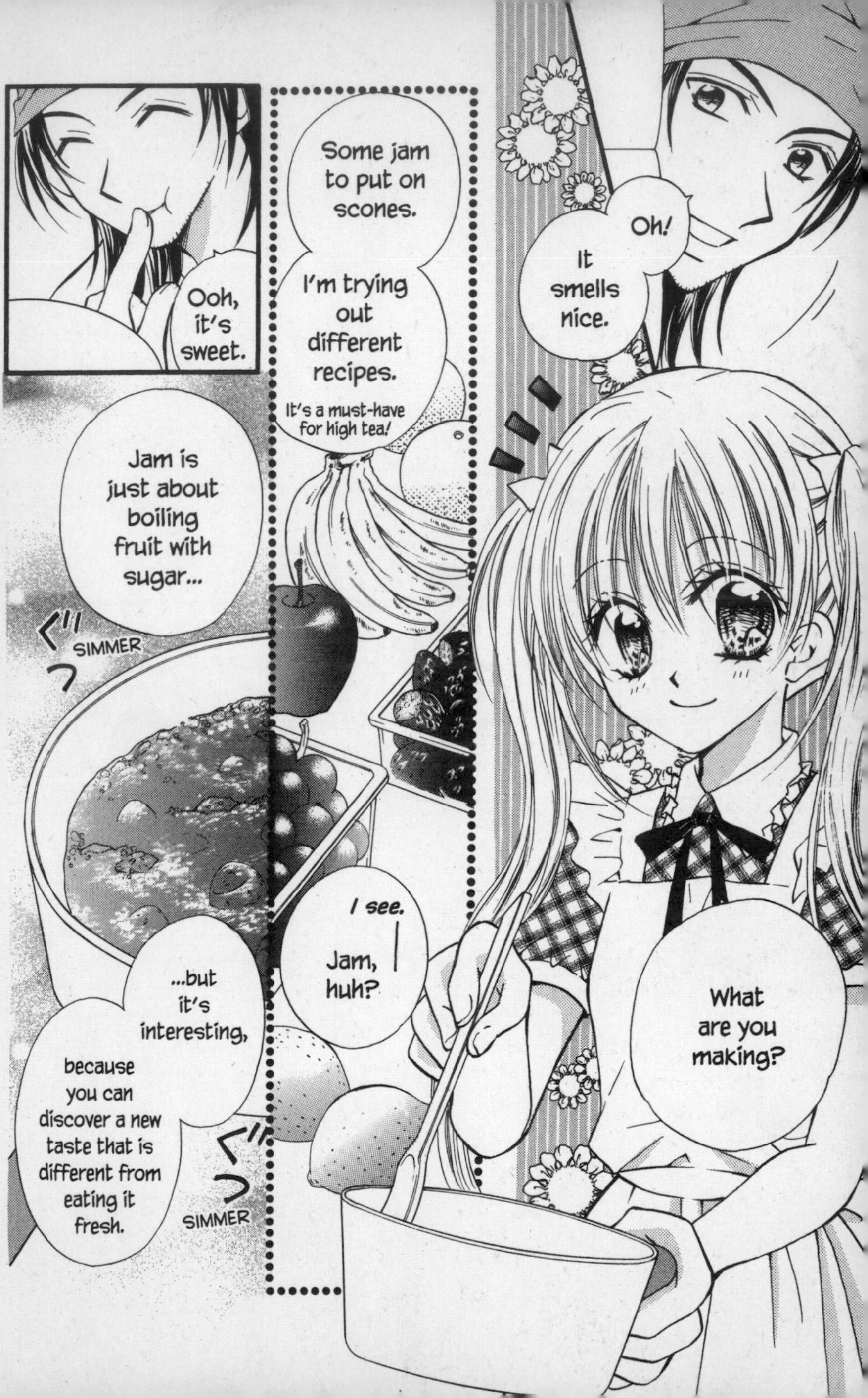
Oh!
It smells nice.
What are you making?
Some jam to put on scones.
I'm trying out different recipes.
It's a must-have for high tea!
I see.
Jam, huh?
Ooh, it's sweet.
Jam is just about boiling fruit with sugar...
SIMMER
...but it's interesting,
because you can discover a new taste that is different from eating it fresh.
SIMMER

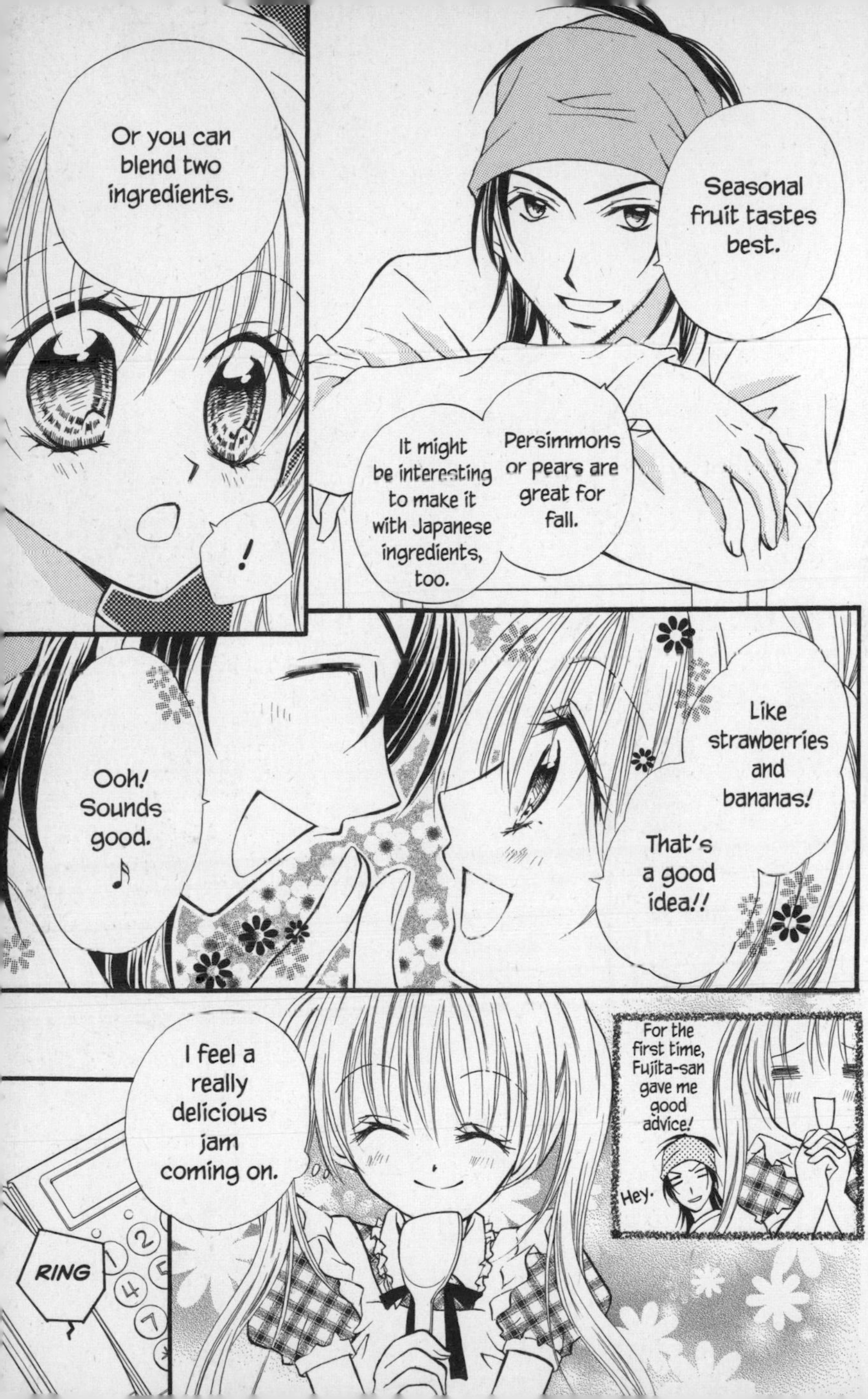
Seasonal fruit tastes best.
Persimmons or pears are great for fall.
It might be interesting to make it with Japanese ingredients, too.
Or you can blend two ingredients.
!
Like strawberries and bananas!
That's a good idea!!
Ooh! Sounds good. ♪
For the first time, Fujita-san gave me good advice!
Hey.
I feel a really delicious jam coming on.
RING

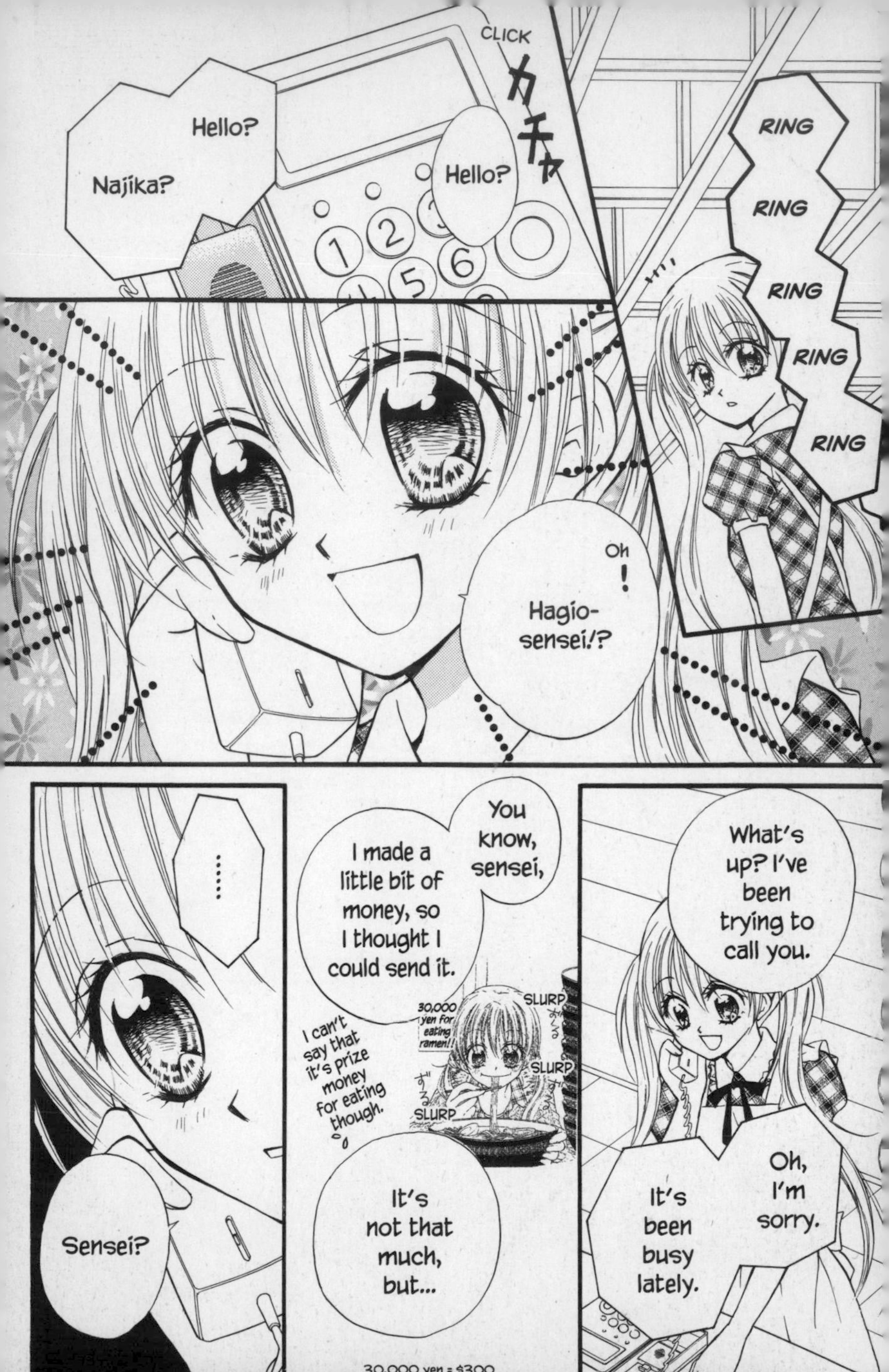
RING
RING
RING
RING
RING
CLICK
カチャ
Hello?
Hello?
Najika?
Oh!
Hagio-sensei!?
What's up? I've been trying to call you.
Oh, I'm sorry.
It's been busy lately.
You know, sensei,
I made a little bit of money, so I thought I could send it.
30,000 yen for eating ramen!!
I can't say that it's prize money for eating though.
SLURP
SLURP
SLURP
It's not that much, but...
......
Sensei?
30,000 yen = $300

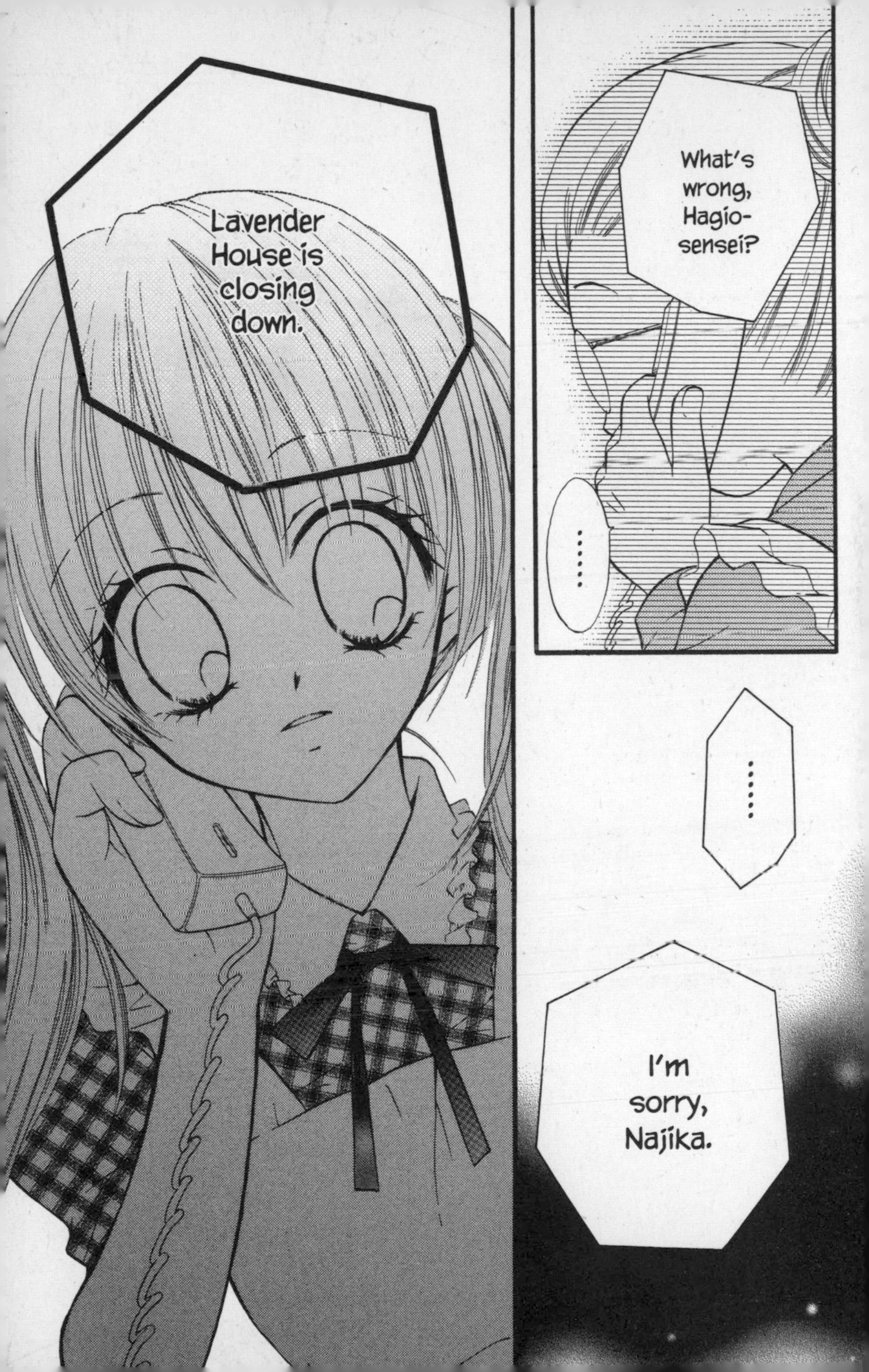
What's wrong, Hagio-sensei?
......
......
I'm sorry, Najika.
Lavender House is closing down.

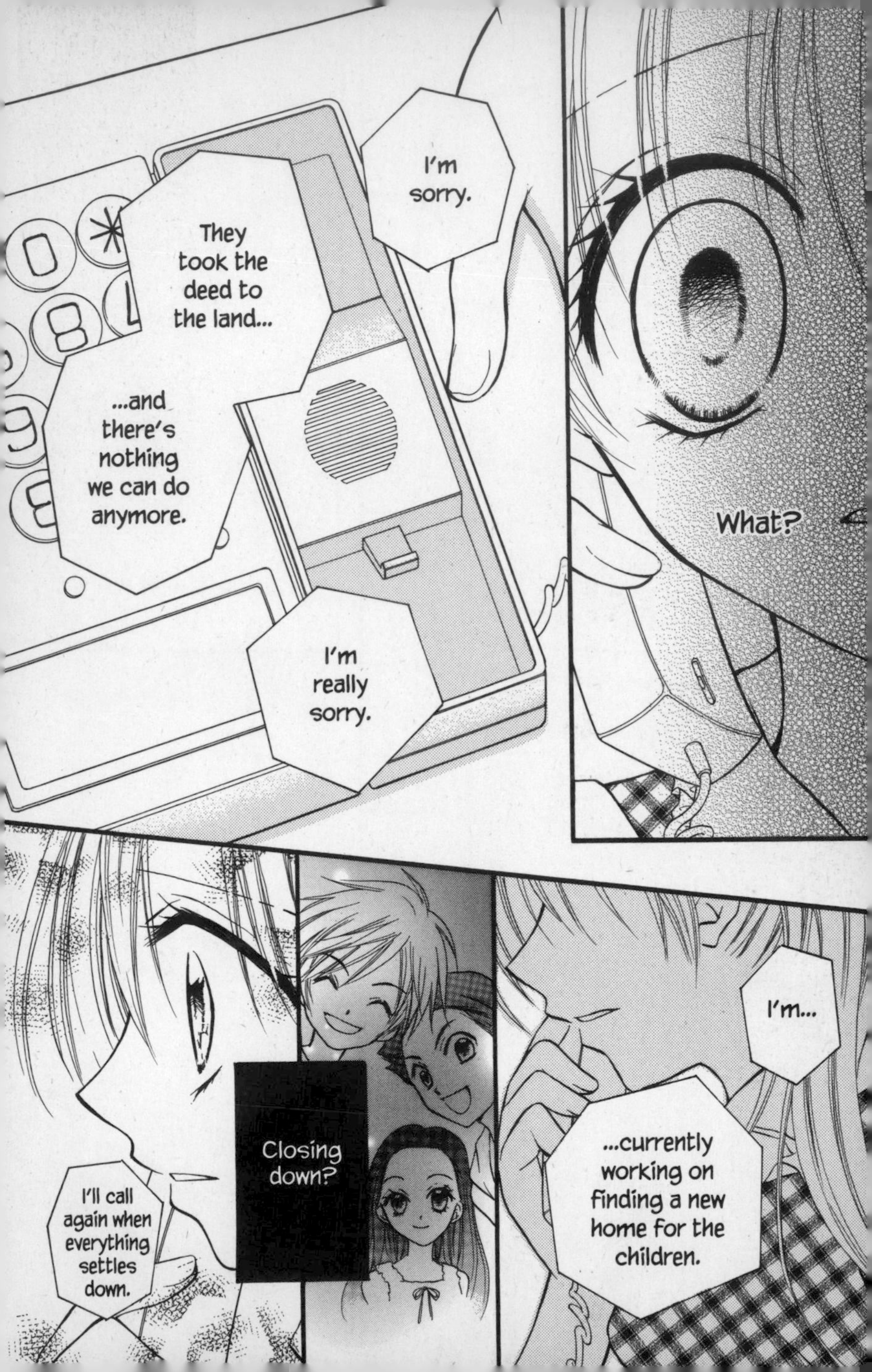
What?
I'm sorry.
They took the deed to the land...
...and there's nothing we can do anymore.
I'm really sorry.
I'm...
...currently working on finding a new home for the children.
Closing down?
I'll call again when everything settles down.

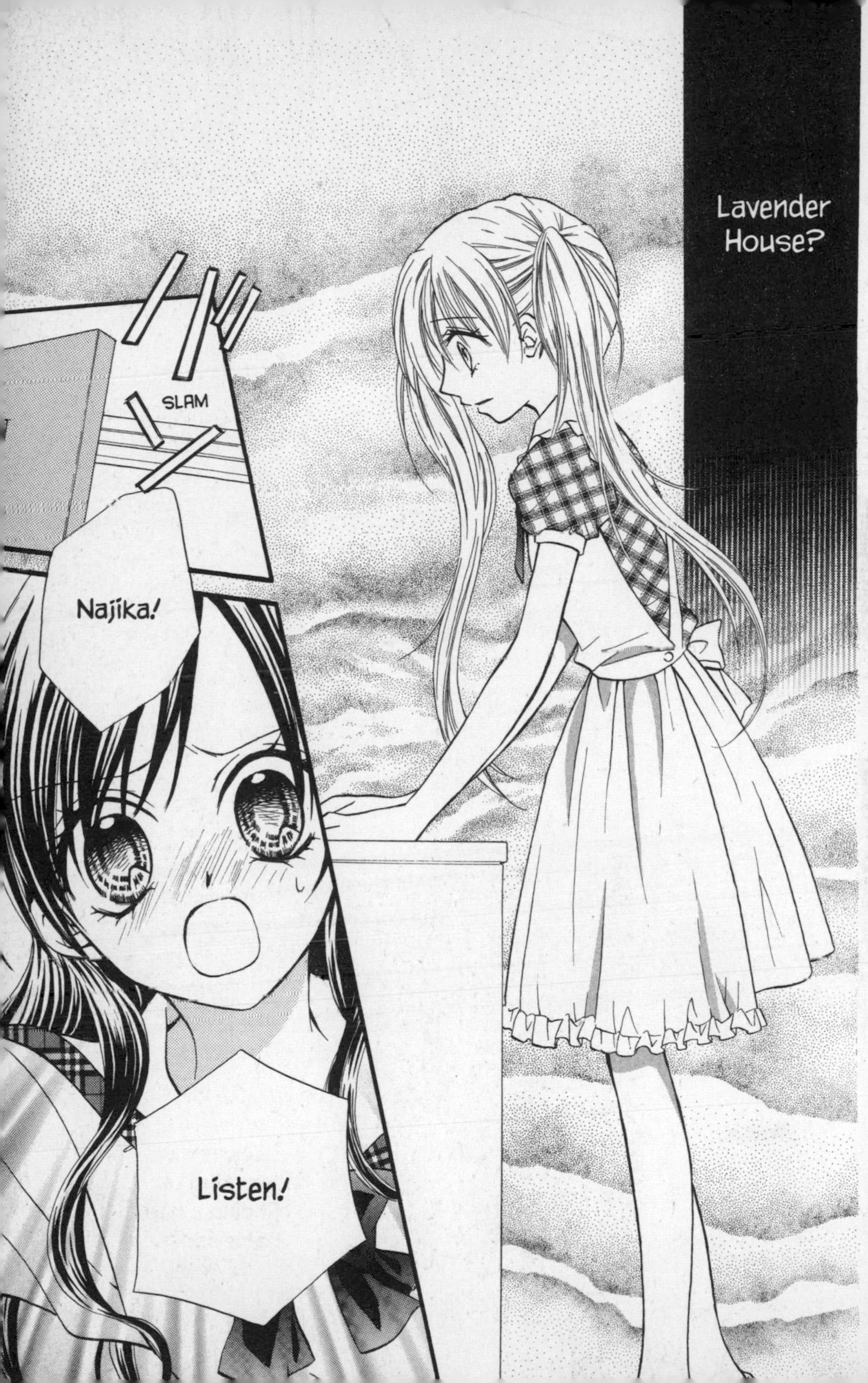
Lavender House?
SLAM
Najika!
Listen!

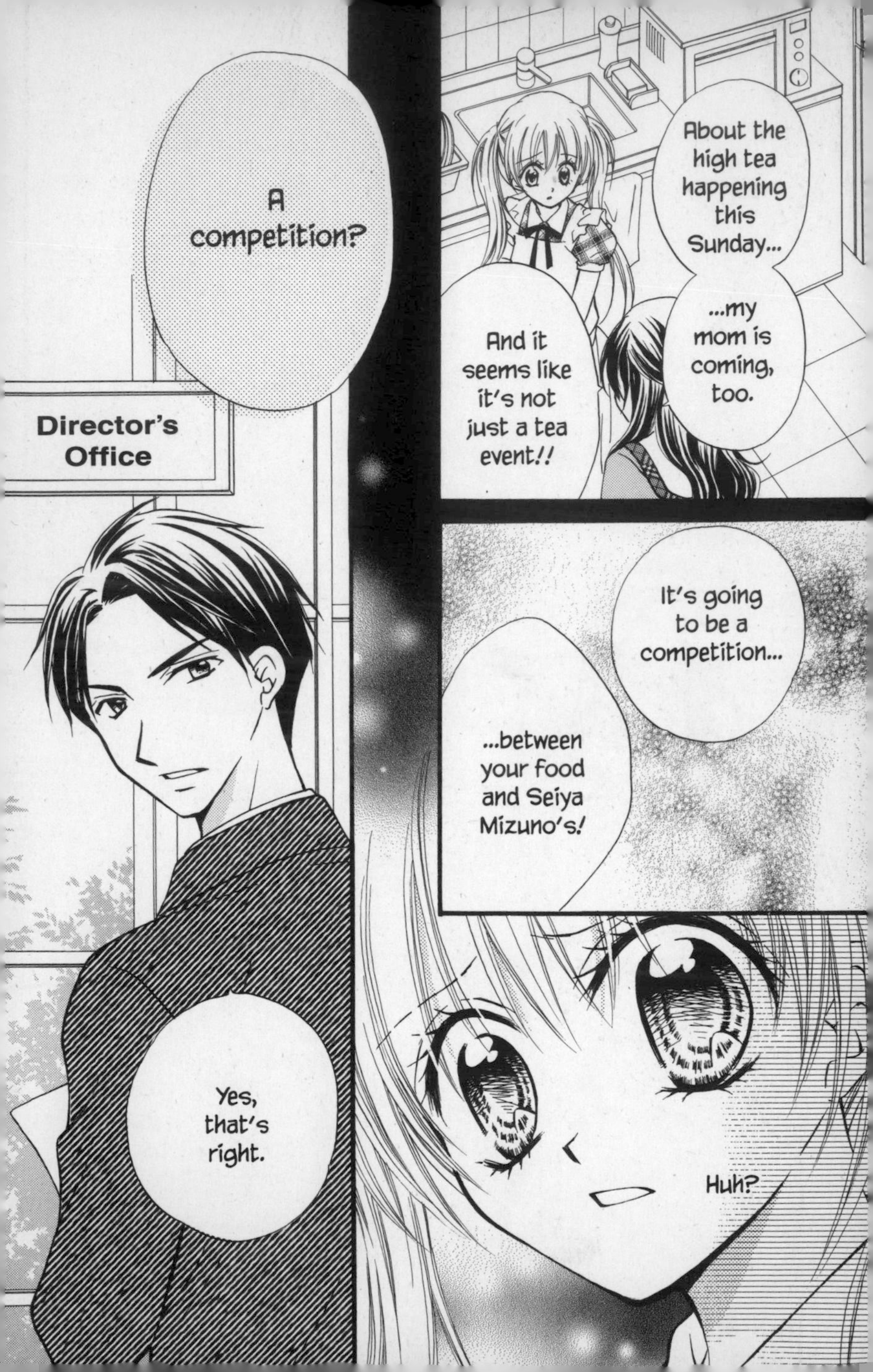
About the high tea happening this Sunday...
...my mom is coming, too.
And it seems like it's not just a tea event!!
It's going to be a competition...
...between your food and Seiya Mizuno's!
Huh?
A competition?
Director's Office
Yes, that's right.

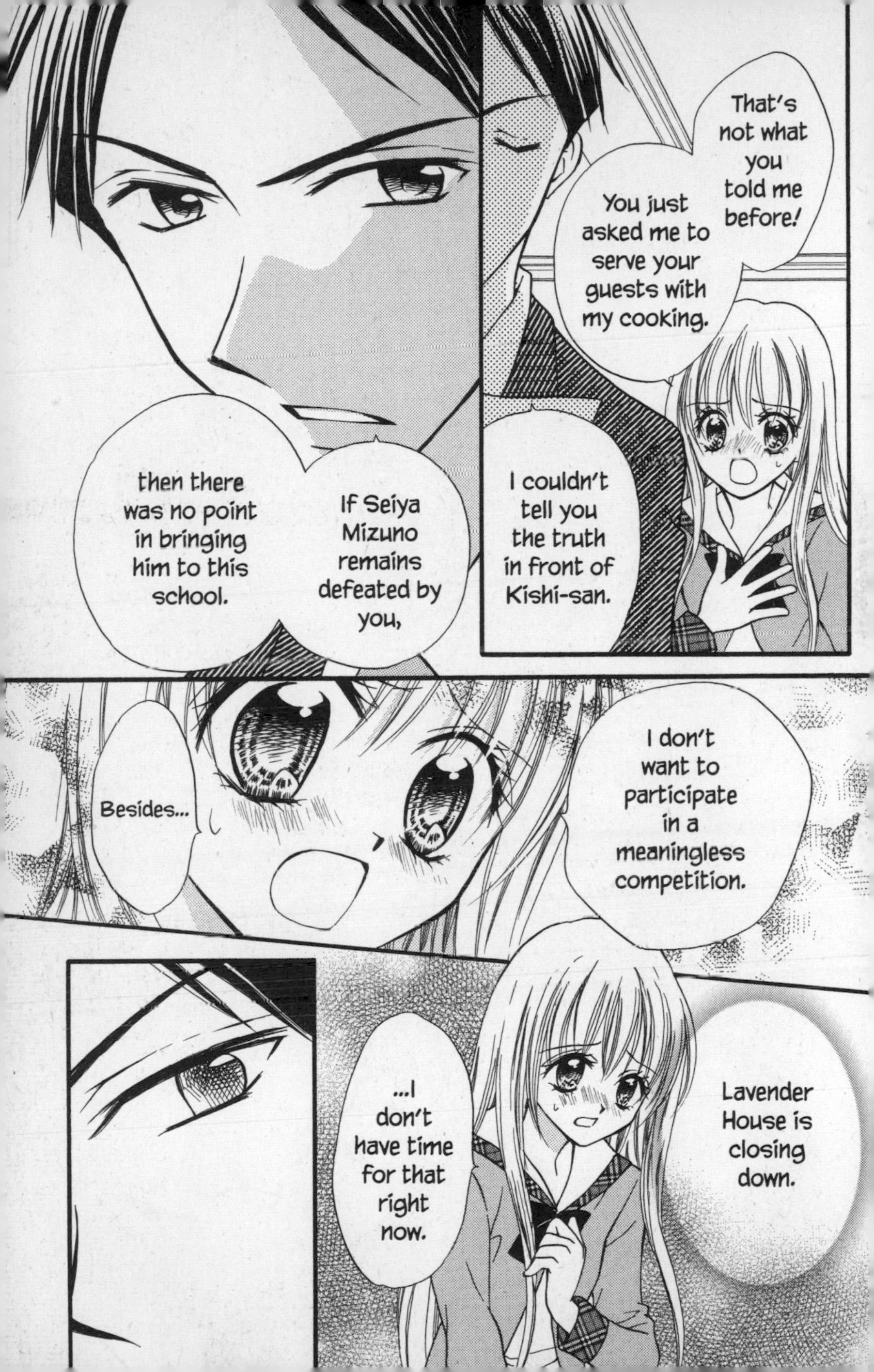
That's not what you told me before!
You just asked me to serve your guests with my cooking.
I couldn't tell you the truth in front of Kishi-san.
If Seiya Mizuno remains defeated by you,
then there was no point in bringing him to this school.
I don't want to participate in a meaningless competition.
Besides...
Lavender House is closing down.
...I don't have time for that right now.

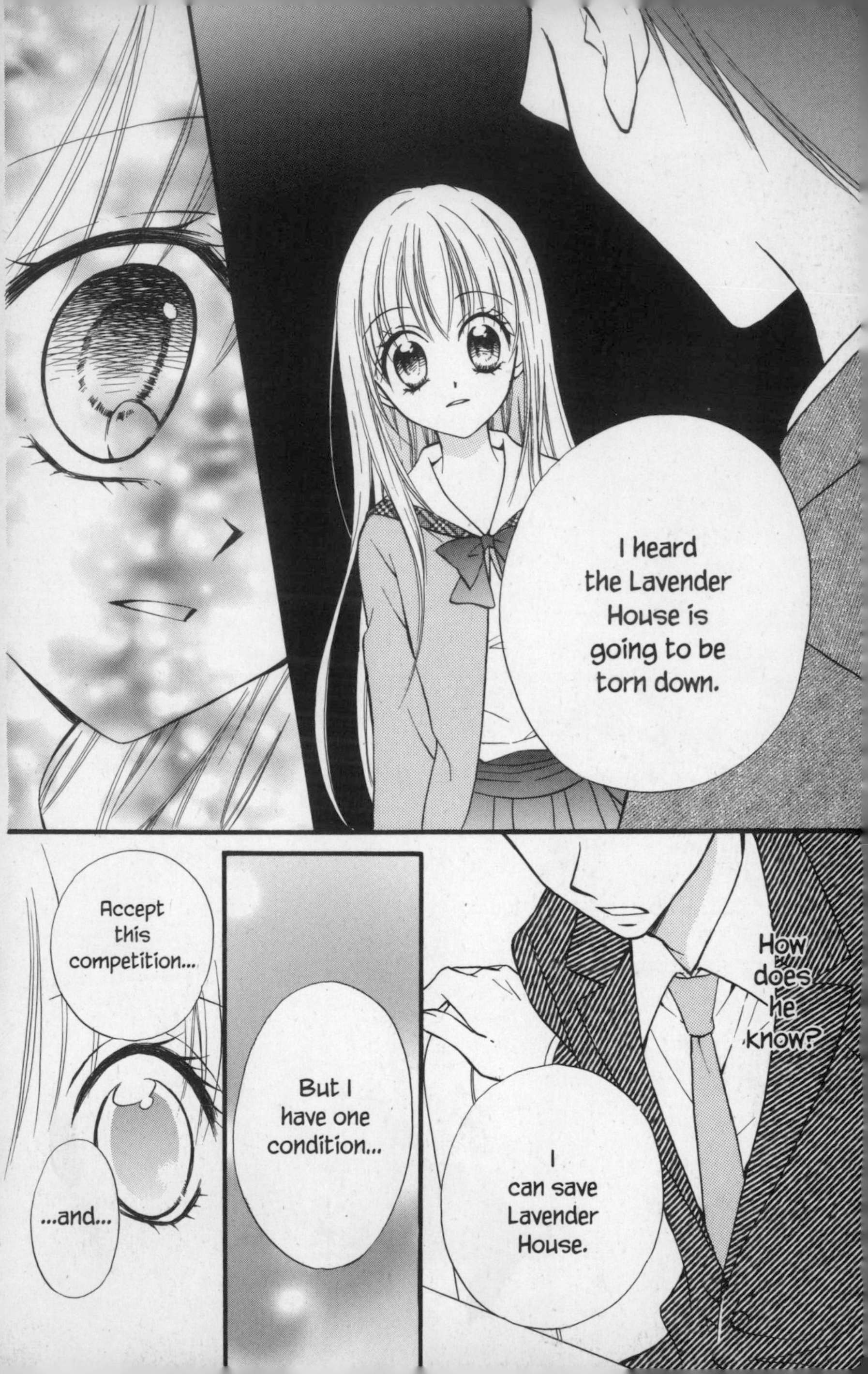
I heard the Lavender House is going to be torn down.
How does he know?
I can save Lavender House.
But I have one condition...
Accept this competition...
...and...

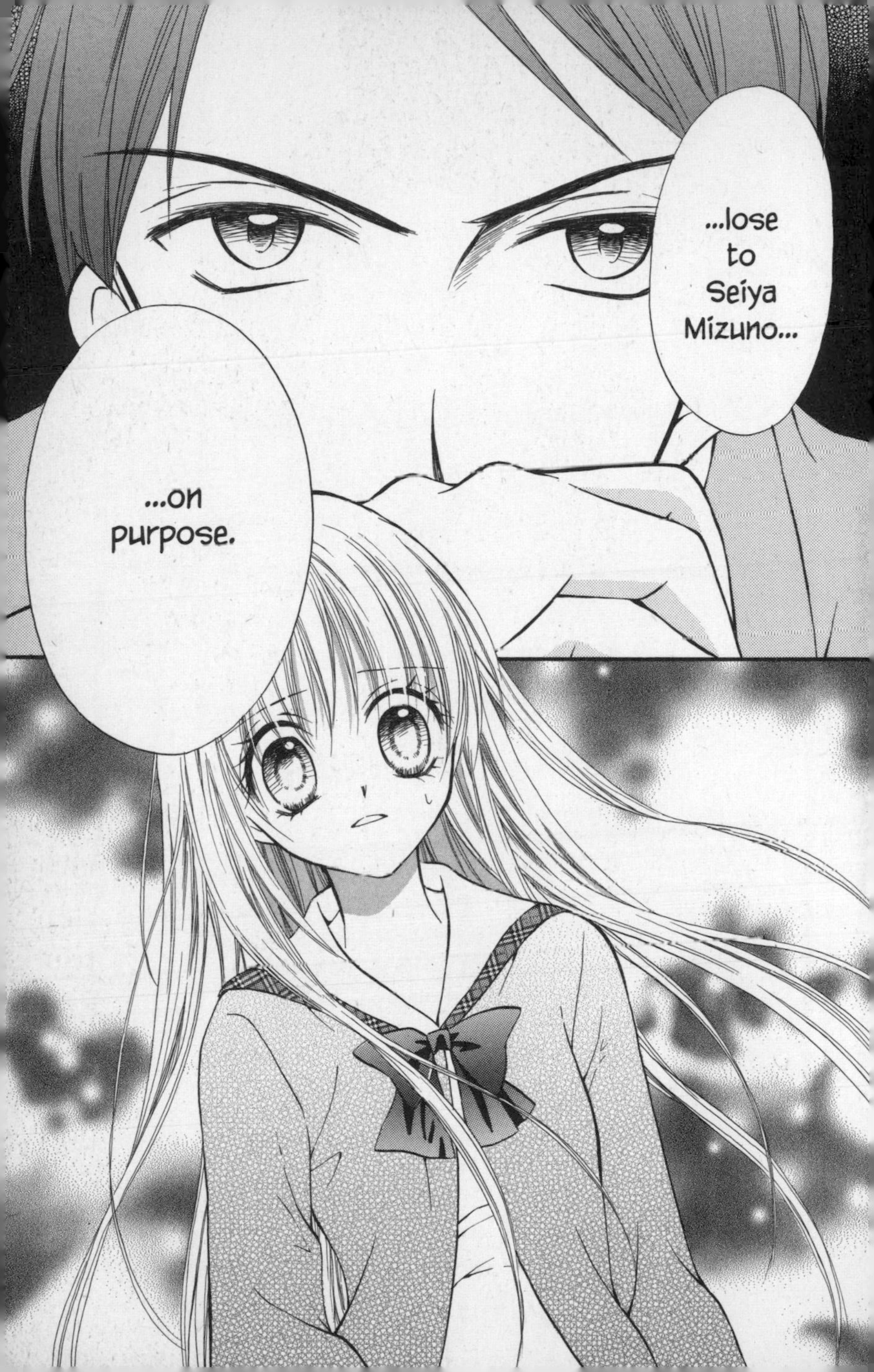
...lose to Seiya Mizuno...
...on purpose.

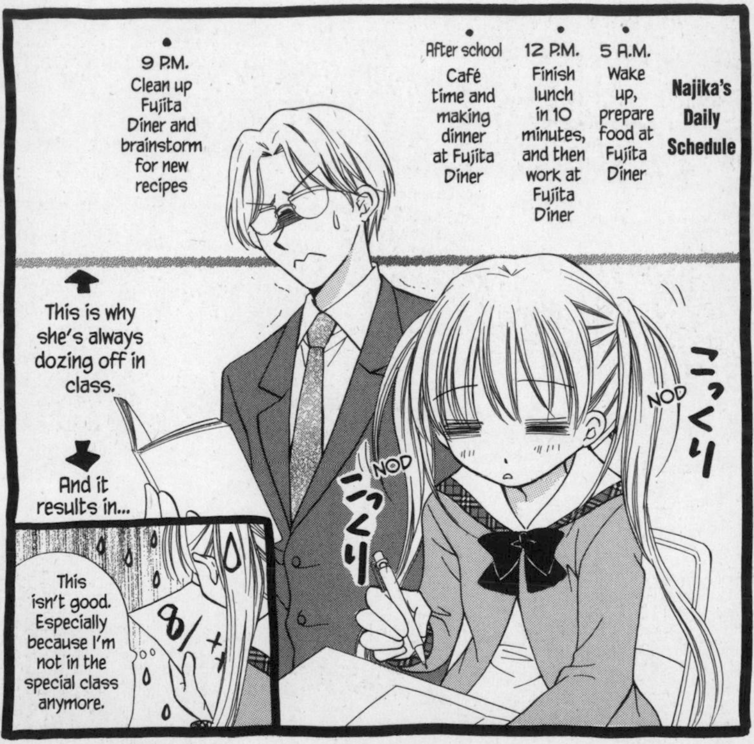
Najika's Daily Schedule
5 A.M. Wake up, prepare food at Fujita Diner
12 P.M. Finish lunch in 10 minutes, and then work at Fujita Diner
After school Café time and making dinner at Fujita Diner
9 P.M. Clean up Fujita Diner and brainstorm for new recipes
NOD こっくり
NOD こっくり
This is why she's always dozing off in class.
And it results in...
This isn't good. Especially because I'm not in the special class anymore.

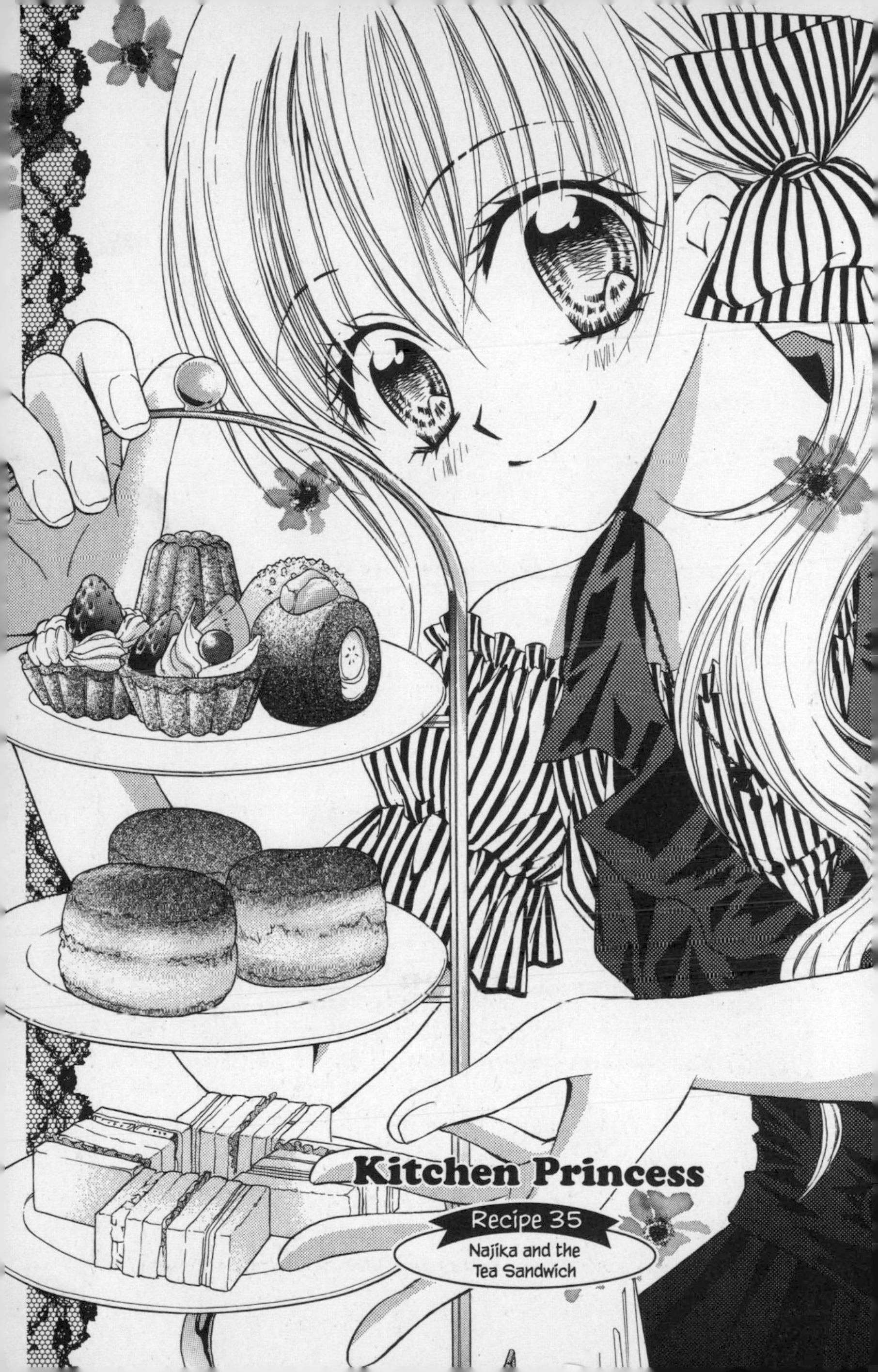
Kitchen Princess
Recipe 35
Najika and the Tea Sandwich

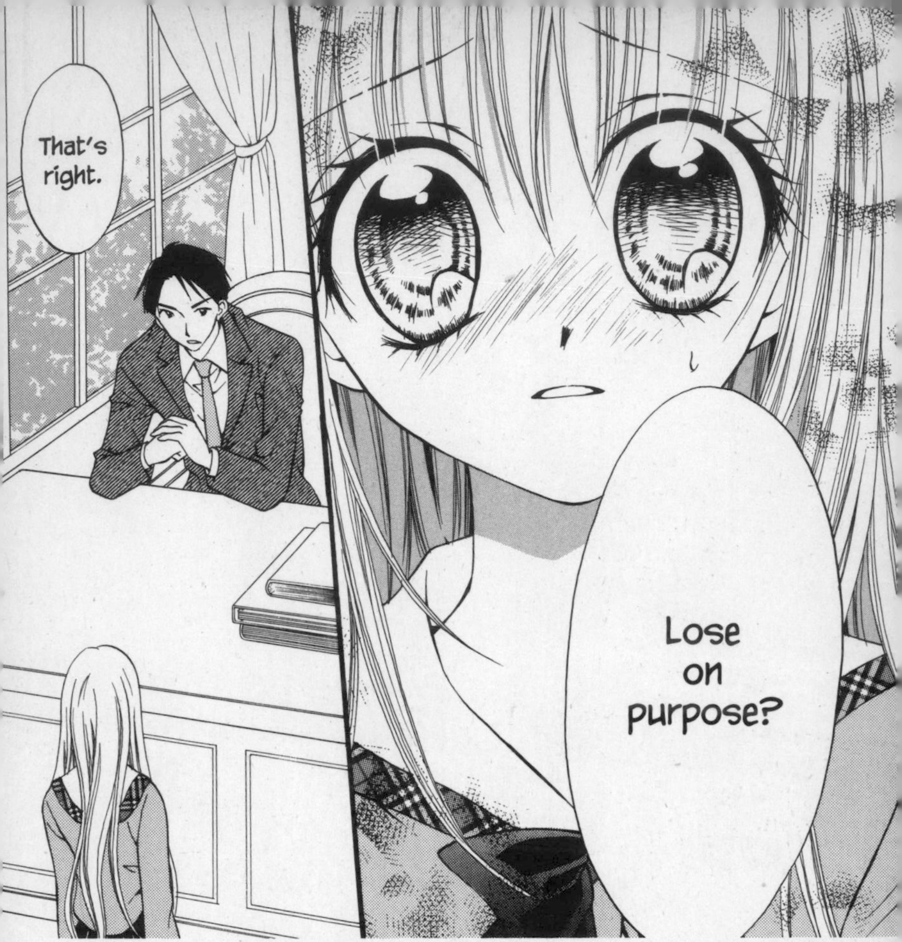
Lose on purpose?
That's right.

About Recipe 35's Splash Page

It's exactly what the chapter title is. I think it's one of the few splash pages that has something to do with the actual story!

Najika's note ideas were thought up by my assistants, and it really helped me! Thank you. ♡

But there's a line that says, "put a 5 mm piece of dragée into the Madeline," and I accidentally wrote "5 m piece of dragée." No way! That's too big!!

I realized it later, and fixed it immediately. That was close. ०००

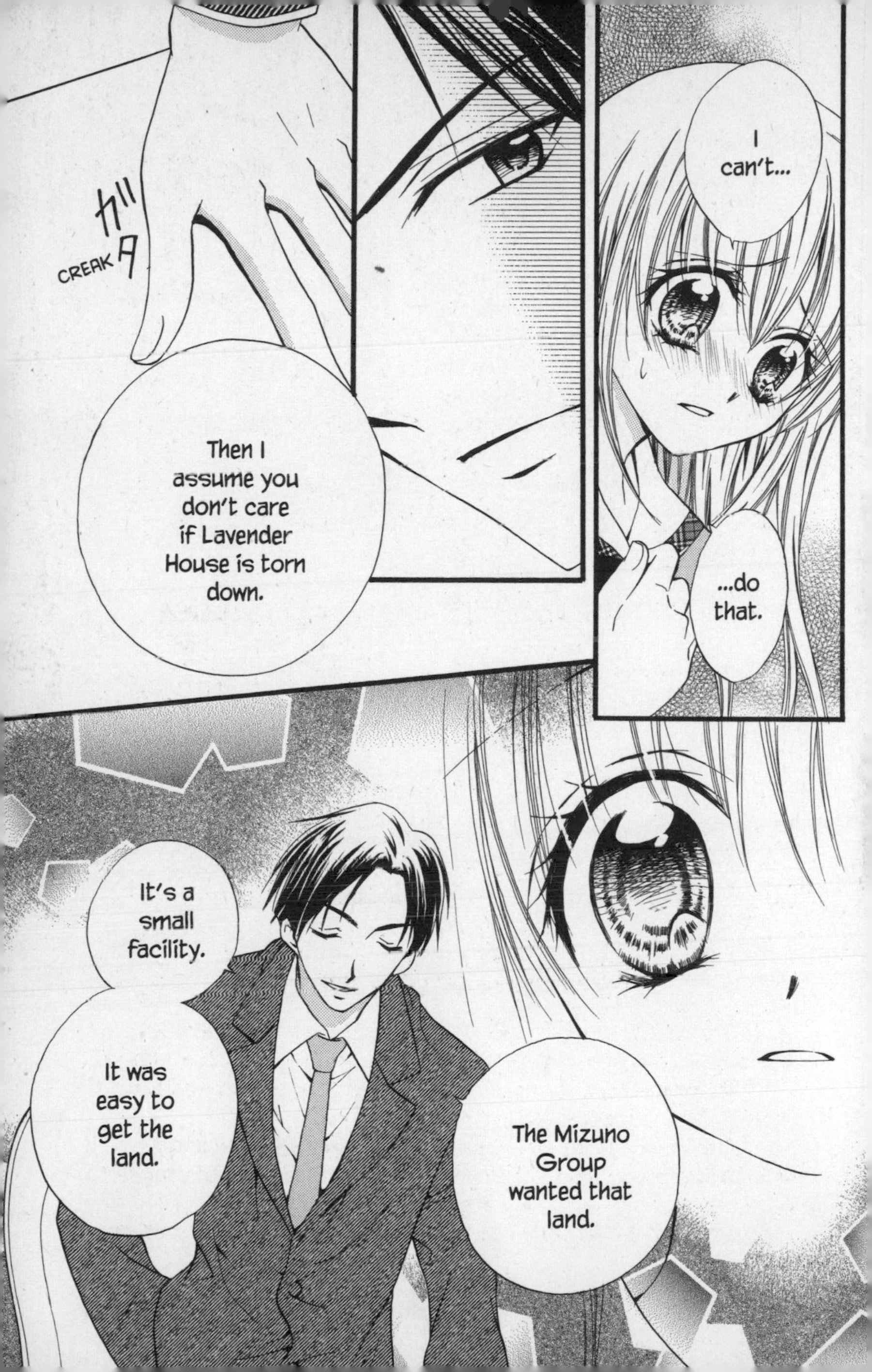
I can't...
...do that.
CREAK
Then I assume you don't care if Lavender House is torn down.
The Mizuno Group wanted that land.
It's a small facility.
It was easy to get the land.

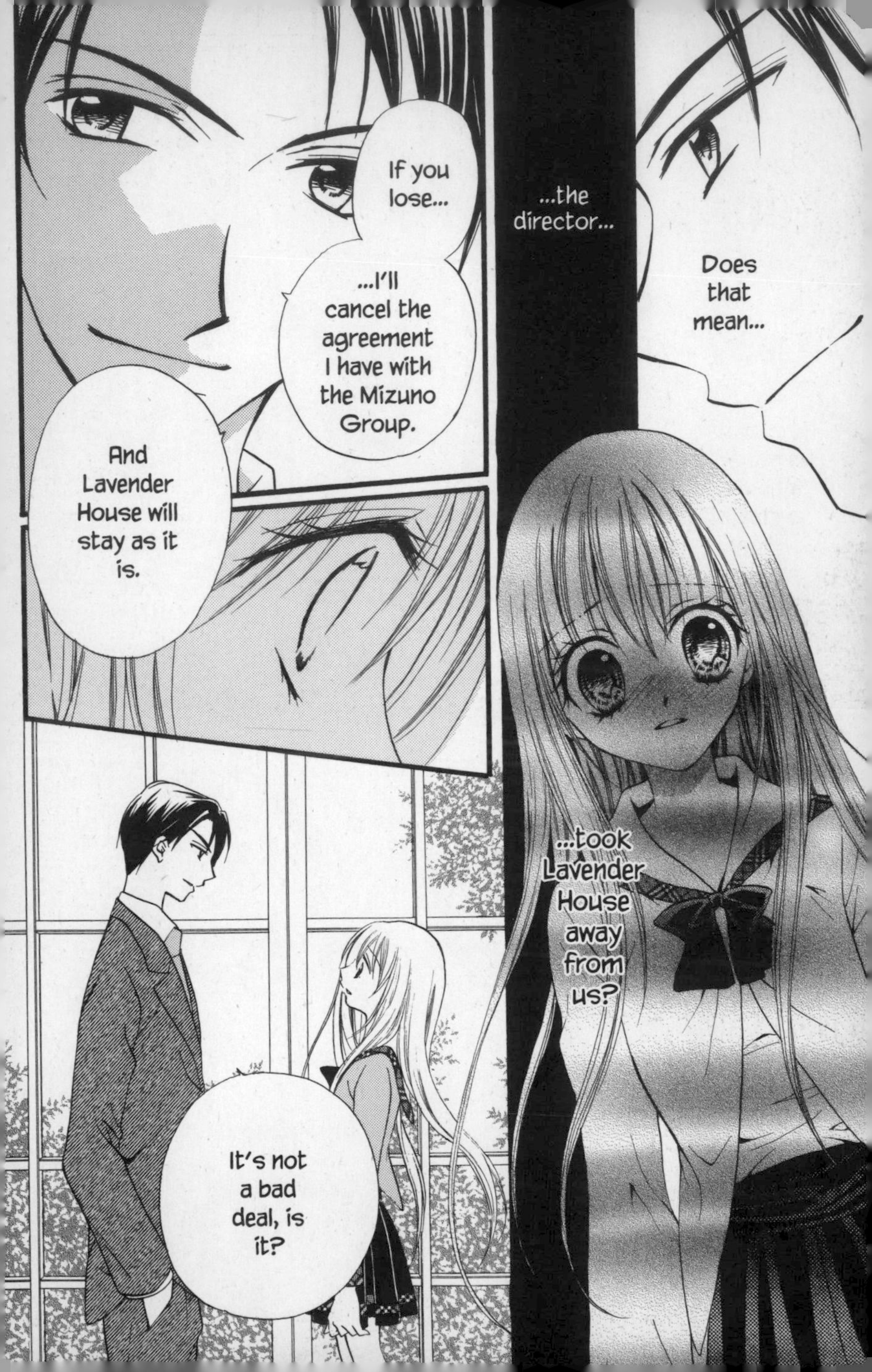
If you lose...
...I'll cancel the agreement I have with the Mizuno Group.
And Lavender House will stay as it is.
It's not a bad deal, is it?
Does that mean...
...the director...
...took Lavender House away from us?

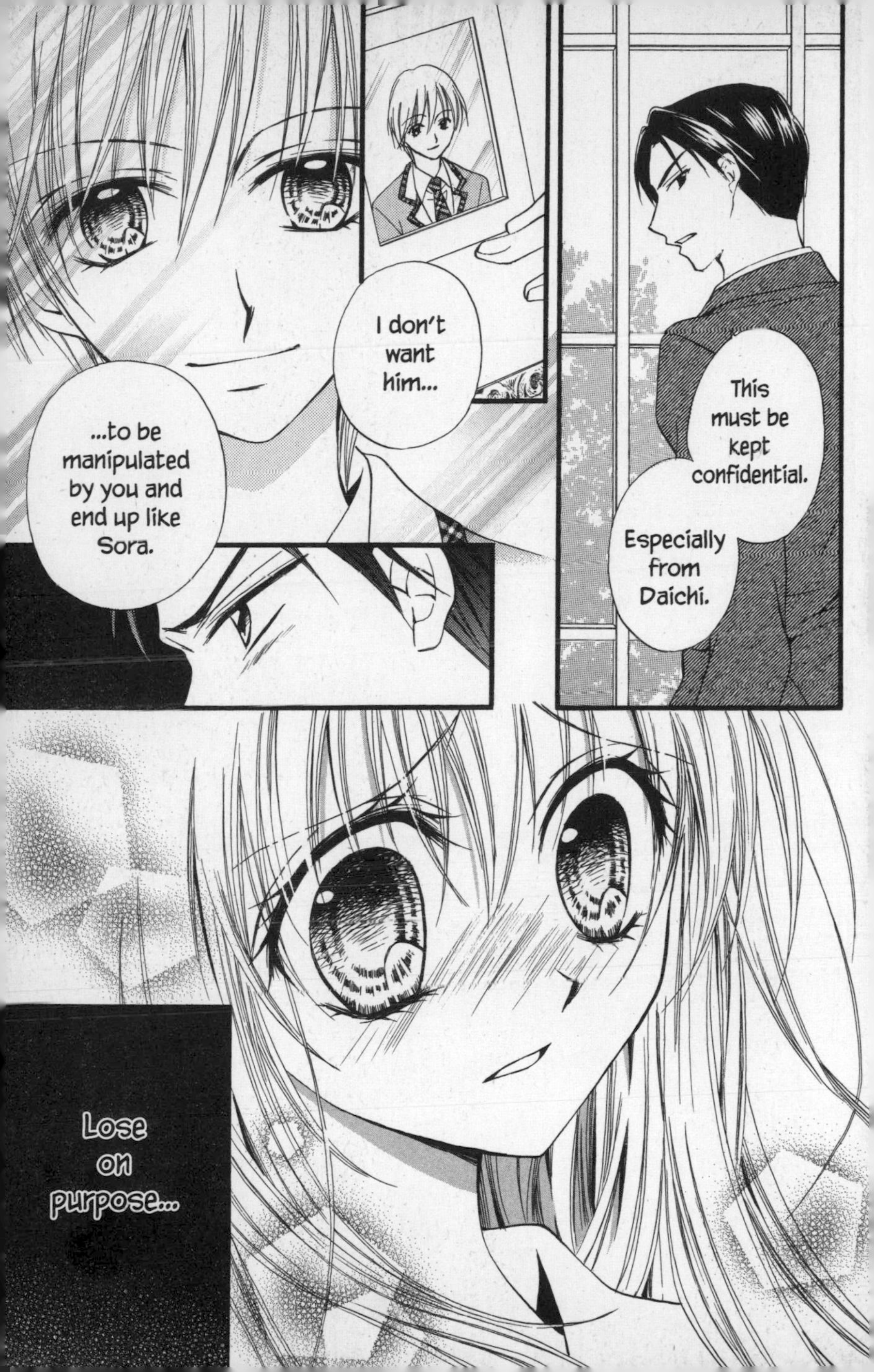
This must be kept confidential.
Especially from Daichi.
I don't want him...
...to be manipulated by you and end up like Sora.
Lose on purpose...

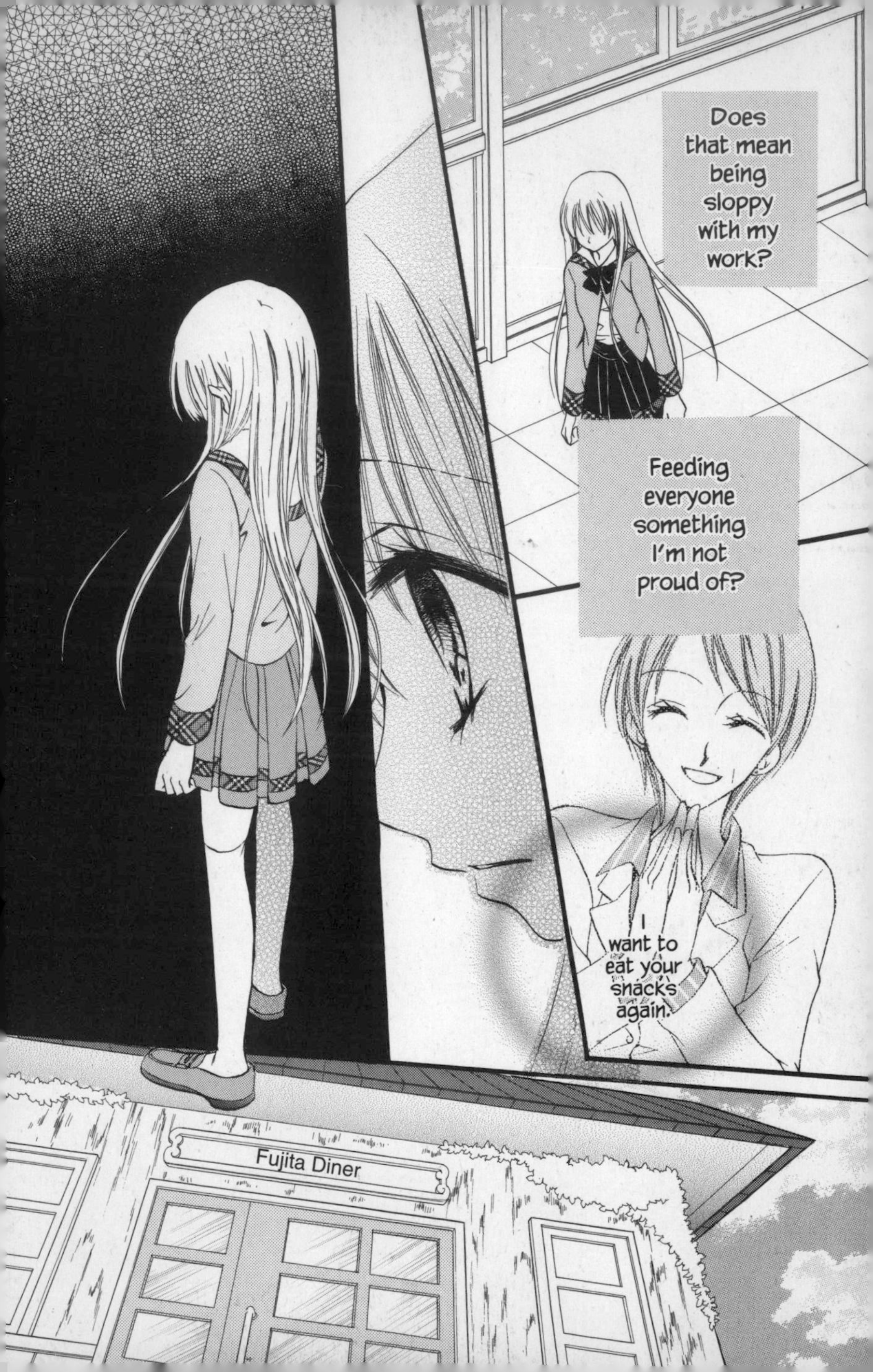
Does that mean being sloppy with my work?
Feeding everyone something I'm not proud of?
I want to eat your snacks again.
Fujita Diner

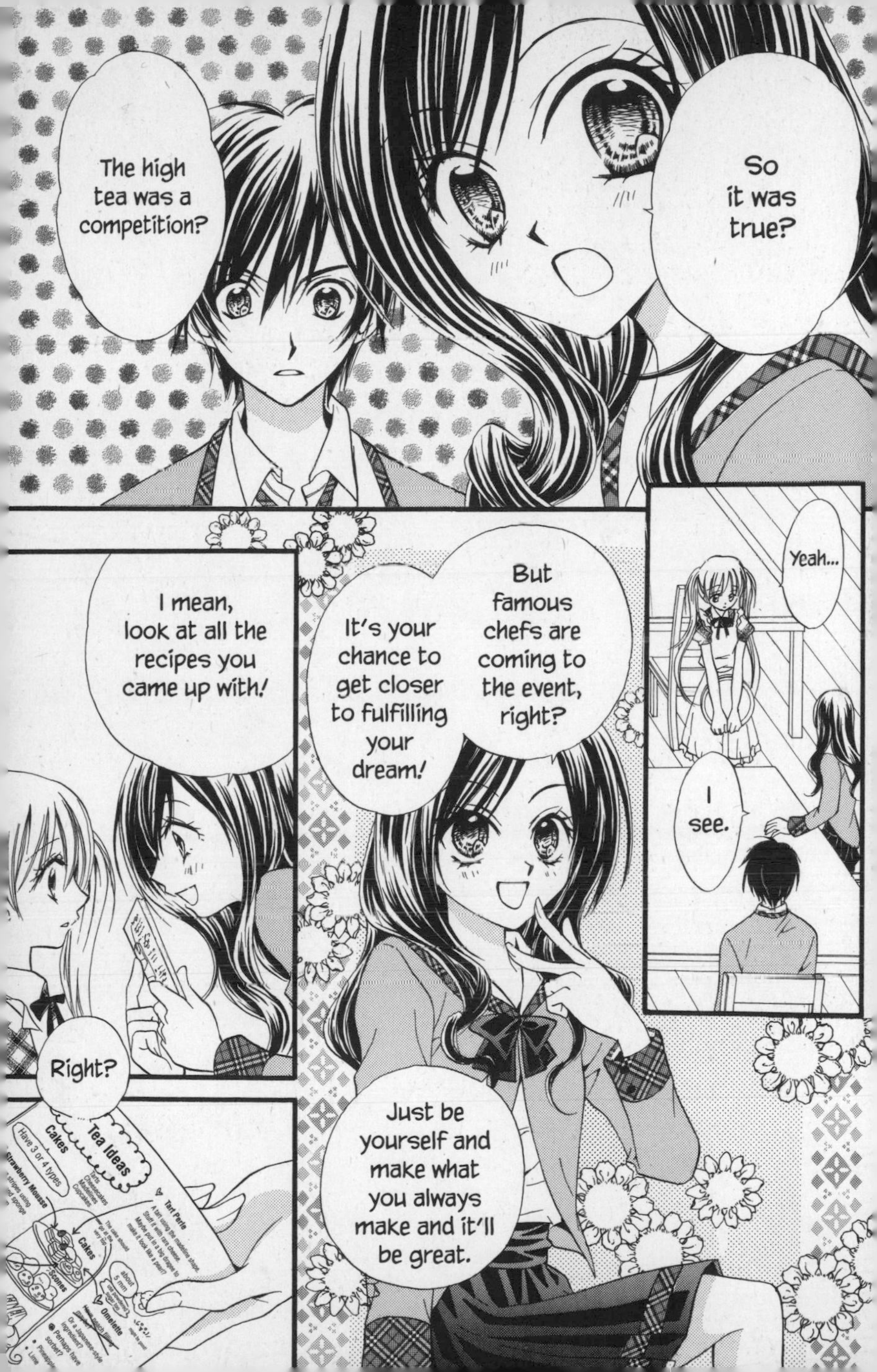
So it was true?
The high tea was a competition?
Yeah...
I see.
But famous chefs are coming to the event, right?
It's your chance to get closer to fulfilling your dream!
Just be yourself and make what you always make and it'll be great.
I mean, look at all the recipes you came up with!
Right?
Tea Ideas
Cakes
Have 3 or 4 types

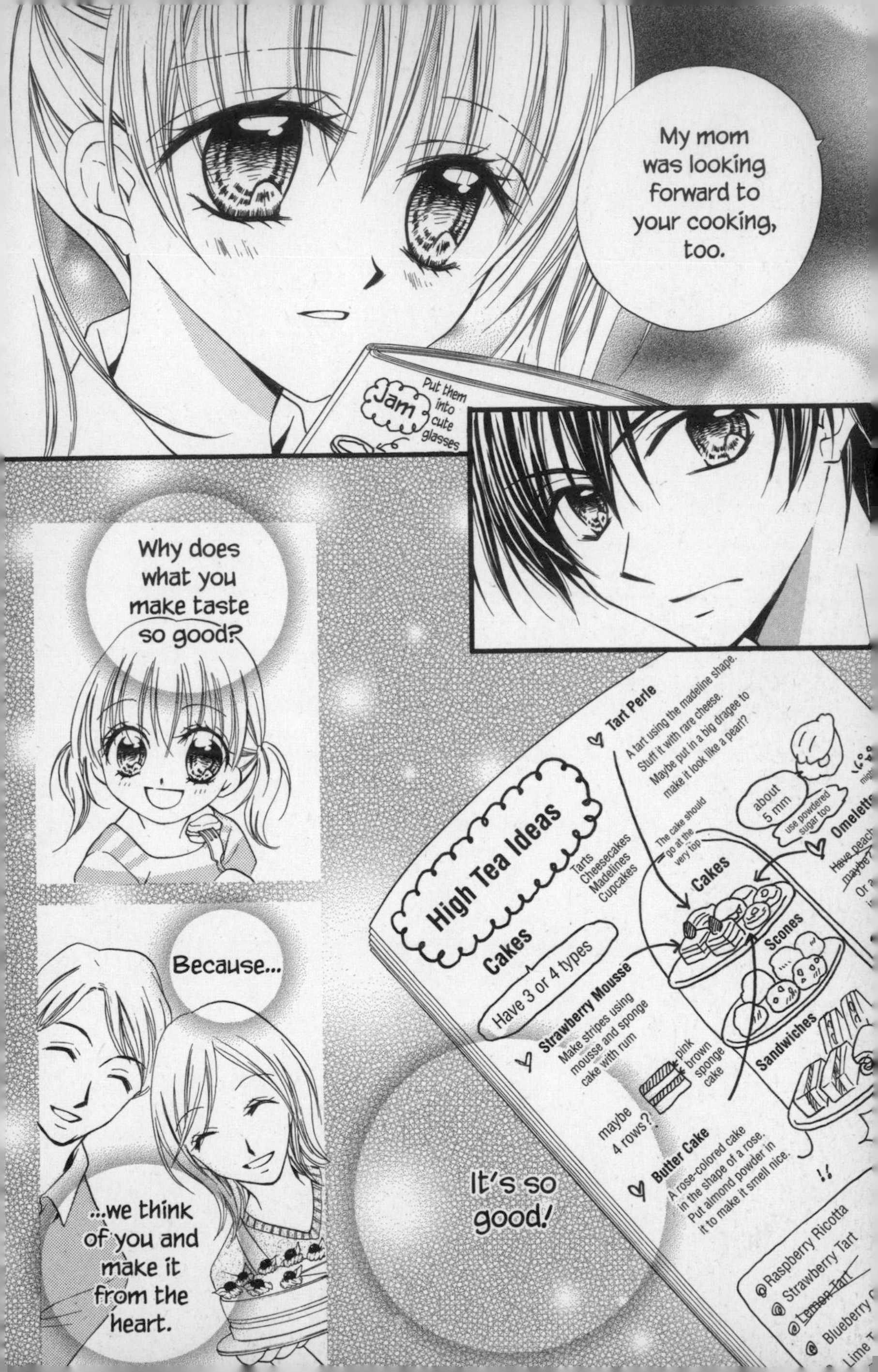
My mom was looking forward to your cooking, too.
Jam
Put them into cute glasses
High Tea Ideas
Tarts
Cheesecakes
Madelines
Cupcakes
Cakes
Have 3 or 4 types
Tart Perle
A tart using the madeline shape. Stuff it with rare cheese. Maybe put in a big dragee to make it look like a pearl?
about 5 mm
use powdered sugar too
The cake should go at the very top
Cakes
Scones
Sandwiches
Strawberry Mousse
Make stripes using mousse and sponge cake with rum
pink
brown
sponge cake
maybe 4 rows?
Butter Cake
A rose-colored cake in the shape of a rose. Put almond powder in it to make it smell nice.
Raspberry Ricotta
Strawberry Tart
Lemon Tart
It's so good!
Why does what you make taste so good?
Because...
...we think of you and make it from the heart.

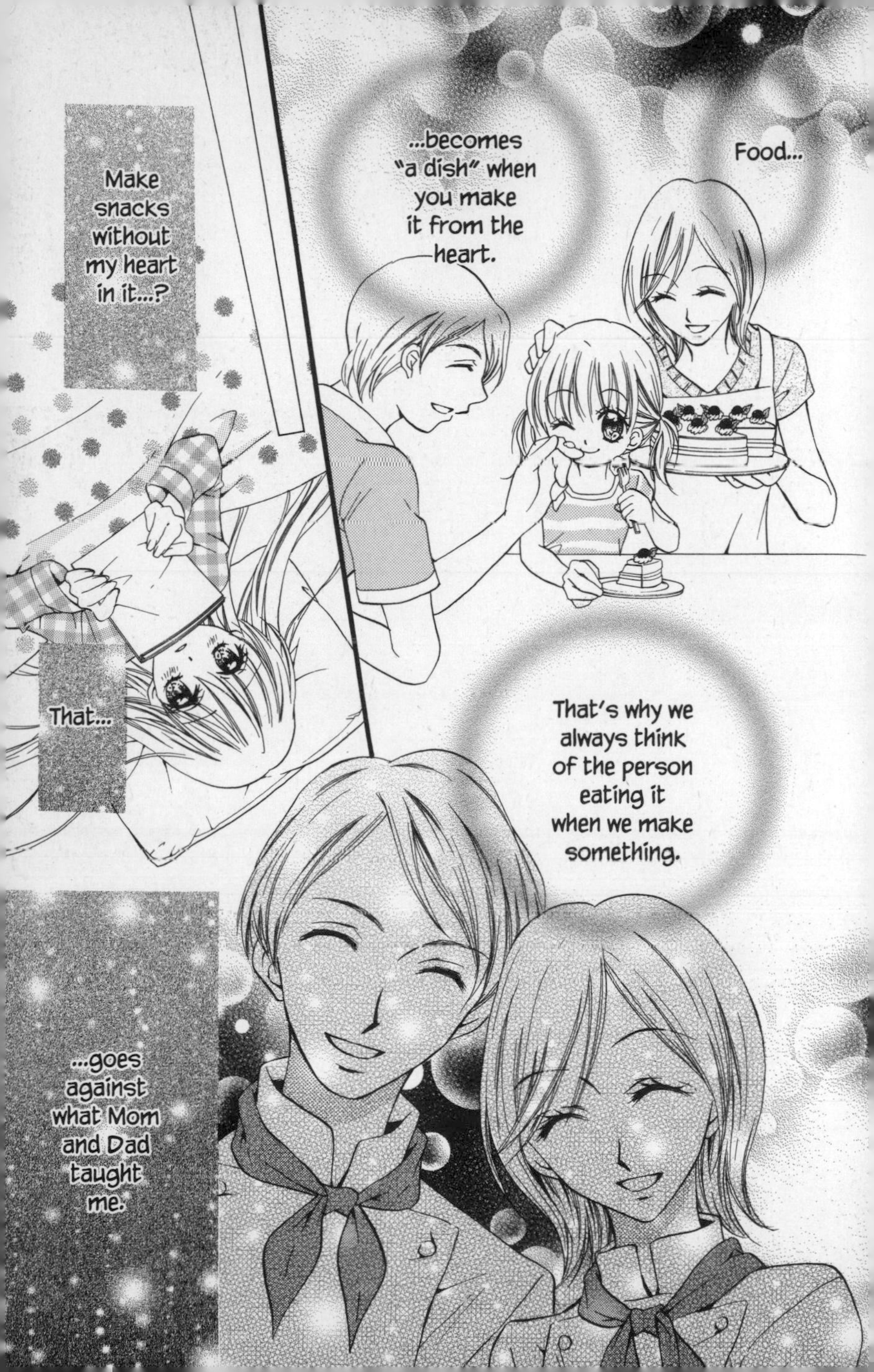
Food...
...becomes "a dish" when you make it from the heart.
That's why we always think of the person eating it when we make something.
Make snacks without my heart in it...?
That...
...goes against what Mom and Dad taught me.

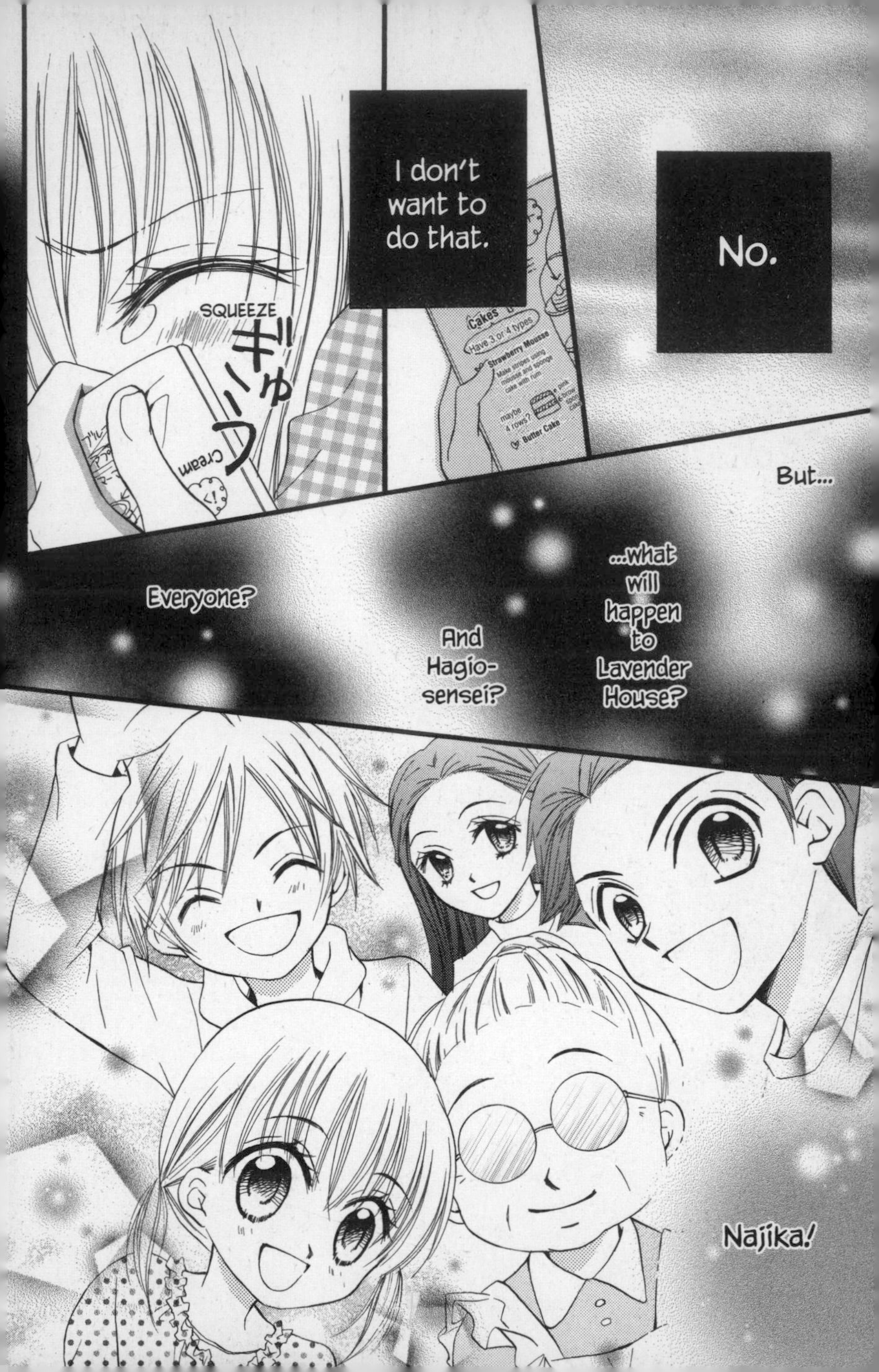
No.
I don't want to do that.
Cakes
Have 3 or 4 types
Strawberry Mousse
Make stripes using mousse and sponge cake with rum
maybe 4 rows?
Butter Cake
SQUEEZE
Cream
But...
...what will happen to Lavender House?
And Hagio-sensei?
Everyone?
Najika!

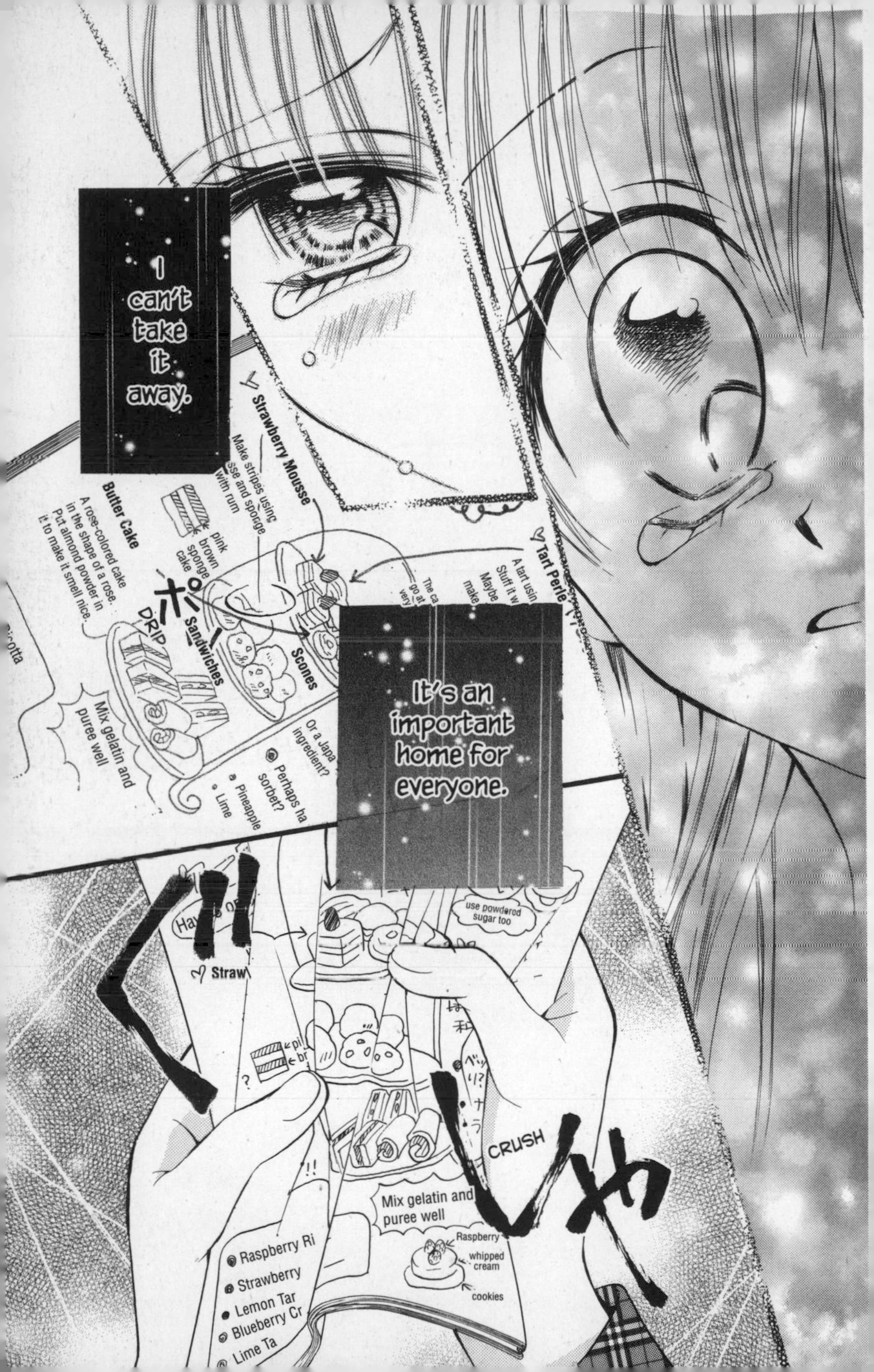
I can't take it away.
It's an important home for everyone.
DRIP
CRUSH

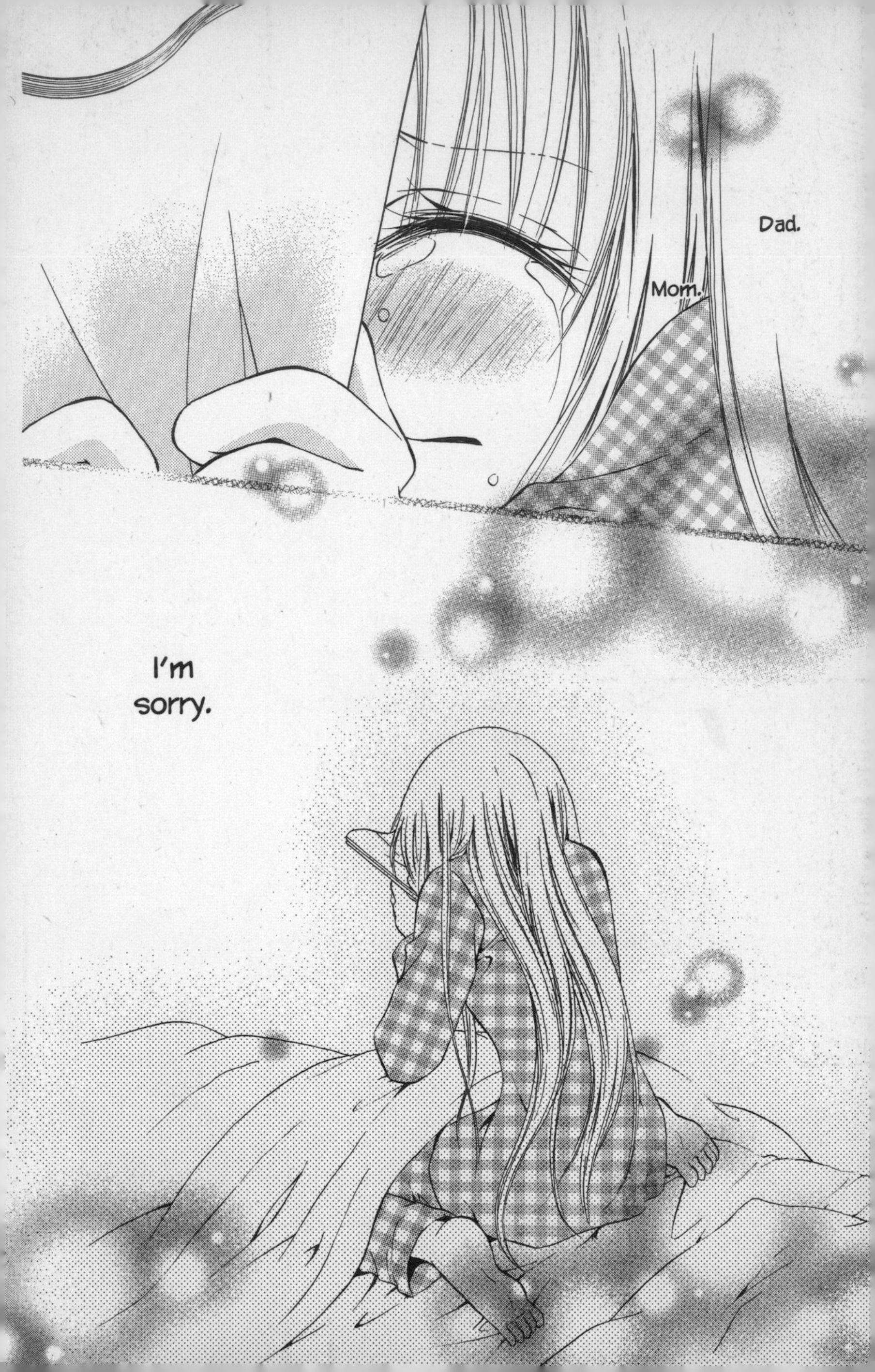
Dad.
Mom.
I'm sorry.

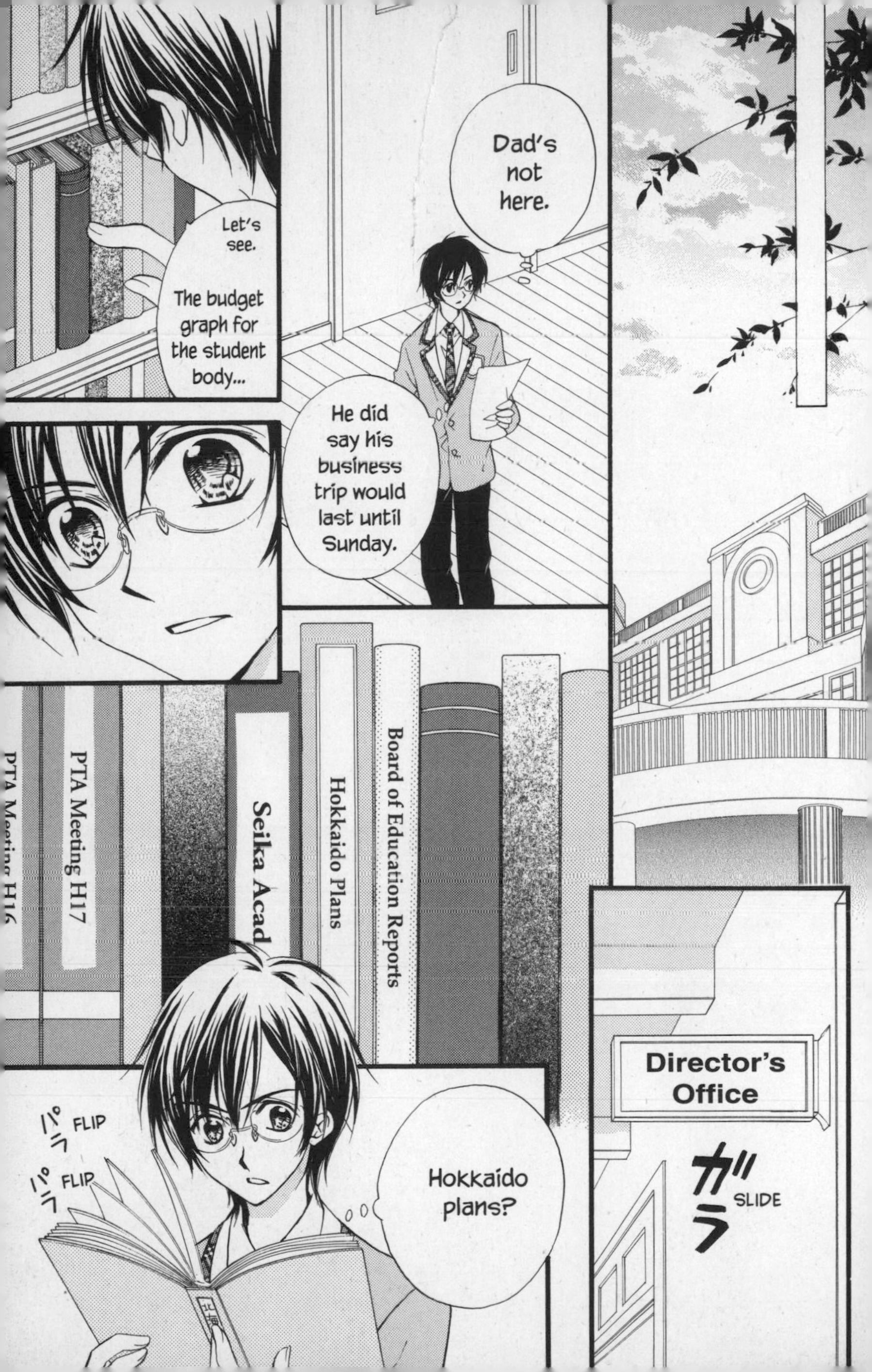

Dad's not here.
He did say his business trip would last until Sunday.
Let's see.
The budget graph for the student body...
Director's Office
ガラ SLIDE
Board of Education Reports
Hokkaido Plans
Seika Acad
PTA Meeting H17
PTA Meeting H16
パラ FLIP
パラ FLIP
Hokkaido plans?

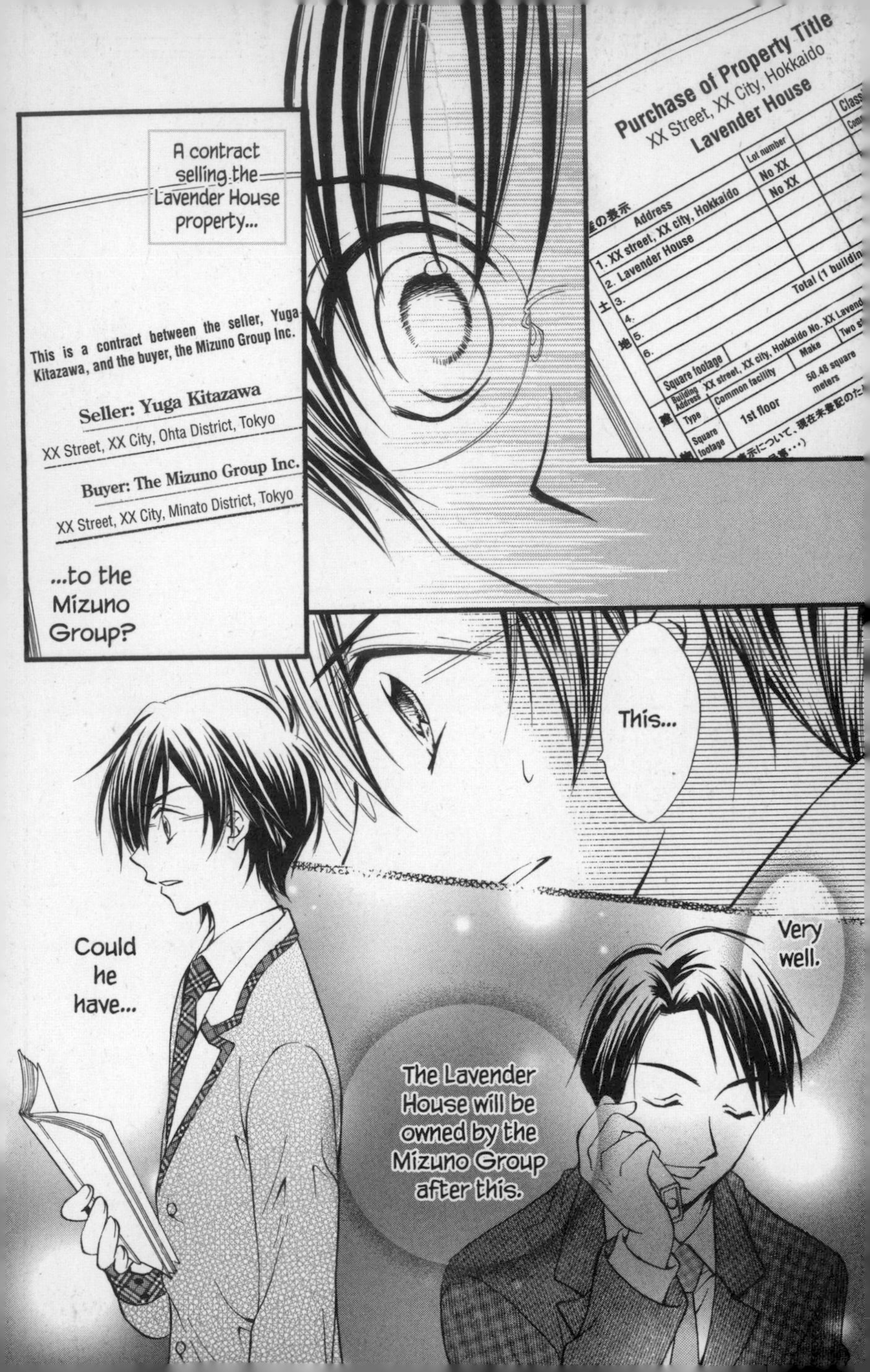

Purchase of Property Title
XX Street, XX City, Hokkaido
Lavender House
Lot number
Address
No XX
No XX
1. XX street, XX city, Hokkaido
2. Lavender House
3.
4.
5.
6.
Square footage
Building Address
XX street, XX city, Hokkaido No. XX
Type
Common facility
Make
Square footage
1st floor
50.48 square meters
A contract selling the Lavender House property...
This is a contract between the seller, Yuga Kitazawa, and the buyer, the Mizuno Group Inc.
Seller: Yuga Kitazawa
XX Street, XX City, Ohta District, Tokyo
Buyer: The Mizuno Group Inc.
XX Street, XX City, Minato District, Tokyo
...to the Mizuno Group?
This...
Very well.
The Lavender House will be owned by the Mizuno Group after this.
Could he have...

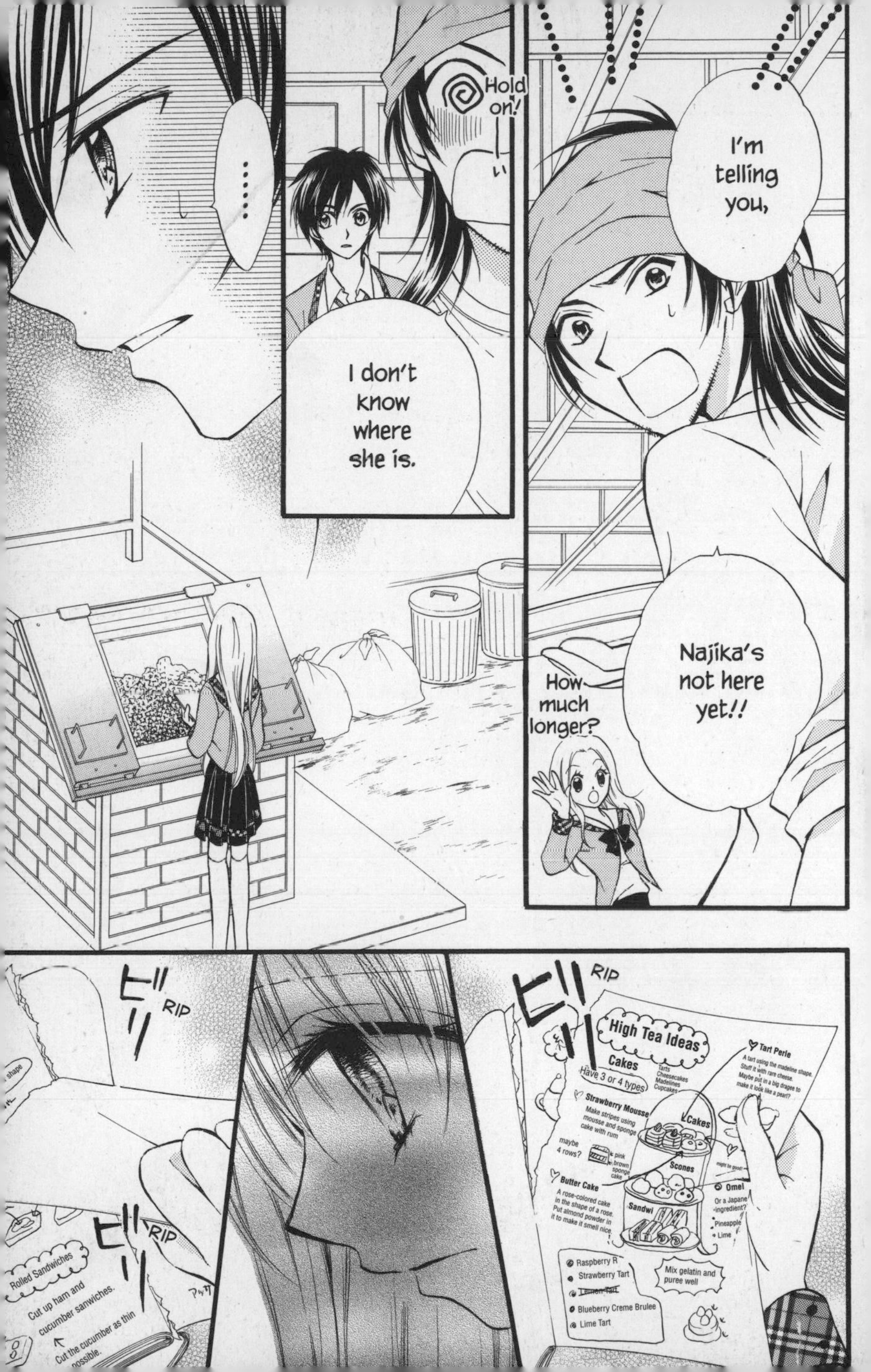
I'm telling you,
Najika's not here yet!!
How much longer?
Hold on!
I don't know where she is.
......
ビリ
RIP
High Tea Ideas
Cakes
Have 3 or 4 types
Tarts
Cheesecakes
Madelines
Cupcakes
Tart Perle
A tart using the madeline shape. Stuff it with rare cheese. Maybe put in a big dragee to make it look like a pearl?
Strawberry Mousse
Make stripes using mousse and sponge cake with rum
maybe 4 rows?
pink
brown
sponge cake
Cakes
Scones
might be good!
Butter Cake
A rose-colored cake in the shape of a rose. Put almond powder in it to make it smell nice.
Sandwi
Omel
Or a Japane ingredient?
Pineapple
Lime
Raspberry R
Strawberry Tart
Lemon Tart
Blueberry Creme Brulee
Lime Tart
Mix gelatin and puree well
ビリ
RIP
shape
ビリ
RIP
Rolled Sandwiches
Cut up ham and cucumber sanwiches.
Cut the cucumber as thin possible.

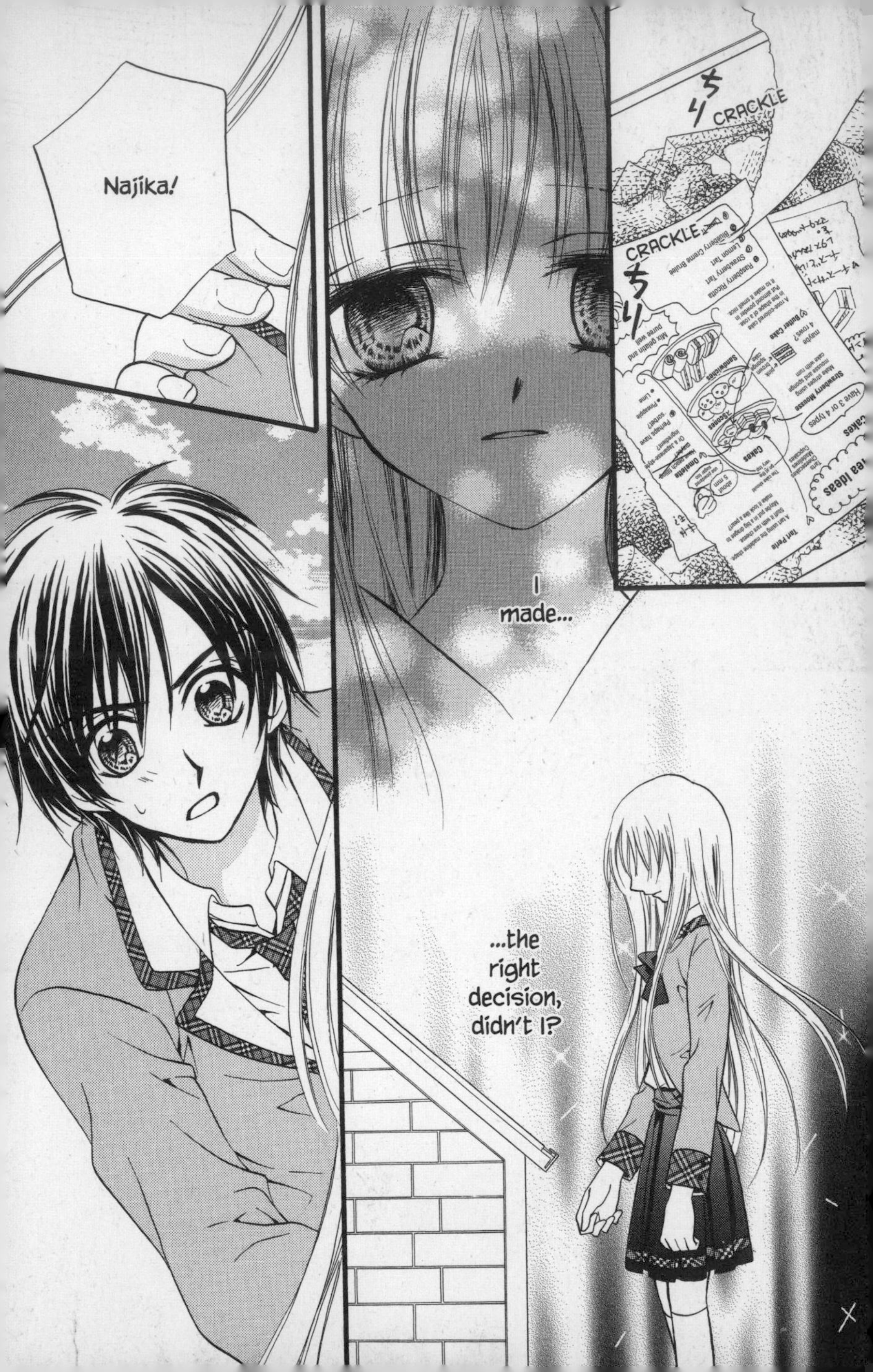
CRACKLE
CRACKLE
I made...
...the right decision, didn't I?
Najika!

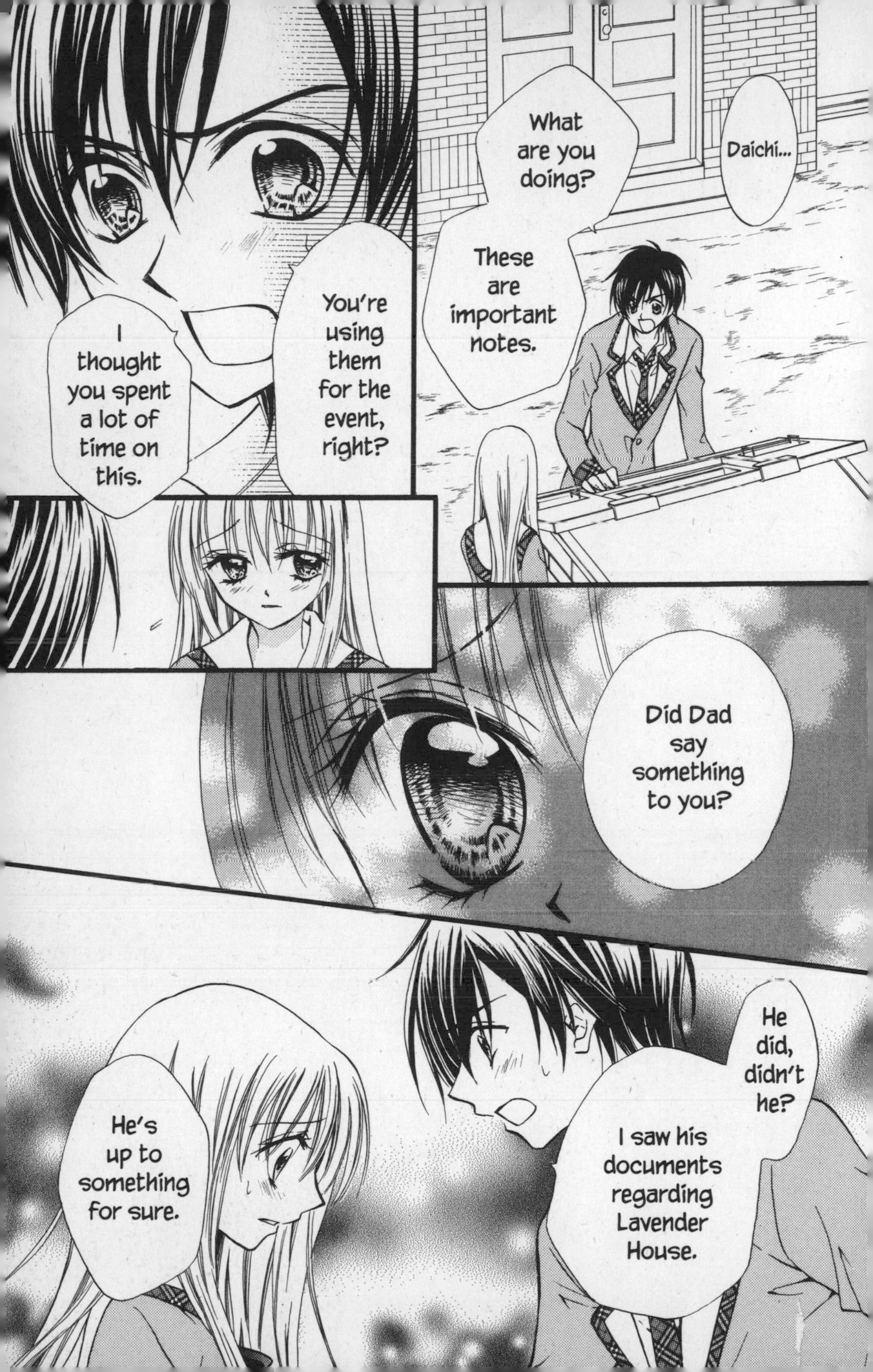
Daichi...
What are you doing?
These are important notes.
You're using them for the event, right?
I thought you spent a lot of time on this.
Did Dad say something to you?
He did, didn't he?
I saw his documents regarding Lavender House.
He's up to something for sure.

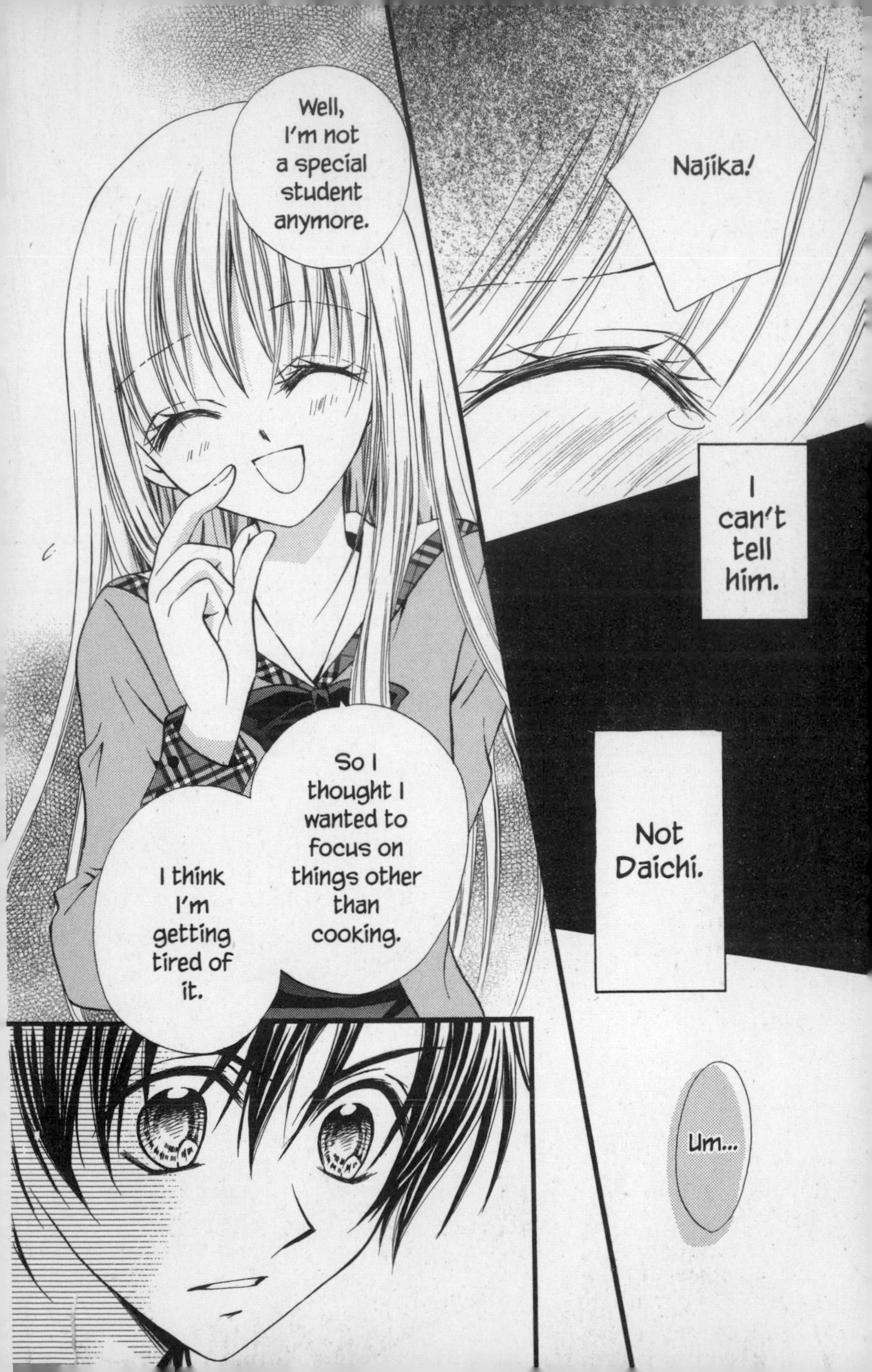
Najika!
I can't tell him.
Not Daichi.
Um...
Well, I'm not a special student anymore.
So I thought I wanted to focus on things other than cooking.
I think I'm getting tired of it.

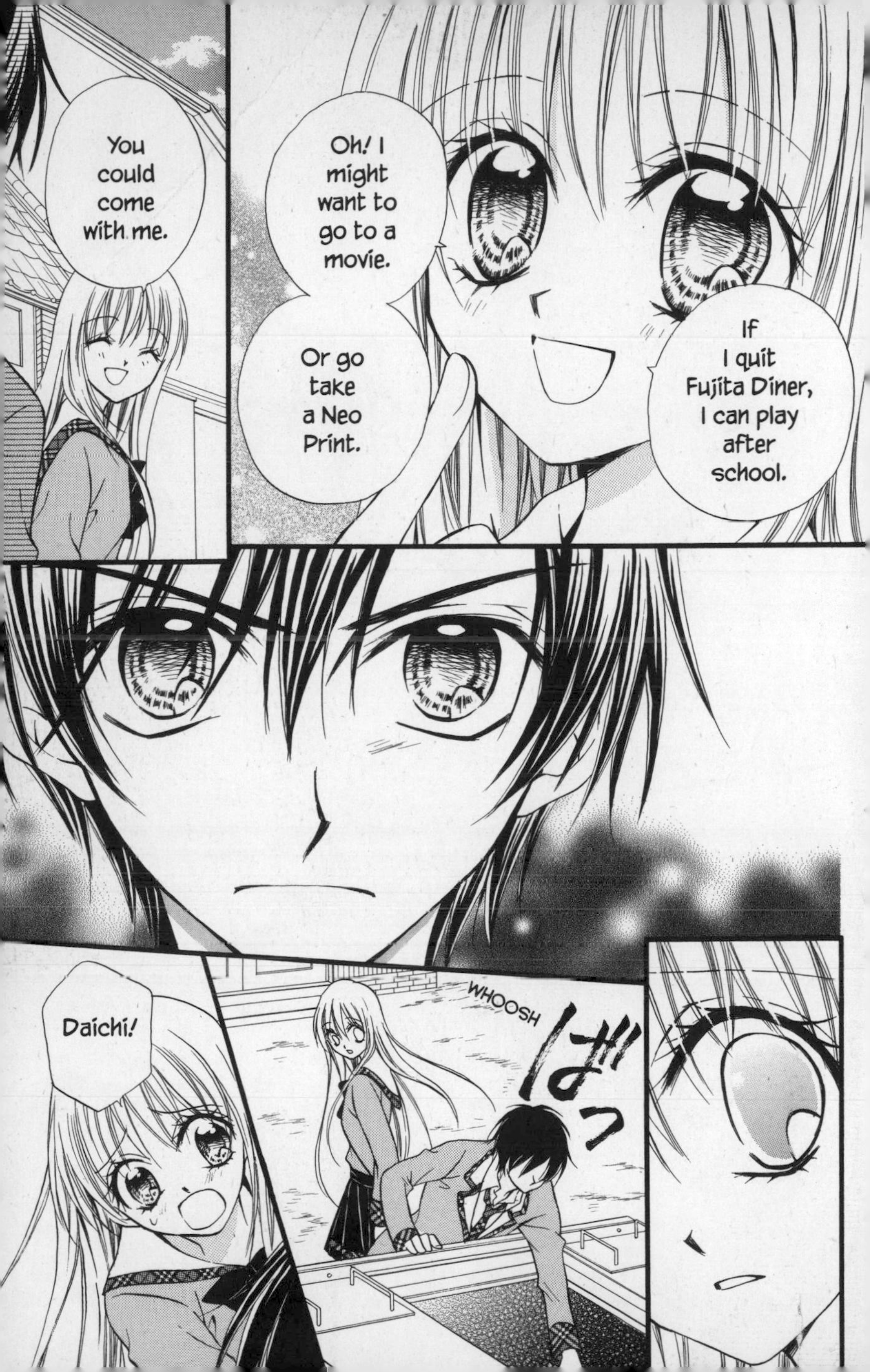
If I quit Fujita Diner, I can play after school.
Oh! I might want to go to a movie.
Or go take a Neo Print.
You could come with me.
WHOOSH
ぱっ
Daichi!

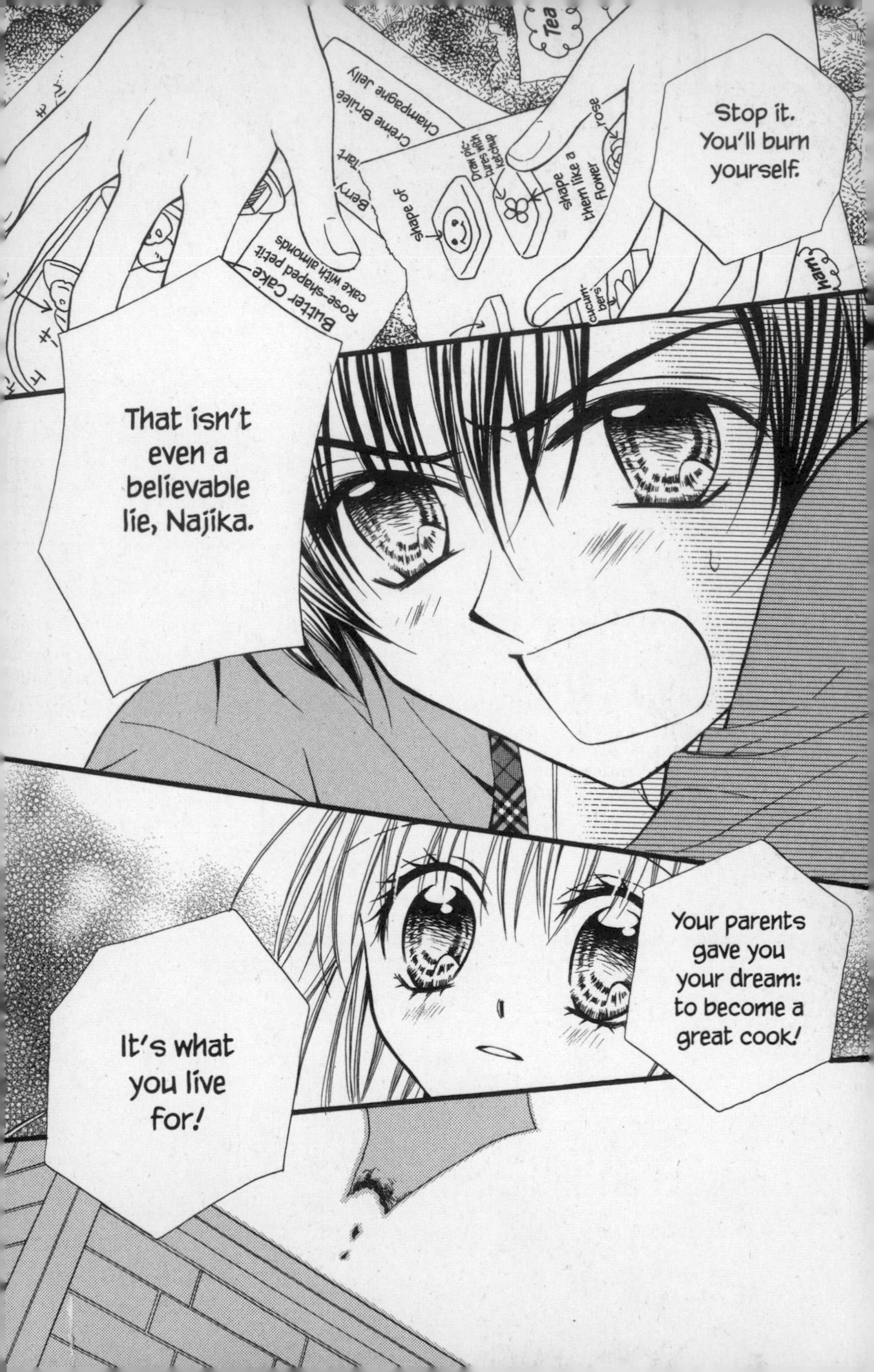
Tea
ham
rose
shape them like a flower
Draw pictures with ketchup
shape of
cucumbers
Champagne Jelly
Creme Brulee
Berry Tart
Butter Cake
Rose-shaped petit cake with almonds
Stop it. You'll burn yourself.
That isn't even a believable lie, Najika.
Your parents gave you your dream: to become a great cook!
It's what you live for!

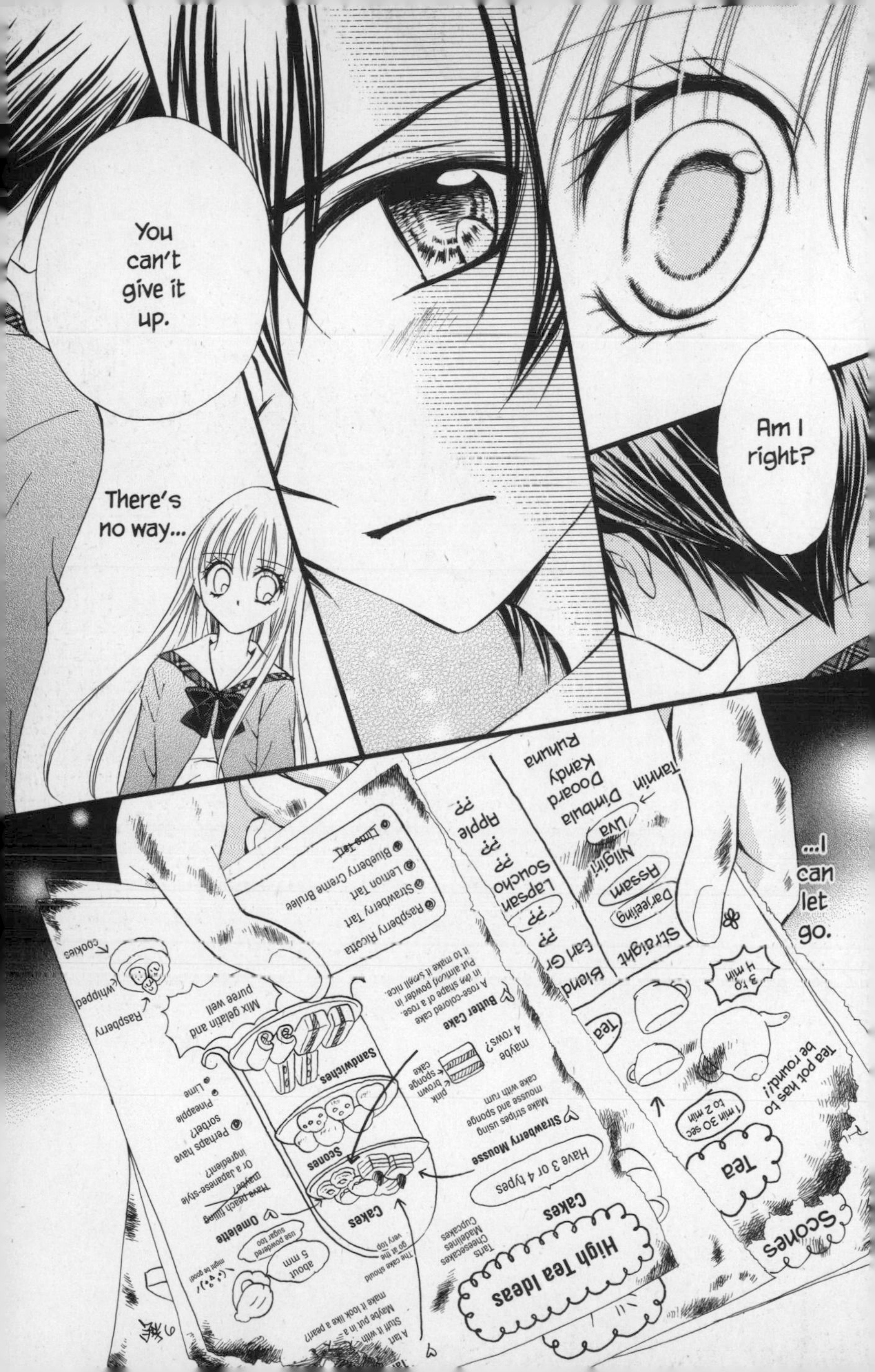
Am I right?
You can't give it up.
There's no way...
...I can let go.
High Tea Ideas
Cakes
Tarts Cheesecakes Madeleines Cupcakes
Have 3 or 4 types
Strawberry Mousse
Make stripes using mousse and sponge cake with rum
Butter Cake
Sandwiches
Scones
Cakes
Omelete
Raspberry Ricotta
Strawberry Tart
Lemon Tart
Blueberry Creme Brulee
Lime Tart
Straight
Darjeeling
Assam
Nilgiri
Uva
Tannin
Dimbula
Dooard
Kandy
Ruhuna
Blend
Earl Gr
Lapsan Soucho
Apple
Tea
3 to 4 min
1 min 30 sec to 2 min
Tea pot has to be round!!
Scones

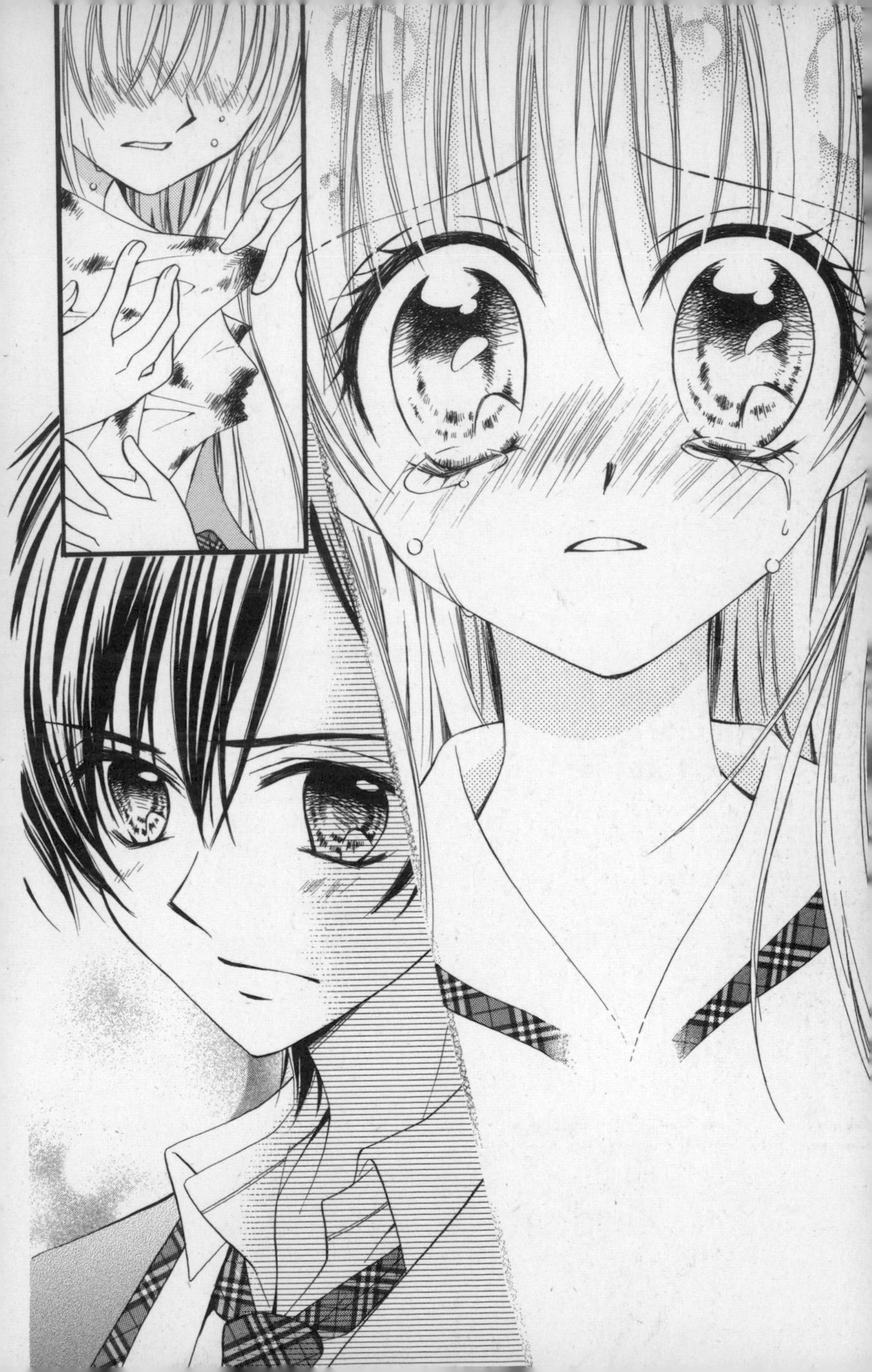

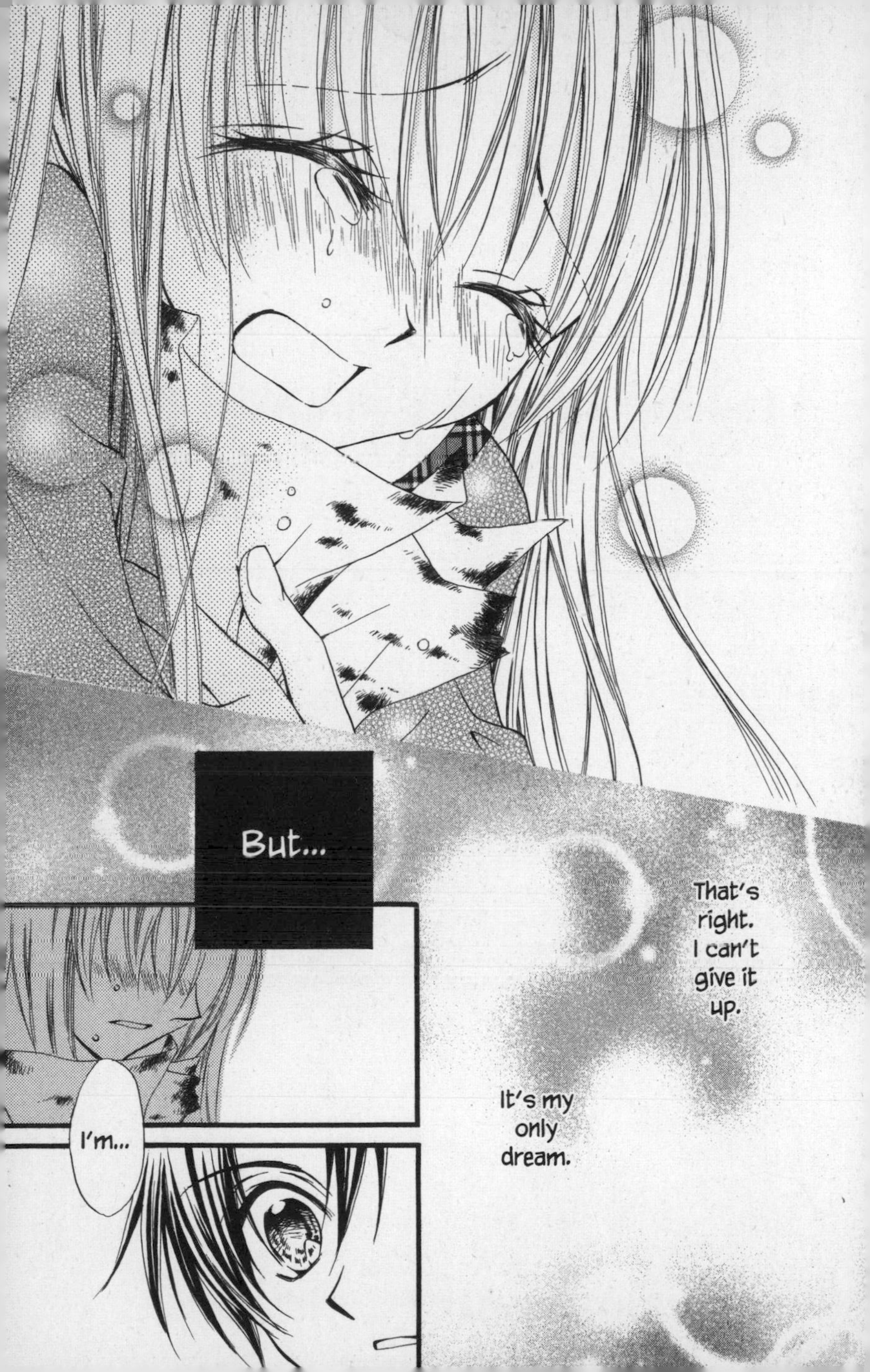
But...
That's right. I can't give it up.
It's my only dream.
I'm...

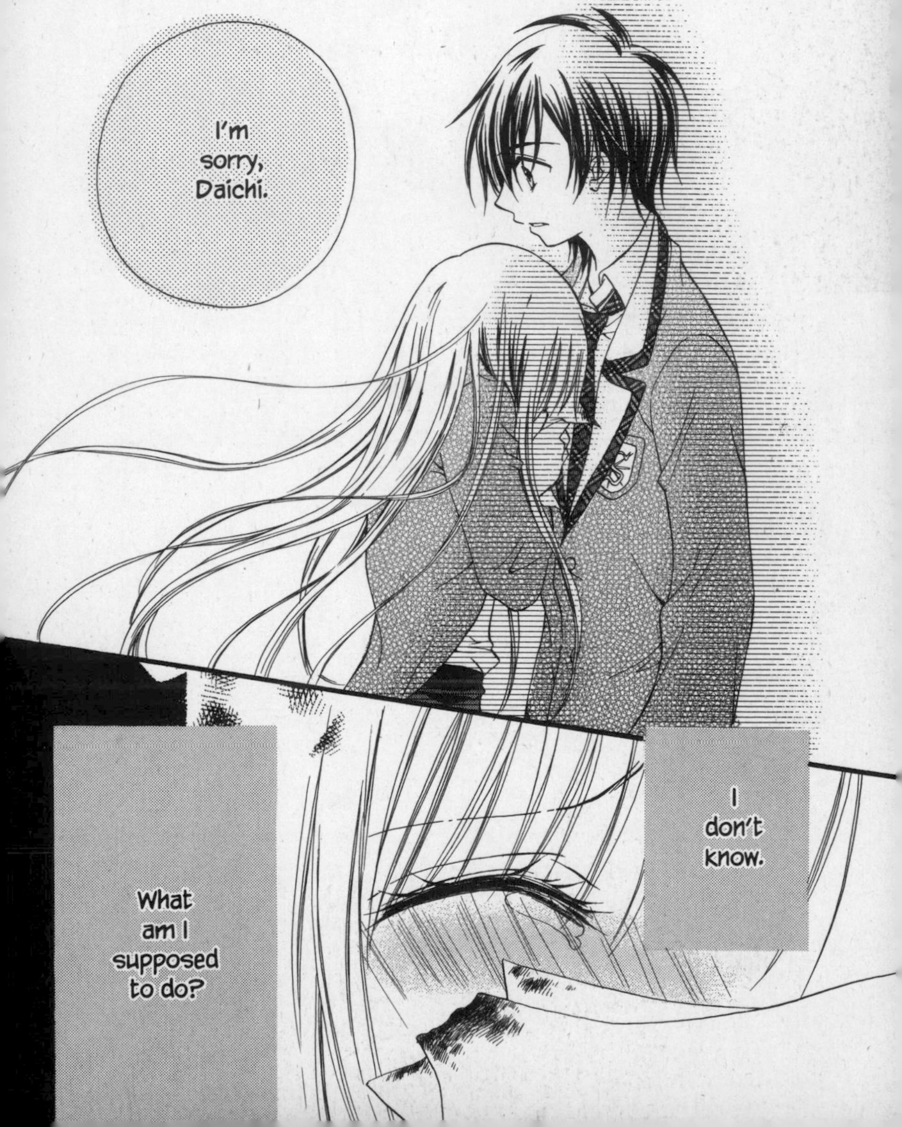
I'm sorry, Daichi.
I don't know.
What am I supposed to do?

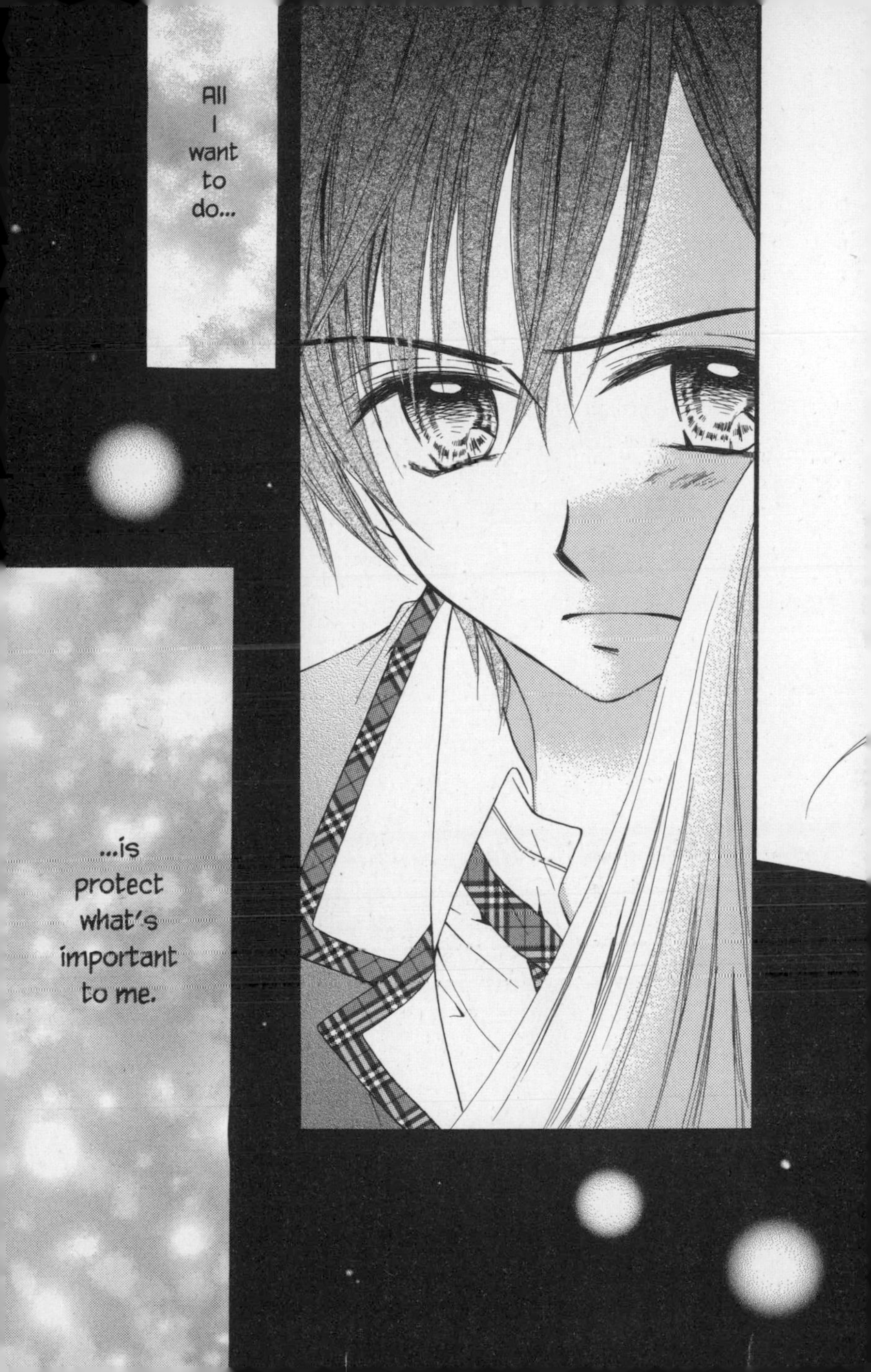
All I want to do...
...is protect what's important to me.

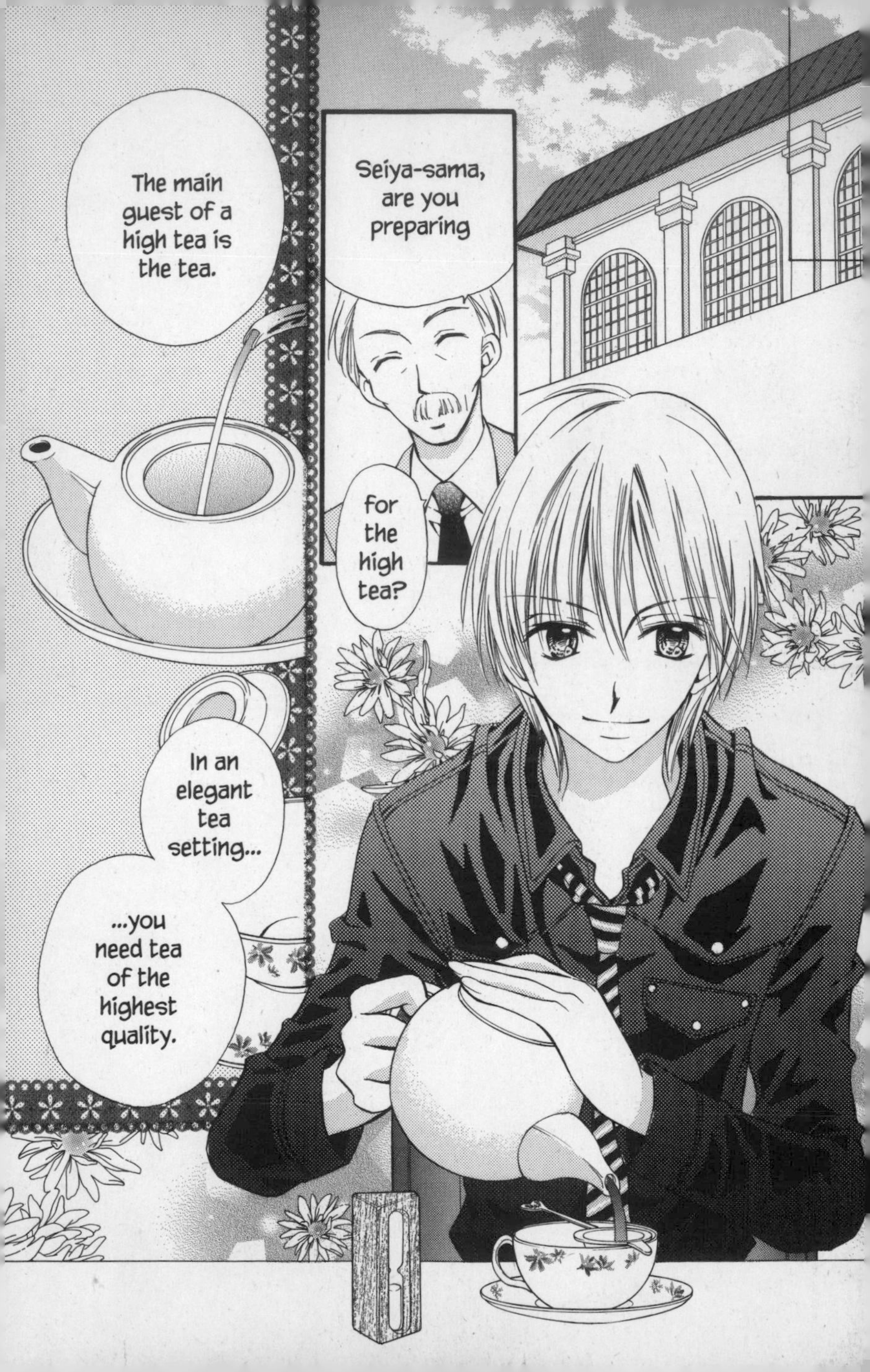
Seiya-sama, are you preparing
for the high tea?
The main guest of a high tea is the tea.
In an elegant tea setting...
...you need tea of the highest quality.

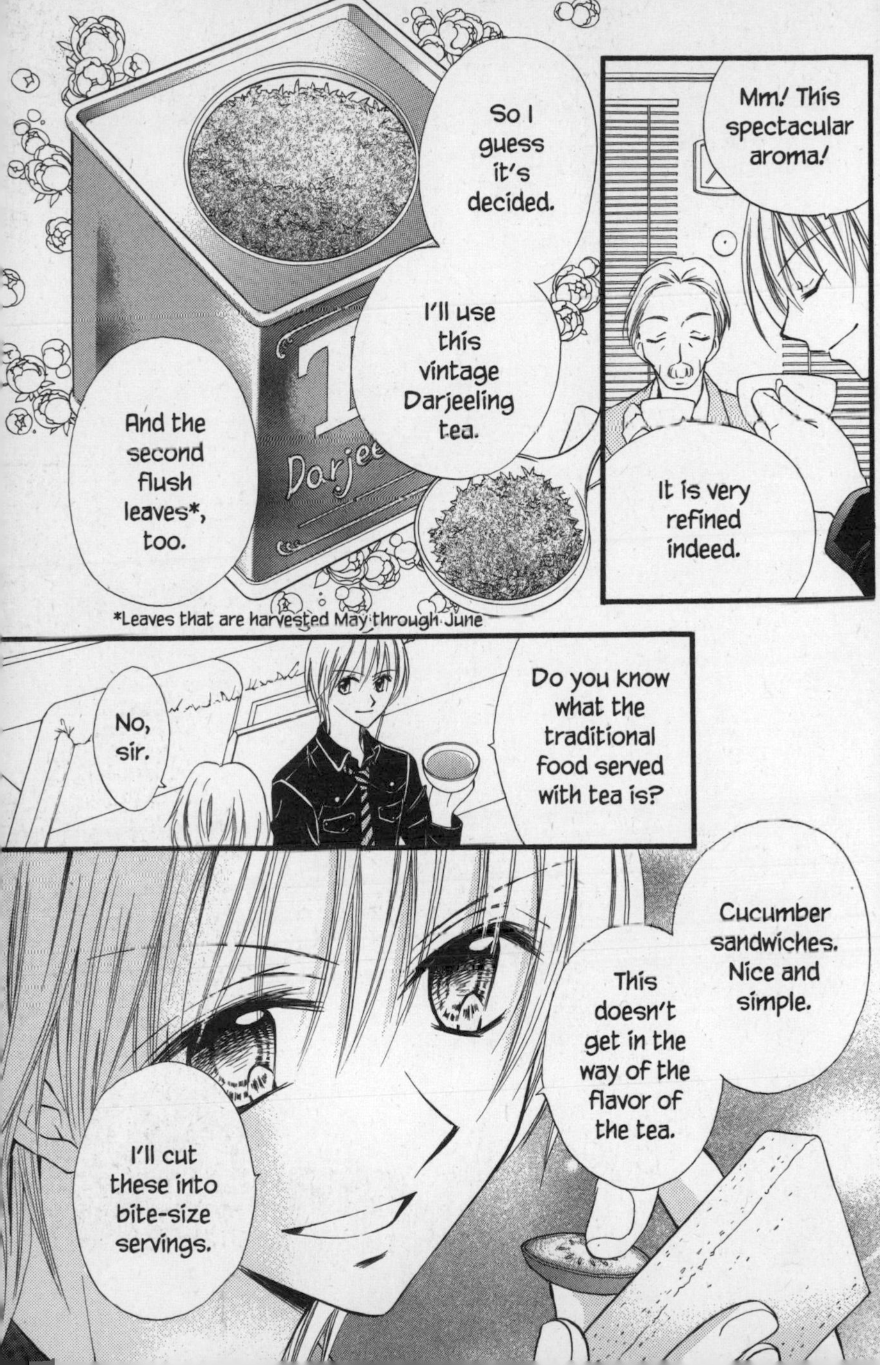
Mm! This spectacular aroma!
It is very refined indeed.
So I guess it's decided.
I'll use this vintage Darjeeling tea.
And the second flush leaves*, too.
*Leaves that are harvested May through June
Do you know what the traditional food served with tea is?
No, sir.
Cucumber sandwiches. Nice and simple.
This doesn't get in the way of the flavor of the tea.
I'll cut these into bite-size servings.

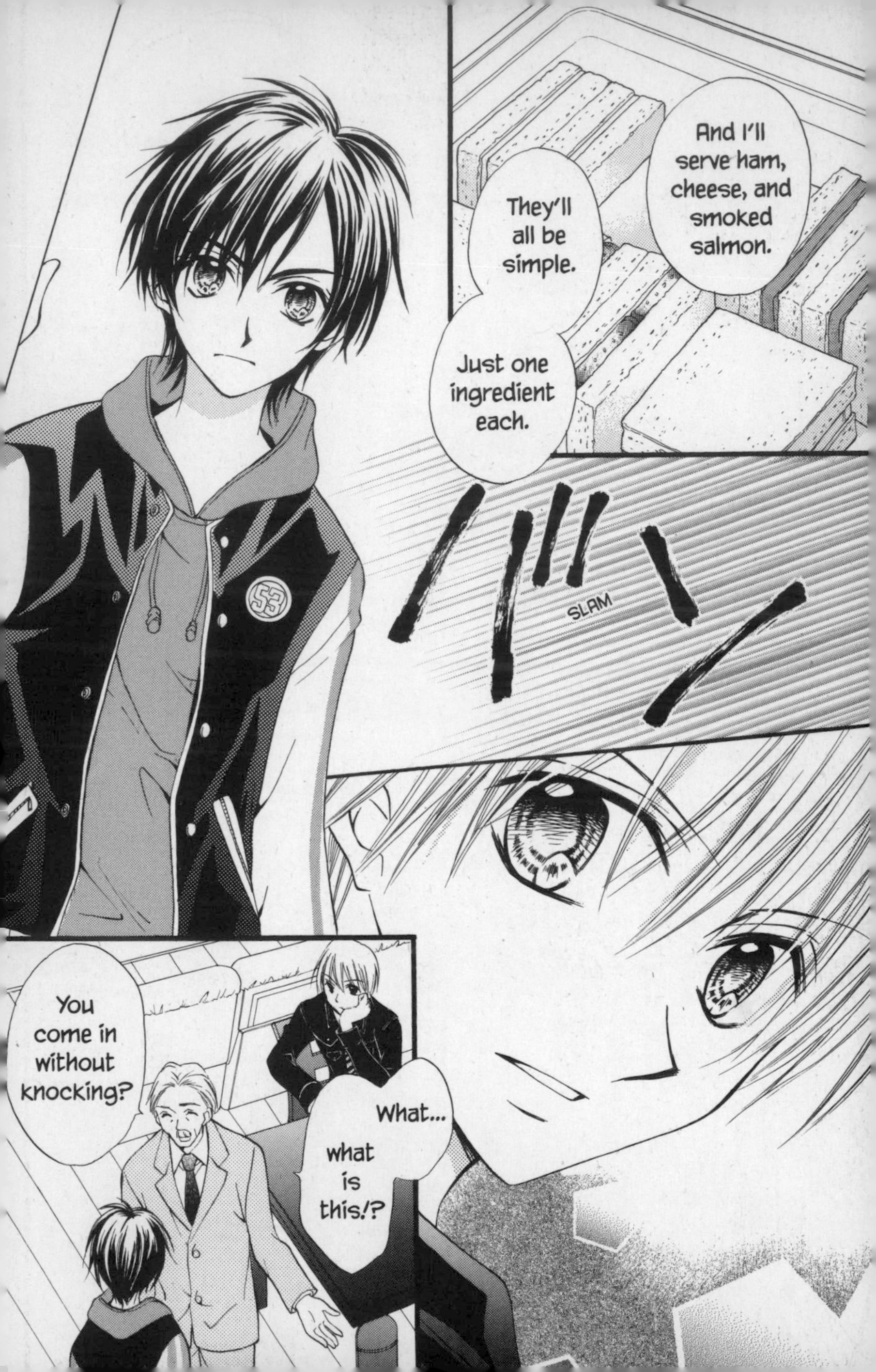
And I'll serve ham, cheese, and smoked salmon.
They'll all be simple.
Just one ingredient each.
SLAM
What... what is this!?
You come in without knocking?

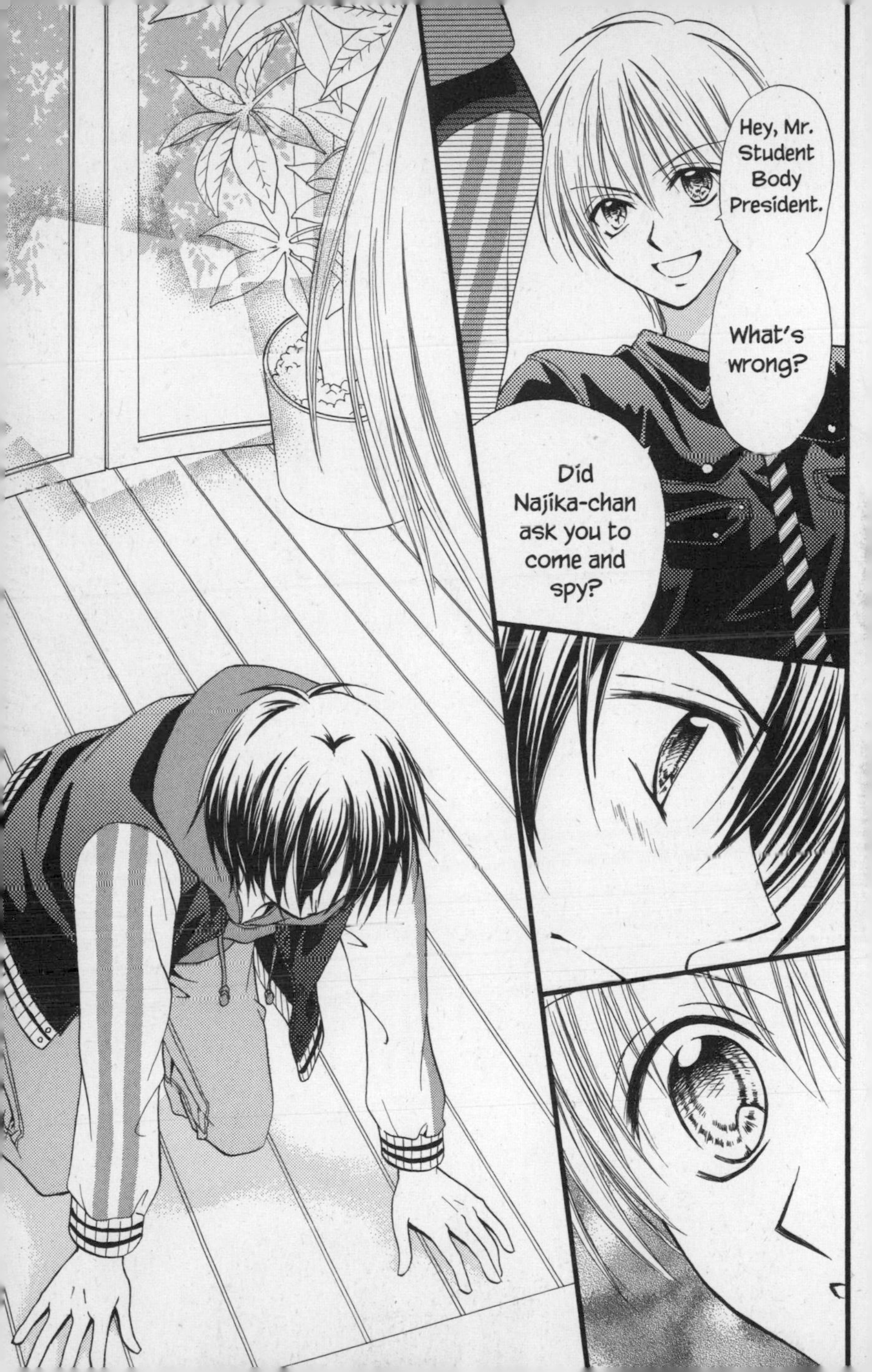
Hey, Mr. Student Body President.
What's wrong?
Did Najika-chan ask you to come and spy?

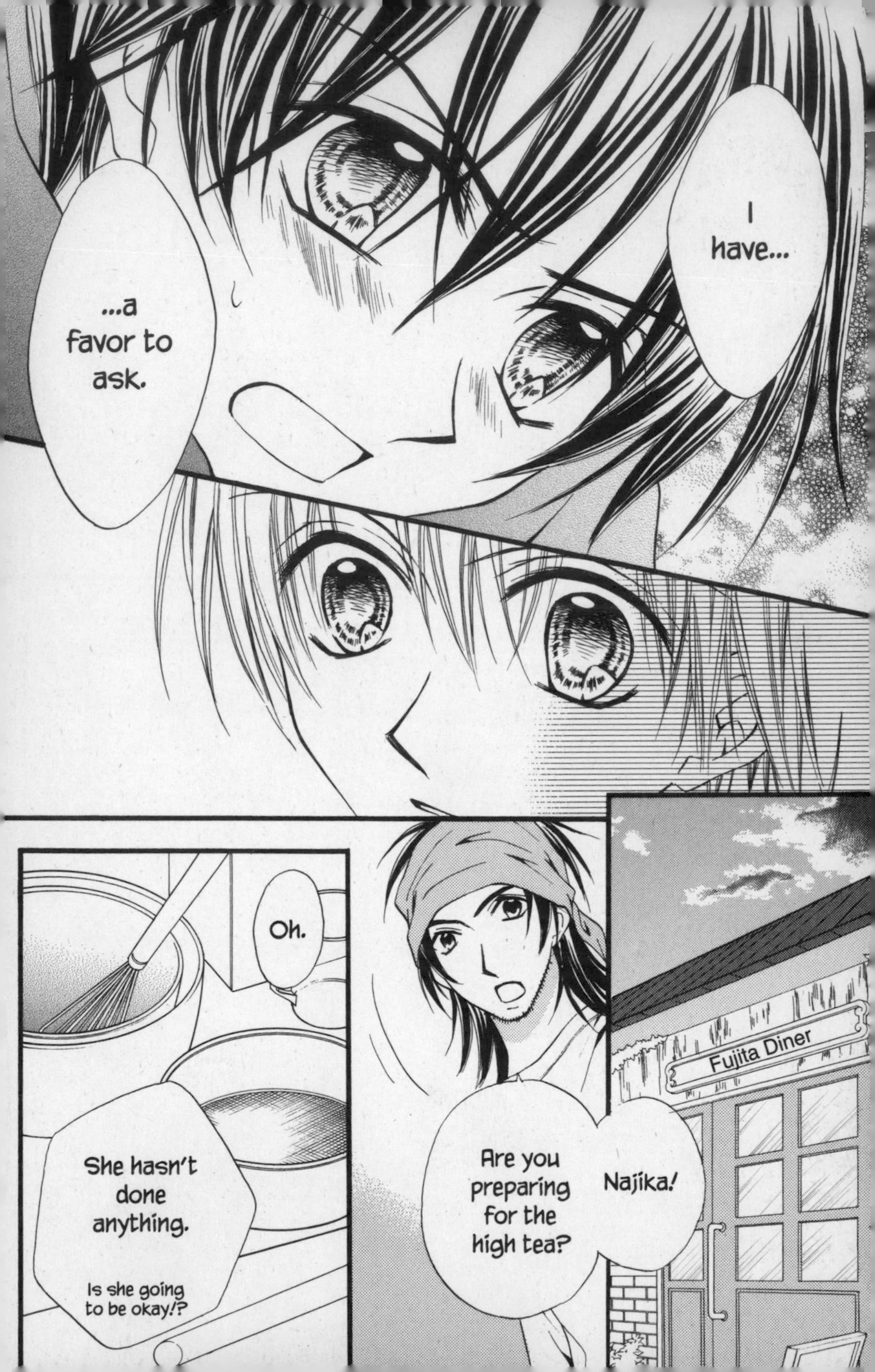

I have...
...a favor to ask.
Fujita Diner
Najika!
Are you preparing for the high tea?
Oh.
She hasn't done anything.
Is she going to be okay!?

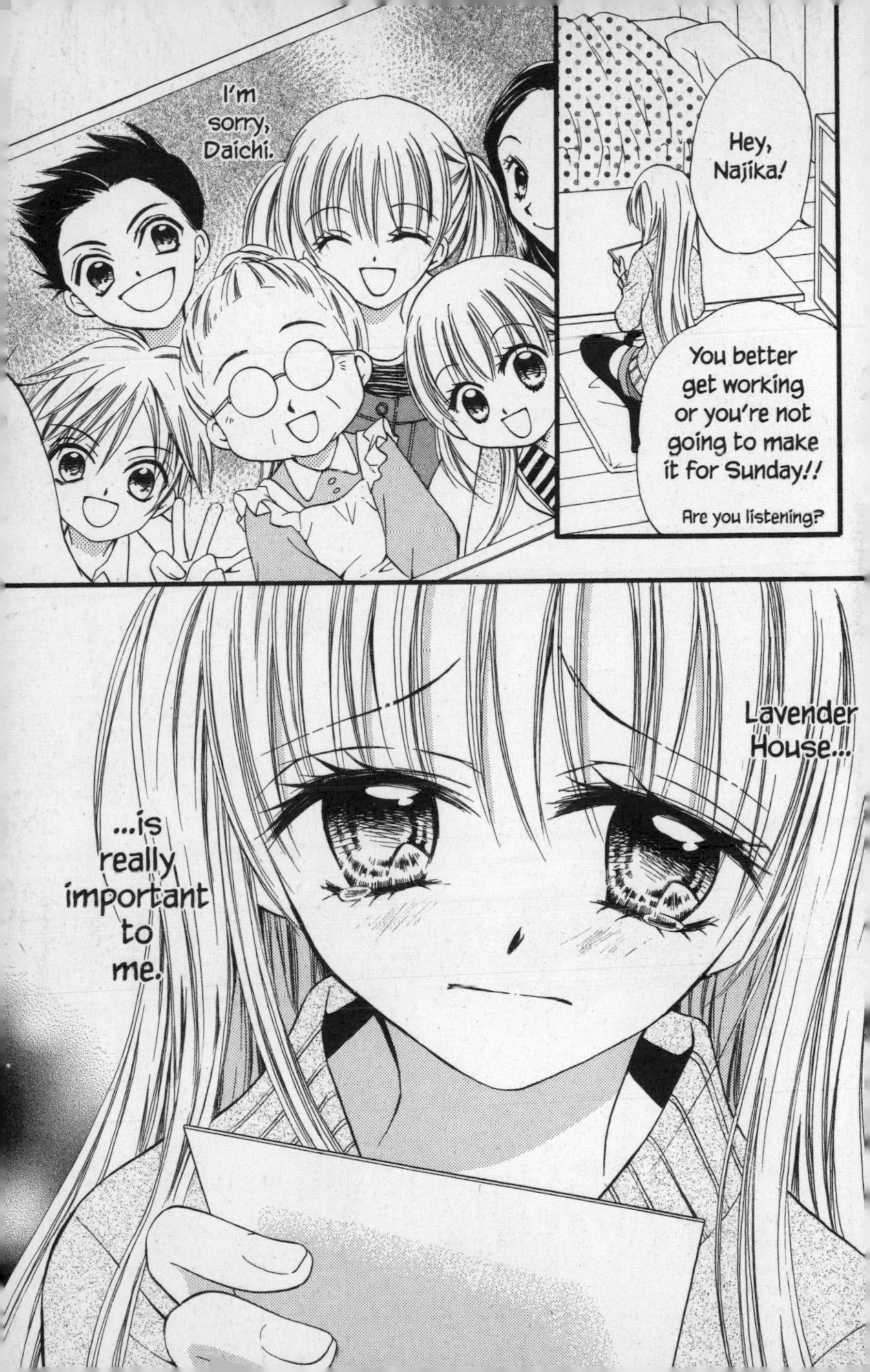
Hey, Najika!
You better get working or you're not going to make it for Sunday!!
Are you listening?
I'm sorry, Daichi.
Lavender House...
...is really important to me.

Seiya's Daily Schedule

6 A.M. Wake up, prepare for lunch

Go to school around the middle of second period

(sometimes third period)

12 P.M. Lunch

The afternoon classes become a drag, so he ditches to go think about dinner

At night he goes to restaurants he read about on the Internet.

And he complains about them...

What is this? It's not all that. The taste is boring, they undercooked it, and besides, if they use fake ingredients like this...

He's going to be stabbed in the back one day.

And it results in...

Sir...

As long as my cooking is okay, it's fine.

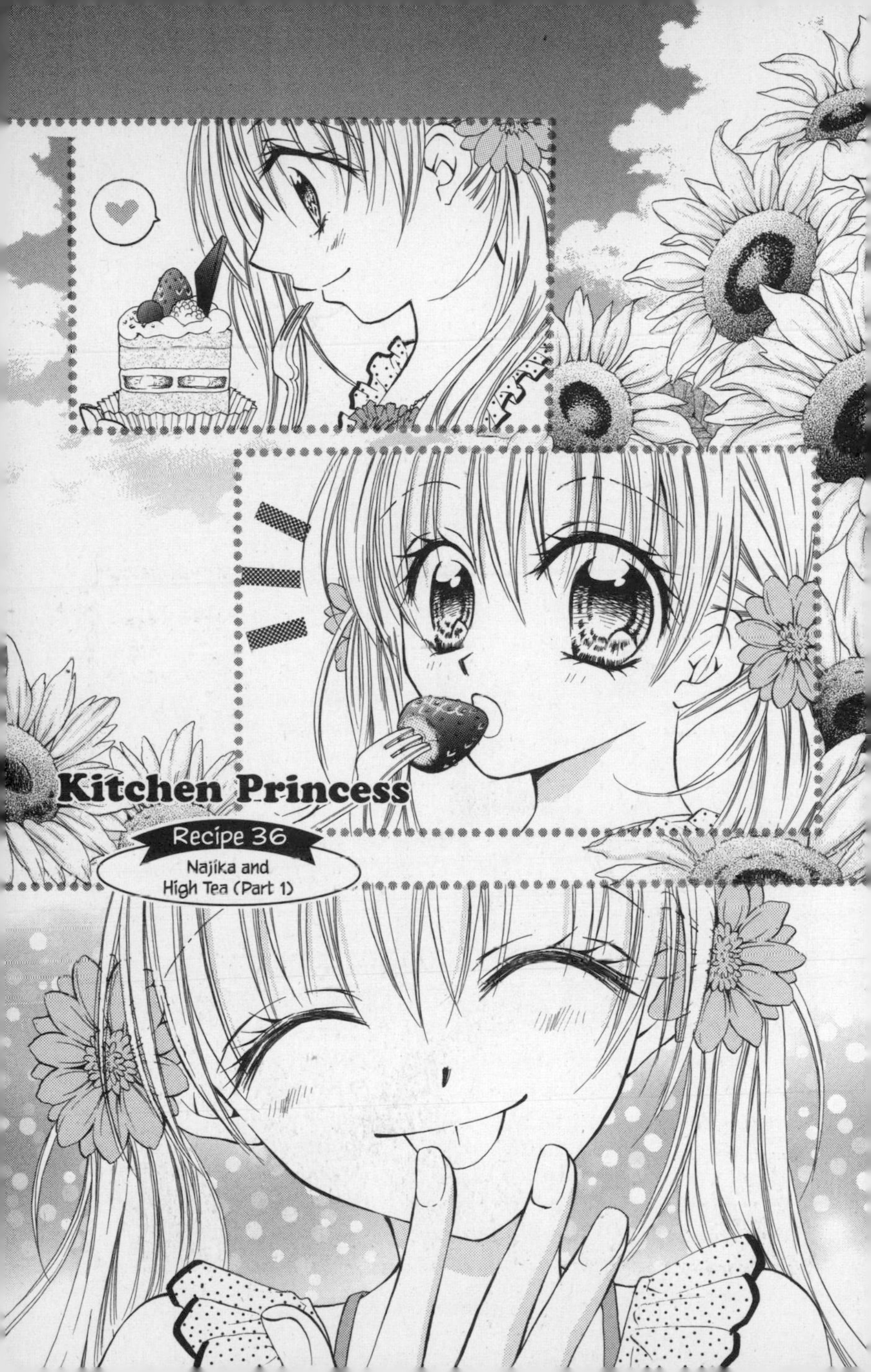
Kitchen Princess
Recipe 36
Najika and
High Tea (Part 1)

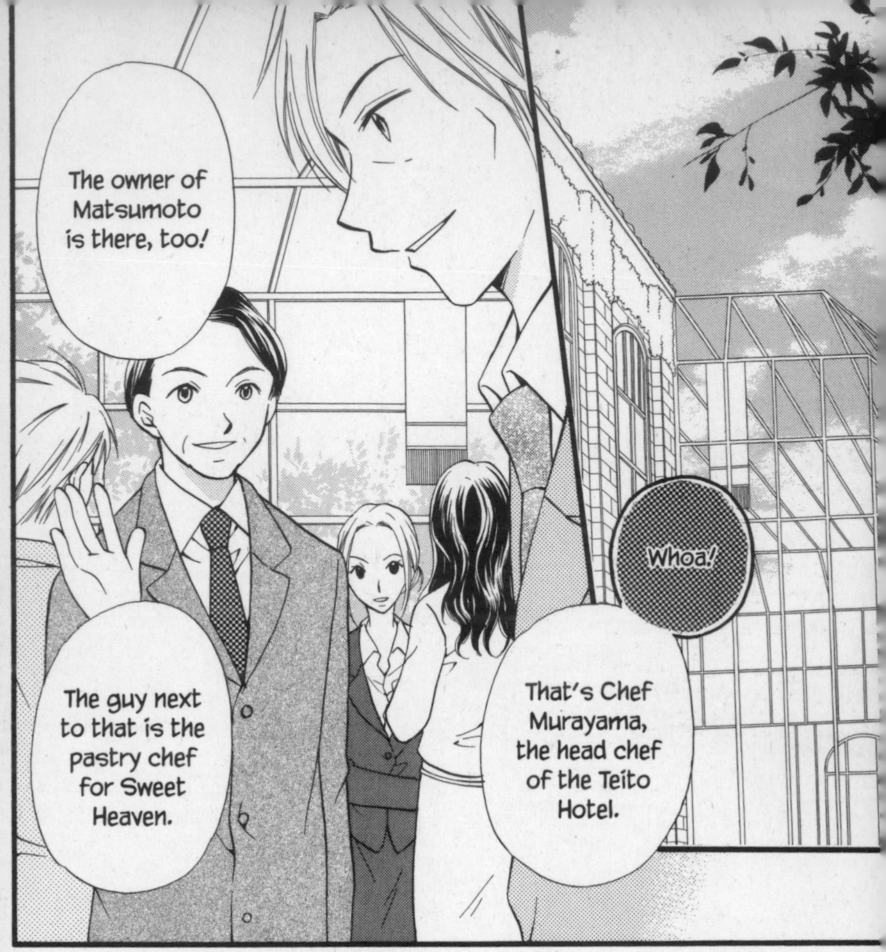
Whoa!
That's Chef Murayama, the head chef of the Teito Hotel.
The guy next to that is the pastry chef for Sweet Heaven.
The owner of Matsumoto is there, too!

About Recipe 36's Splash Page

Three shots of Najika. It's like someone took three consecutive pictures.
When this chapter was released, it was right in the middle of summer, but the story takes place in the fall. I was sweating just from drawing people in long sleeves.
So I tried to make the splash page fresh and fit for summer.
By the way, I used Excel for the first time when I was creating the documents for the Lavender House contract. I was amazed at how handy it is. It's like the feeling I felt when I used a mechanical pencil for the first time!
But...it's too bad that I hardly have the chance to use it!

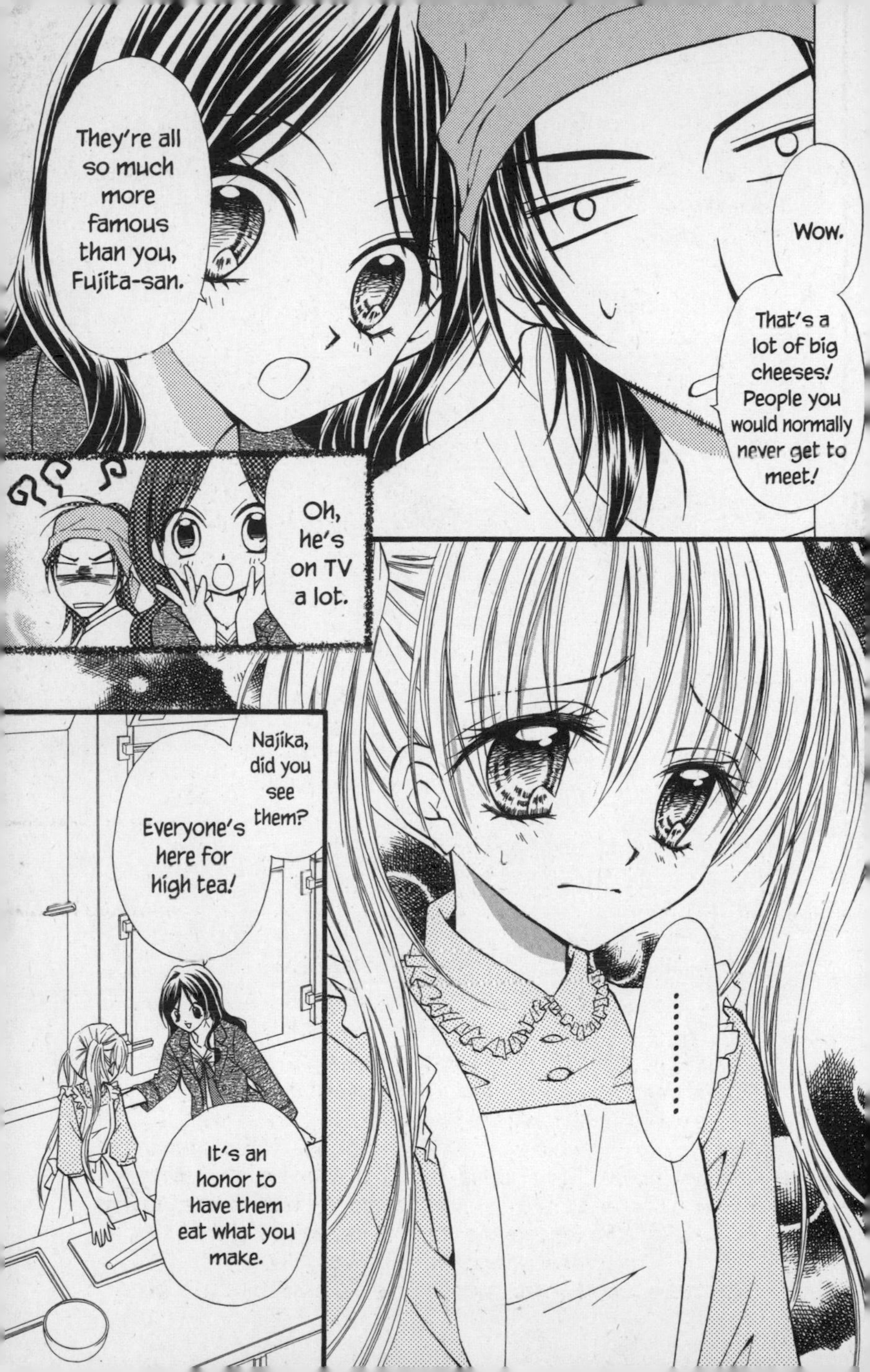
Wow.
That's a lot of big cheeses! People you would normally never get to meet!
They're all so much more famous than you, Fujita-san.
......
Oh, he's on TV a lot.
Najika, did you see them?
Everyone's here for high tea!
It's an honor to have them eat what you make.

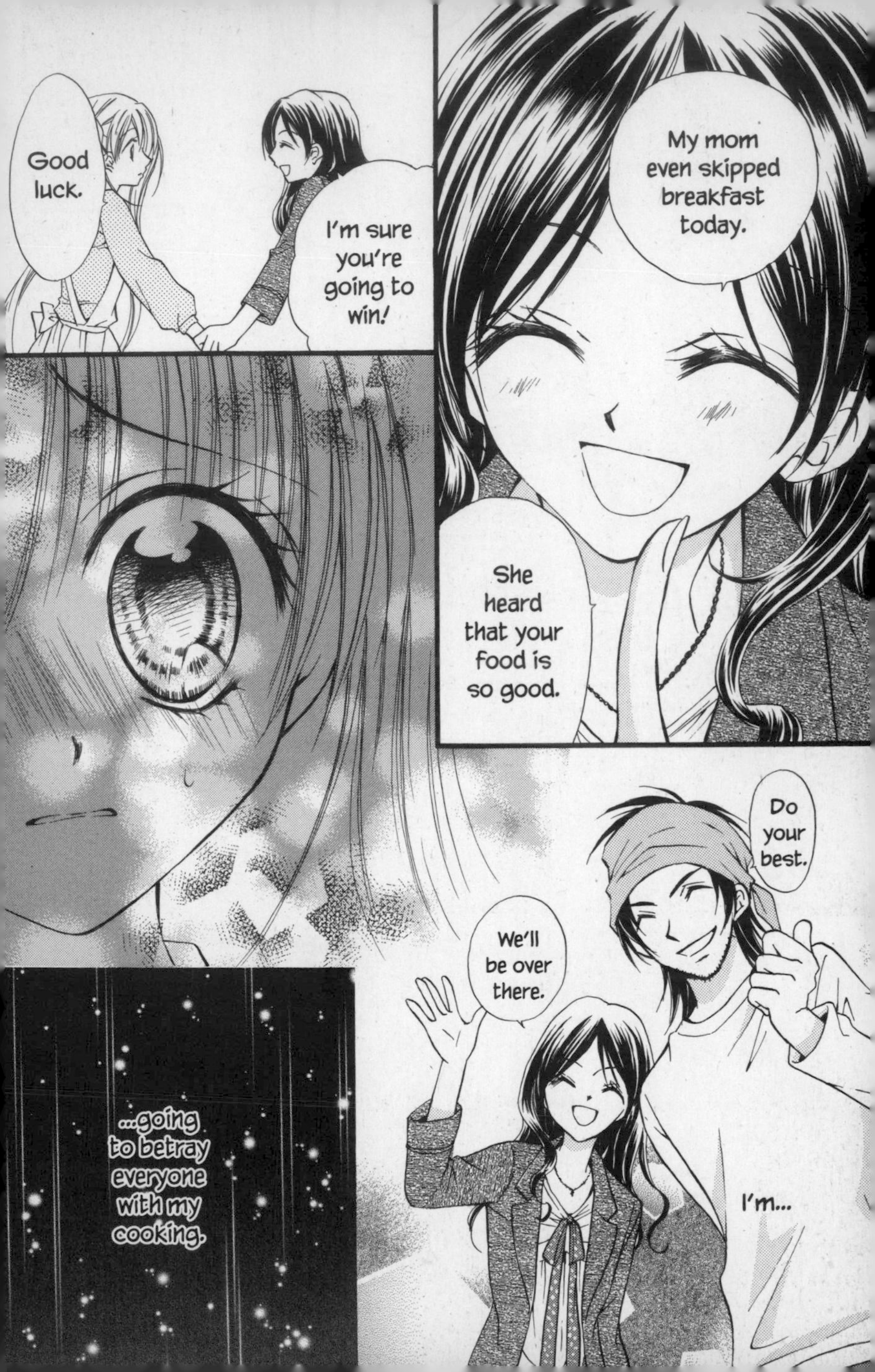
My mom even skipped breakfast today.
She heard that your food is so good.
I'm sure you're going to win!
Good luck.
Do your best.
We'll be over there.
I'm...
...going to betray everyone with my cooking.

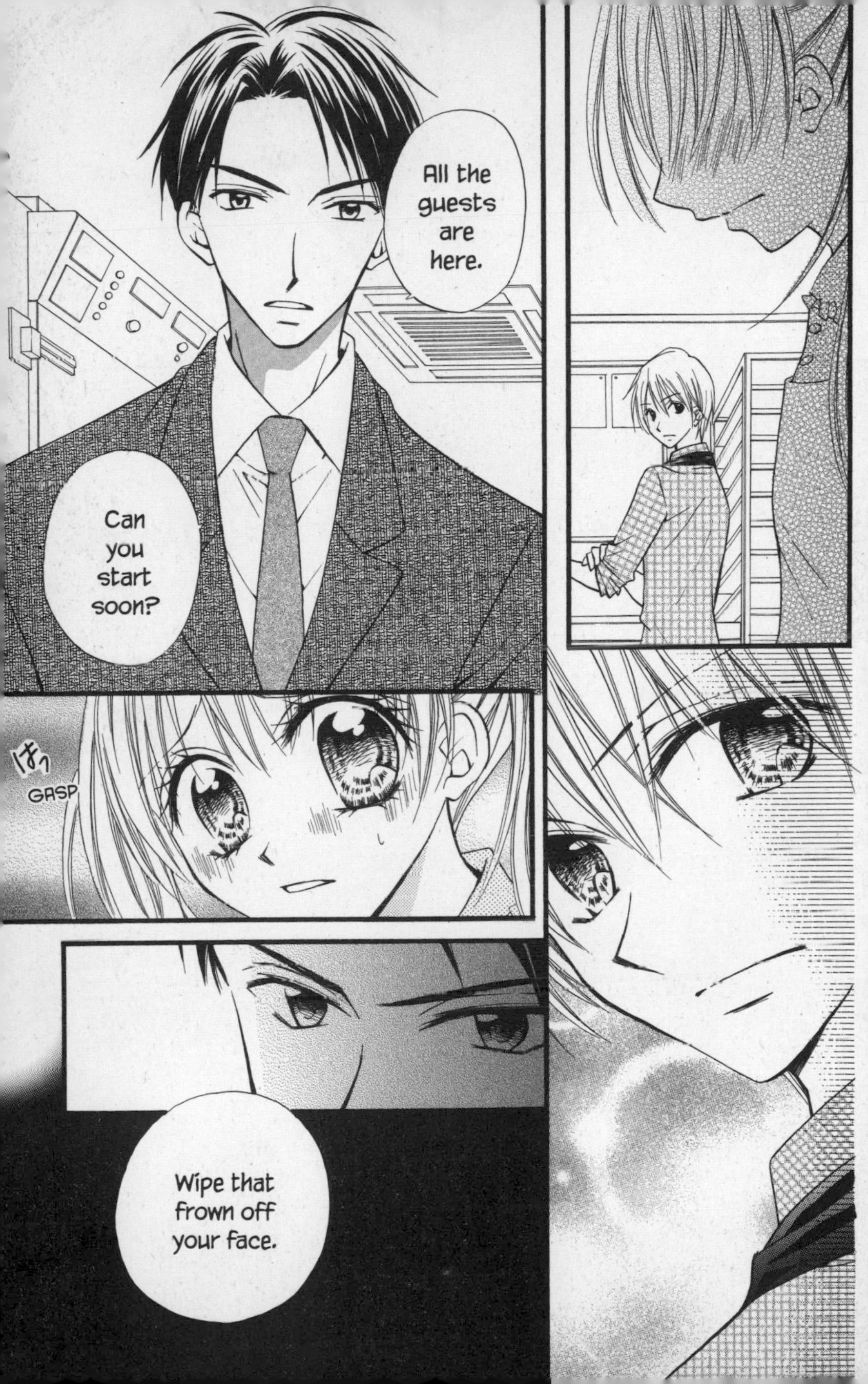
All the guests are here.
Can you start soon?
はっ
GASP
Wipe that frown off your face.

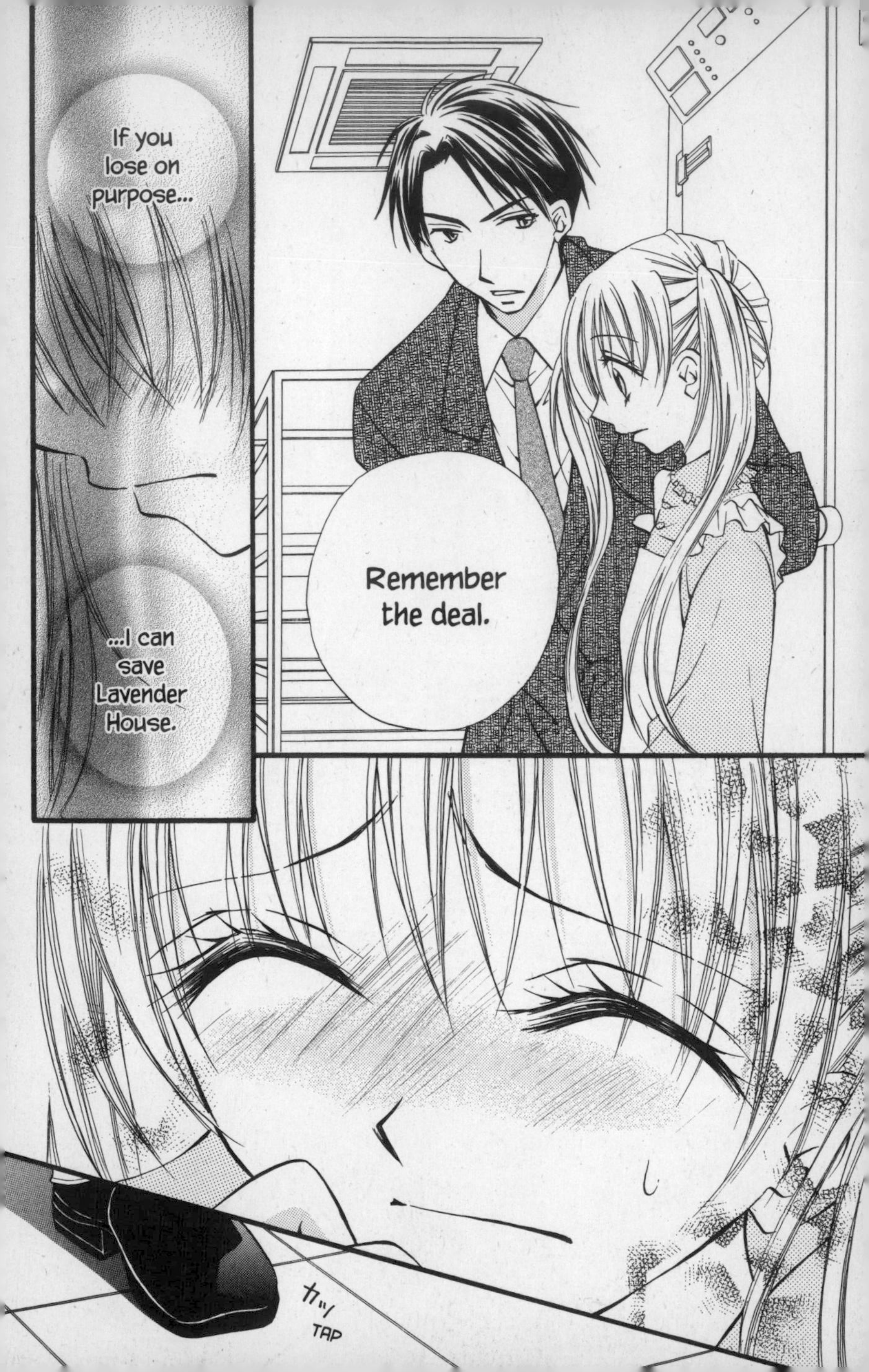
Remember the deal.
If you lose on purpose...
...I can save Lavender House.
カッ
TAP

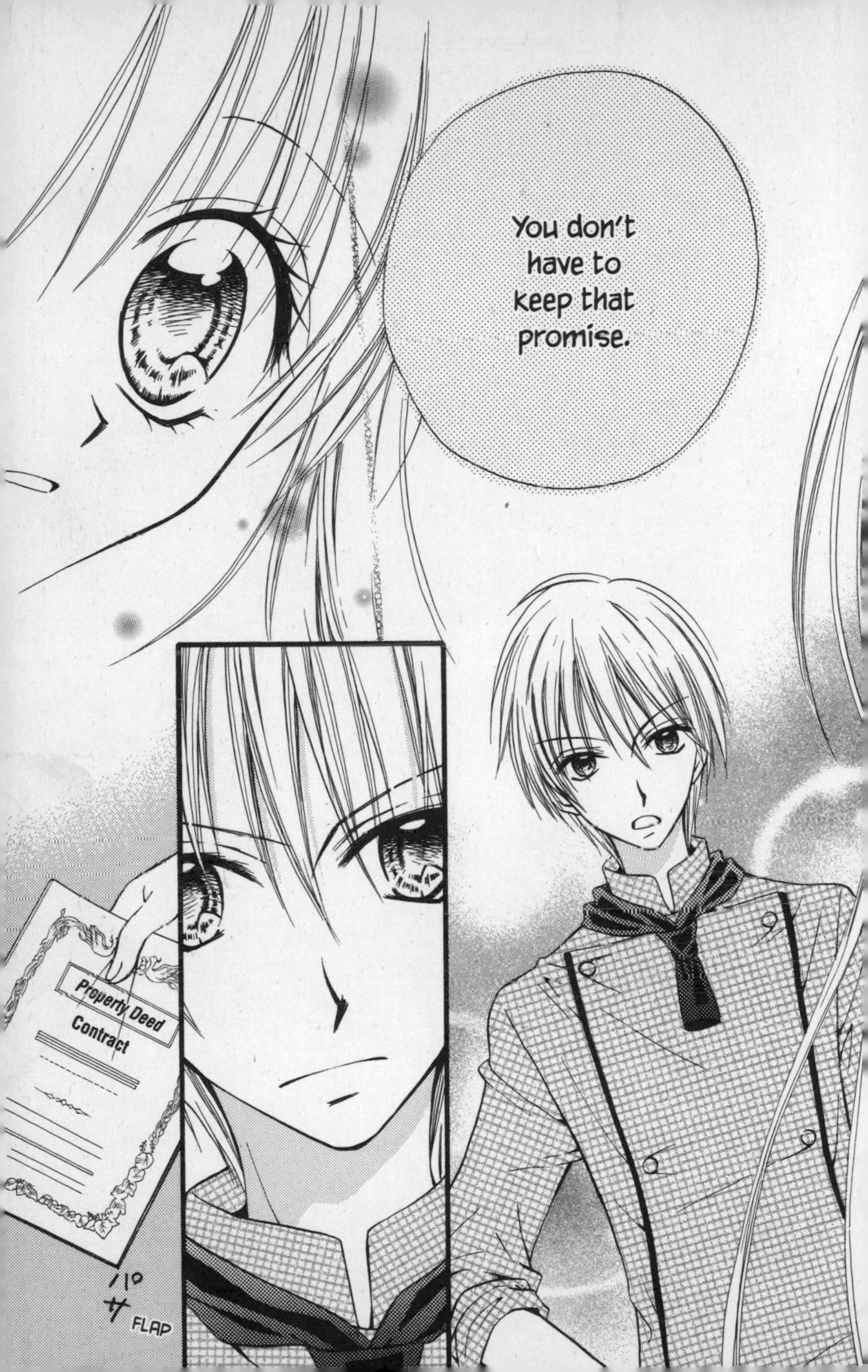
You don't have to keep that promise.
Property Deed
Contract
FLAP

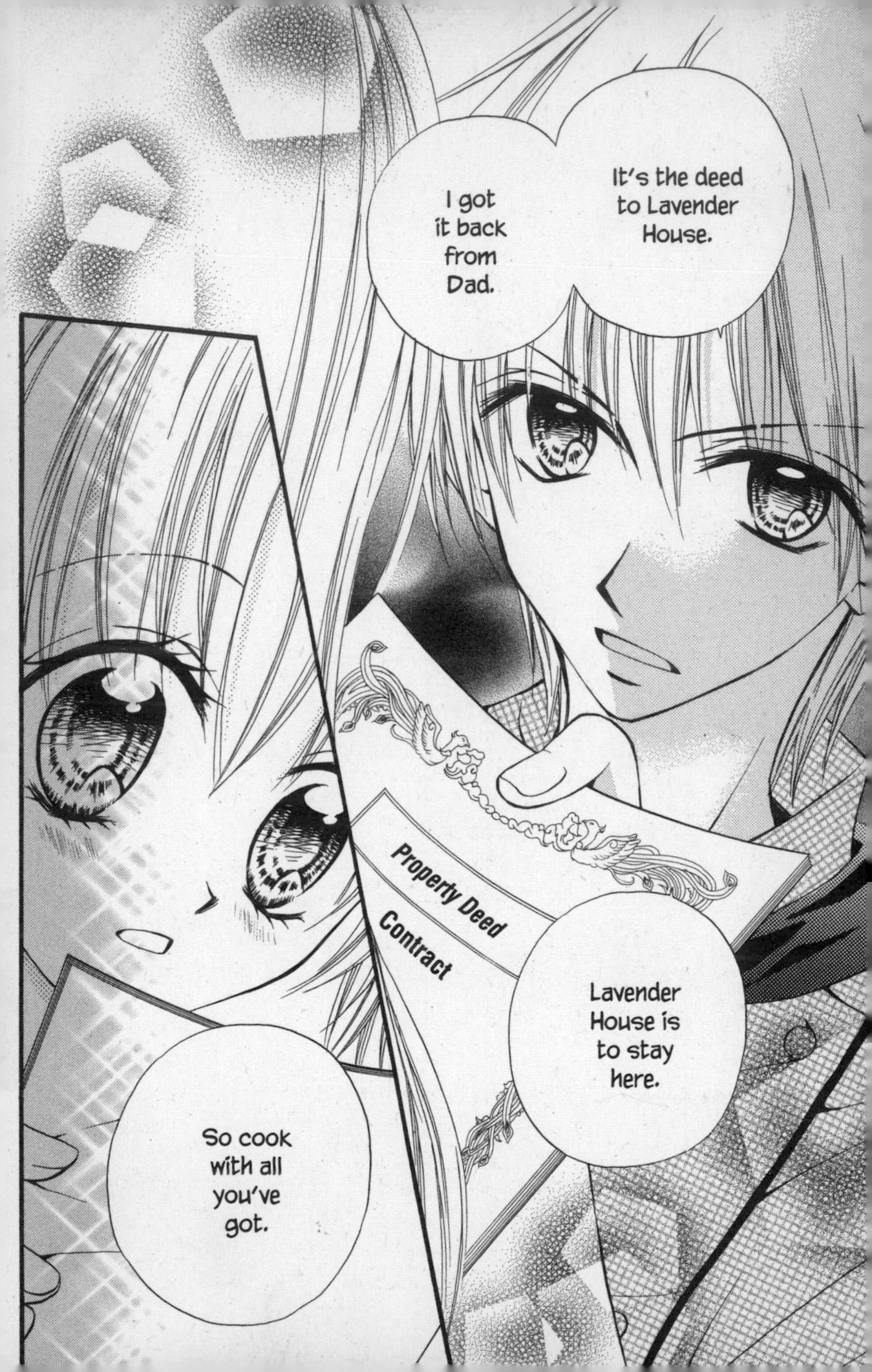
It's the deed to Lavender House.
I got it back from Dad.
Property Deed
Contract
Lavender House is to stay here.
So cook with all you've got.

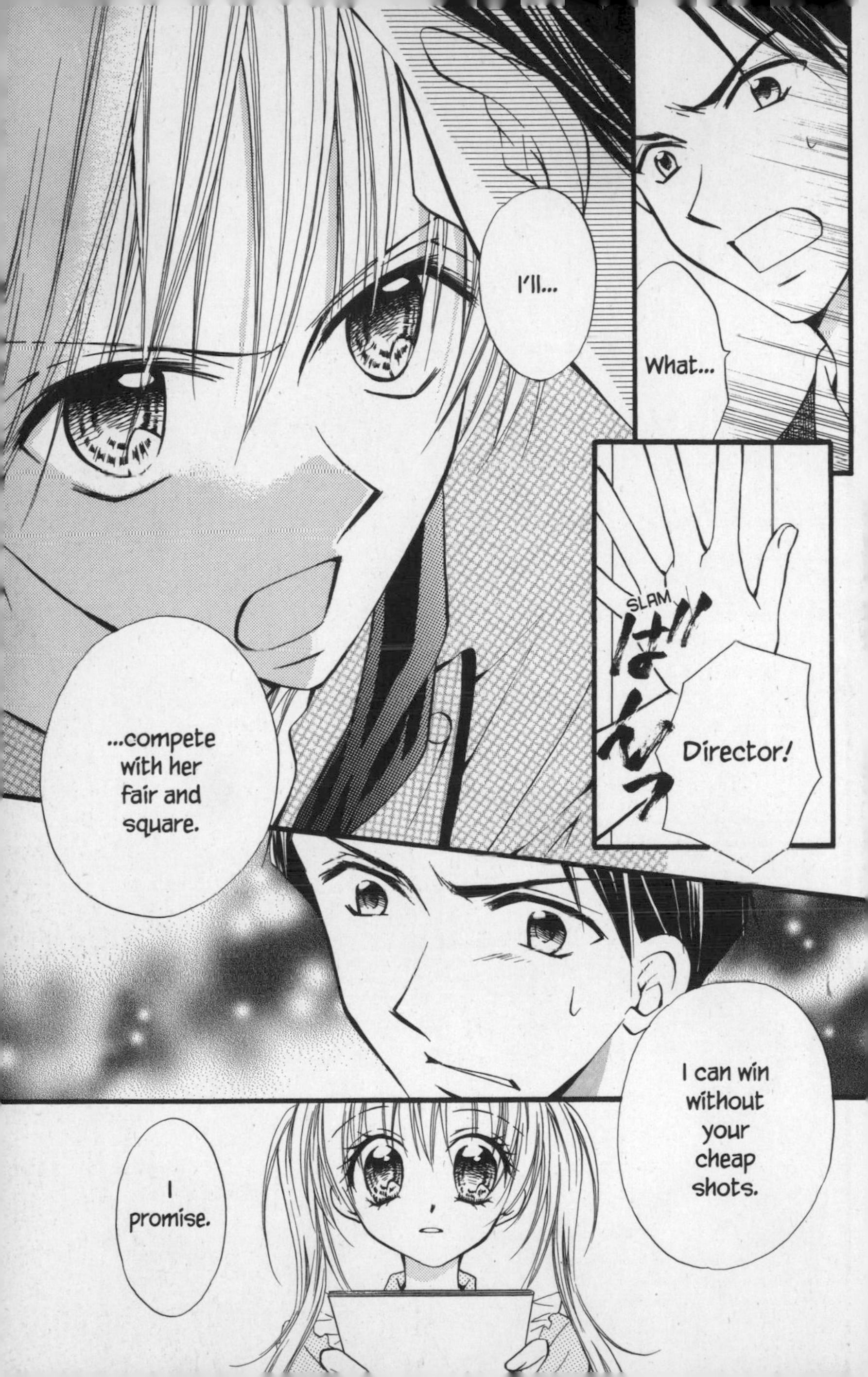
What...
SLAM
ばんっ
Director!
I'll...
...compete with her fair and square.
I can win without your cheap shots.
I promise.

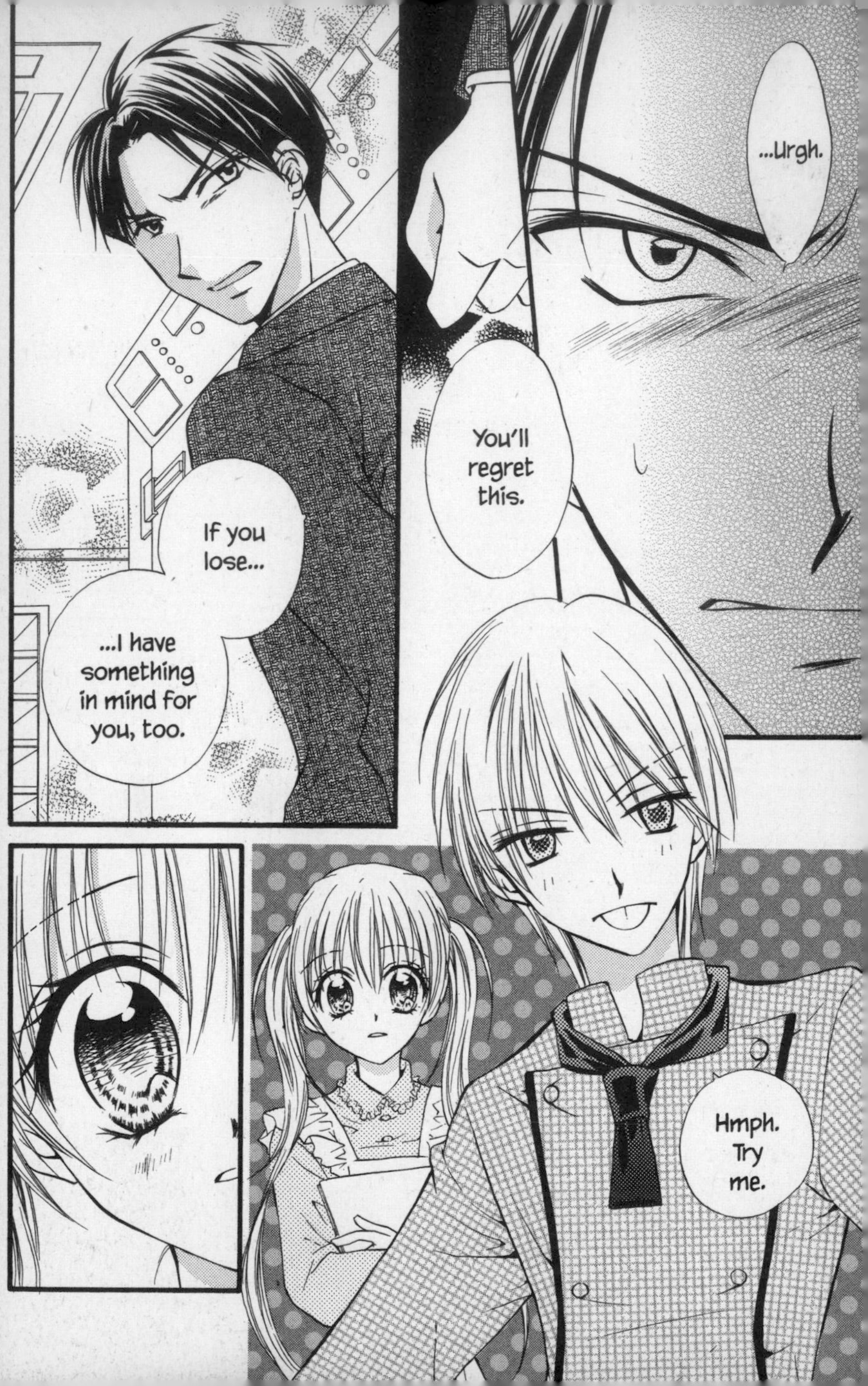
...Urgh.
You'll regret this.
If you lose...
...I have something in mind for you, too.
Hmph. Try me.

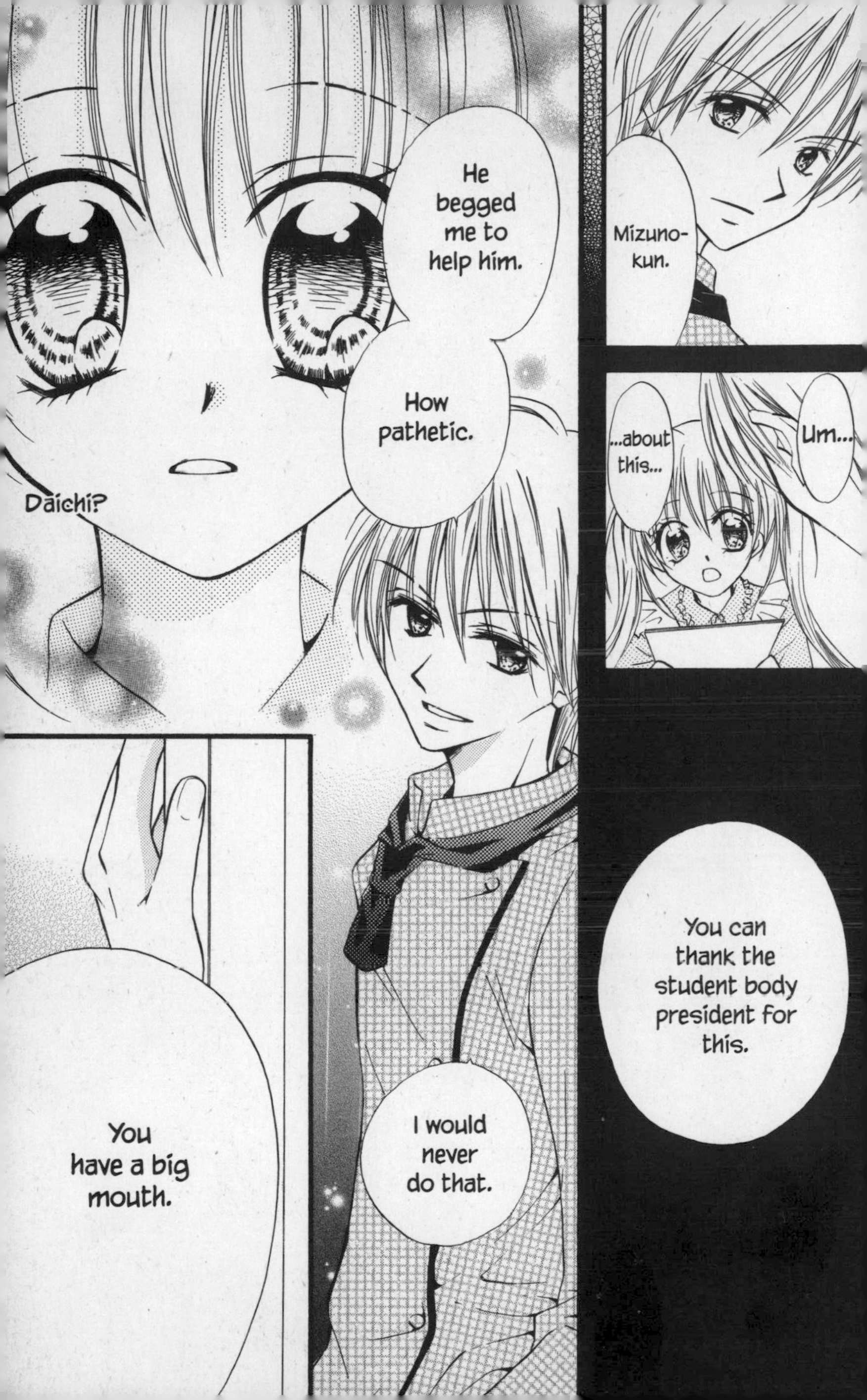
Mizuno-kun.
Um...
...about this...
You can thank the student body president for this.
He begged me to help him.
How pathetic.
Daichi?
I would never do that.
You have a big mouth.

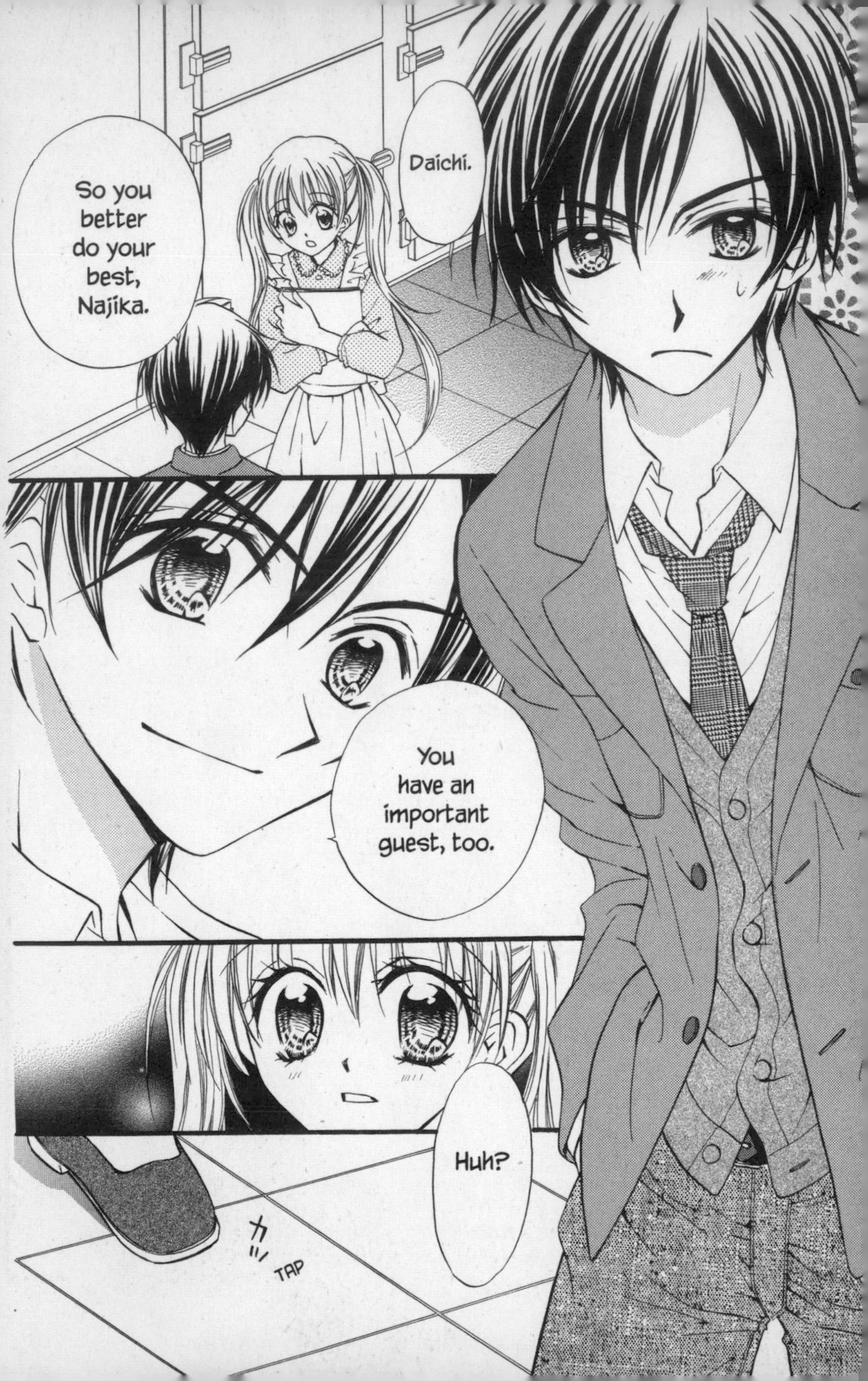
Daichi.
So you better do your best, Najika.
You have an important guest, too.
Huh?
TAP

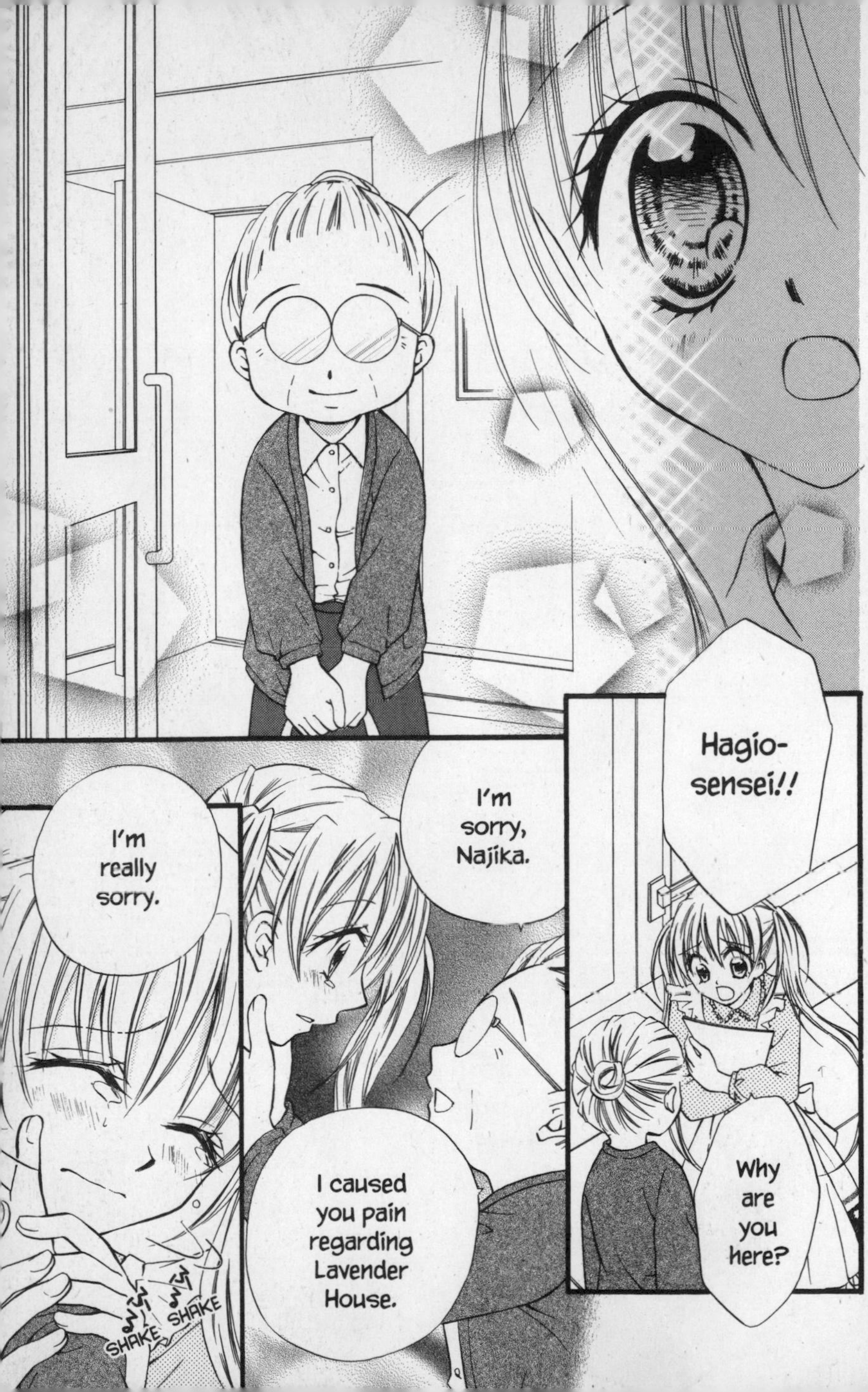
Hagio-sensei!!
Why are you here?
I'm sorry, Najika.
I caused you pain regarding Lavender House.
I'm really sorry.
SHAKE
SHAKE

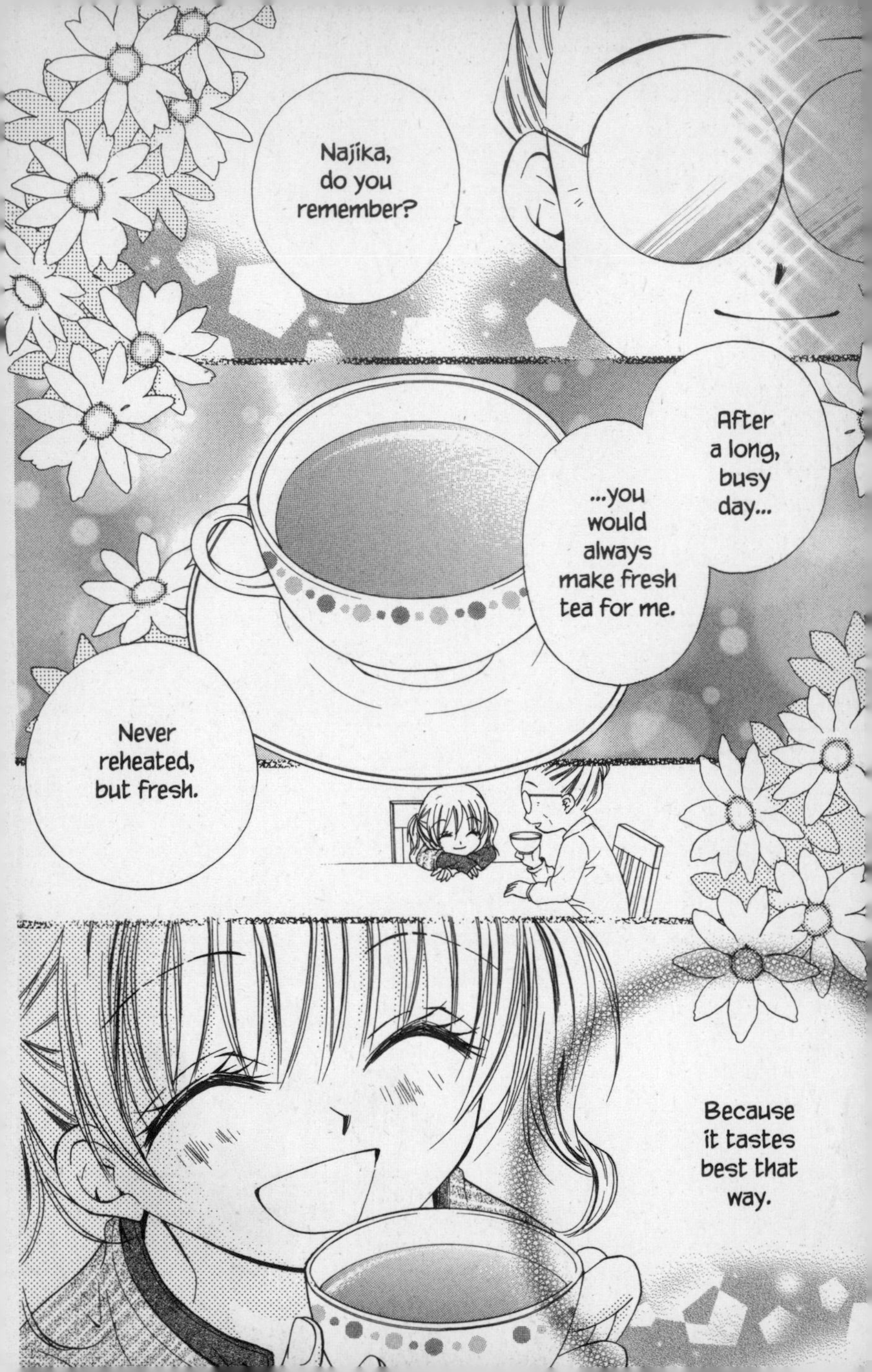
Najika, do you remember?
After a long, busy day...
...you would always make fresh tea for me.
Never reheated, but fresh.
Because it tastes best that way.

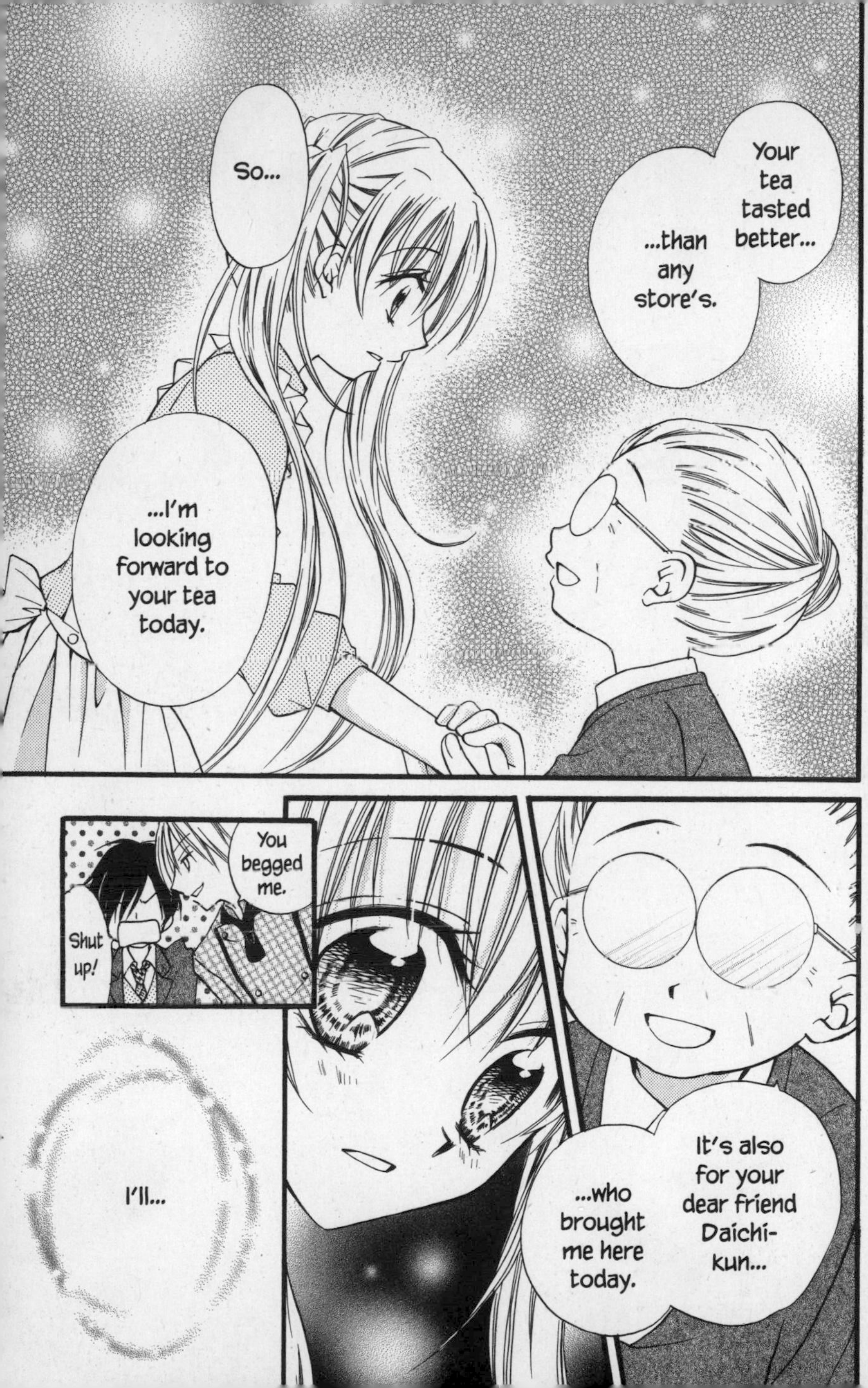
Your tea tasted better...
...than any store's.
So...
...I'm looking forward to your tea today.
It's also for your dear friend Daichi-kun...
...who brought me here today.
You begged me.
Shut up!
I'll...

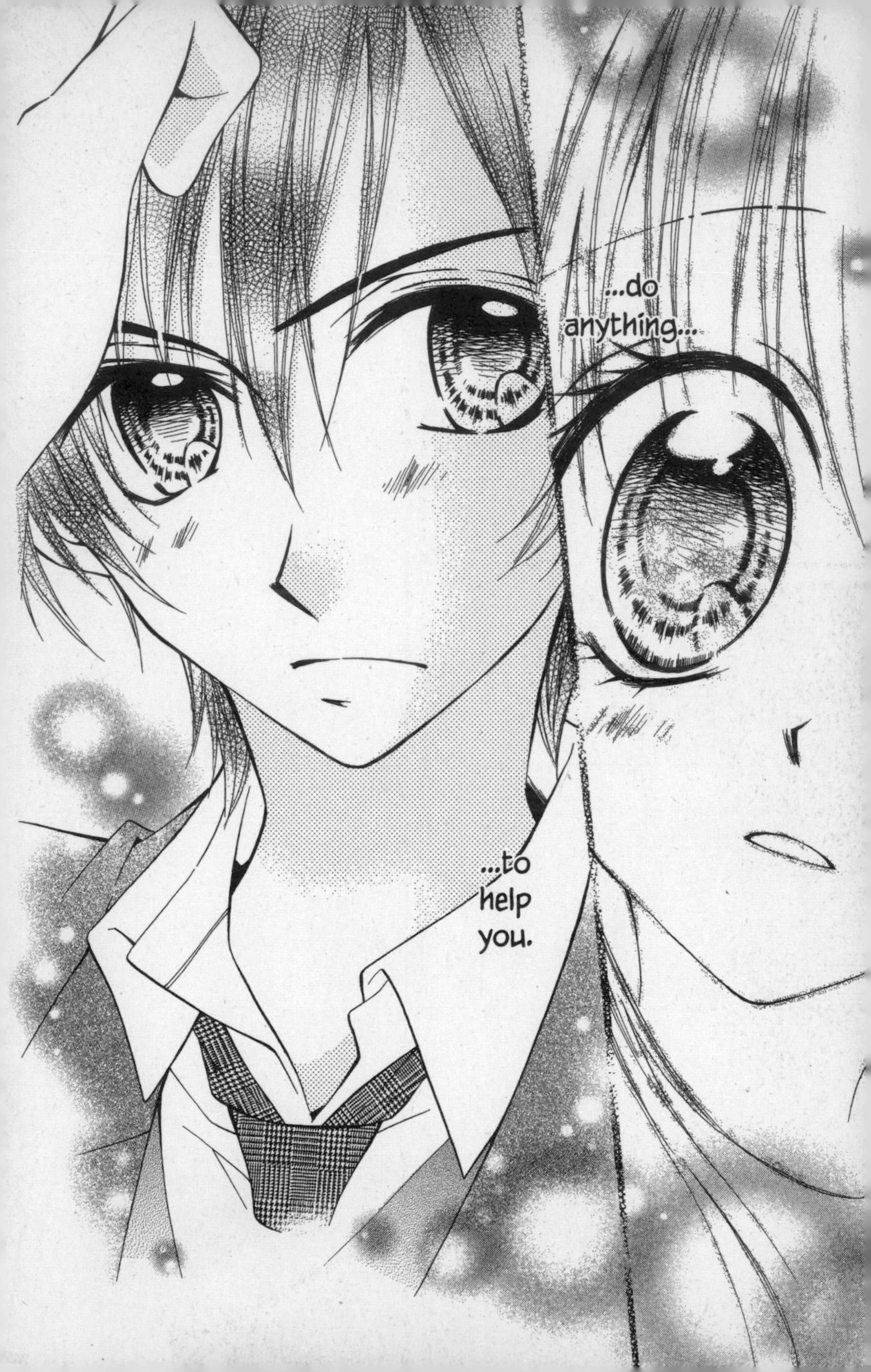
...do anything...
...to help you.

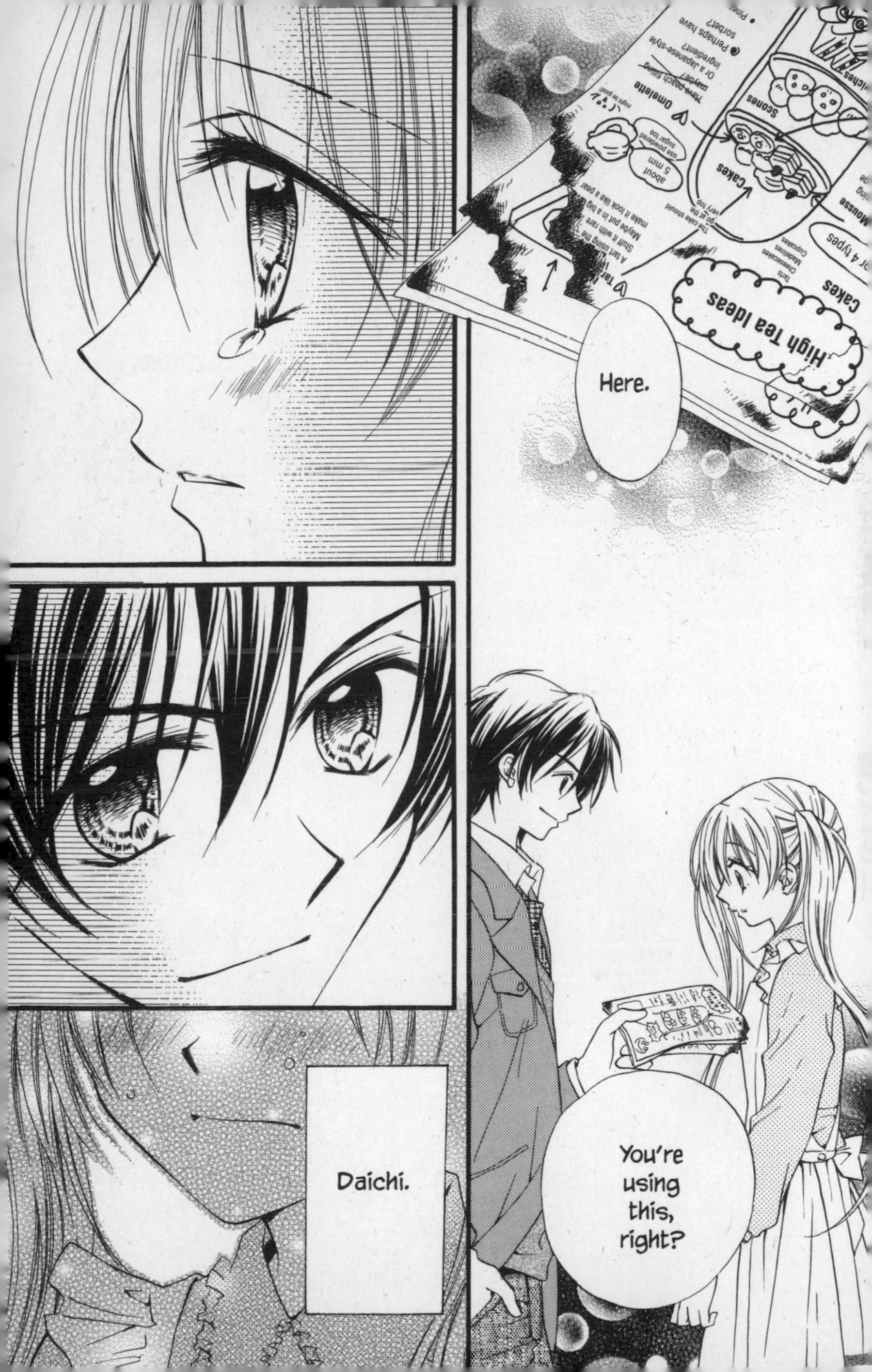
High Tea Ideas
Here.
You're using this, right?
Daichi.

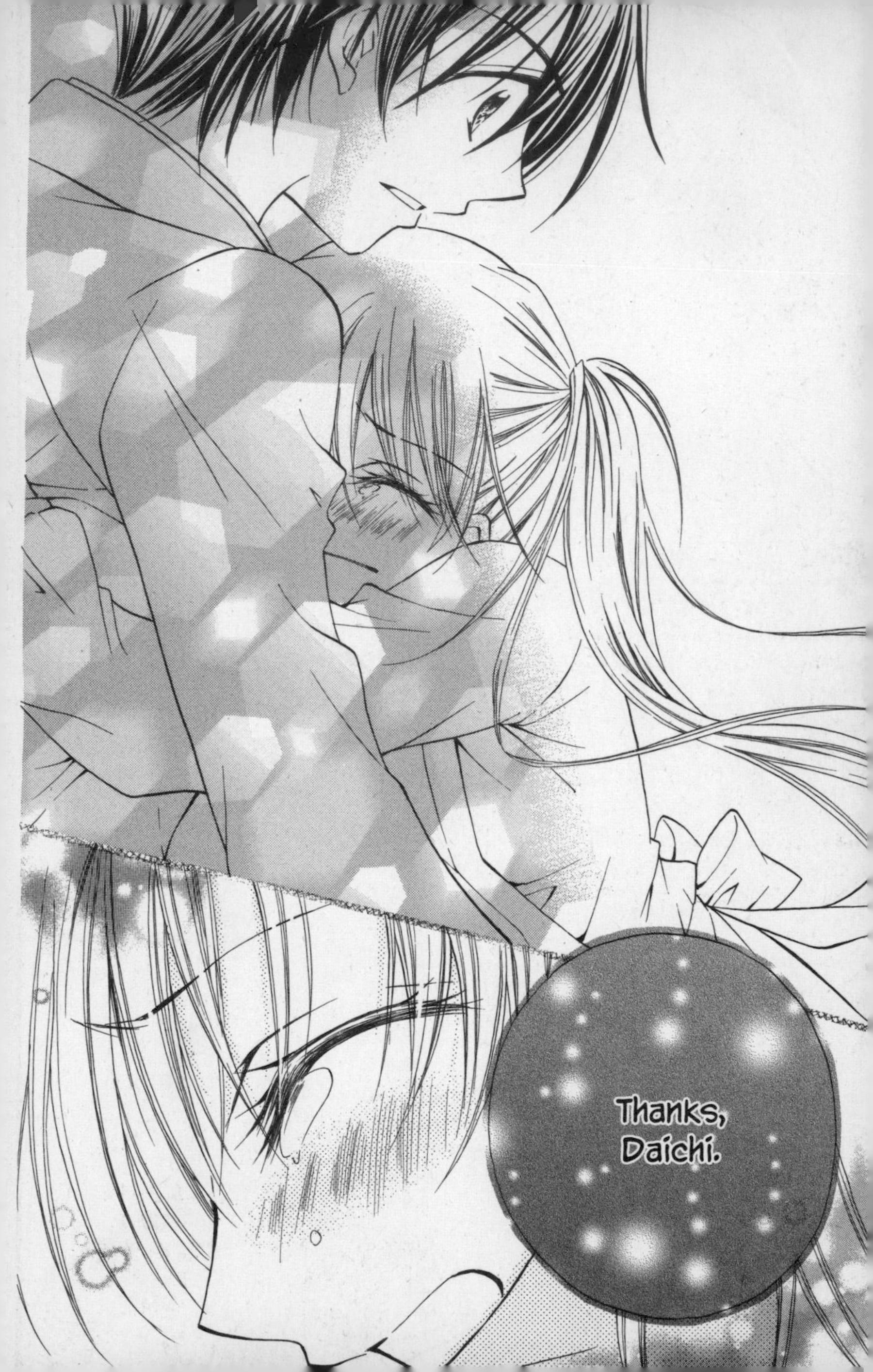
Thanks, Daichi.

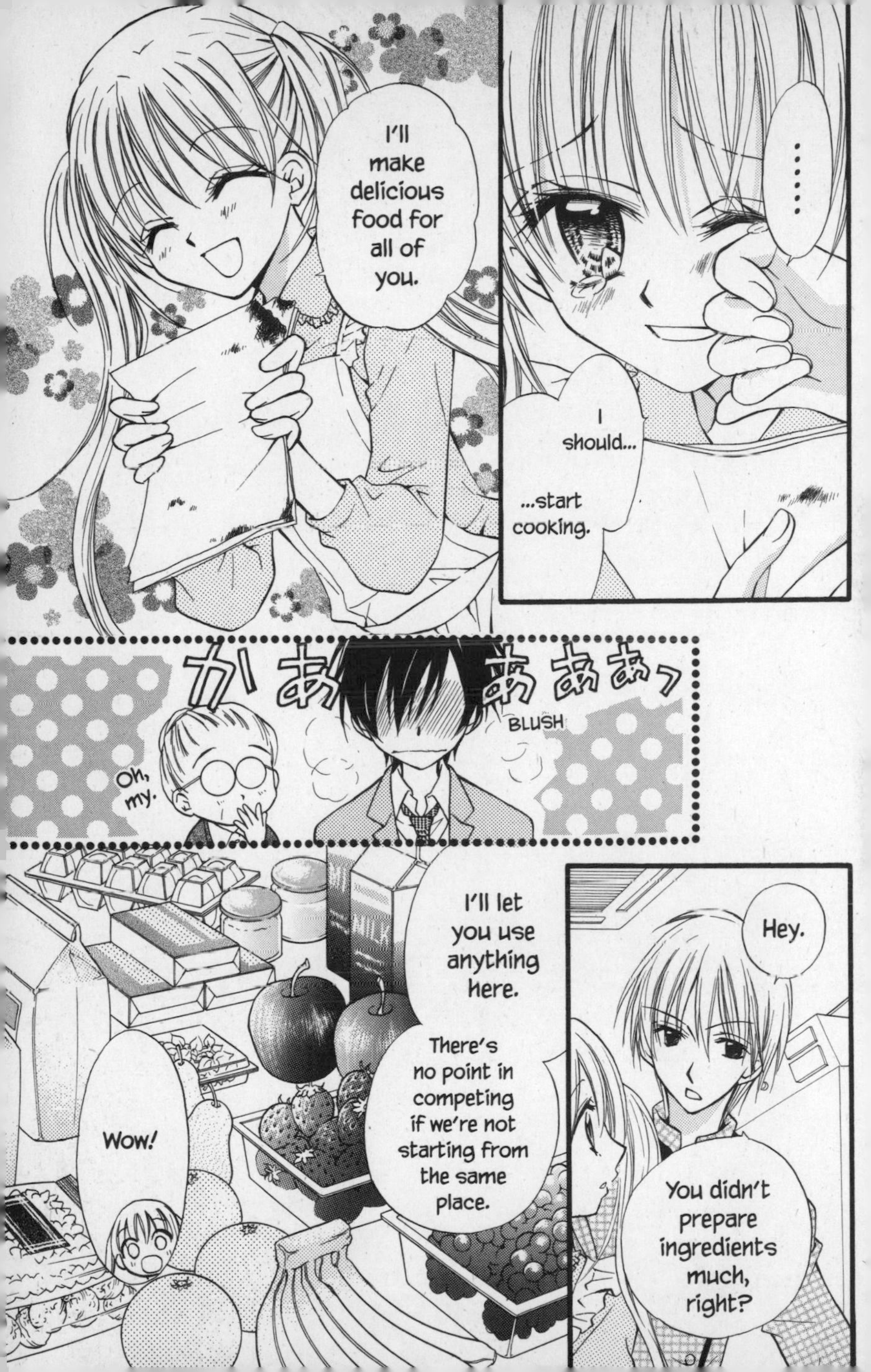

.....
I should...
...start cooking.
I'll make delicious food for all of you.
かあ あああっ
BLUSH
Oh, my.
Hey.
You didn't prepare ingredients much, right?
I'll let you use anything here.
There's no point in competing if we're not starting from the same place.
Wow!

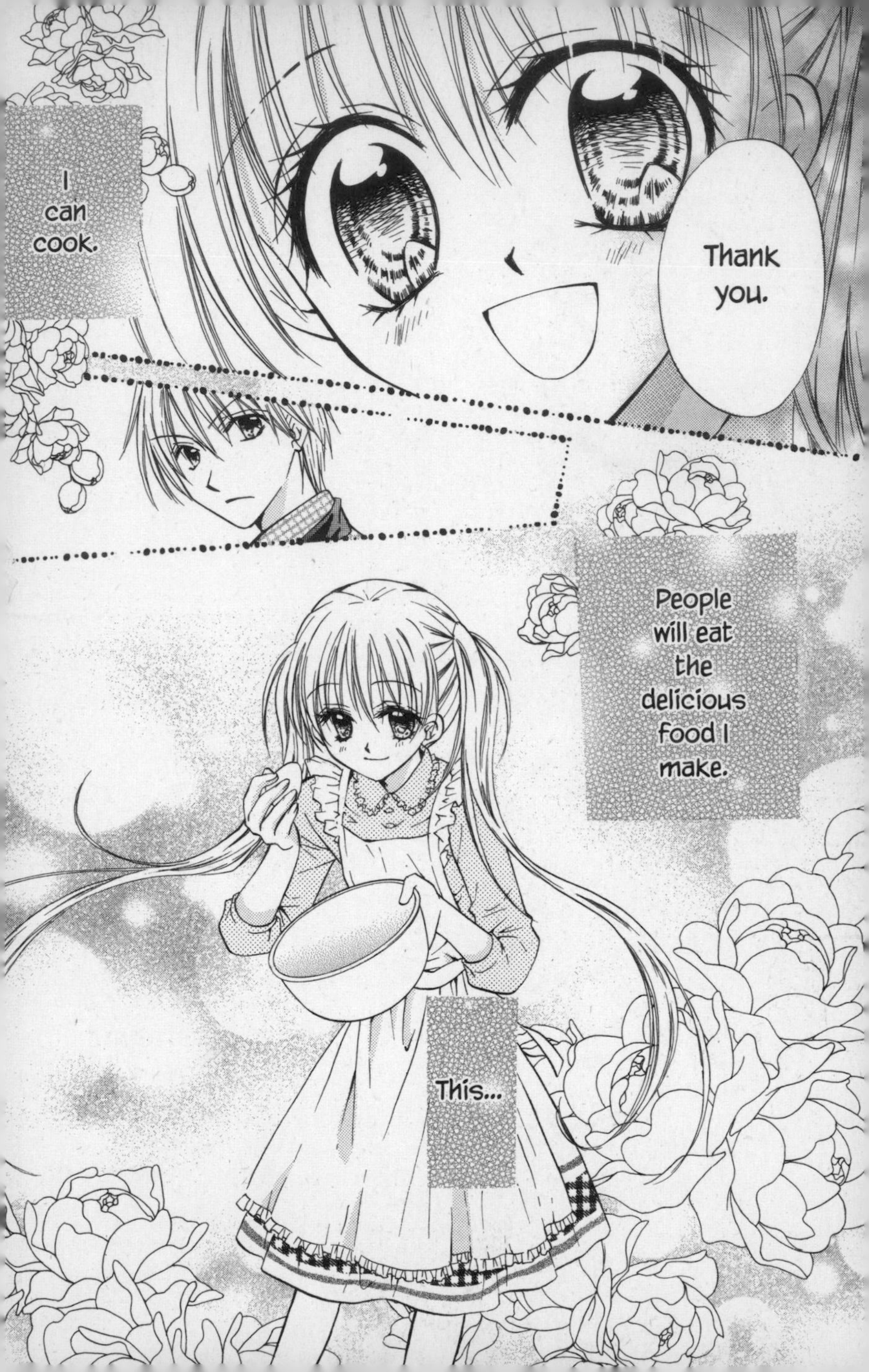
Thank you.
I can cook.
People will eat the delicious food I make.
This...

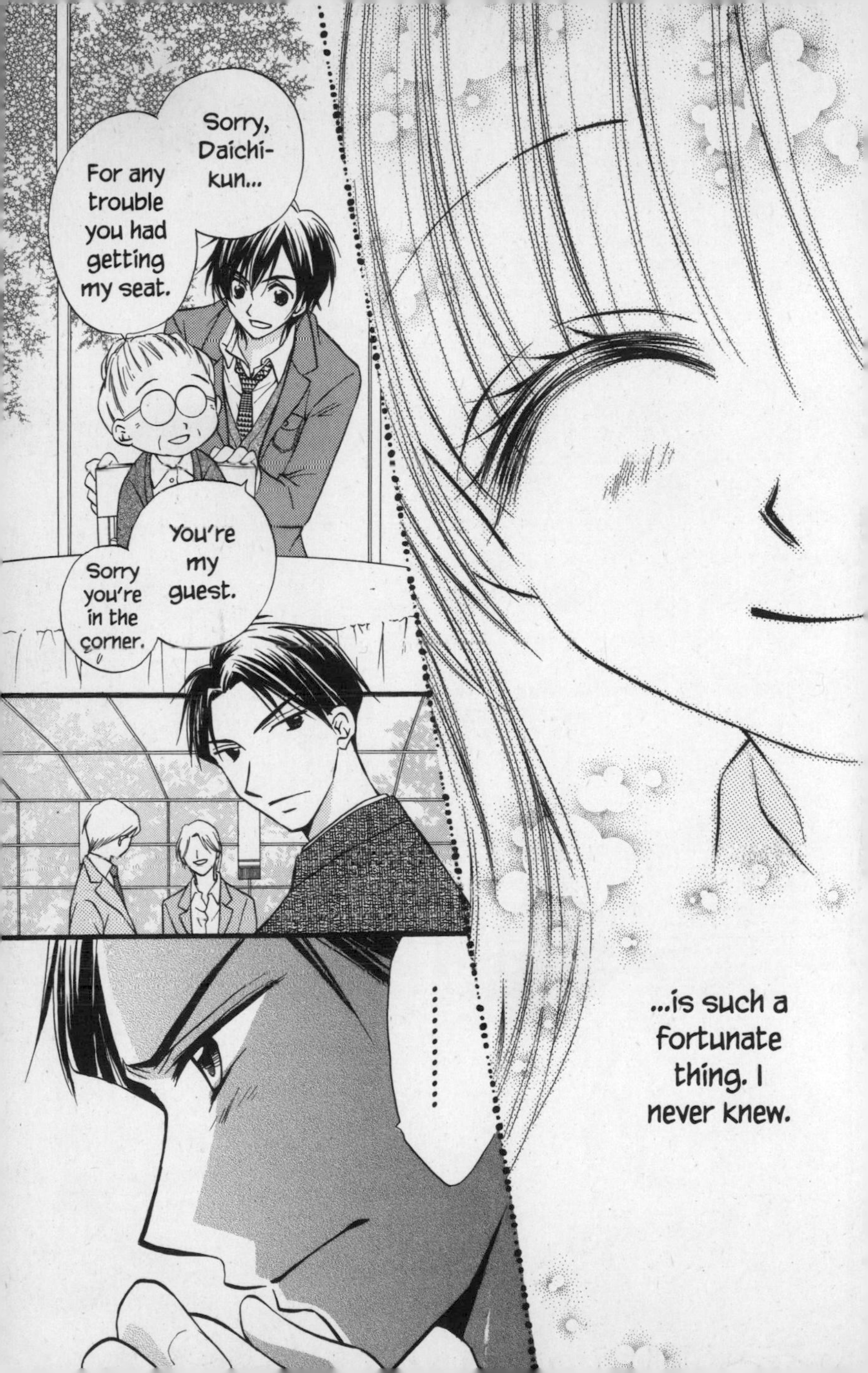
...is such a fortunate thing. I never knew.
Sorry, Daichi-kun...
For any trouble you had getting my seat.
You're my guest.
Sorry you're in the corner.

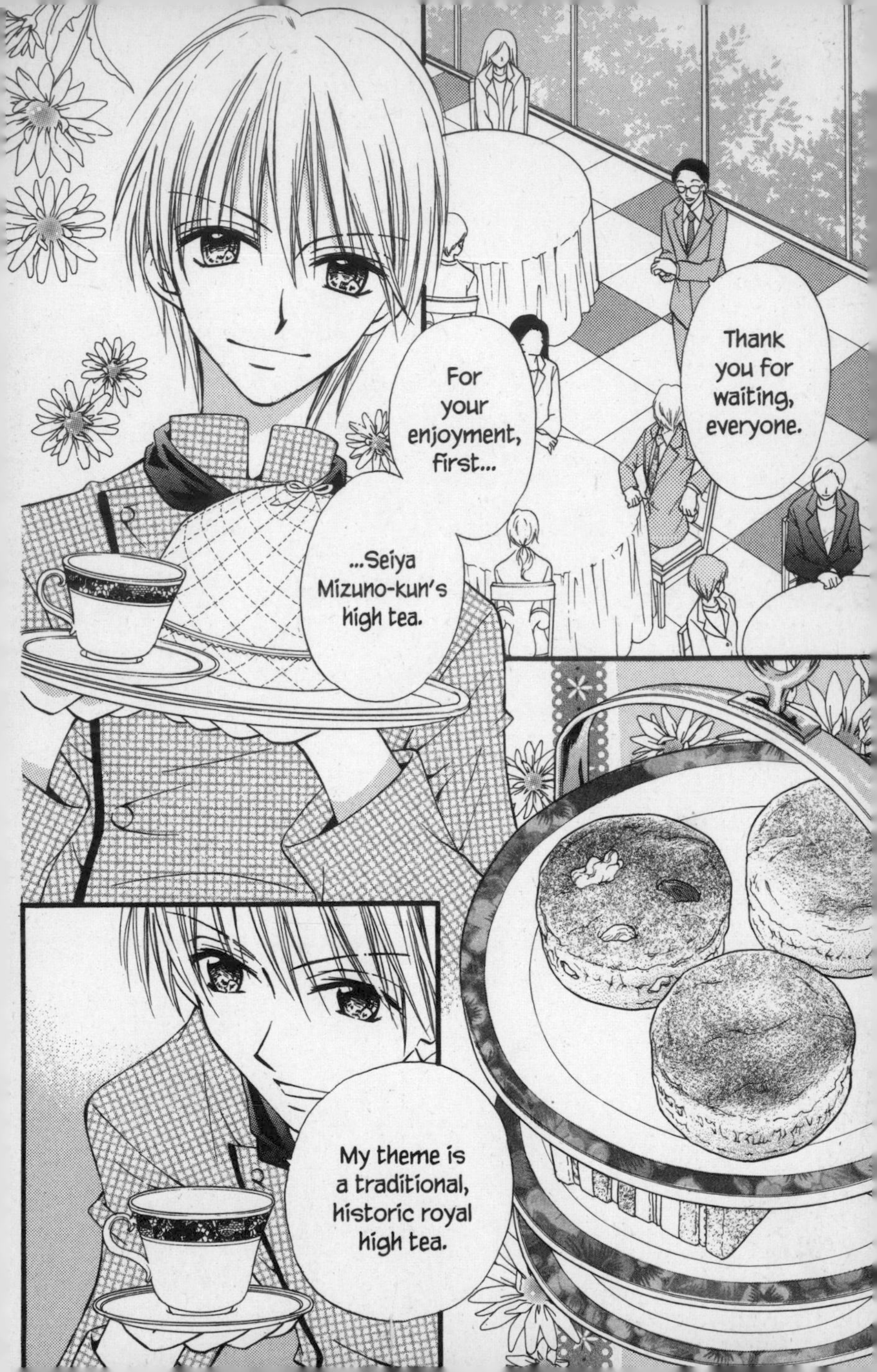
Thank you for waiting, everyone.
For your enjoyment, first...
...Seiya Mizuno-kun's high tea.
My theme is a traditional, historic royal high tea.

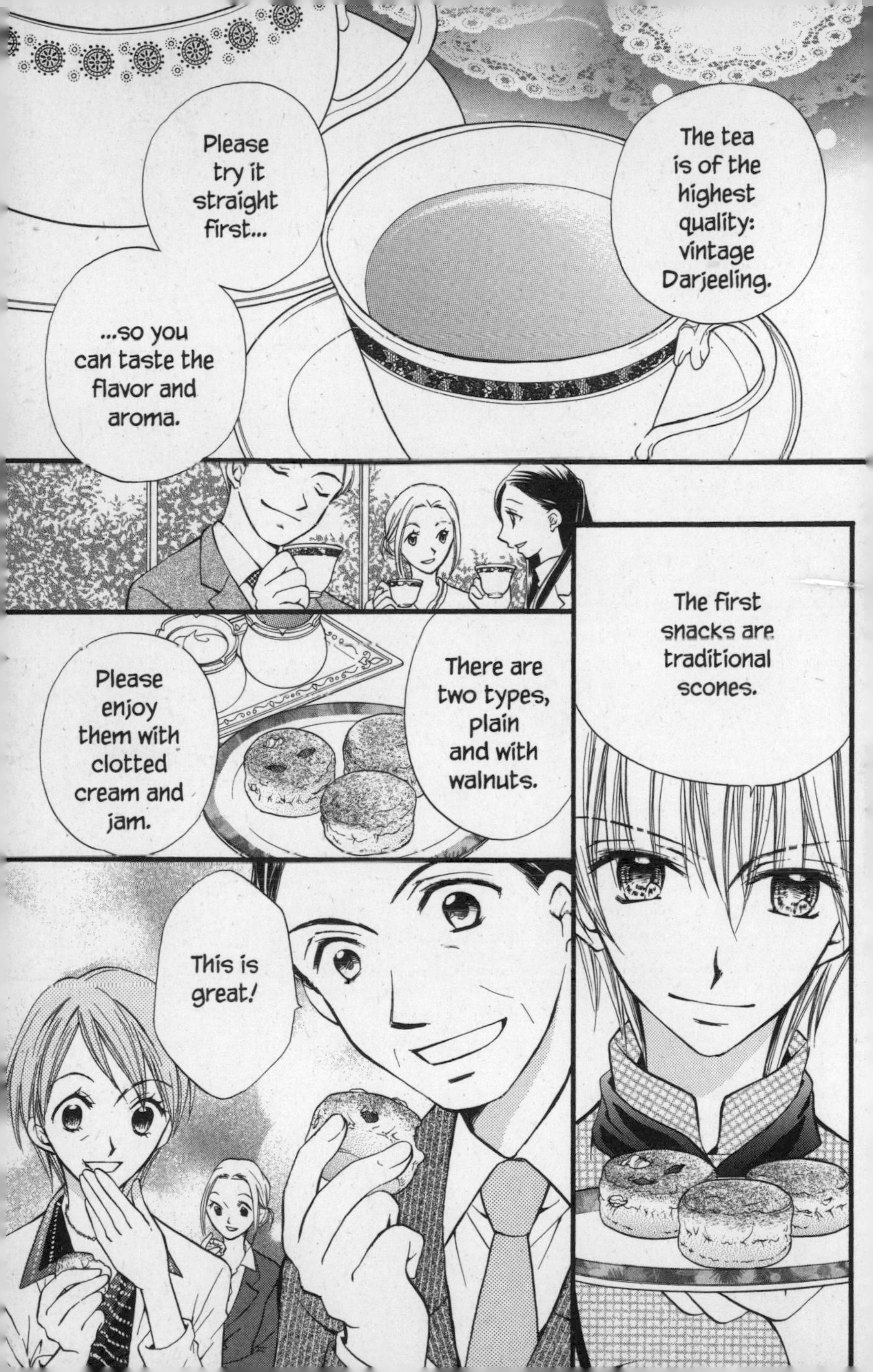
The tea is of the highest quality: vintage Darjeeling.
Please try it straight first...
...so you can taste the flavor and aroma.
The first snacks are traditional scones.
There are two types, plain and with walnuts.
Please enjoy them with clotted cream and jam.
This is great!

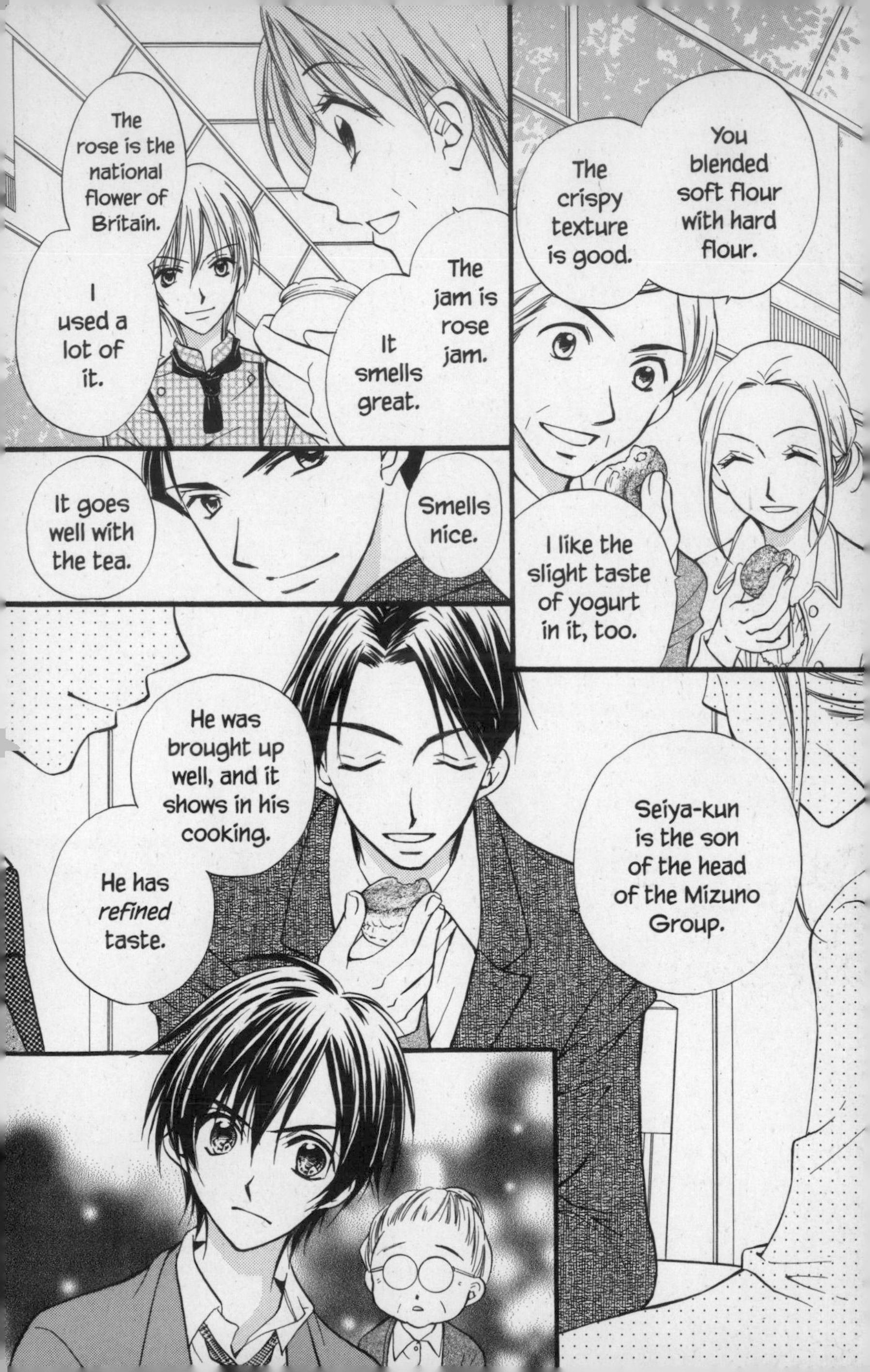
You blended soft flour with hard flour.
The crispy texture is good.
I like the slight taste of yogurt in it, too.
The jam is rose jam.
It smells great.
The rose is the national flower of Britain.
I used a lot of it.
Smells nice.
It goes well with the tea.
Seiya-kun is the son of the head of the Mizuno Group.
He was brought up well, and it shows in his cooking.
He has *refined* taste.

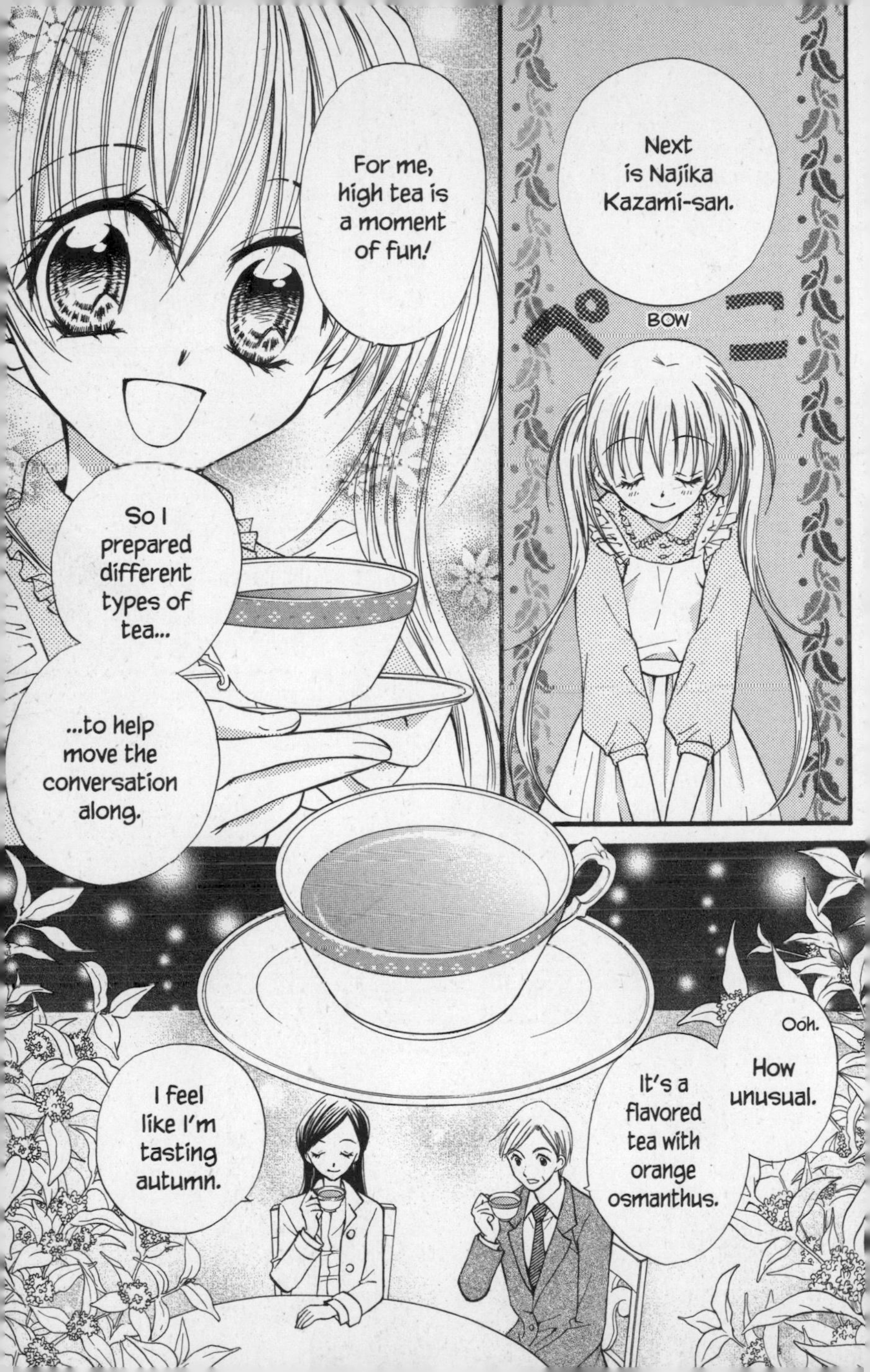
Next is Najika Kazami-san.
BOW
For me, high tea is a moment of fun!
So I prepared different types of tea...
...to help move the conversation along.
Ooh.
How unusual.
It's a flavored tea with orange osmanthus.
I feel like I'm tasting autumn.

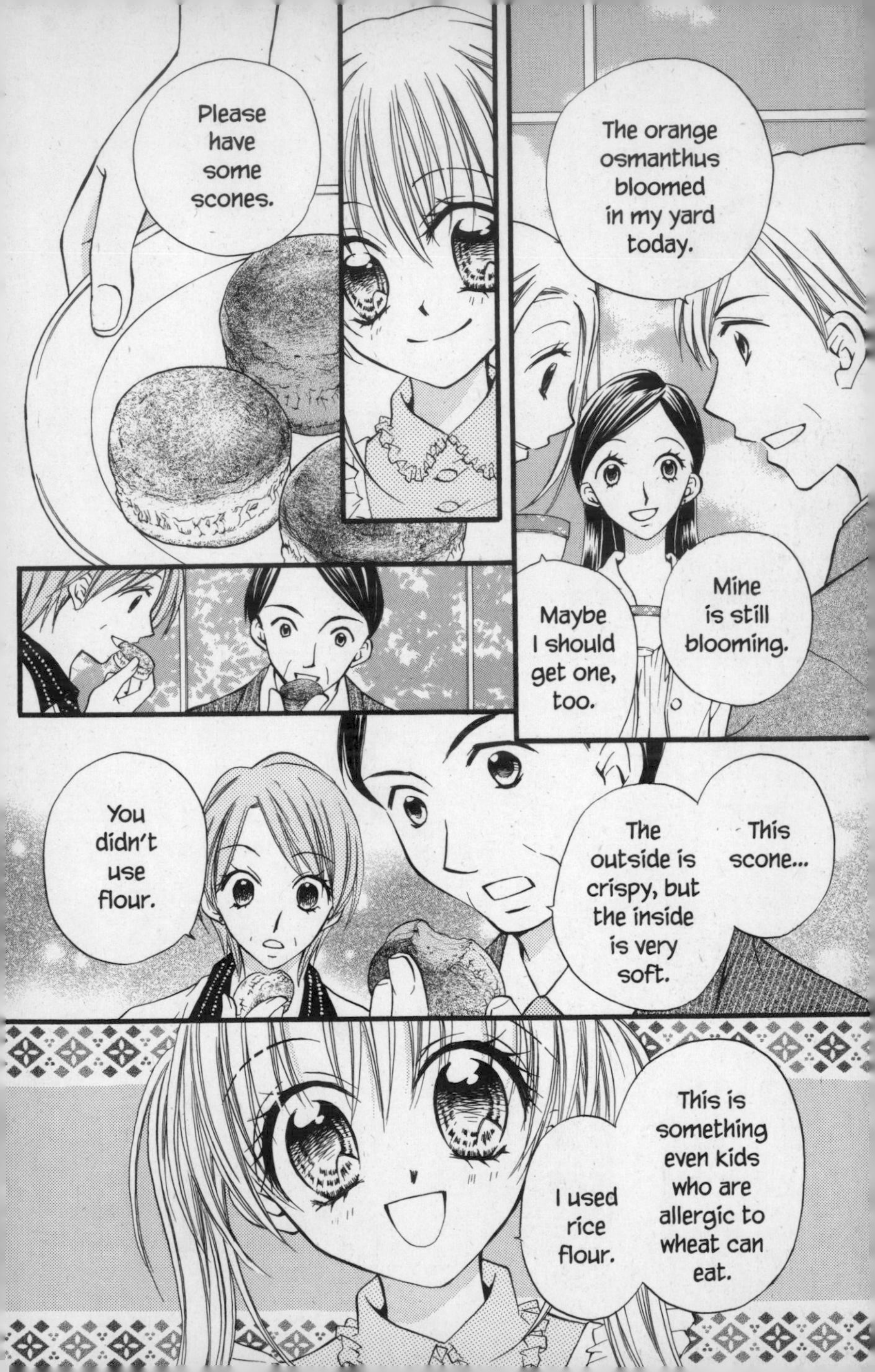
The orange osmanthus bloomed in my yard today.
Mine is still blooming.
Maybe I should get one, too.
Please have some scones.
This scone...
The outside is crispy, but the inside is very soft.
You didn't use flour.
This is something even kids who are allergic to wheat can eat.
I used rice flour.

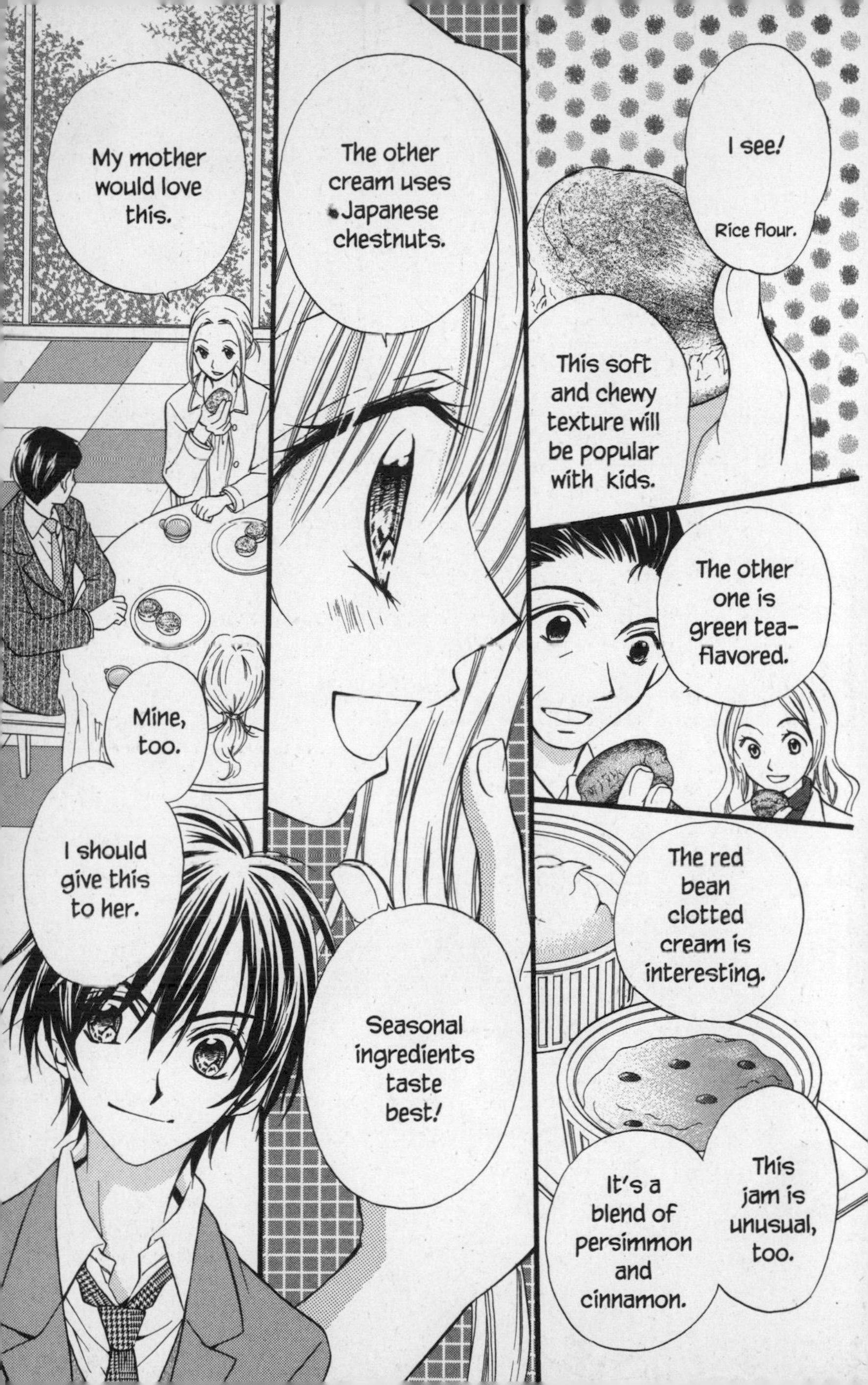
I see!
Rice flour.
This soft and chewy texture will be popular with kids.
The other one is green tea-flavored.
The red bean clotted cream is interesting.
This jam is unusual, too.
It's a blend of persimmon and cinnamon.
The other cream uses Japanese chestnuts.
Seasonal ingredients taste best!
My mother would love this.
Mine, too.
I should give this to her.

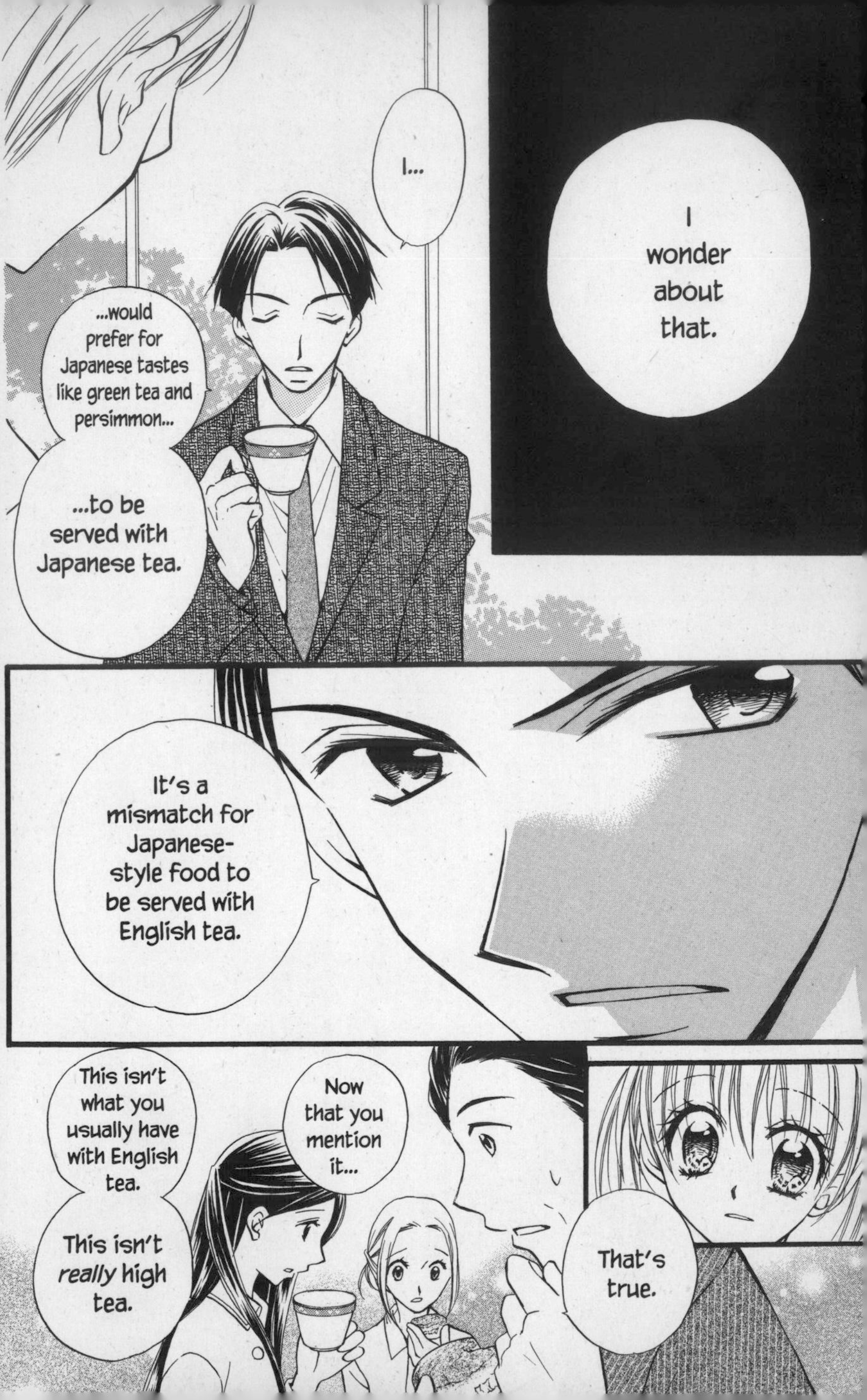
I wonder about that.
I...
...would prefer for Japanese tastes like green tea and persimmon...
...to be served with Japanese tea.
It's a mismatch for Japanese-style food to be served with English tea.
That's true.
Now that you mention it...
This isn't what you usually have with English tea.
This isn't *really* high tea.

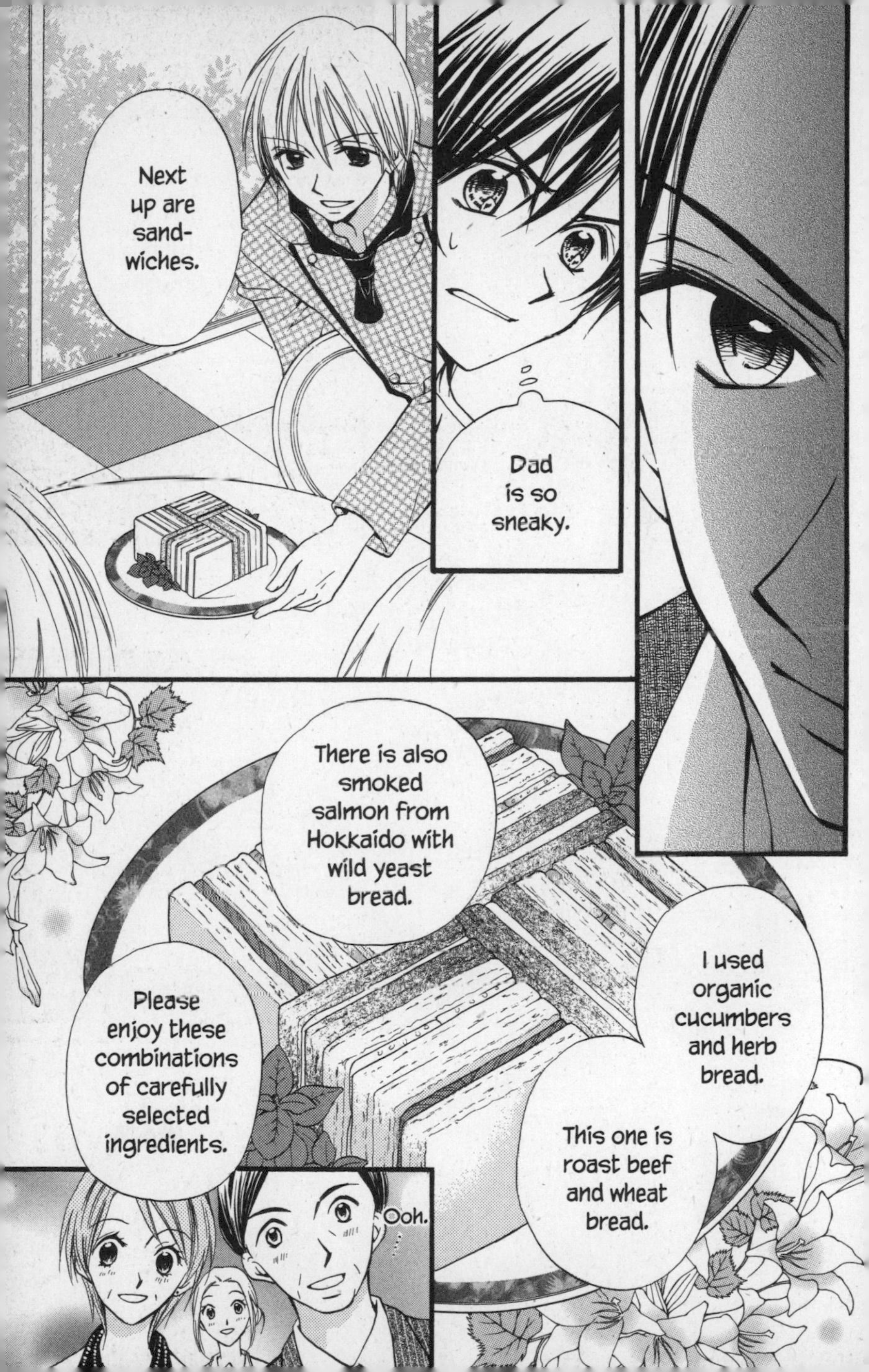

Dad is so sneaky.
Next up are sand-wiches.
This one is roast beef and wheat bread.
I used organic cucumbers and herb bread.
There is also smoked salmon from Hokkaido with wild yeast bread.
Please enjoy these combinations of carefully selected ingredients.
Ooh.

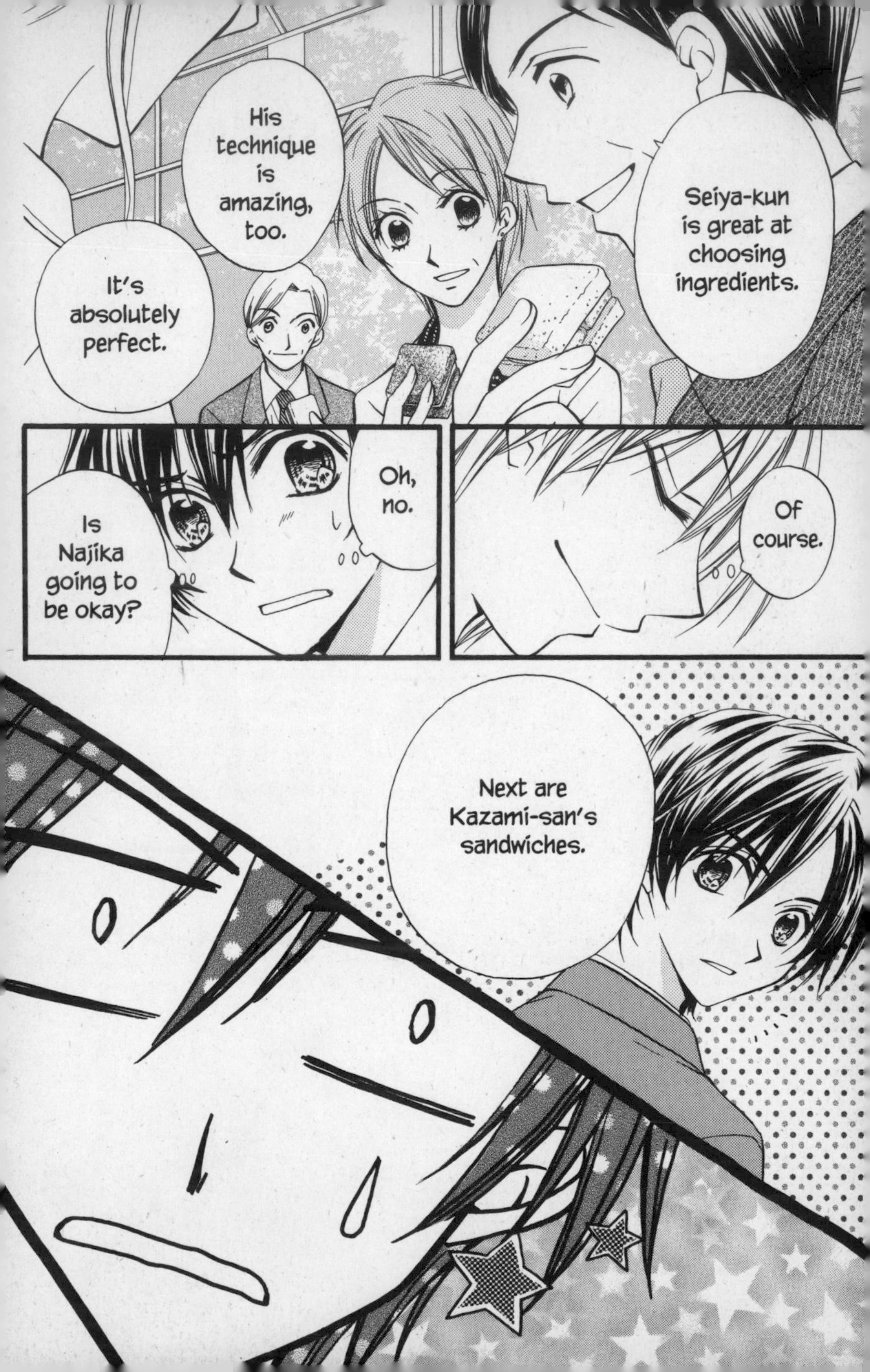
Seiya-kun is great at choosing ingredients.
His technique is amazing, too.
It's absolutely perfect.
Of course.
Oh, no.
Is Najika going to be okay?
Next are Kazami-san's sandwiches.

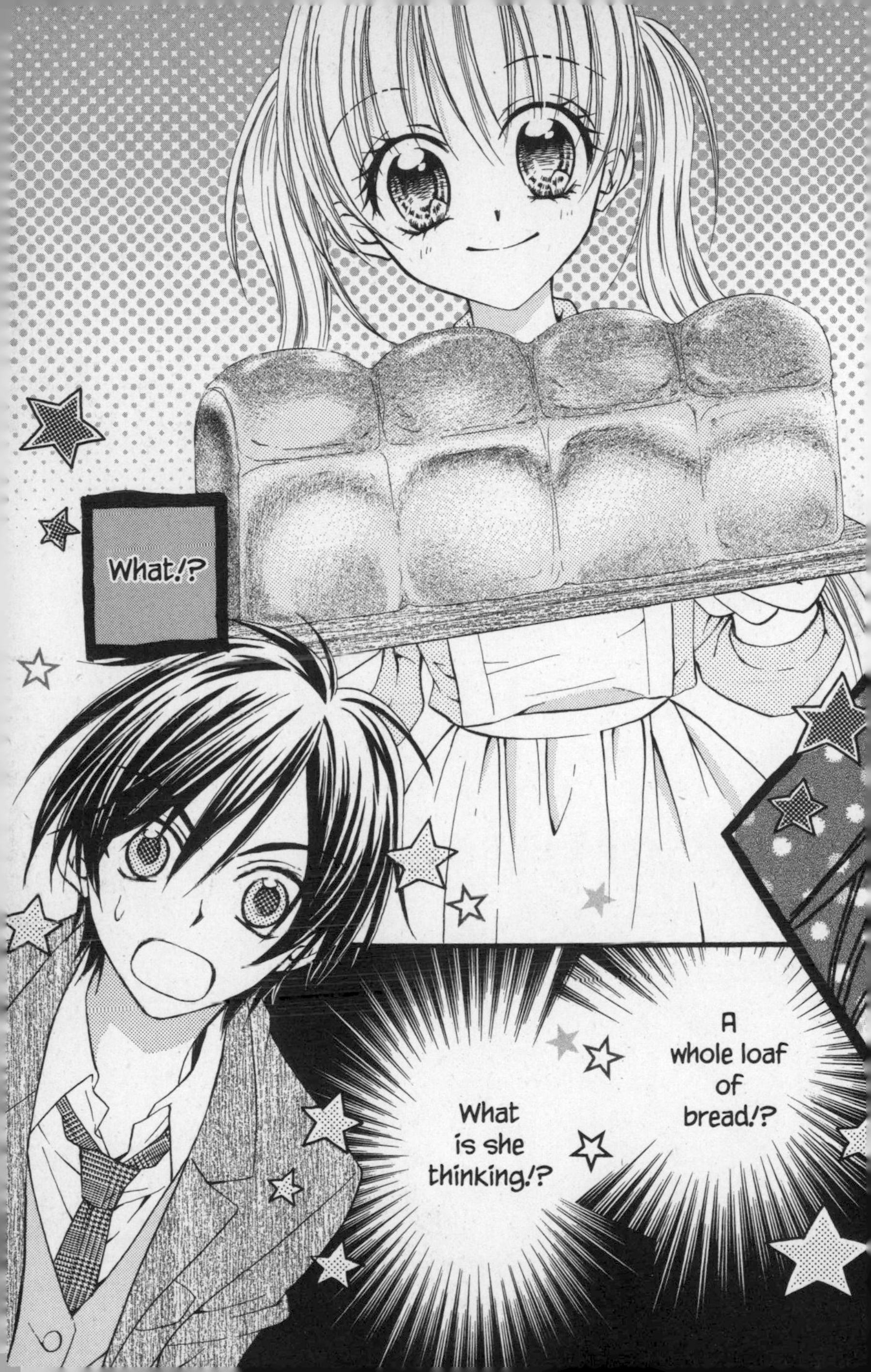
What!?
A whole loaf of bread!?
What is she thinking!?

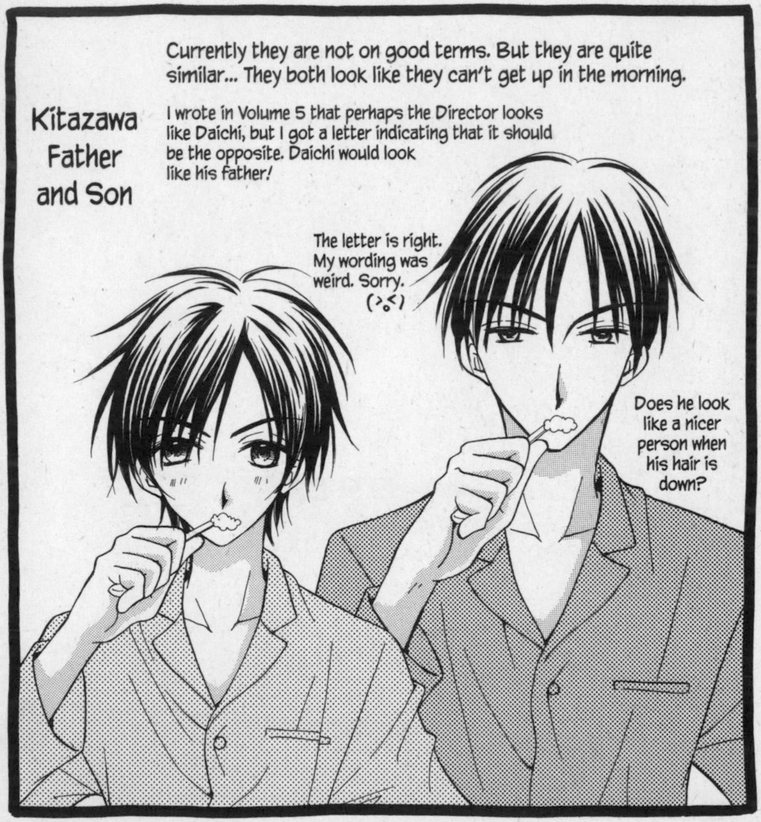
Currently they are not on good terms. But they are quite similar... They both look like they can't get up in the morning.
Kitazawa Father and Son
I wrote in Volume 5 that perhaps the Director looks like Daichi, but I got a letter indicating that it should be the opposite. Daichi would look like his father!
The letter is right. My wording was weird. Sorry. (>o<)
Does he look like a nicer person when his hair is down?

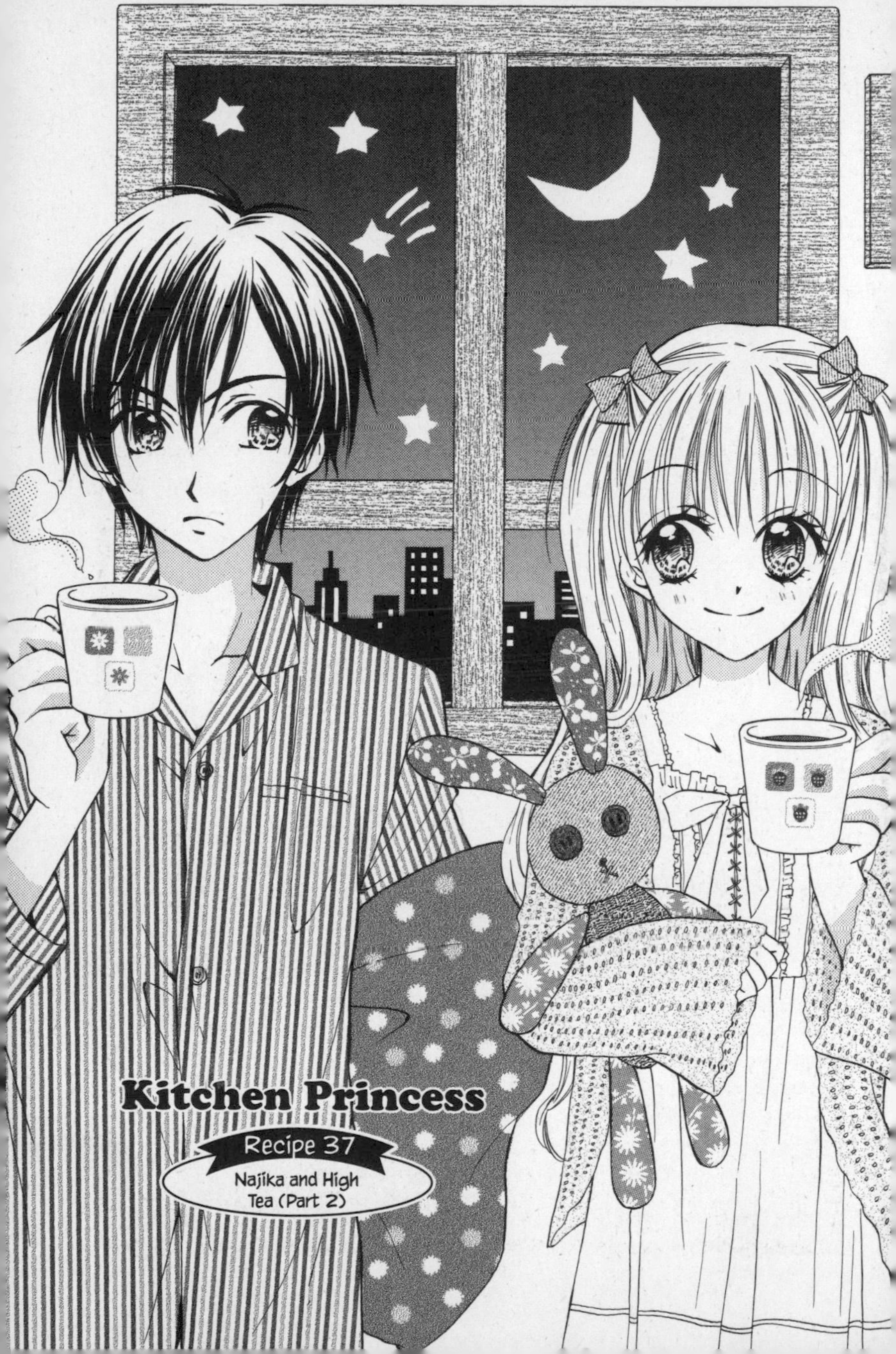
Kitchen Princess
Recipe 37
Najika and High Tea (Part 2)

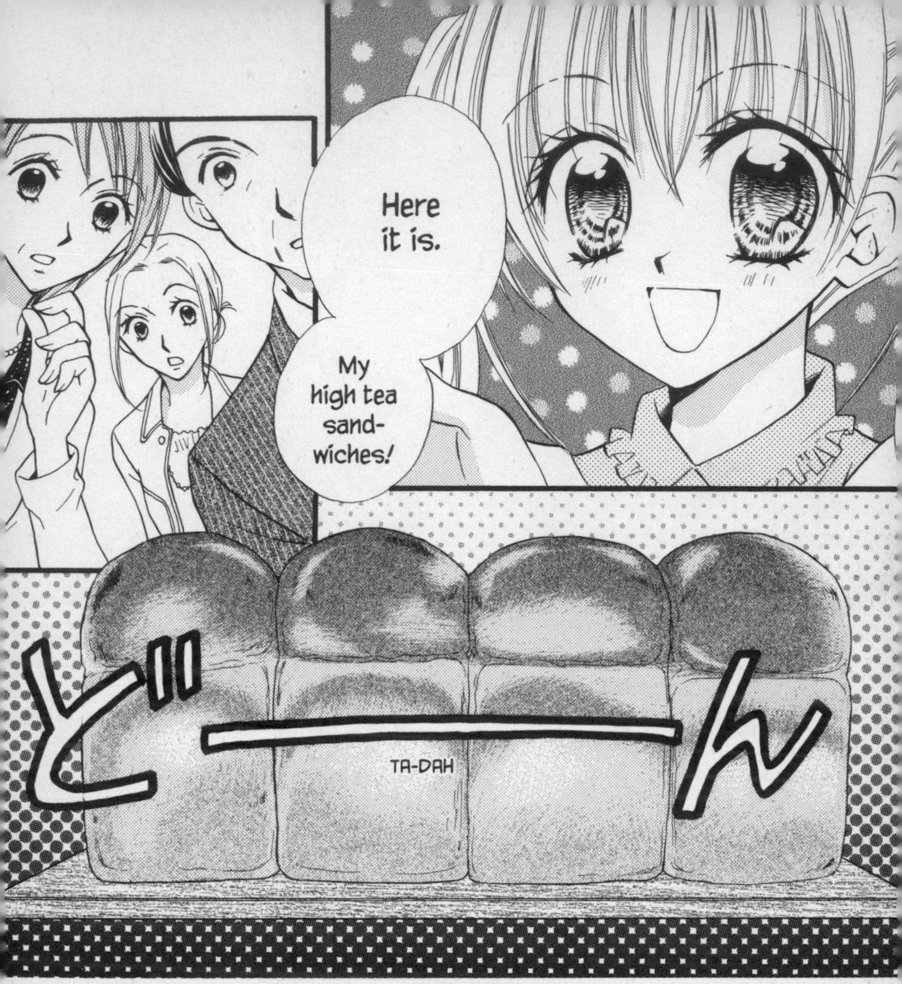
Here it is.
My high tea sandwiches!
ど——ん
TA-DAH

About Recipe 37's Splash Page

I wanted to draw something that was like a storybook...and when I realized that, I drew the two of them in pajamas. I wanted them to wear country-style outfits, but that didn't look as good with the nighttime background... They are both drinking hot chocolate. Speaking of hot chocolate, the Disney Resort's hot chocolate is the best. It probably tastes better because I drink it when it's freezing. When it gets chilly, I crave it.The warmth has saved me so many times... (>.<)

By the way, I drew hot chocolate for Recipe 16, too (in Volume 4). I must really like it. ooo

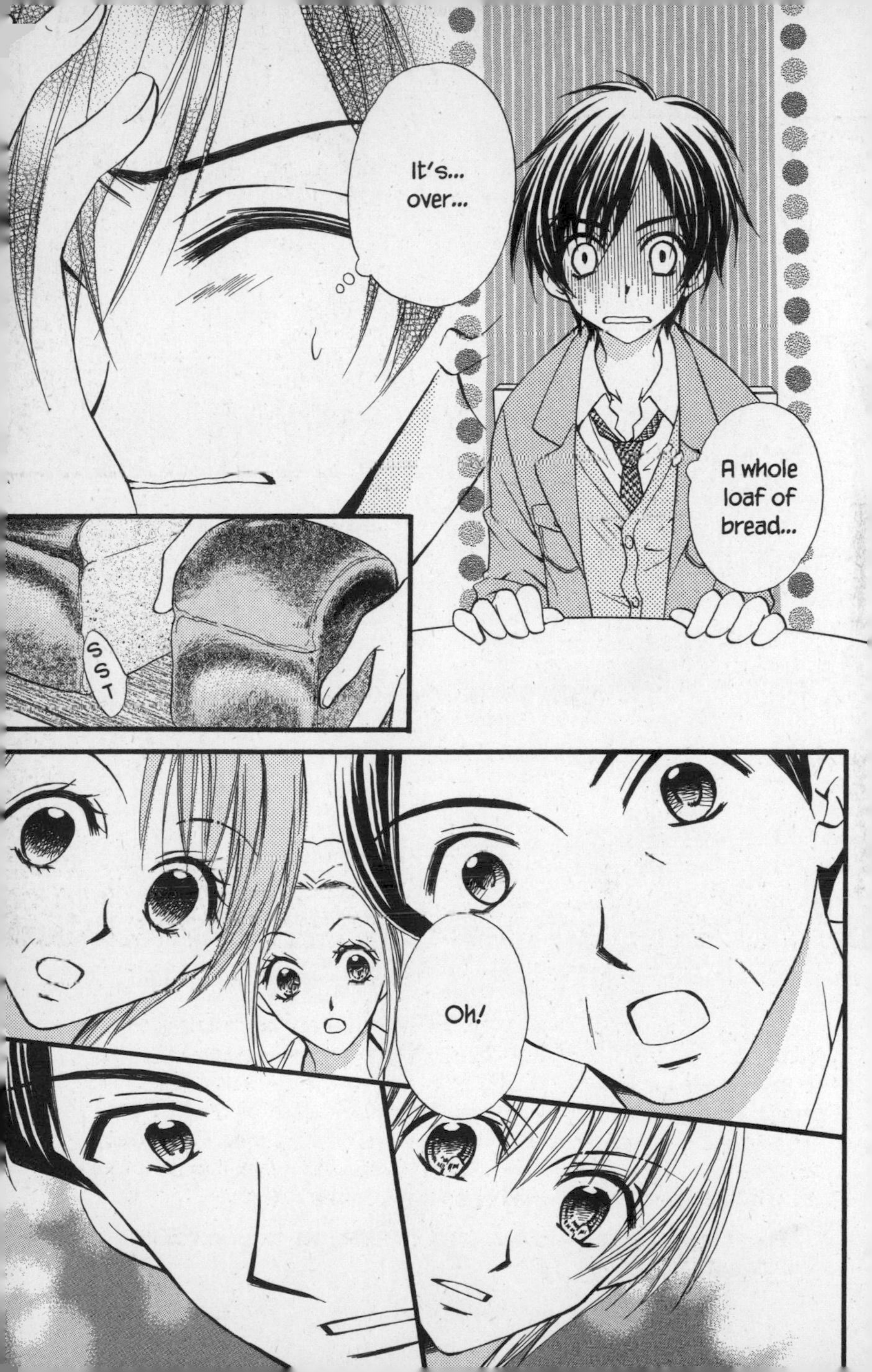
A whole loaf of bread...
It's... over...
SST
Oh!

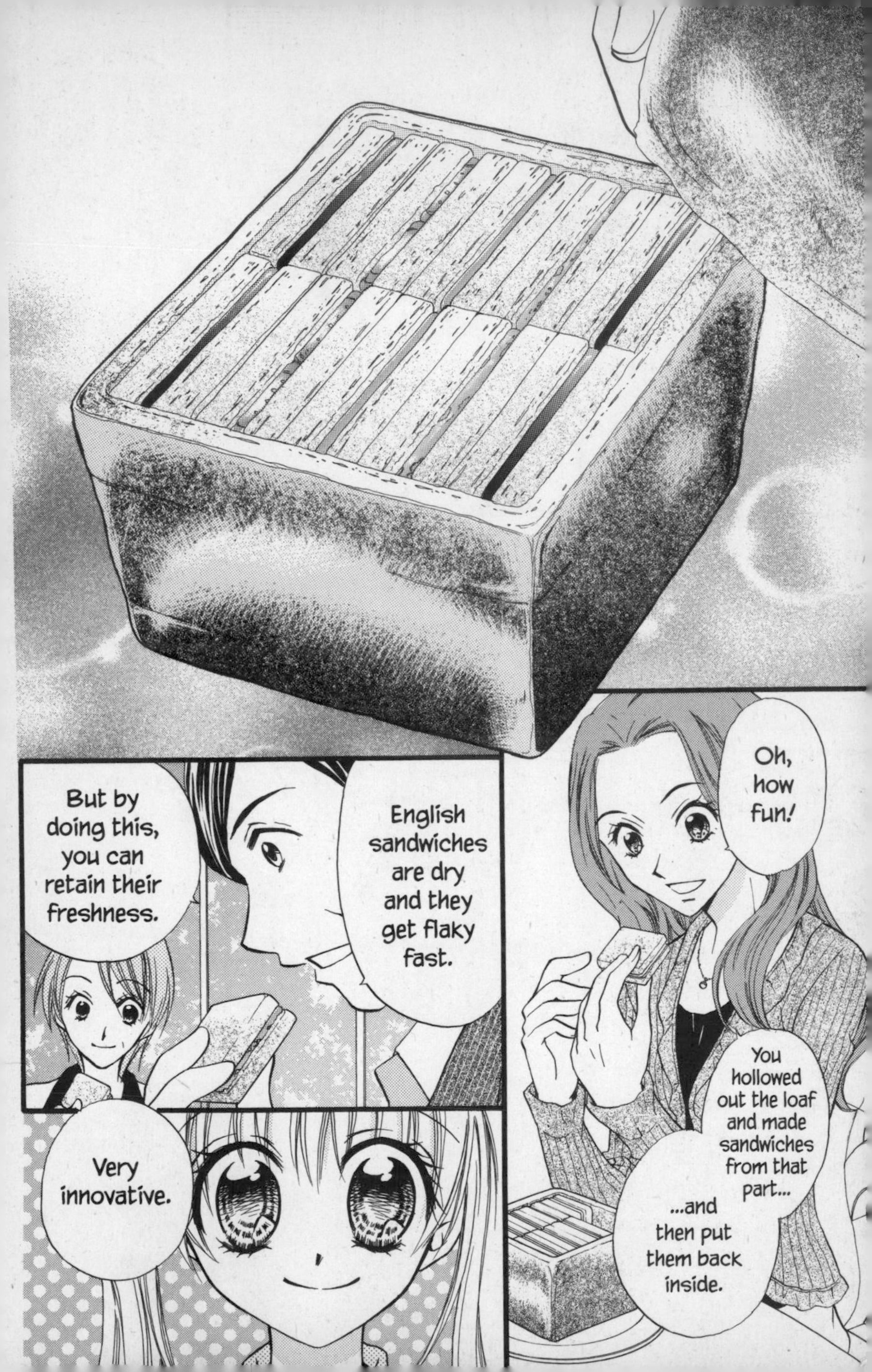
Oh, how fun!
You hollowed out the loaf and made sandwiches from that part...
...and then put them back inside.
English sandwiches are dry and they get flaky fast.
But by doing this, you can retain their freshness.
Very innovative.

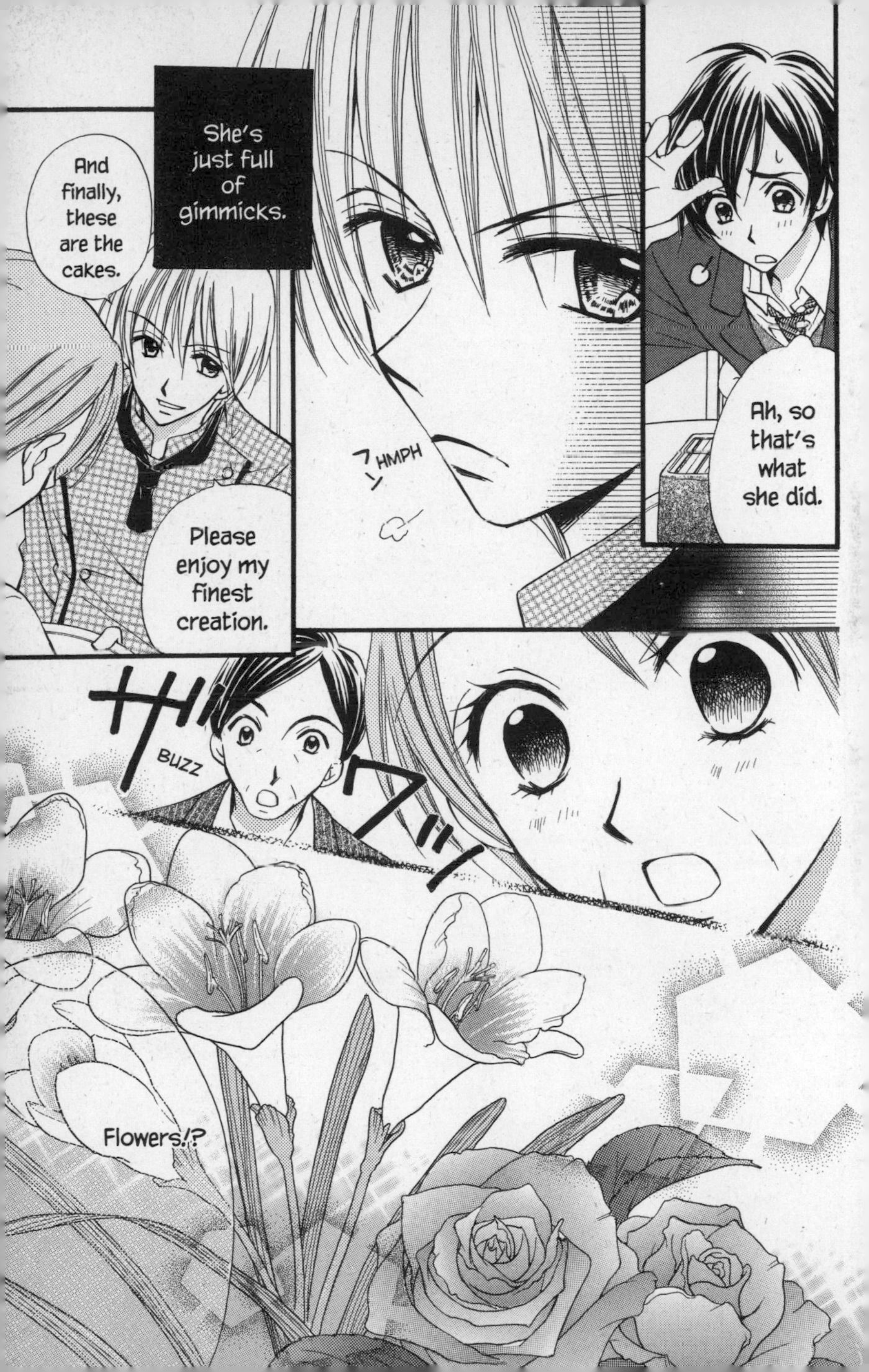
Ah, so that's what she did.
HMPH
She's just full of gimmicks.
And finally, these are the cakes.
Please enjoy my finest creation.
BUZZ
Flowers!?

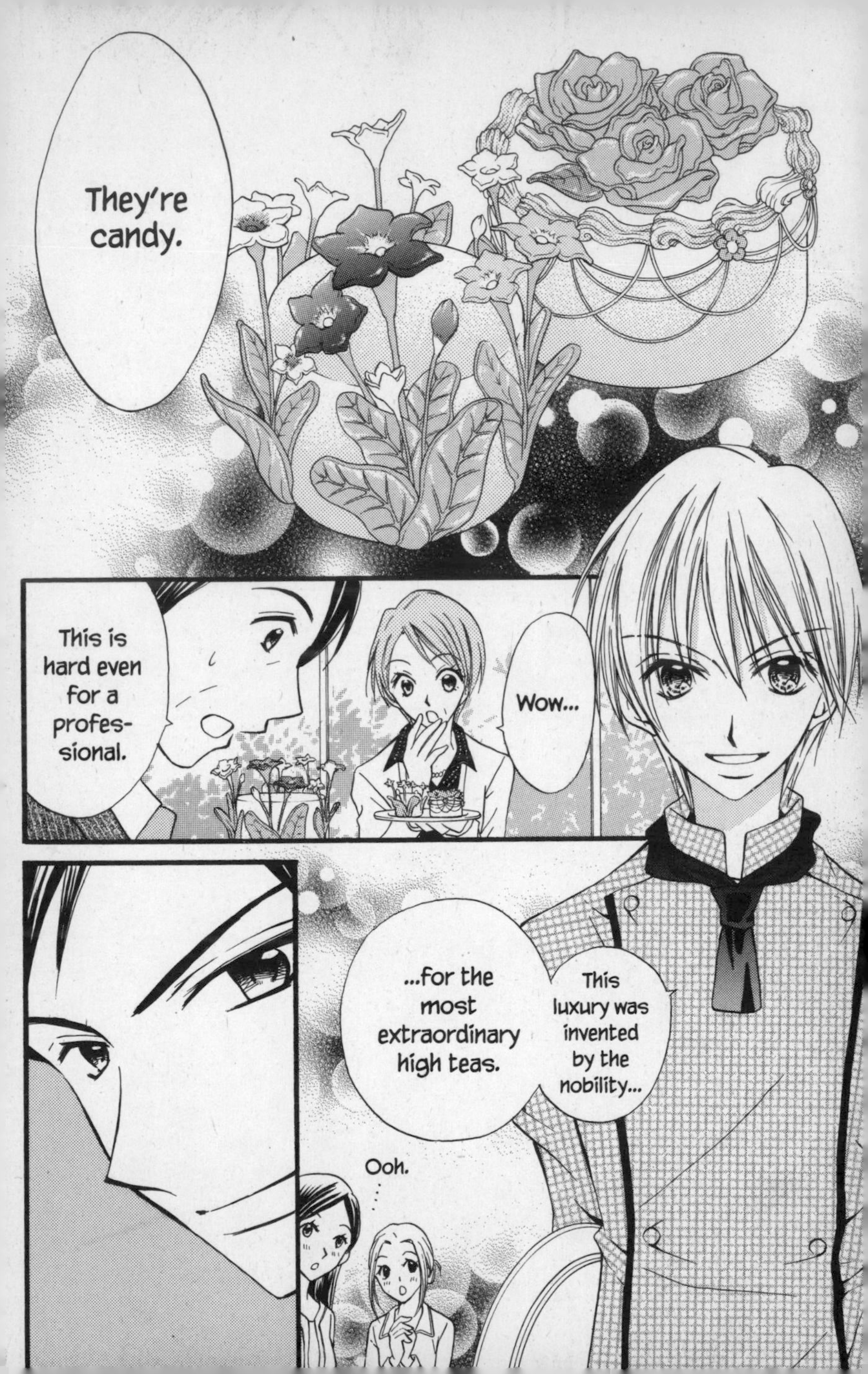
They're candy.
Wow...
This is hard even for a profes-sional.
This luxury was invented by the nobility...
...for the most extraordinary high teas.
Ooh.

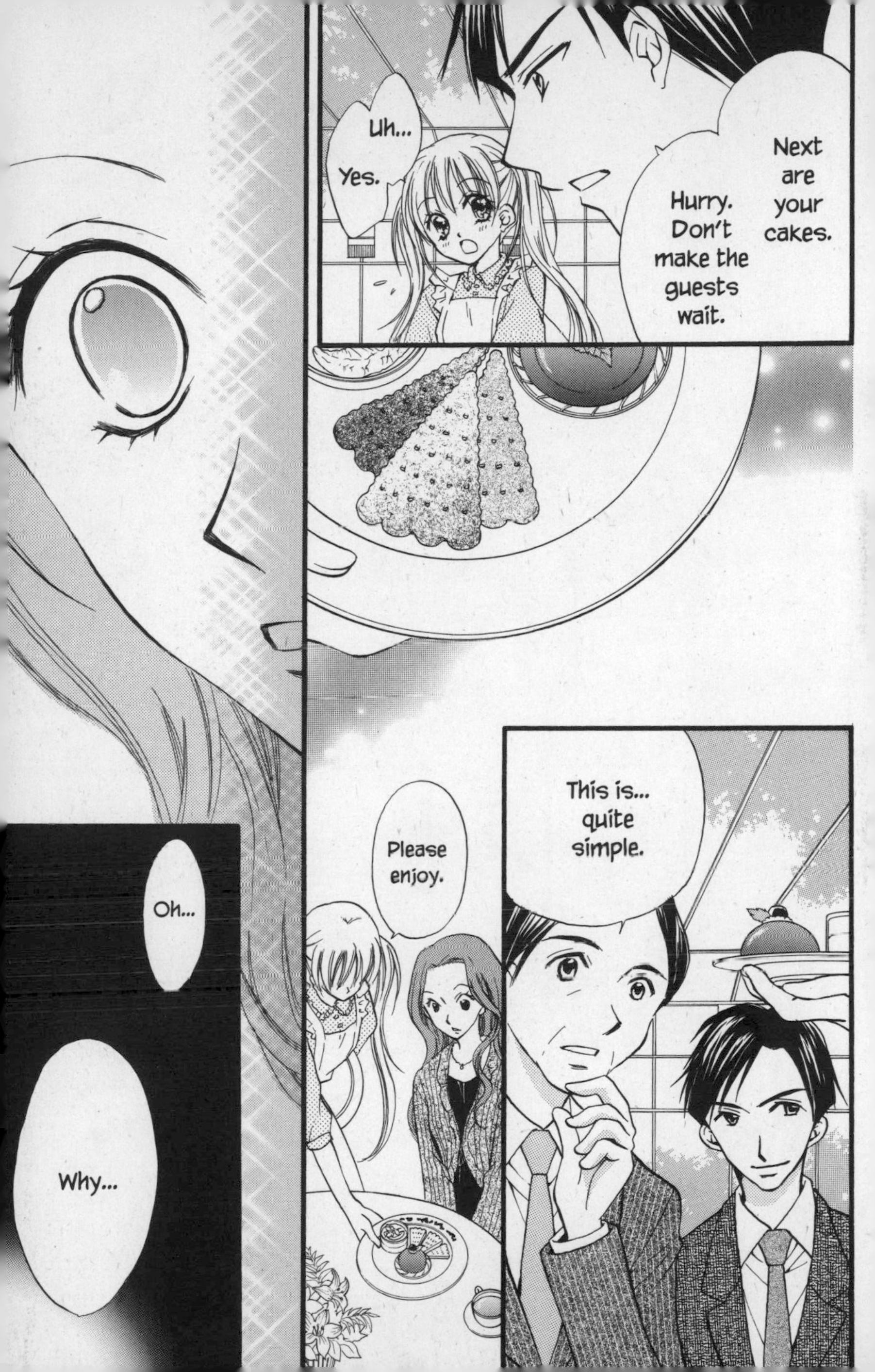

Next are your cakes.
Hurry. Don't make the guests wait.
Uh... Yes.
This is... quite simple.
Please enjoy.
Oh...
Why...

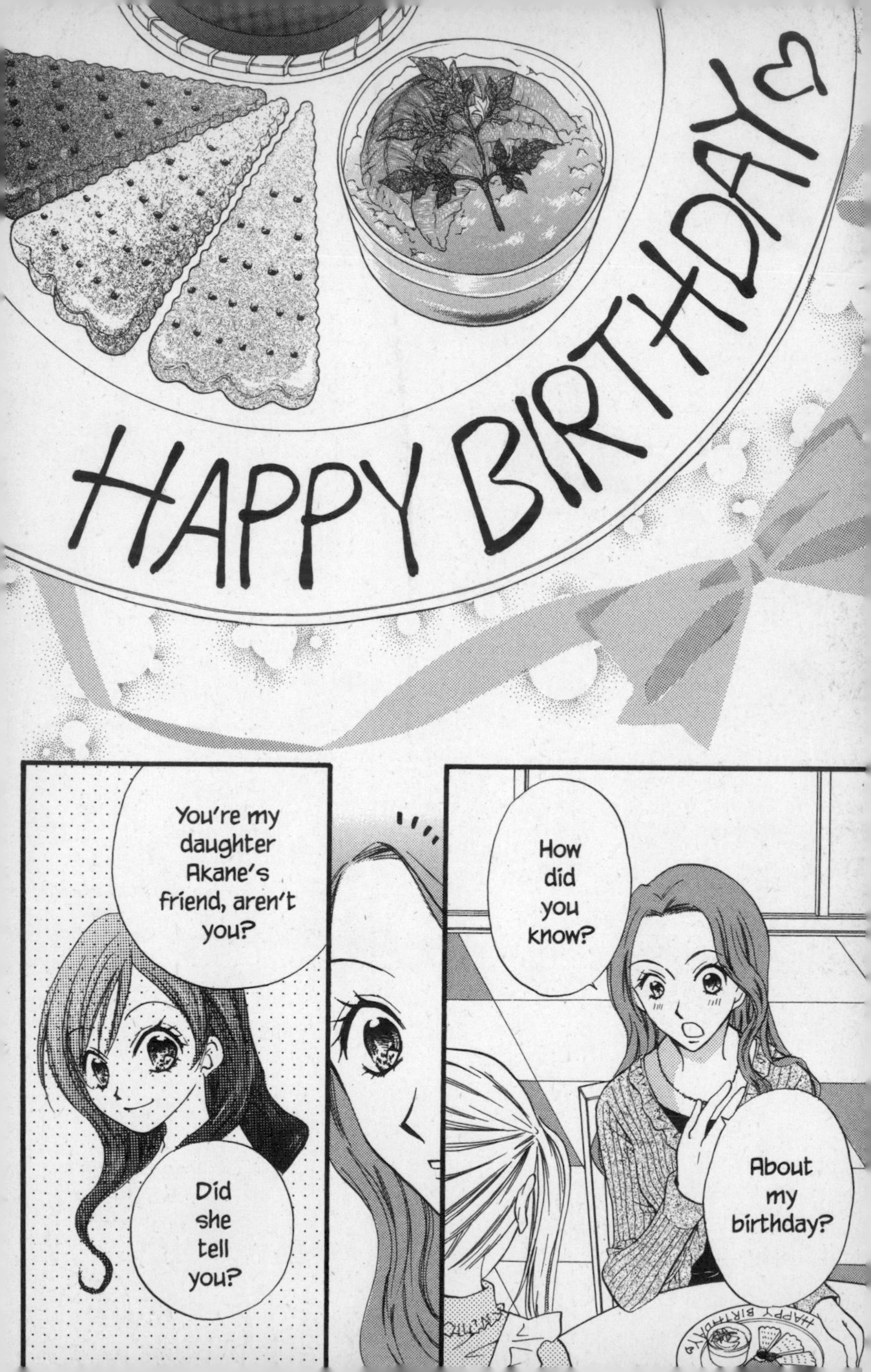
HAPPY BIRTHDAY
How did you know?
About my birthday?
You're my daughter Akane's friend, aren't you?
Did she tell you?

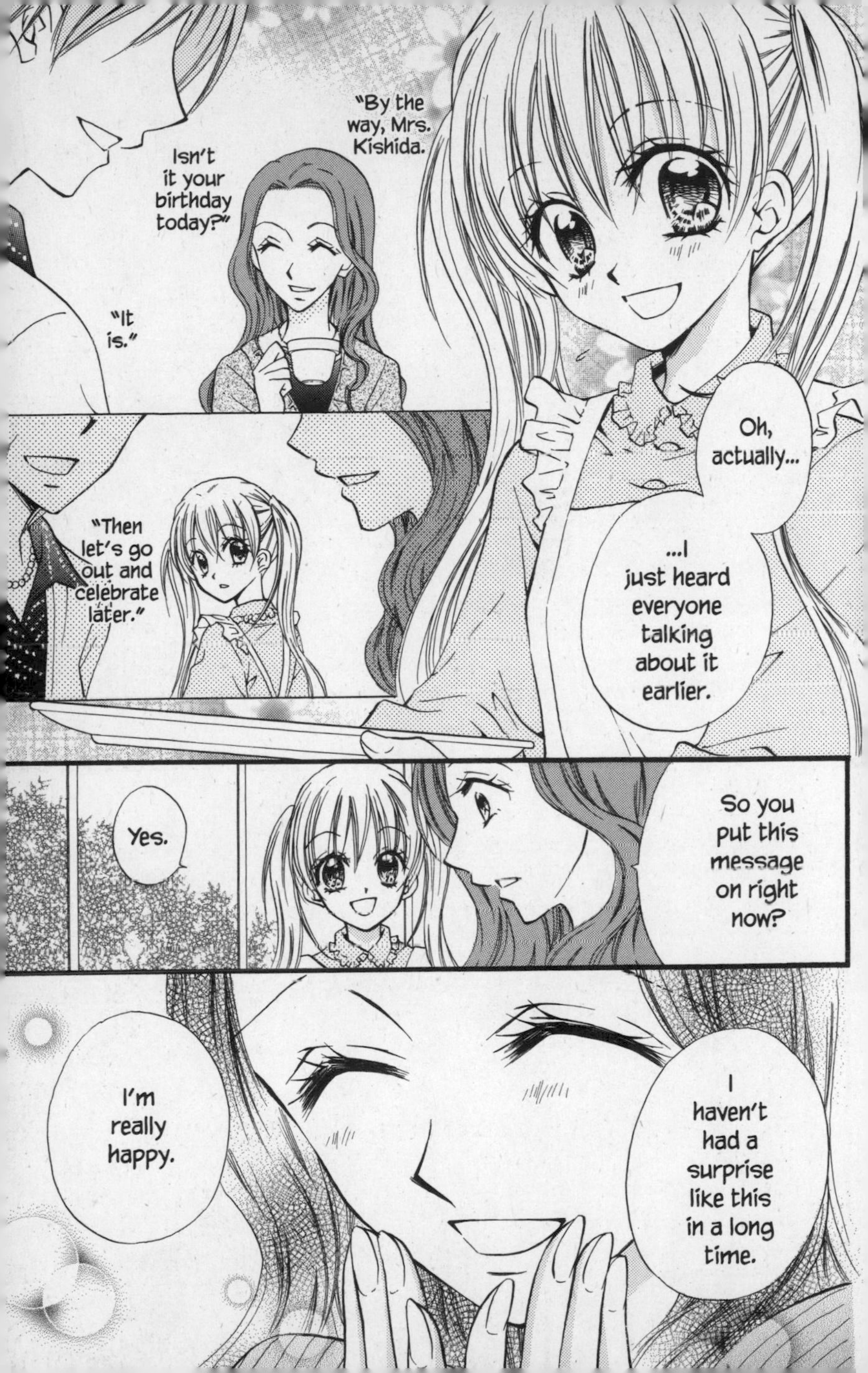
Oh, actually...
...I just heard everyone talking about it earlier.
"By the way, Mrs. Kishida.
Isn't it your birthday today?"
"It is."
"Then let's go out and celebrate later."
So you put this message on right now?
Yes.
I haven't had a surprise like this in a long time.
I'm really happy.

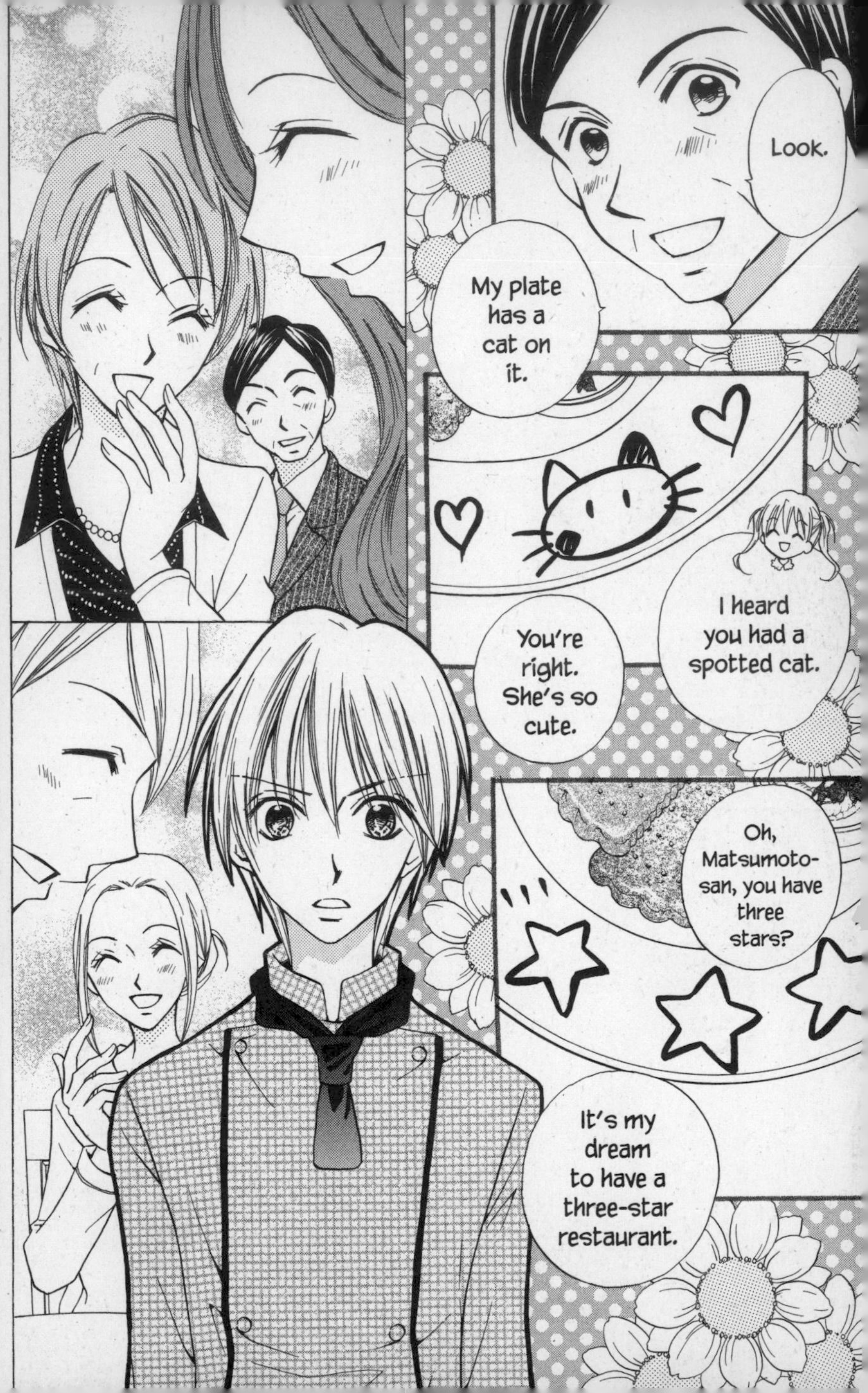

Look.
My plate has a cat on it.
I heard you had a spotted cat.
You're right. She's so cute.
Oh, Matsumoto-san, you have three stars?
It's my dream to have a three-star restaurant.

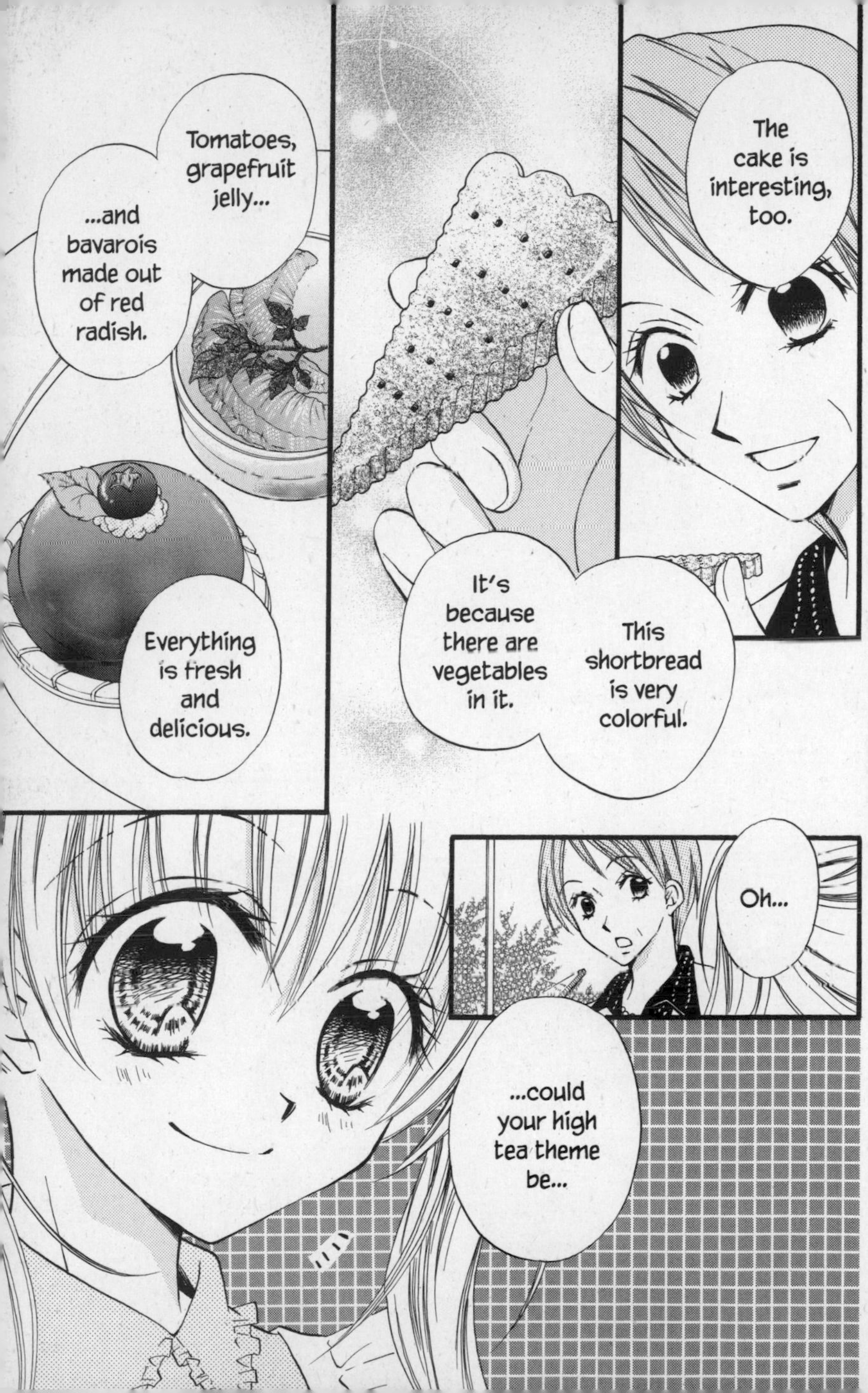
The cake is interesting, too.
This shortbread is very colorful.
It's because there are vegetables in it.
Tomatoes, grapefruit jelly...
...and bavarois made out of red radish.
Everything is fresh and delicious.
Oh...
...could your high tea theme be...

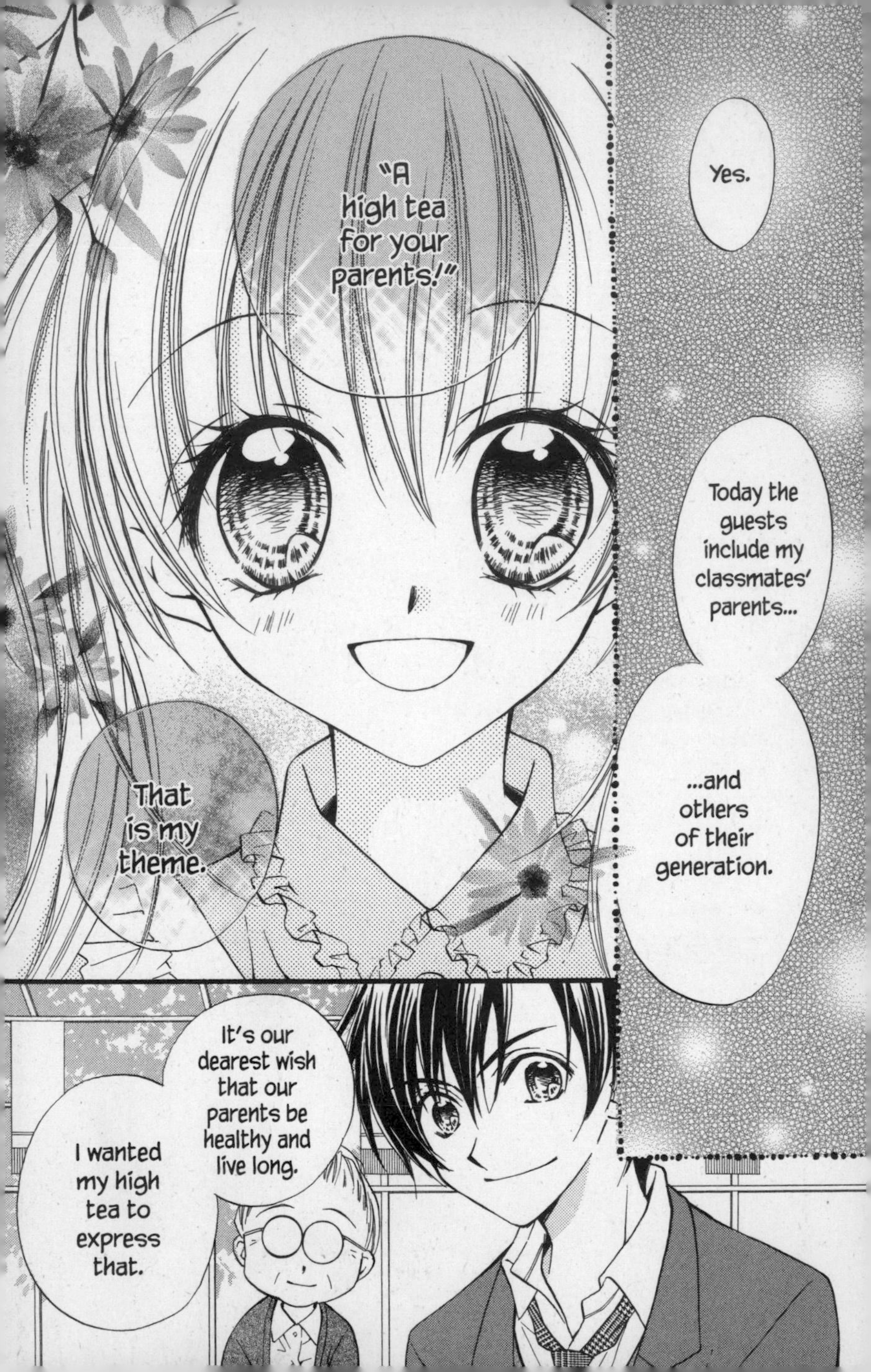
Yes.
Today the guests include my classmates' parents...
...and others of their generation.
"A high tea for your parents!"
That is my theme.
It's our dearest wish that our parents be healthy and live long.
I wanted my high tea to express that.

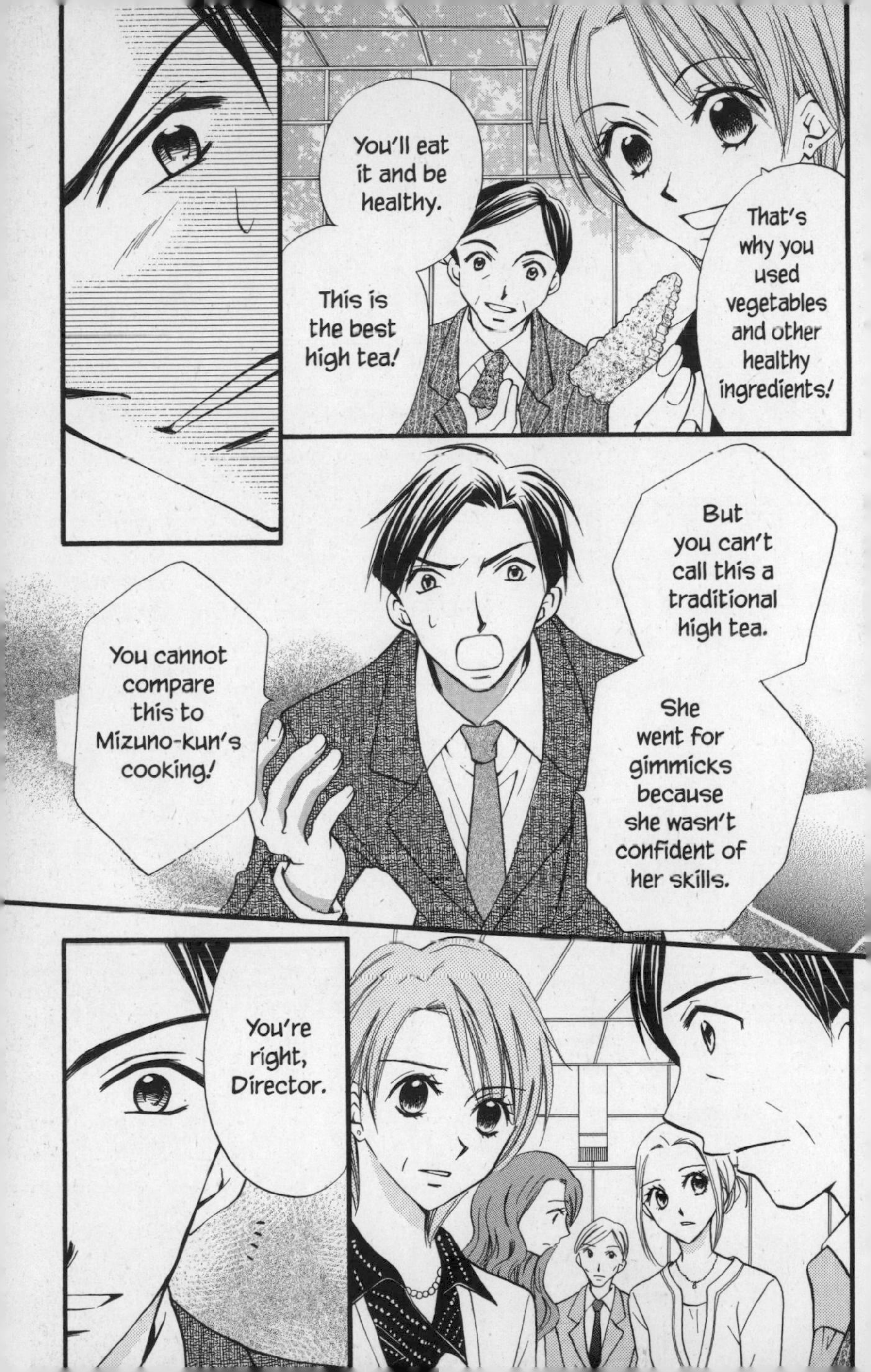

That's why you used vegetables and other healthy ingredients!
You'll eat it and be healthy.
This is the best high tea!
But you can't call this a traditional high tea.
She went for gimmicks because she wasn't confident of her skills.
You cannot compare this to Mizuno-kun's cooking!
You're right, Director.

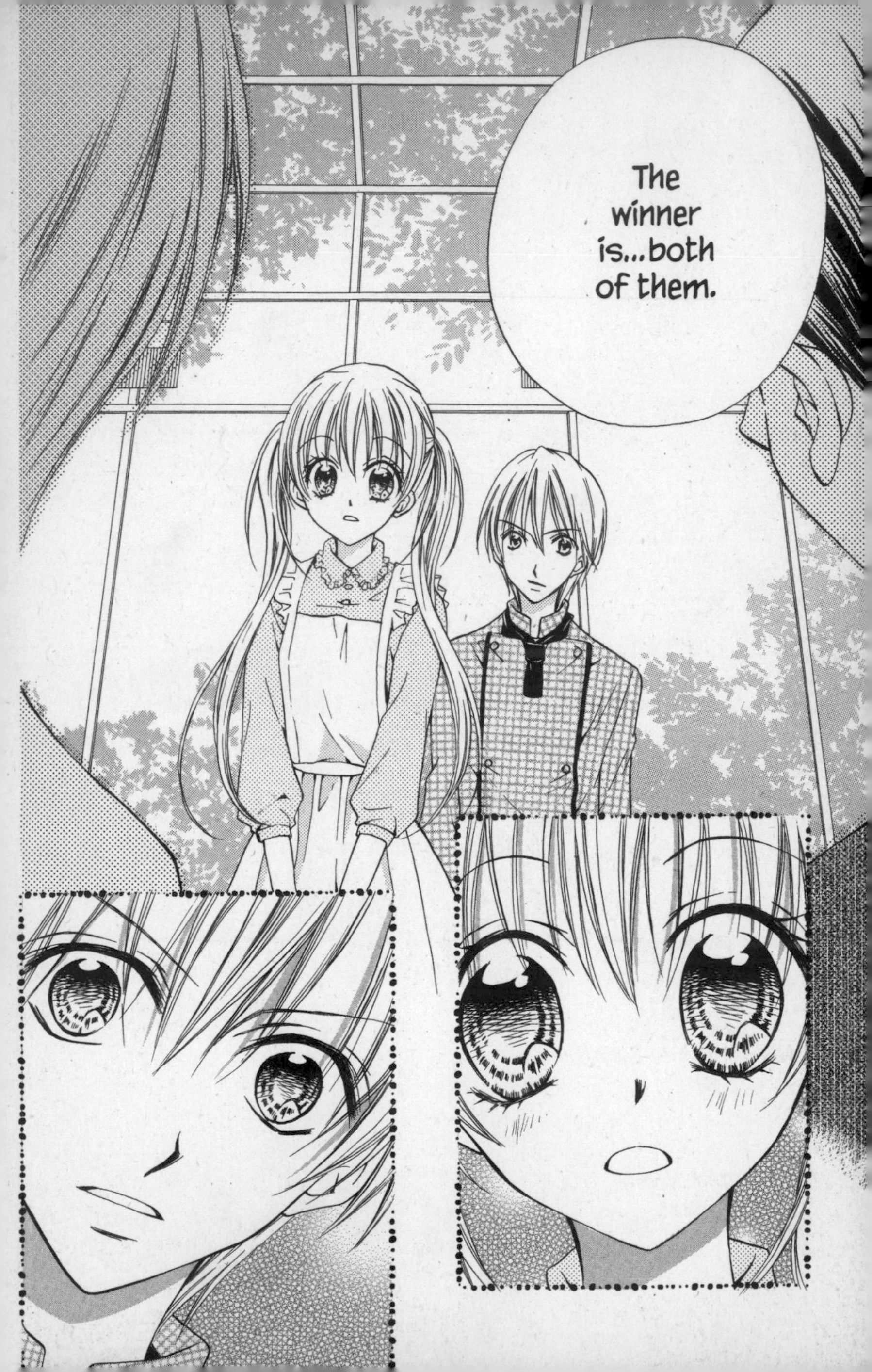
The winner is...both of them.

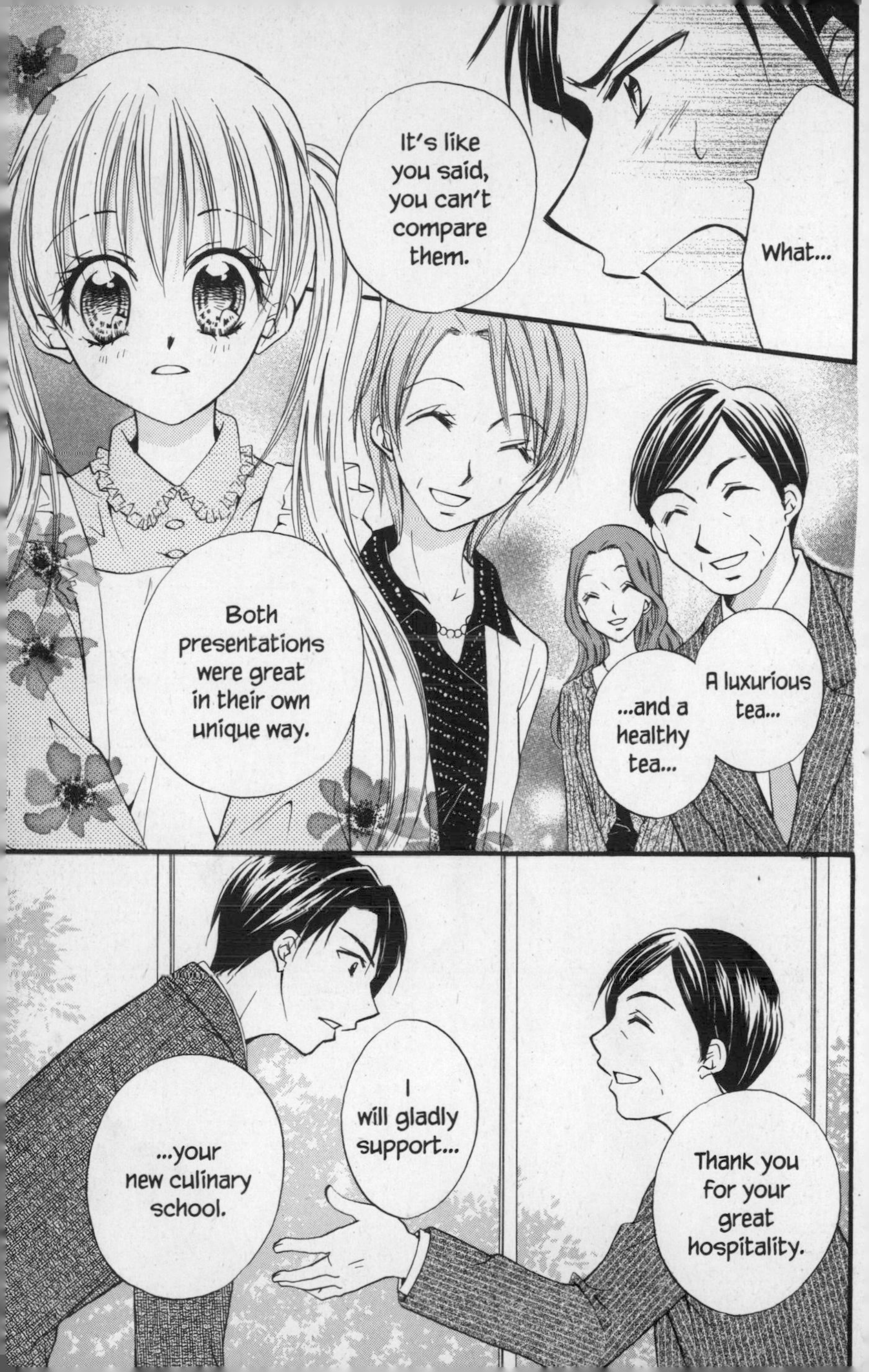
What...
It's like you said, you can't compare them.
A luxurious tea...
...and a healthy tea...
Both presentations were great in their own unique way.
Thank you for your great hospitality.
I will gladly support...
...your new culinary school.

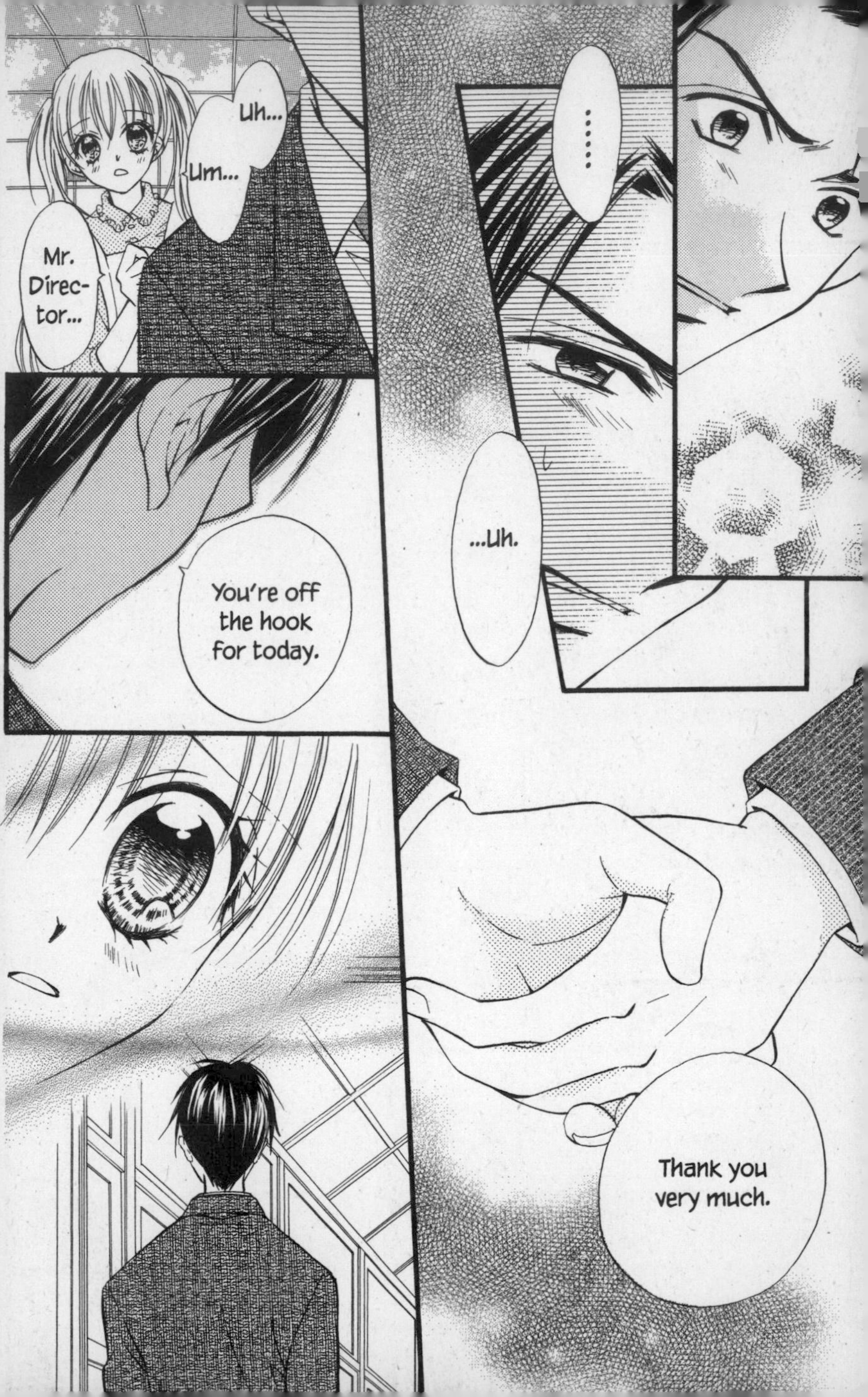
......
Uh...
Um...
Mr. Director...
...Uh.
You're off the hook for today.
Thank you very much.

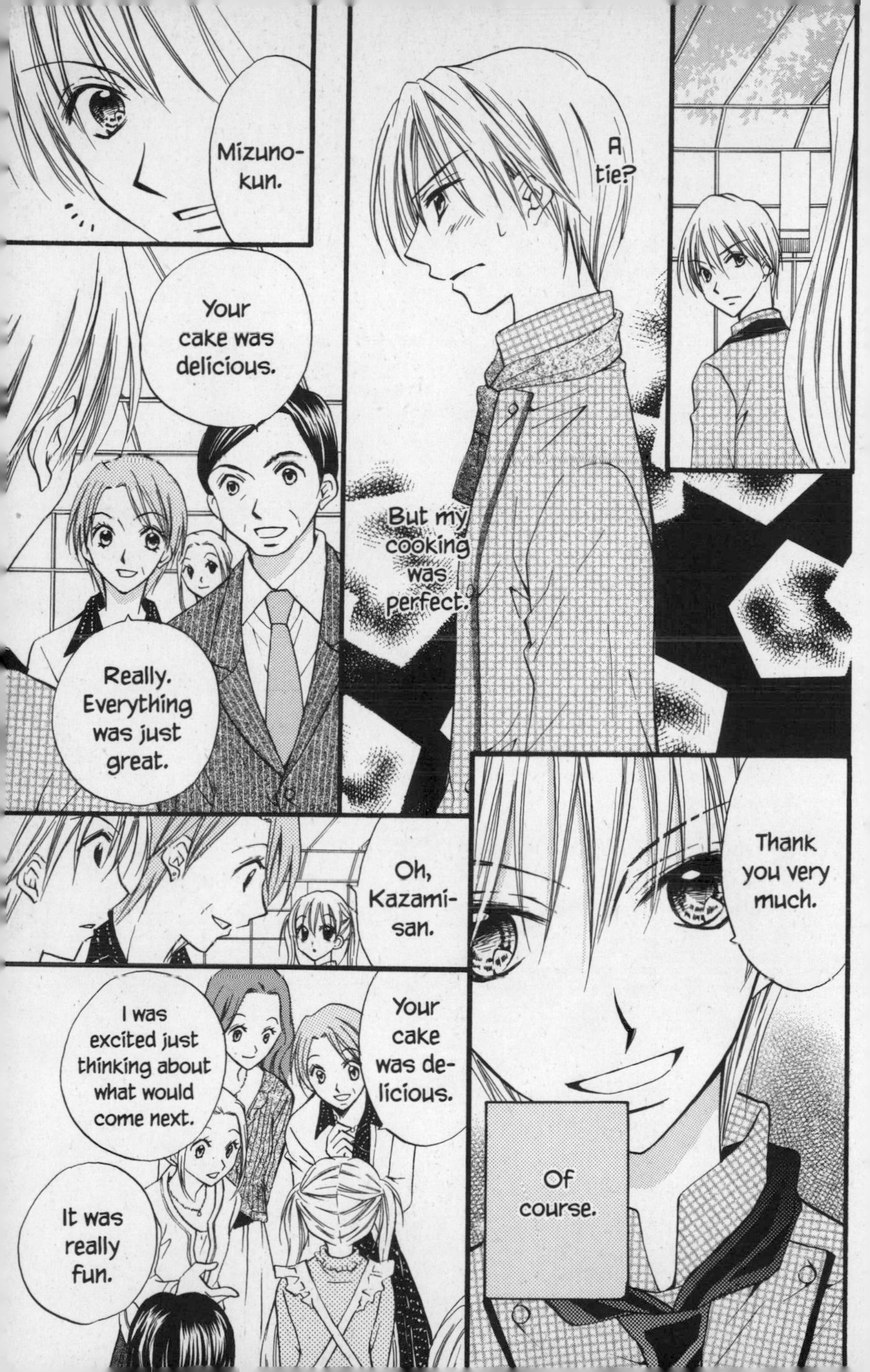
A tie?
But my cooking was perfect.
Mizuno-kun.
Your cake was delicious.
Really. Everything was just great.
Thank you very much.
Of course.
Oh, Kazami-san.
Your cake was de-licious.
I was excited just thinking about what would come next.
It was really fun.

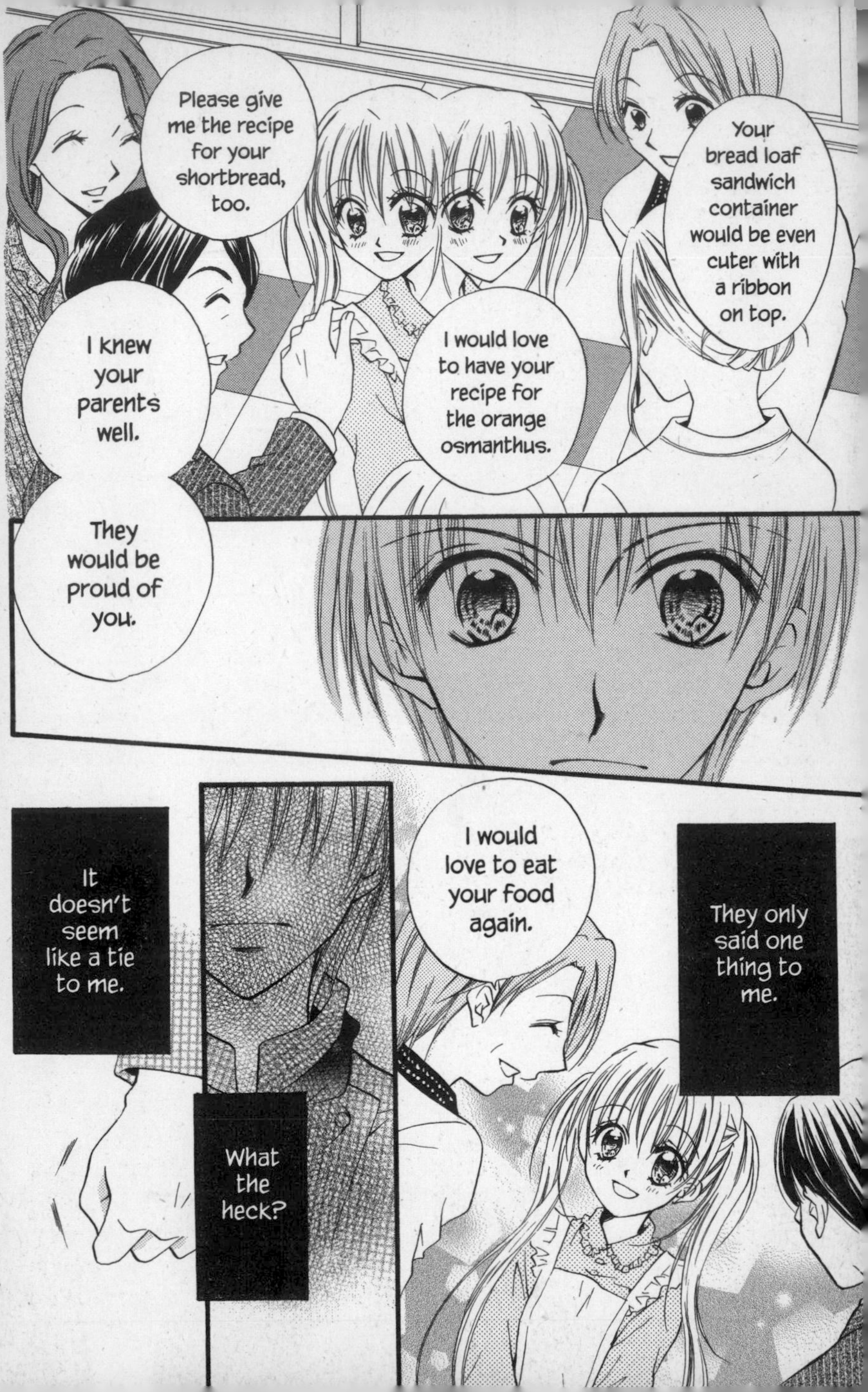
Your bread loaf sandwich container would be even cuter with a ribbon on top.
Please give me the recipe for your shortbread, too.
I would love to have your recipe for the orange osmanthus.
I knew your parents well.
They would be proud of you.
They only said one thing to me.
I would love to eat your food again.
What the heck?
It doesn't seem like a tie to me.

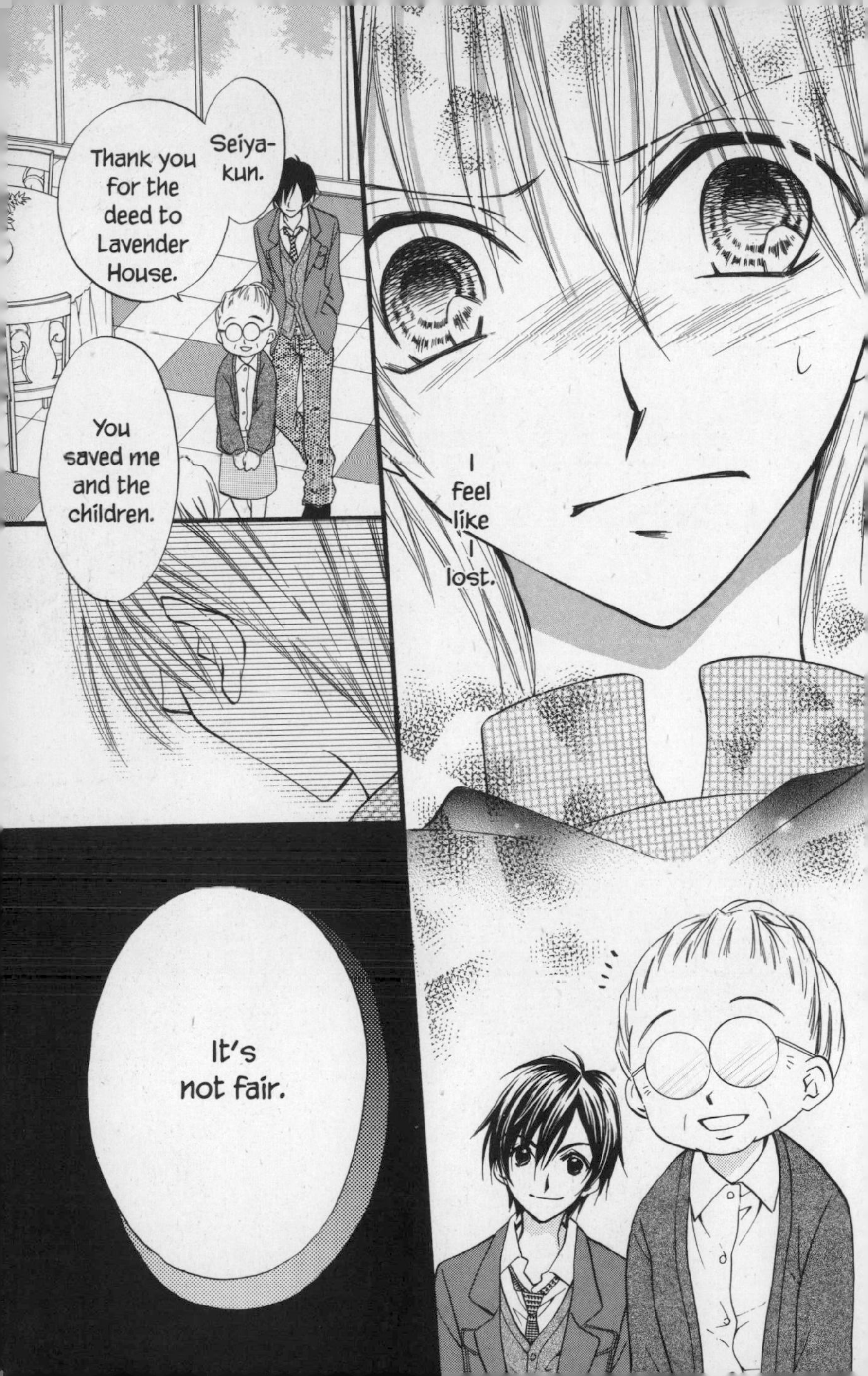
I feel like I lost.
Seiya-kun.
Thank you for the deed to Lavender House.
You saved me and the children.
It's not fair.

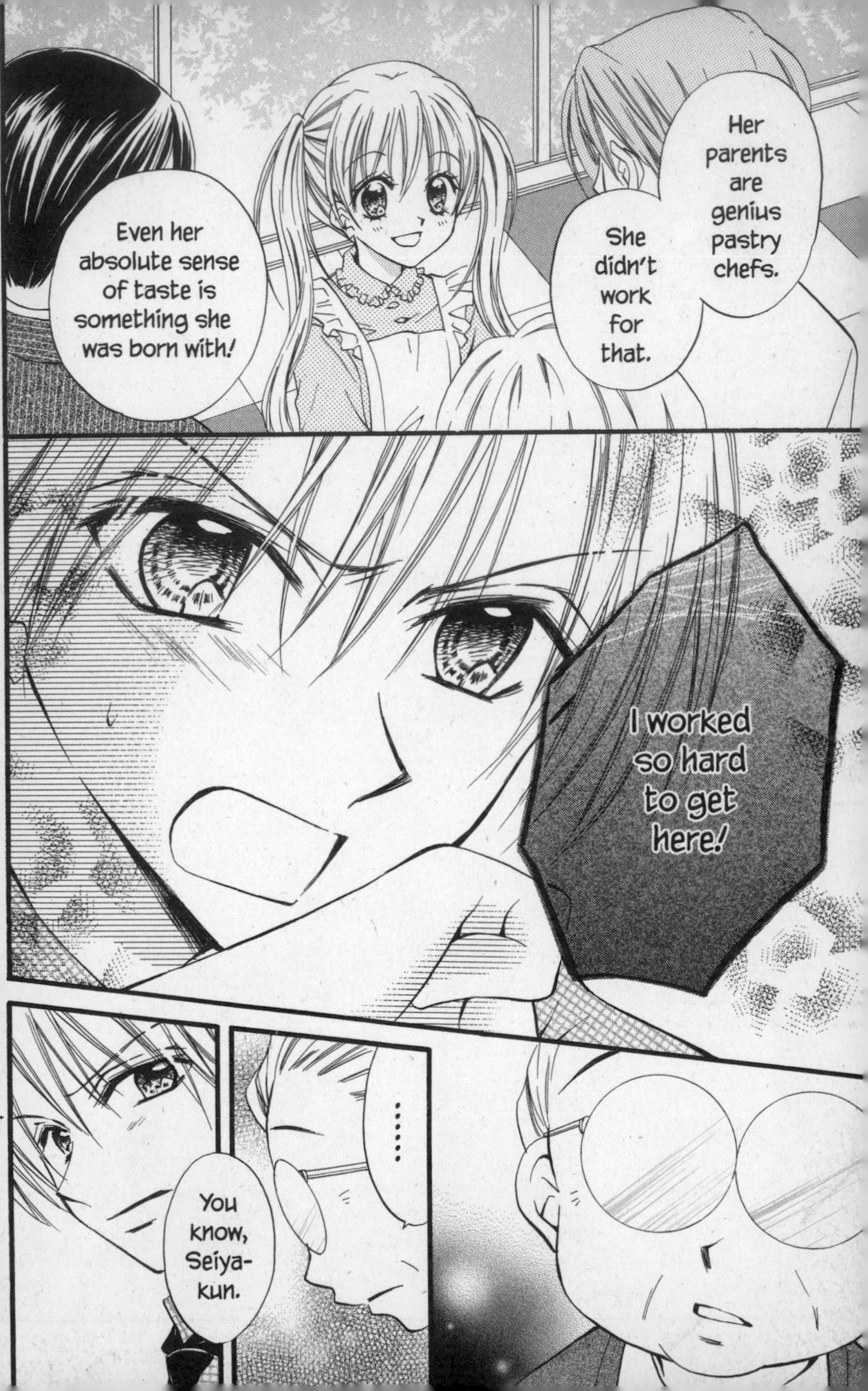
Her parents are genius pastry chefs.
She didn't work for that.
Even her absolute sense of taste is something she was born with!
I worked so hard to get here!
......
You know, Seiya-kun.

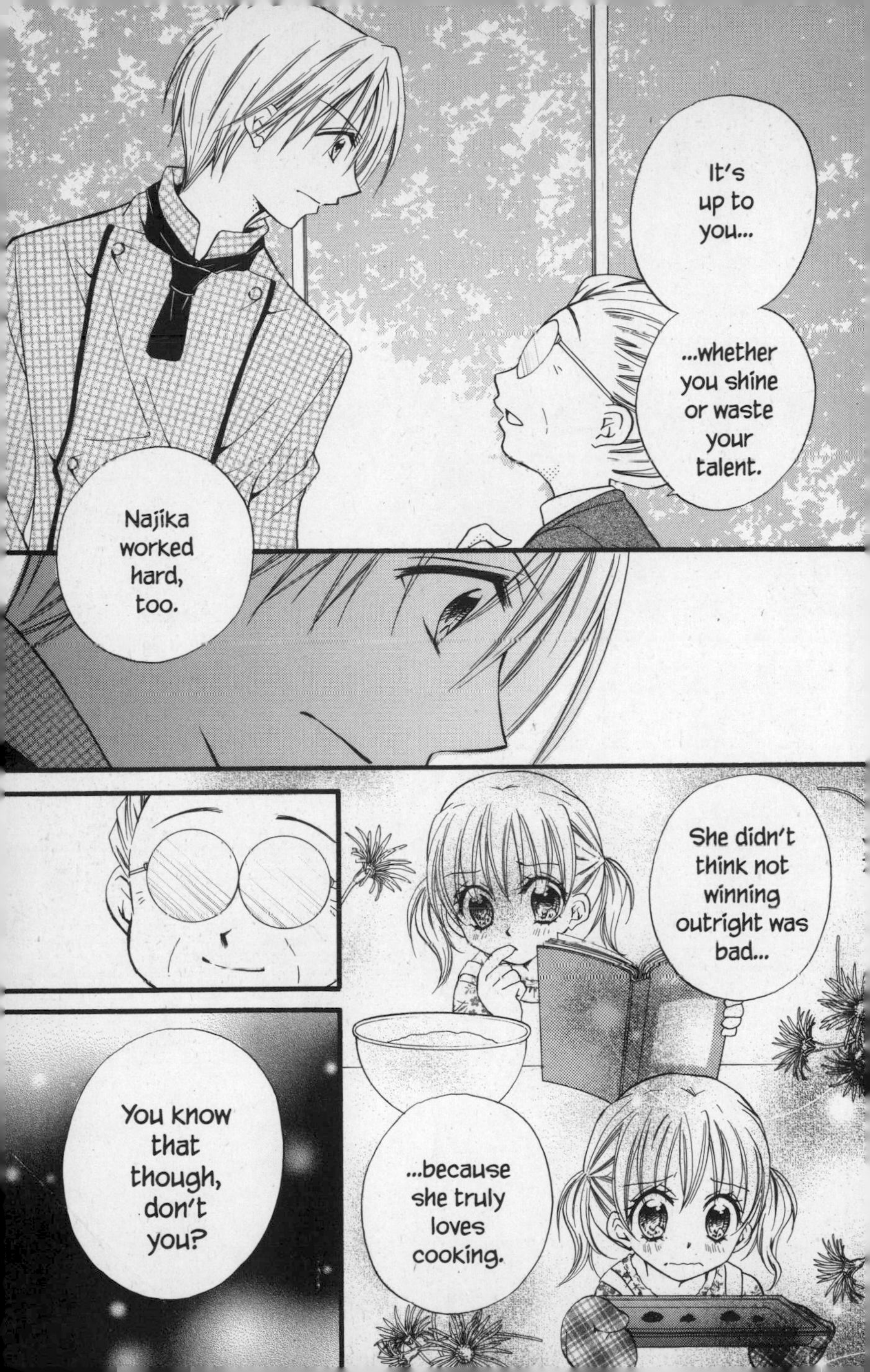
It's up to you...
...whether you shine or waste your talent.
Najika worked hard, too.
She didn't think not winning outright was bad...
...because she truly loves cooking.
You know that though, don't you?

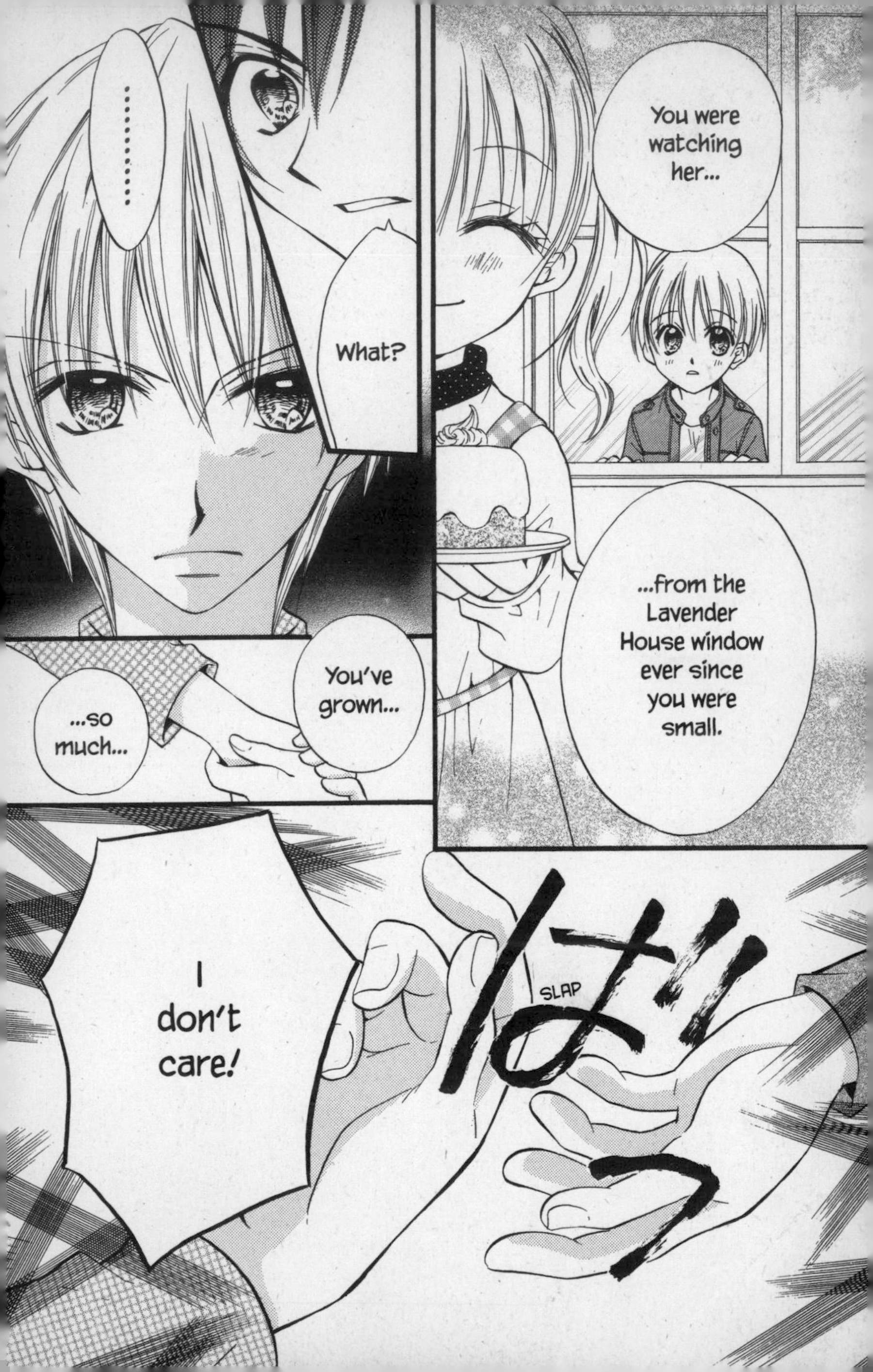
You were watching her...
...from the Lavender House window ever since you were small.
......
What?
You've grown...
...so much...
ばっ
SLAP
I don't care!

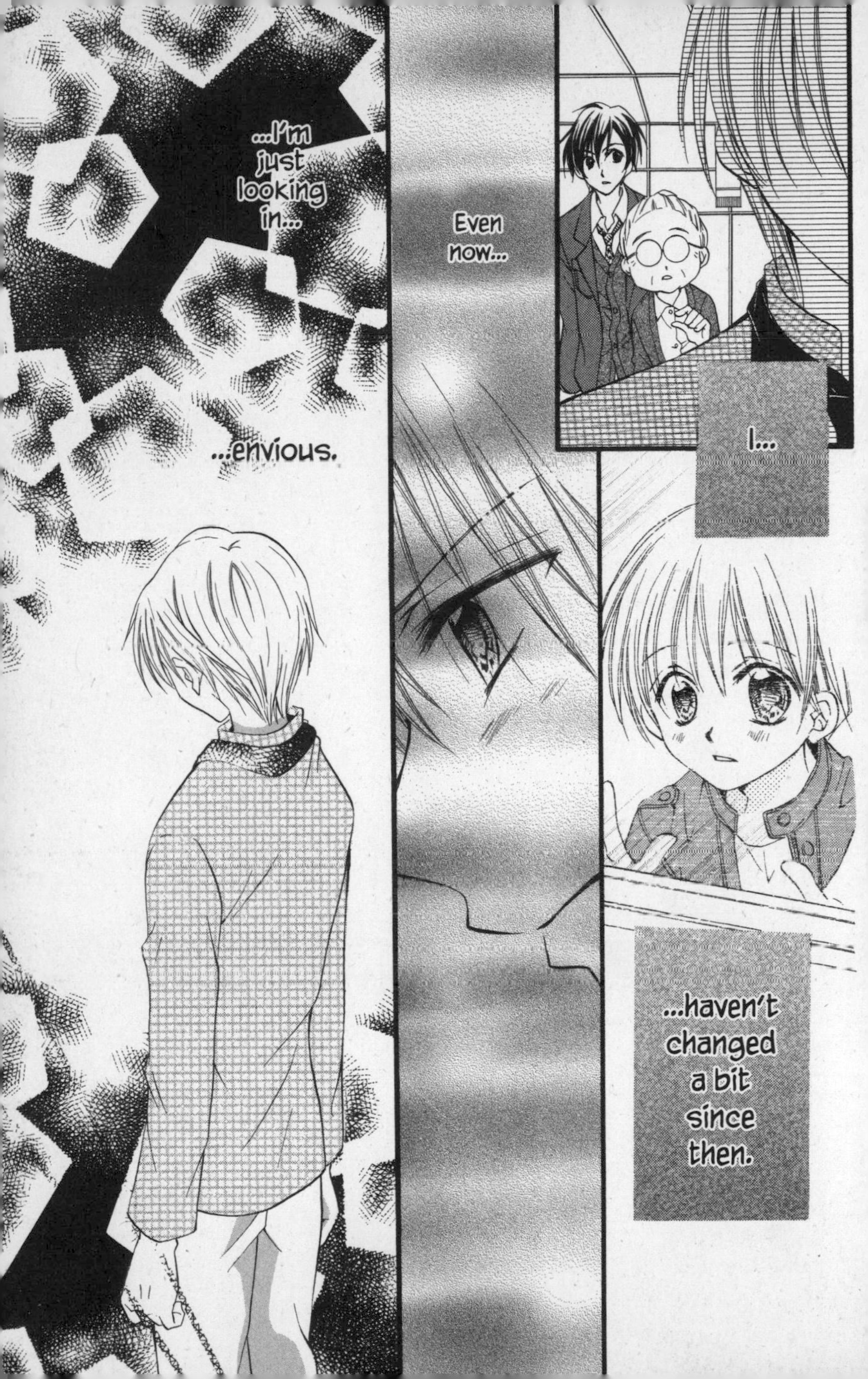
I...
...haven't changed a bit since then.
Even now...
...I'm just looking in...
...envious.

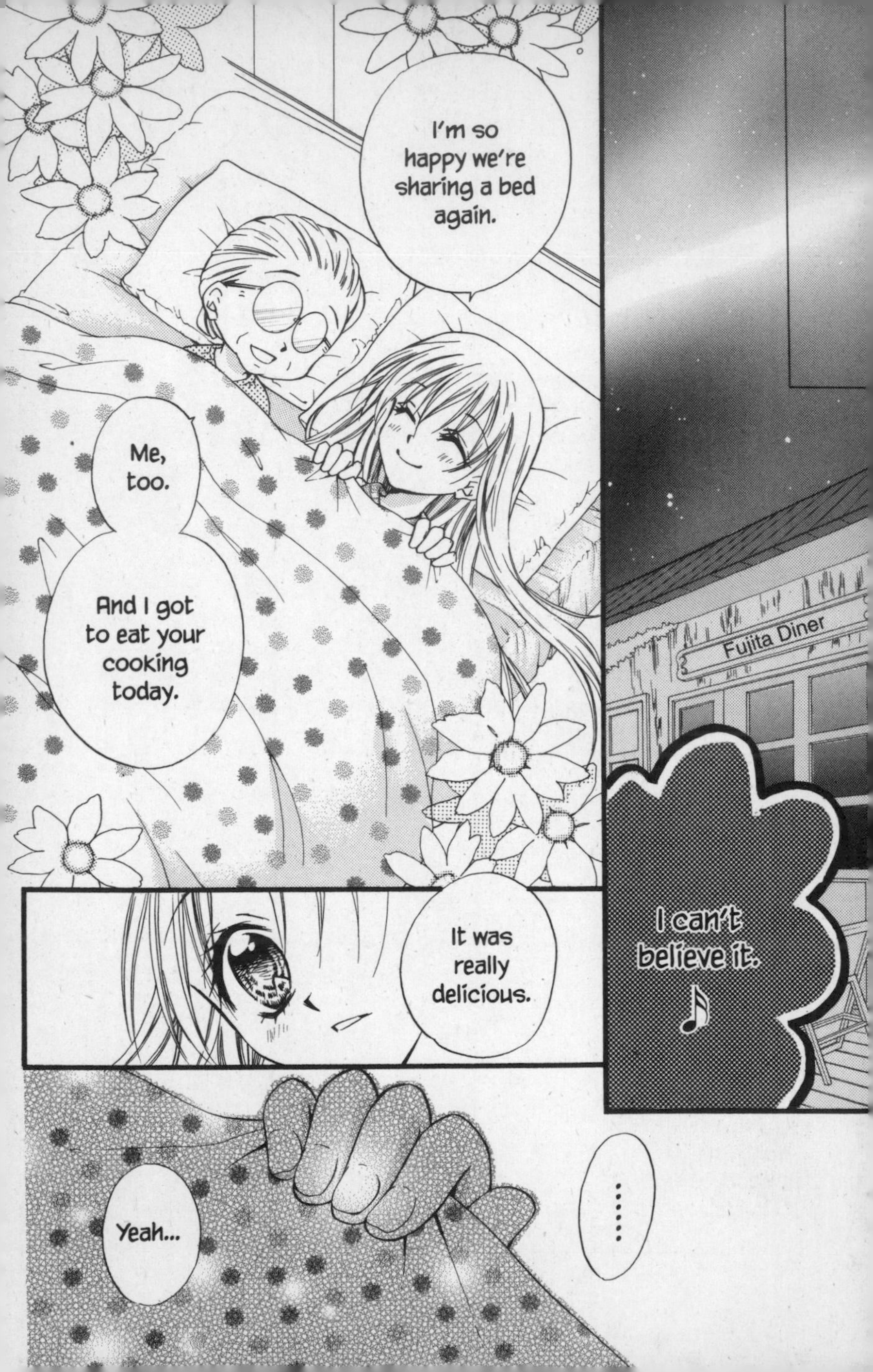
Fujita Diner
I can't believe it. ♪
I'm so happy we're sharing a bed again.
Me, too.
And I got to eat your cooking today.
It was really delicious.
......
Yeah...

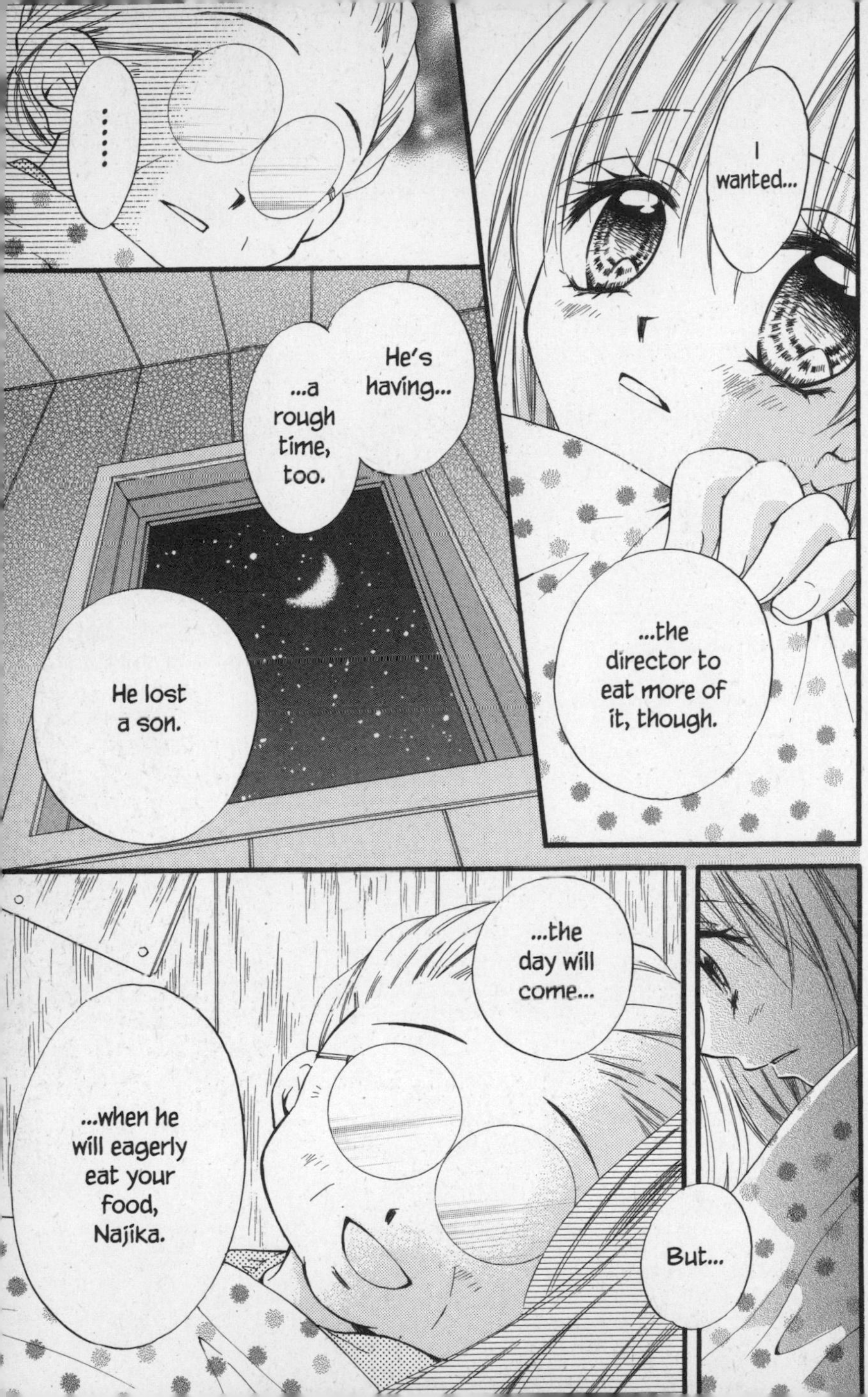
I wanted...
...the director to eat more of it, though.
......
He's having...
...a rough time, too.
He lost a son.
But...
...the day will come...
...when he will eagerly eat your food, Najika.

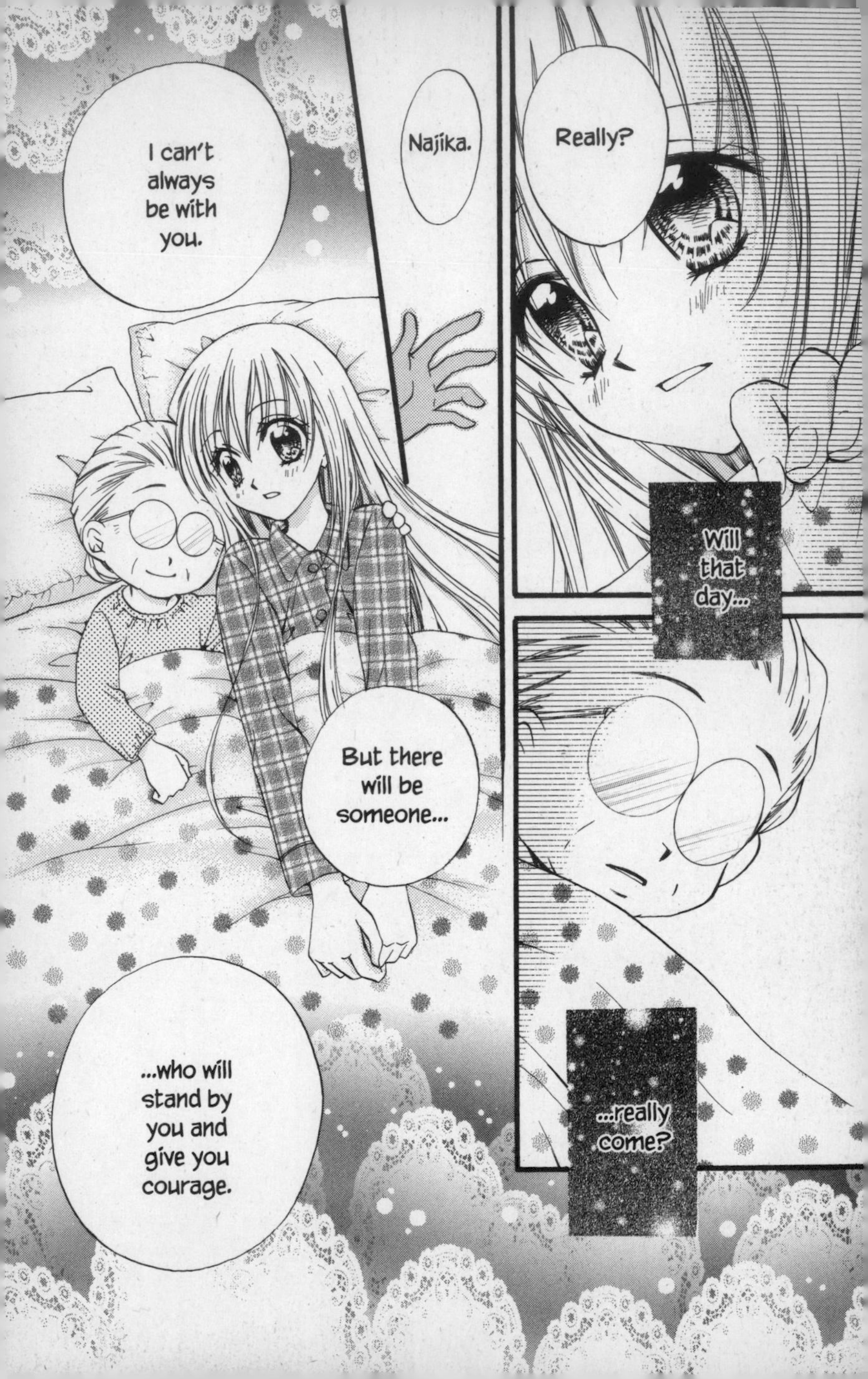
Najika.
I can't always be with you.
But there will be someone...
...who will stand by you and give you courage.
Really?
Will that day...
...really come?

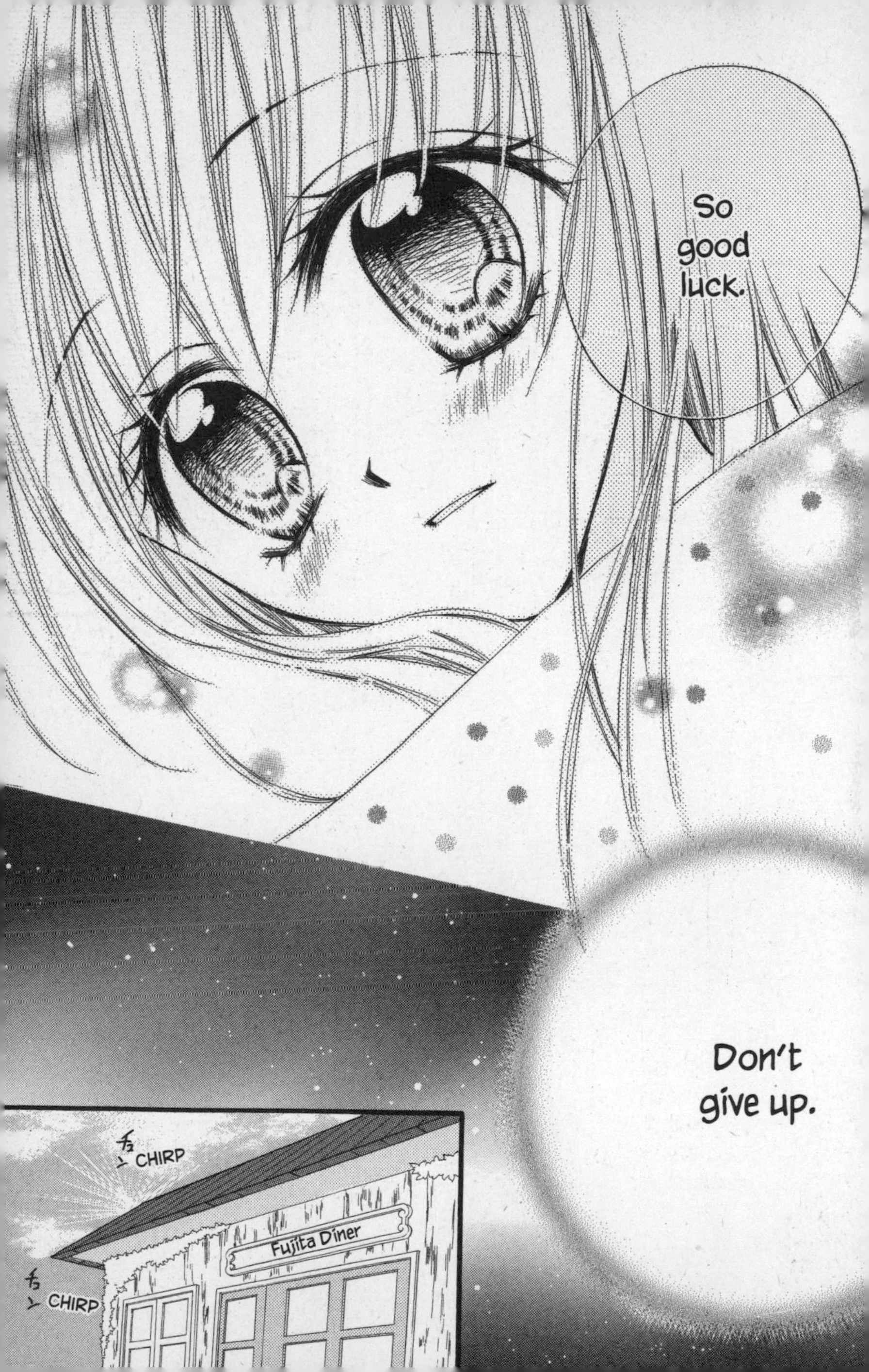
So good luck.
Don't give up.
CHIRP
Fujita Diner
CHIRP

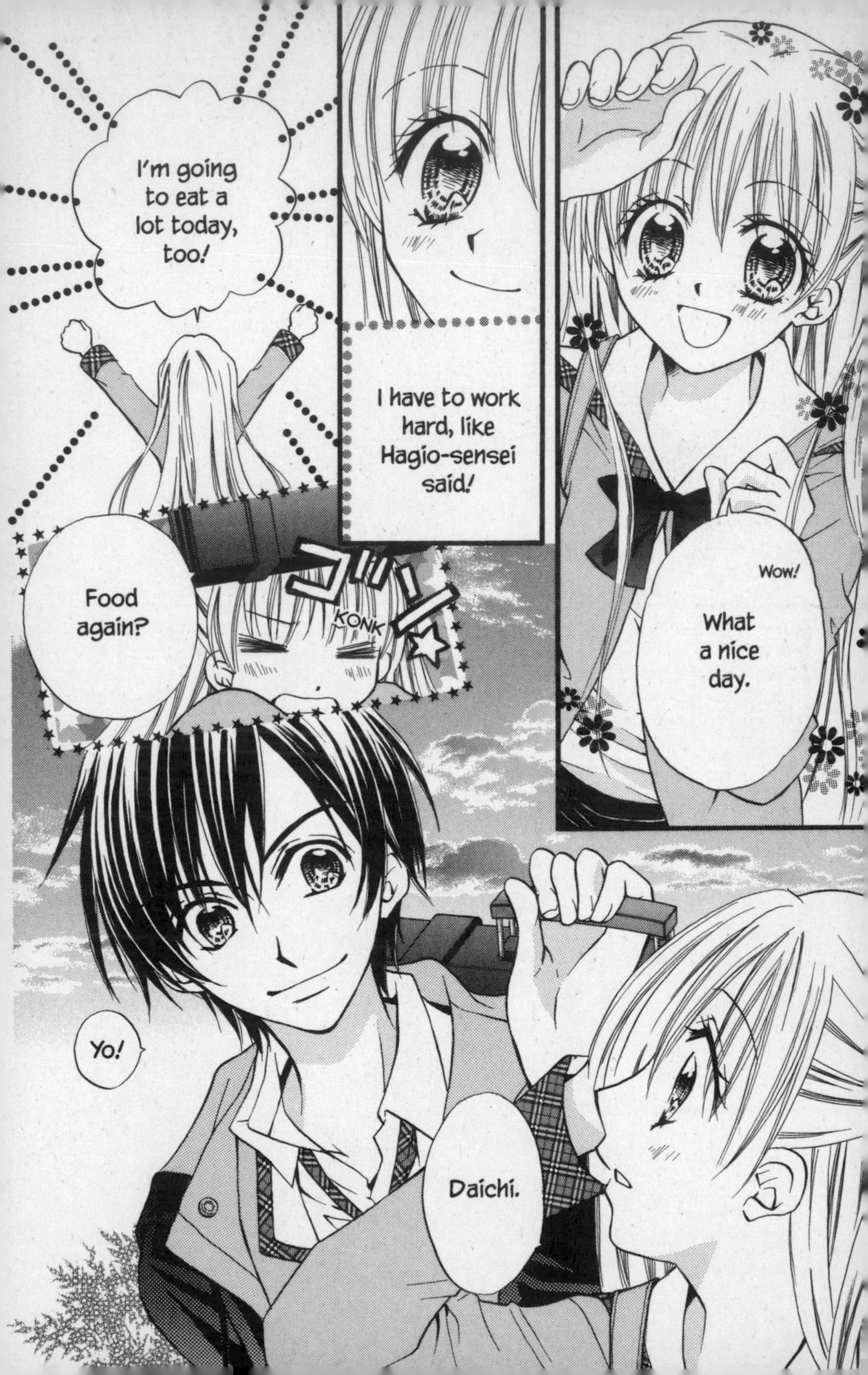
Wow!
What a nice day.
I have to work hard, like Hagio-sensei said!
I'm going to eat a lot today, too!
Food again?
KONK
Yo!
Daichi.

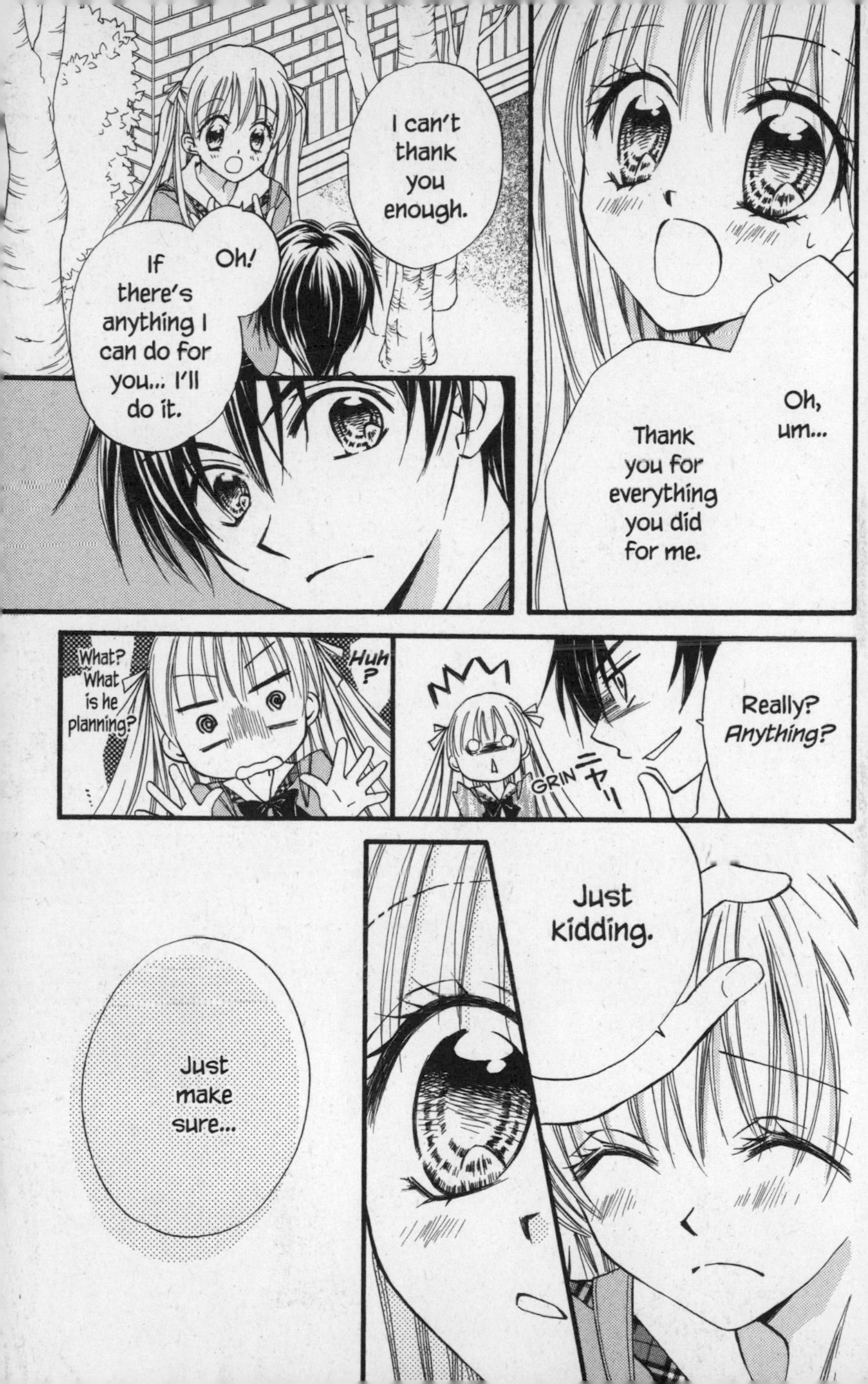
Oh, um...
Thank you for everything you did for me.
I can't thank you enough.
Oh!
If there's anything I can do for you... I'll do it.
Really? Anything?
GRIN
ニヤリ
Huh?
What? What is he planning?
Just kidding.
Just make sure...

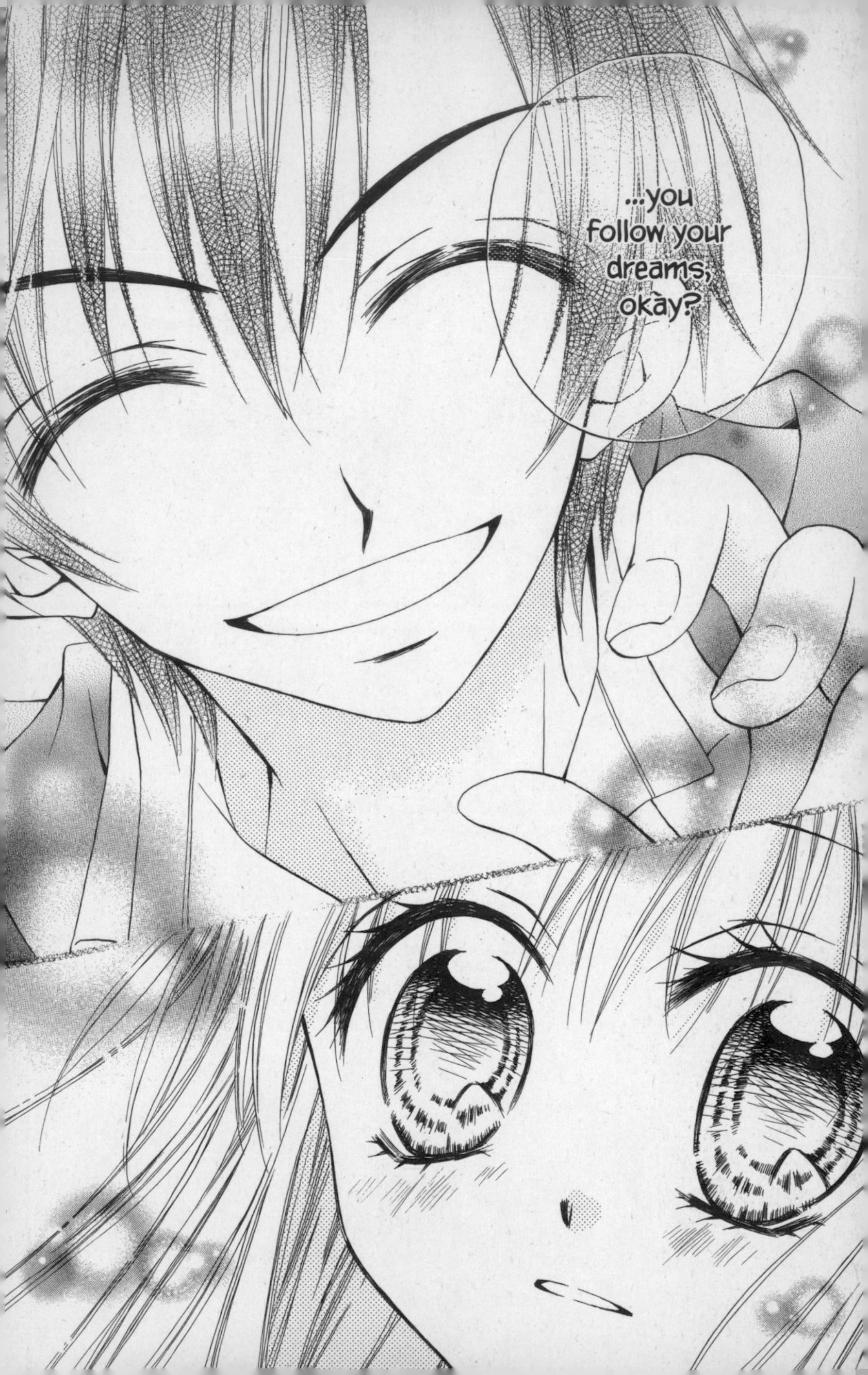
...you follow your dreams, okay?

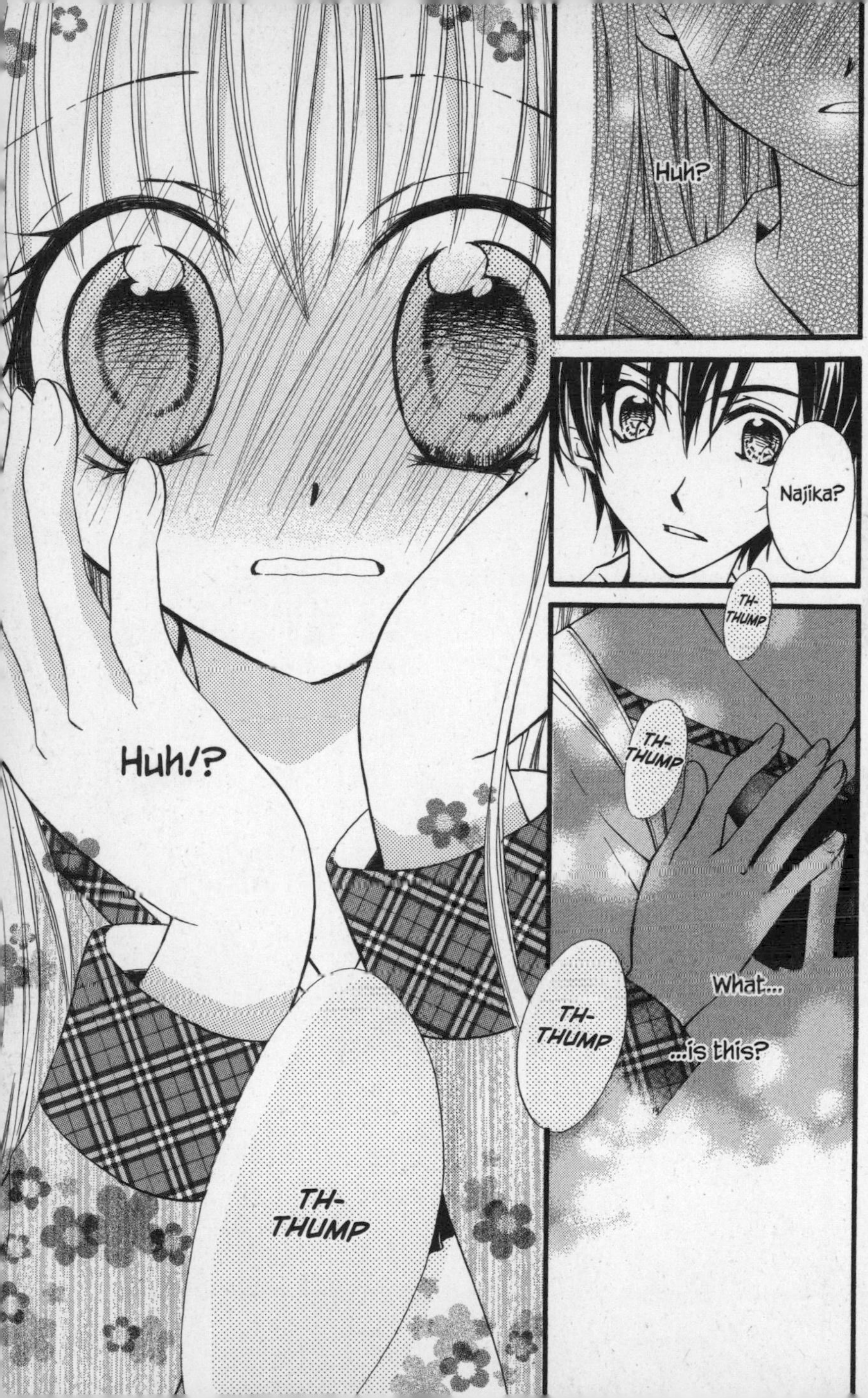
Huh?
Najika?
TH-THUMP
TH-THUMP
What...
...is this?
TH-THUMP
Huh!?
TH-THUMP

Kishida Mother and Daughter

The mother is a former model, and Akane used to feel a lot of pressure from her, but now they have a good relationship.

When they go shopping, they buy a ton of stuff. ♪

→ Akane's mom dyed her hair black recently.

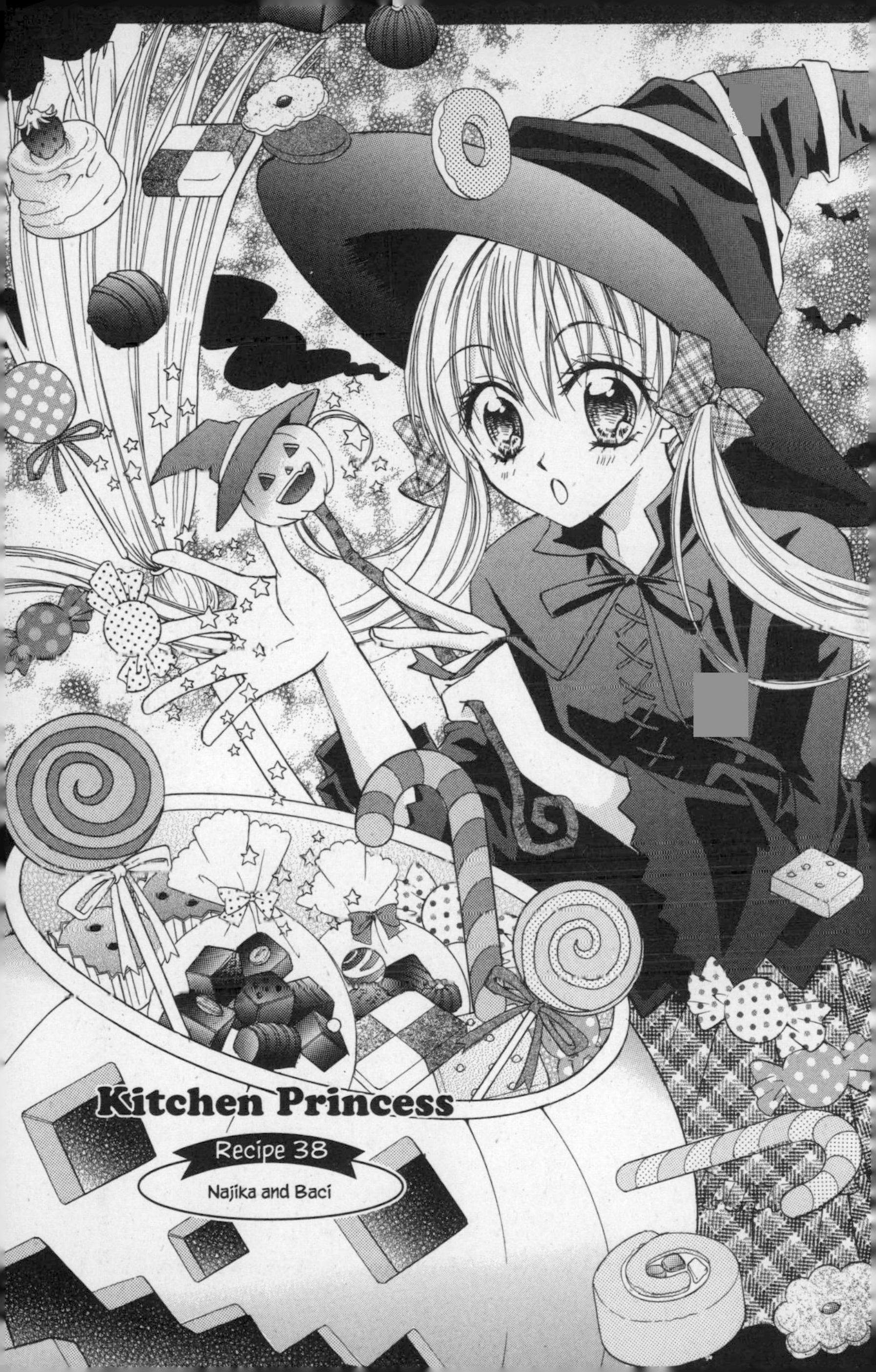
Kitchen Princess
Recipe 38
Najika and Baci

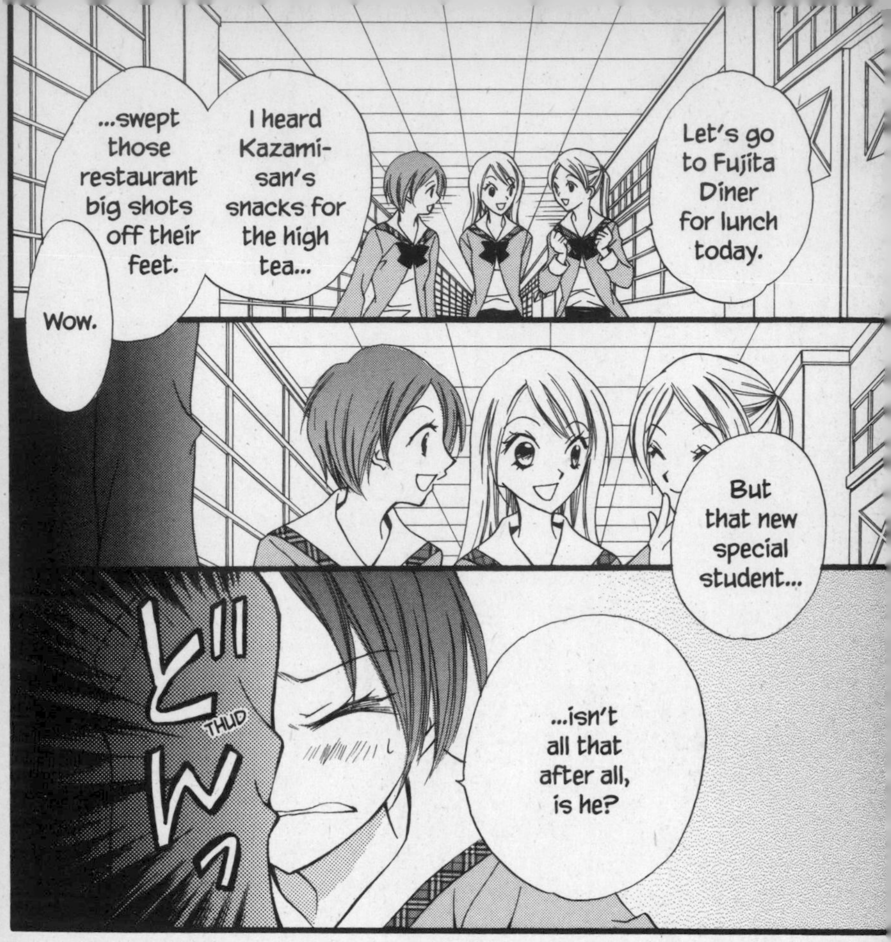
Let's go to Fujita Diner for lunch today.
I heard Kazami-san's snacks for the high tea...
...swept those restaurant big shots off their feet.
Wow.
But that new special student...
THUD
...isn't all that after all, is he?

About Recipe 38's Splash Page

It's Halloween-themed! The magazine came out in October, so...
This may be my first time drawing a splash page for Halloween.
In my head, it was all in color, so I thought I should photocopy it before I put the screentones on and then color it for use for a cover. But I completely forgot to photocopy it... (idiot)
I forgot that I would probably forget the closer it got to my deadline.
But I haven't forgotten to take my work out of the photocopy machines lately. Yes!
Not related? ...

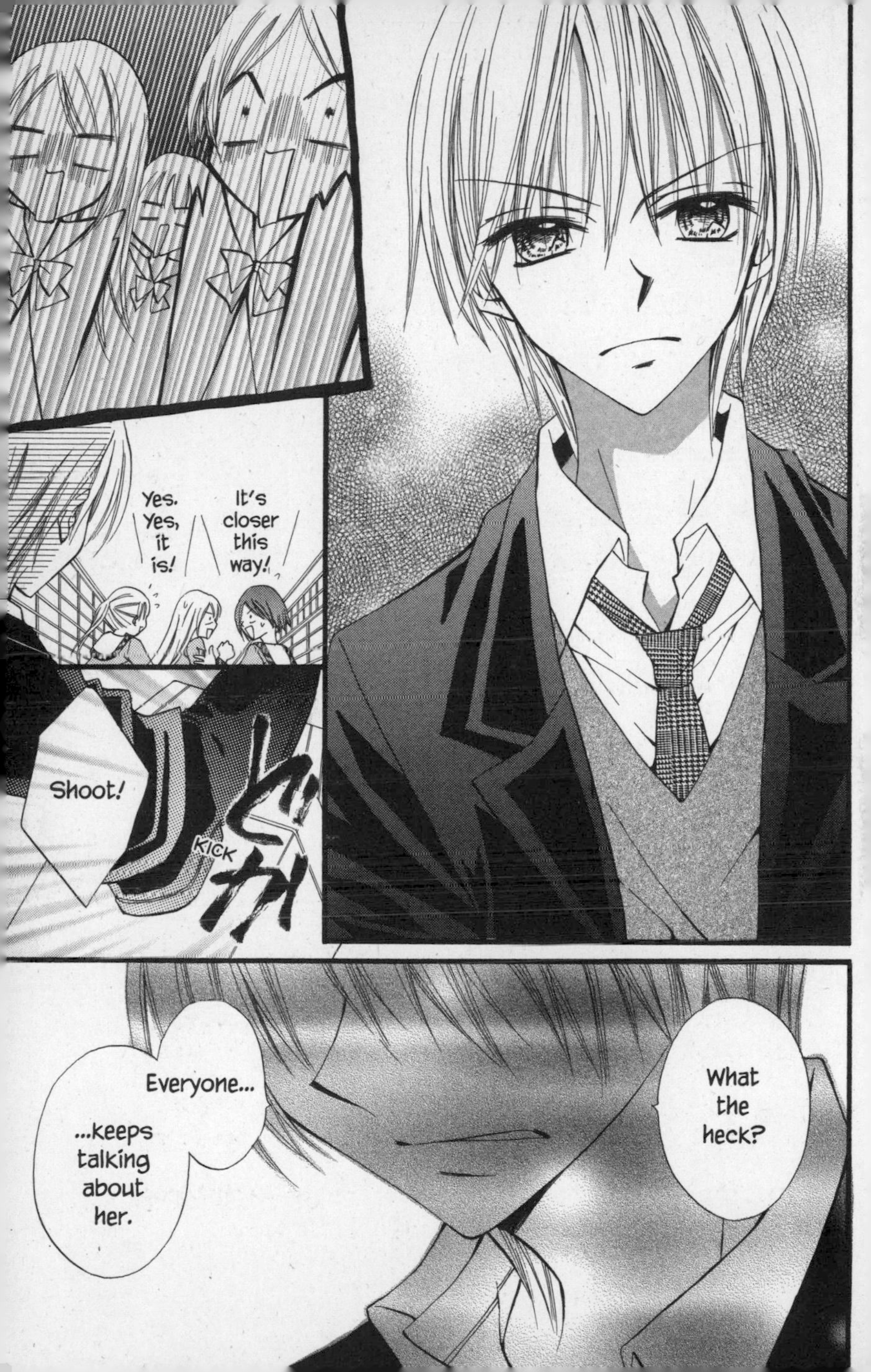
It's closer this way!
Yes. Yes, it is!
Shoot!
KICK
What the heck?
Everyone...
...keeps talking about her.

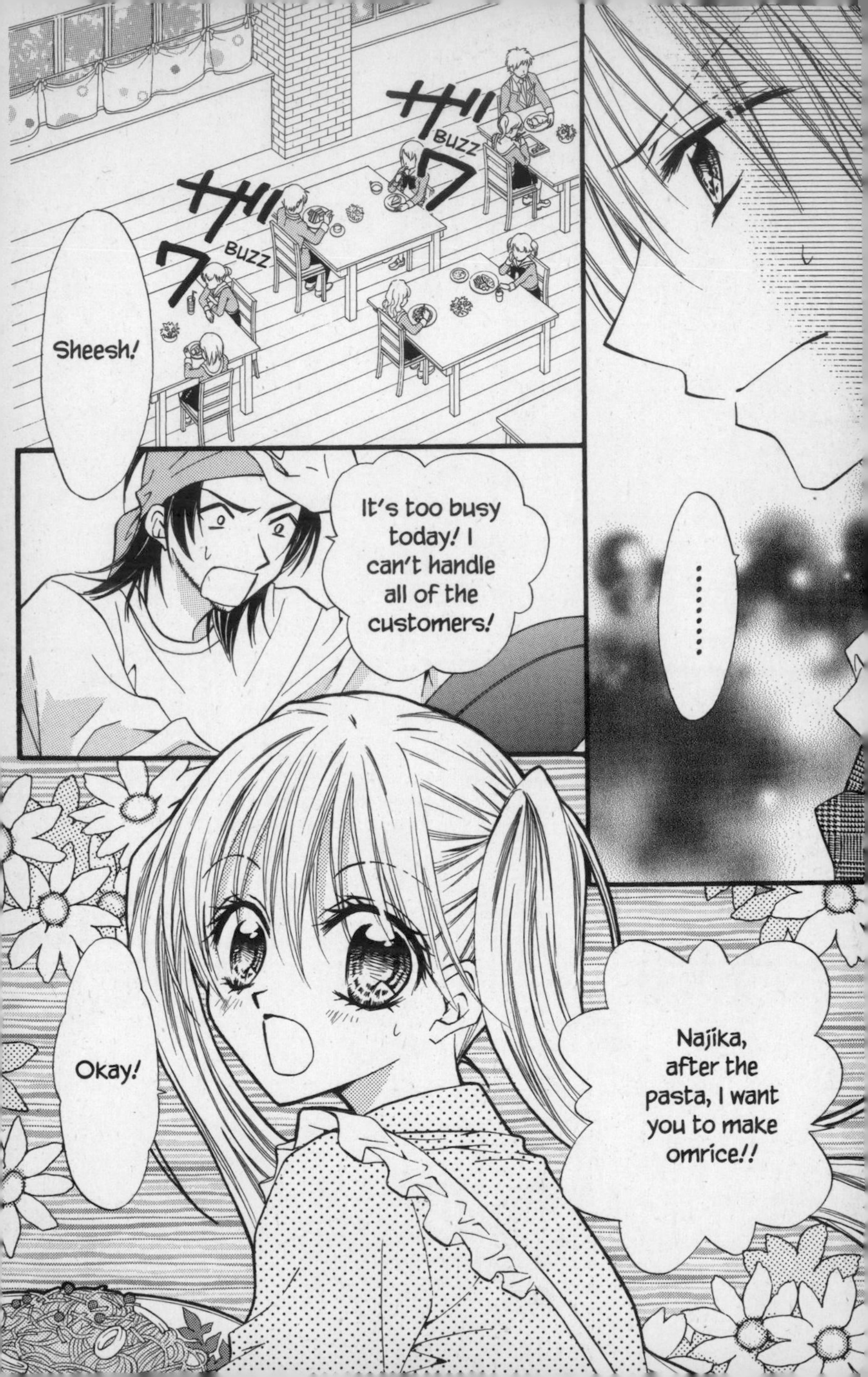
......
BUZZ
BUZZ
Sheesh!
It's too busy today! I can't handle all of the customers!
Najika, after the pasta, I want you to make omrice!!
Okay!

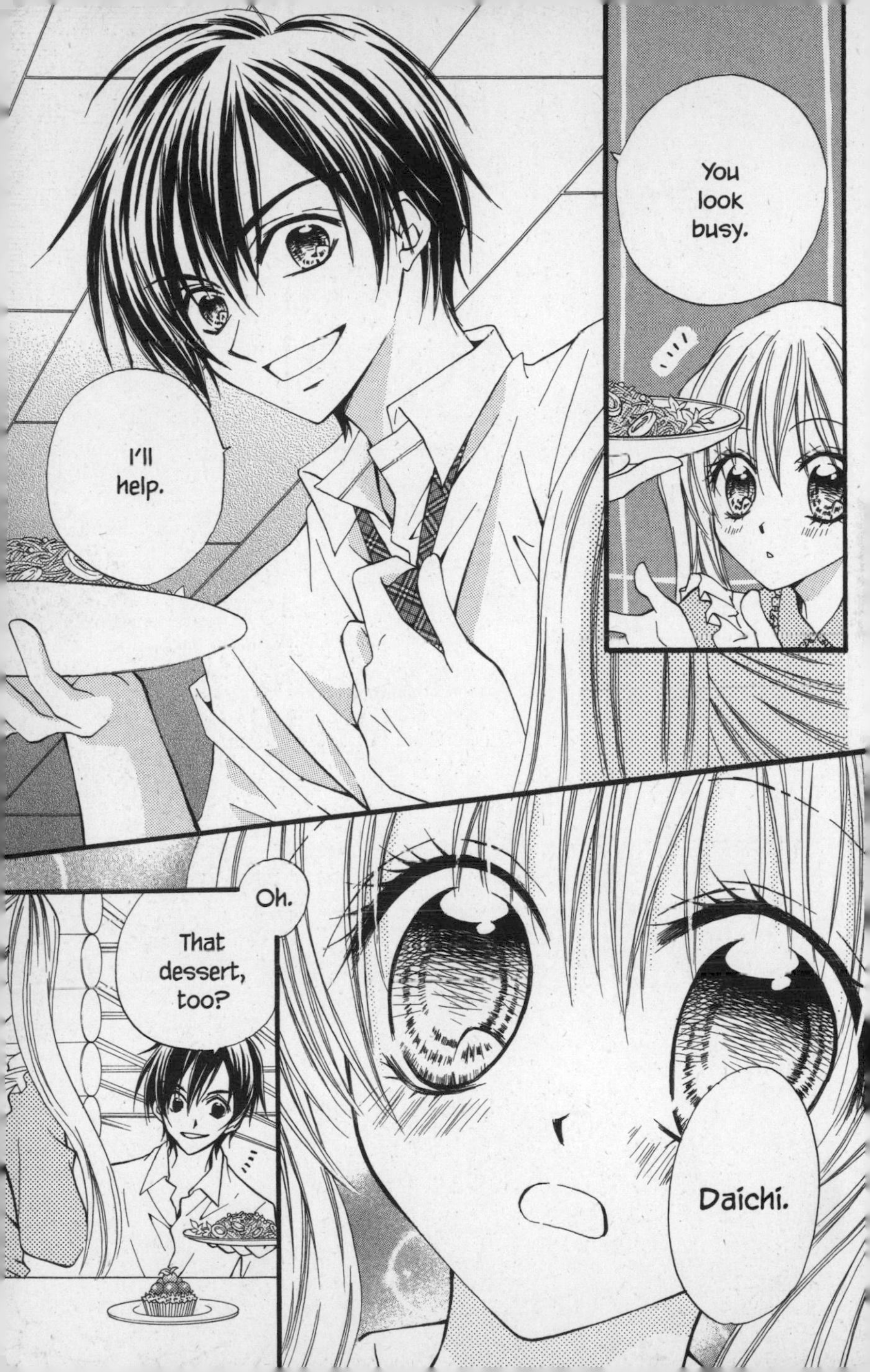
You look busy.
...!
I'll help.
Daichi.
Oh.
That dessert, too?
...

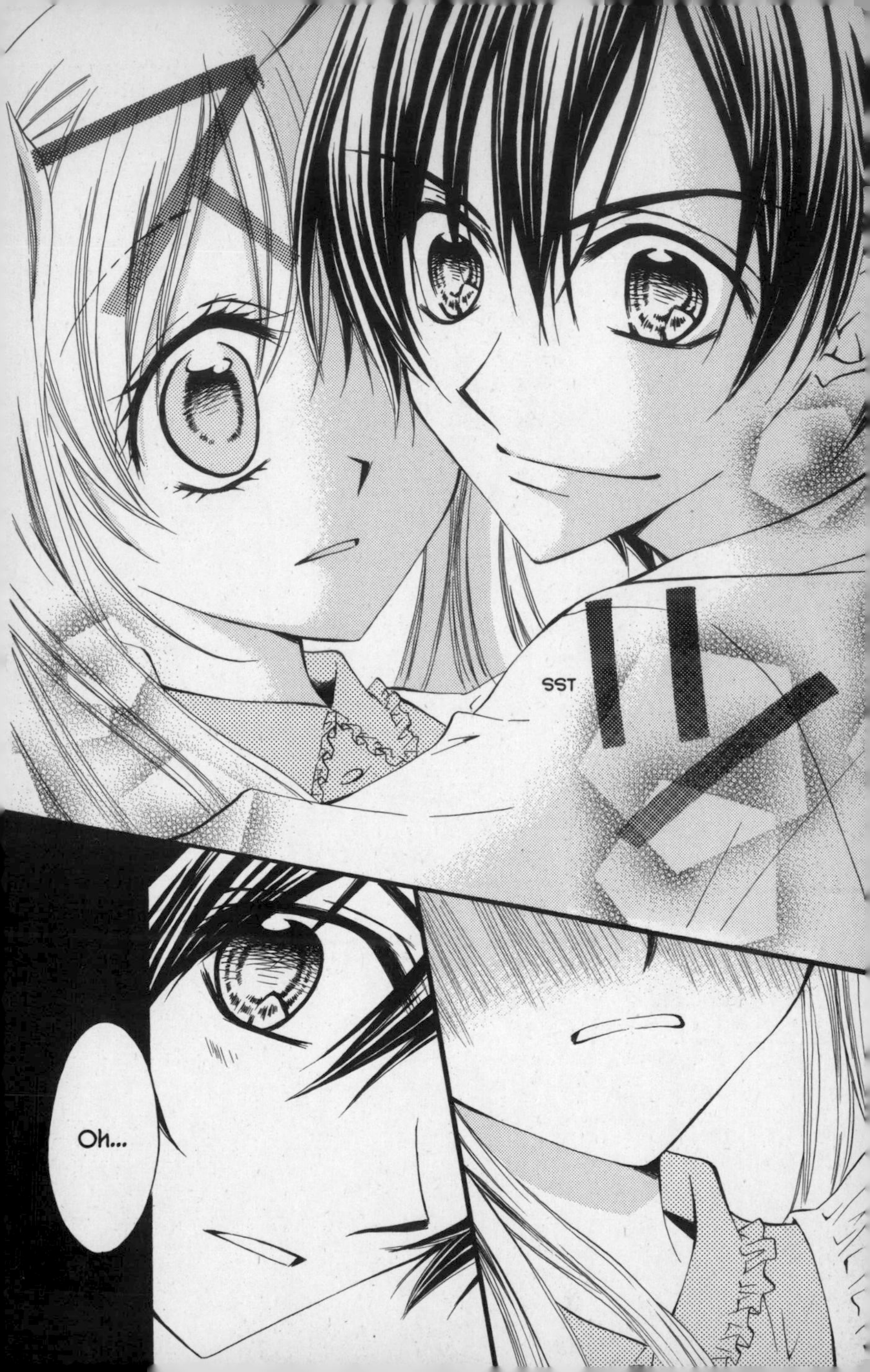
SST
Oh...

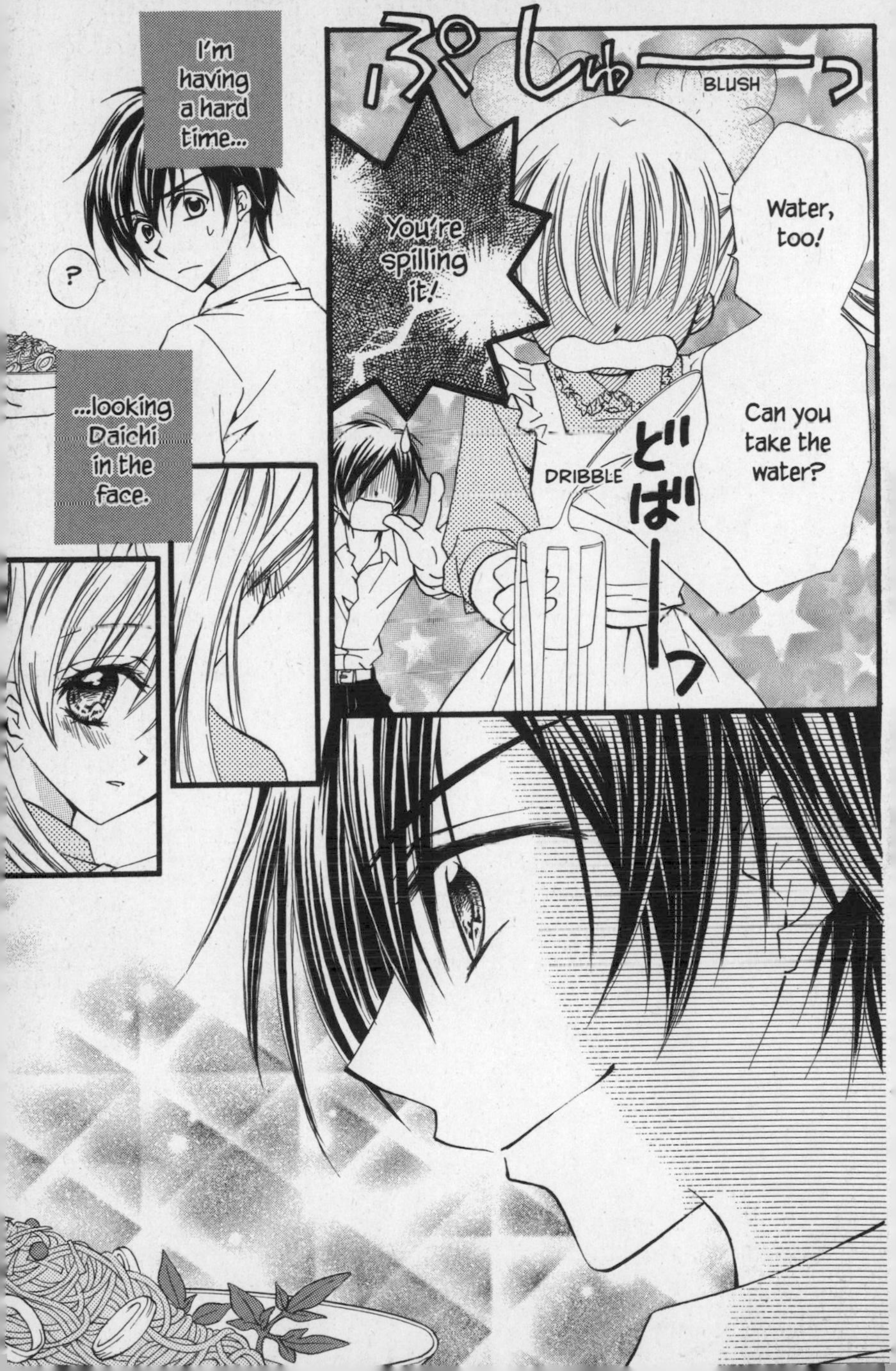
ぷしゅーっ
BLUSH
Water, too!
Can you take the water?
You're spilling it!
どばーっ
DRIBBLE
I'm having a hard time...
?
...looking Daichi in the face.

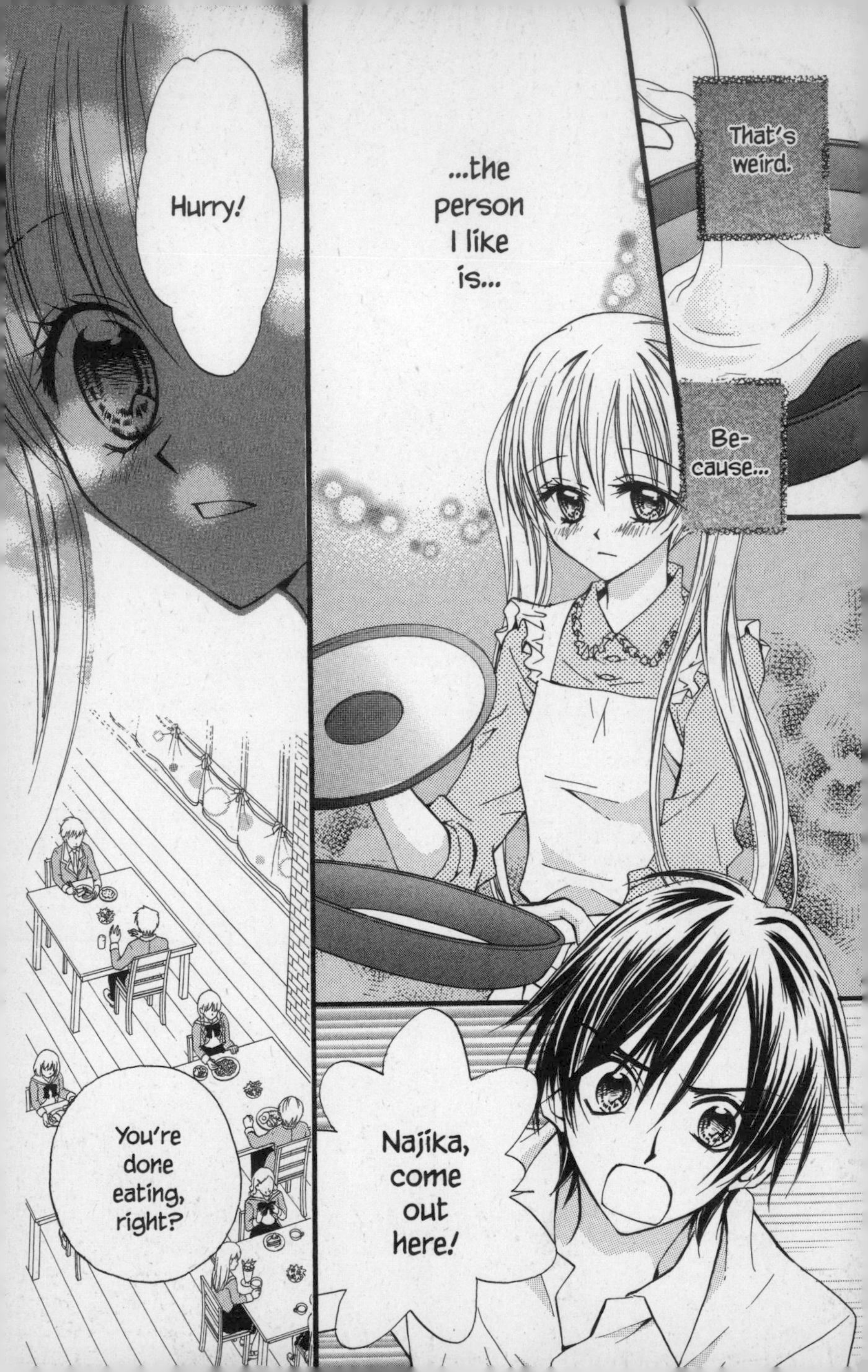
That's weird.
Be-cause...
...the person I like is...
Najika, come out here!
Hurry!
You're done eating, right?

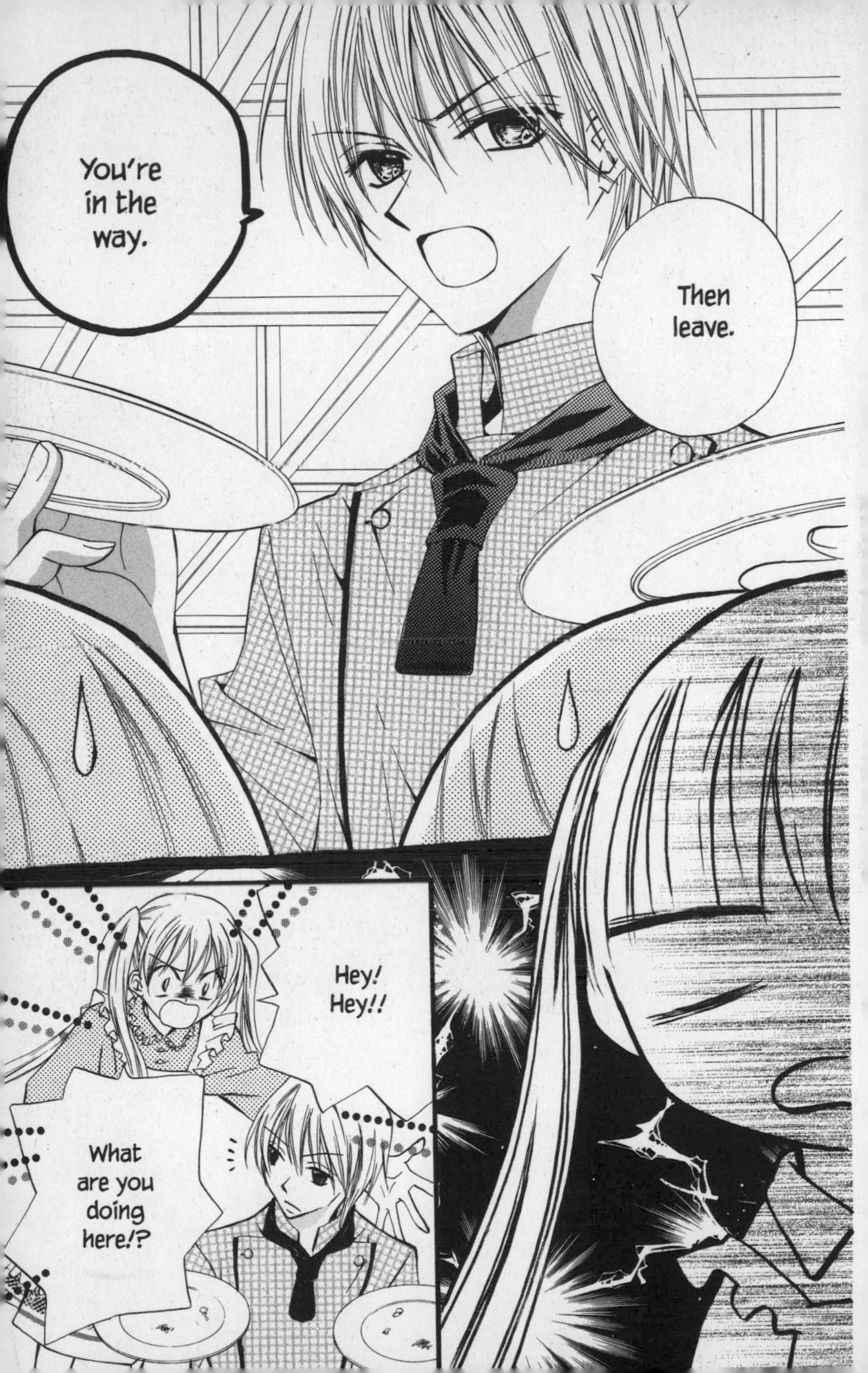
You're in the way.
Then leave.
Hey! Hey!!
What are you doing here!?

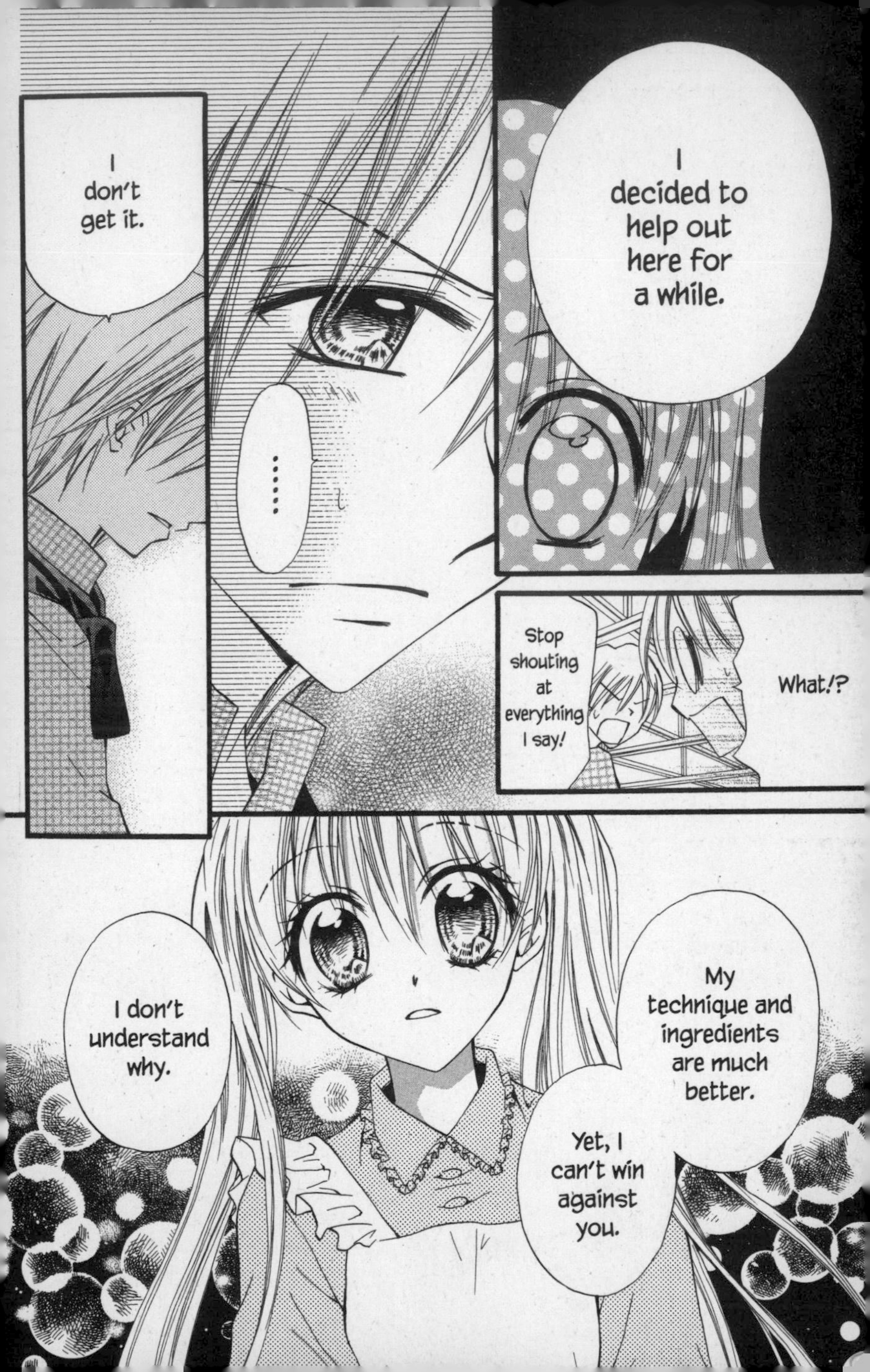
I decided to help out here for a while.
What!?
Stop shouting at everything I say!
......
I don't get it.
My technique and ingredients are much better.
Yet, I can't win against you.
I don't understand why.

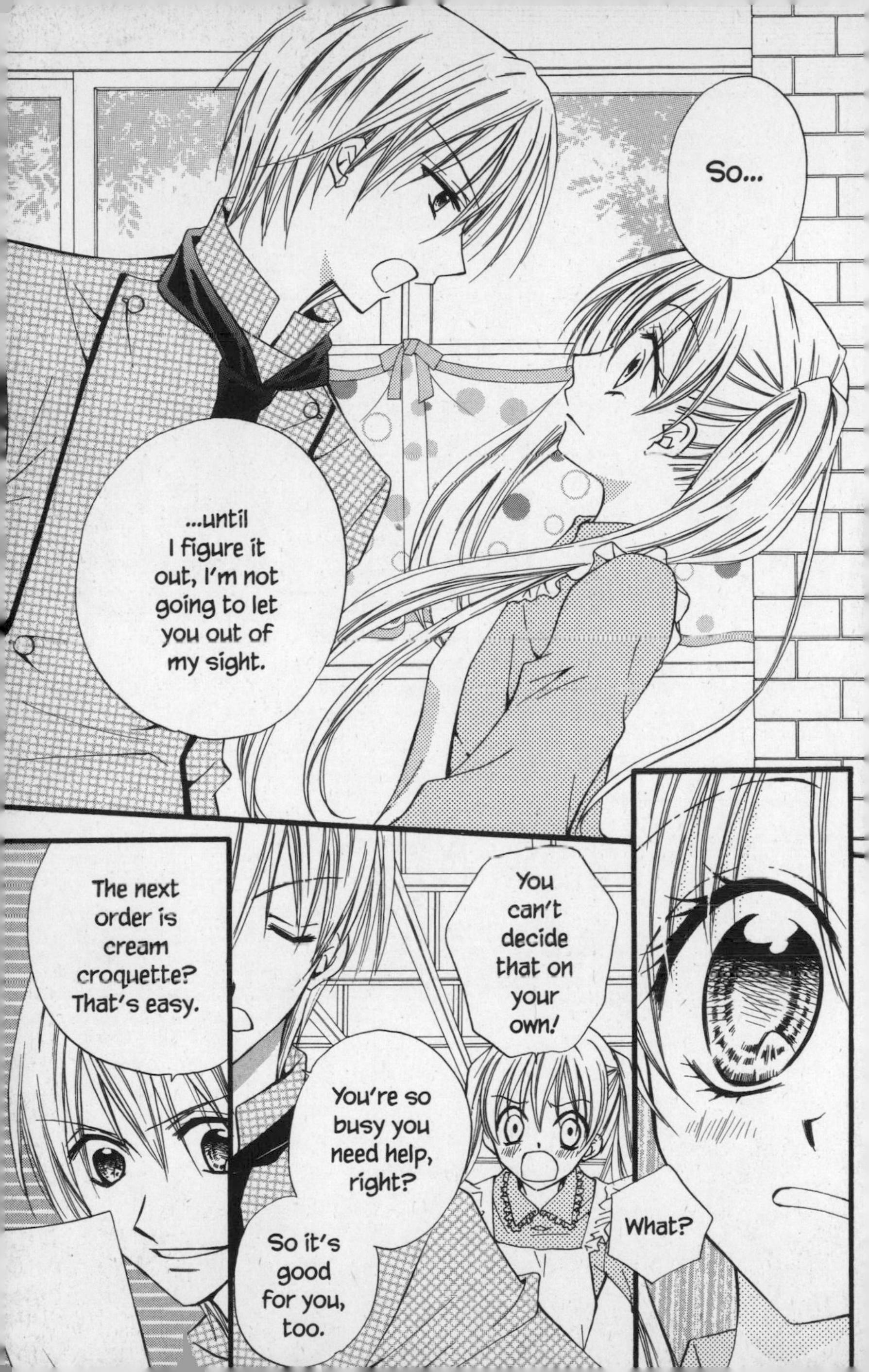
So...
...until I figure it out, I'm not going to let you out of my sight.
What?
You can't decide that on your own!
The next order is cream croquette? That's easy.
You're so busy you need help, right?
So it's good for you, too.

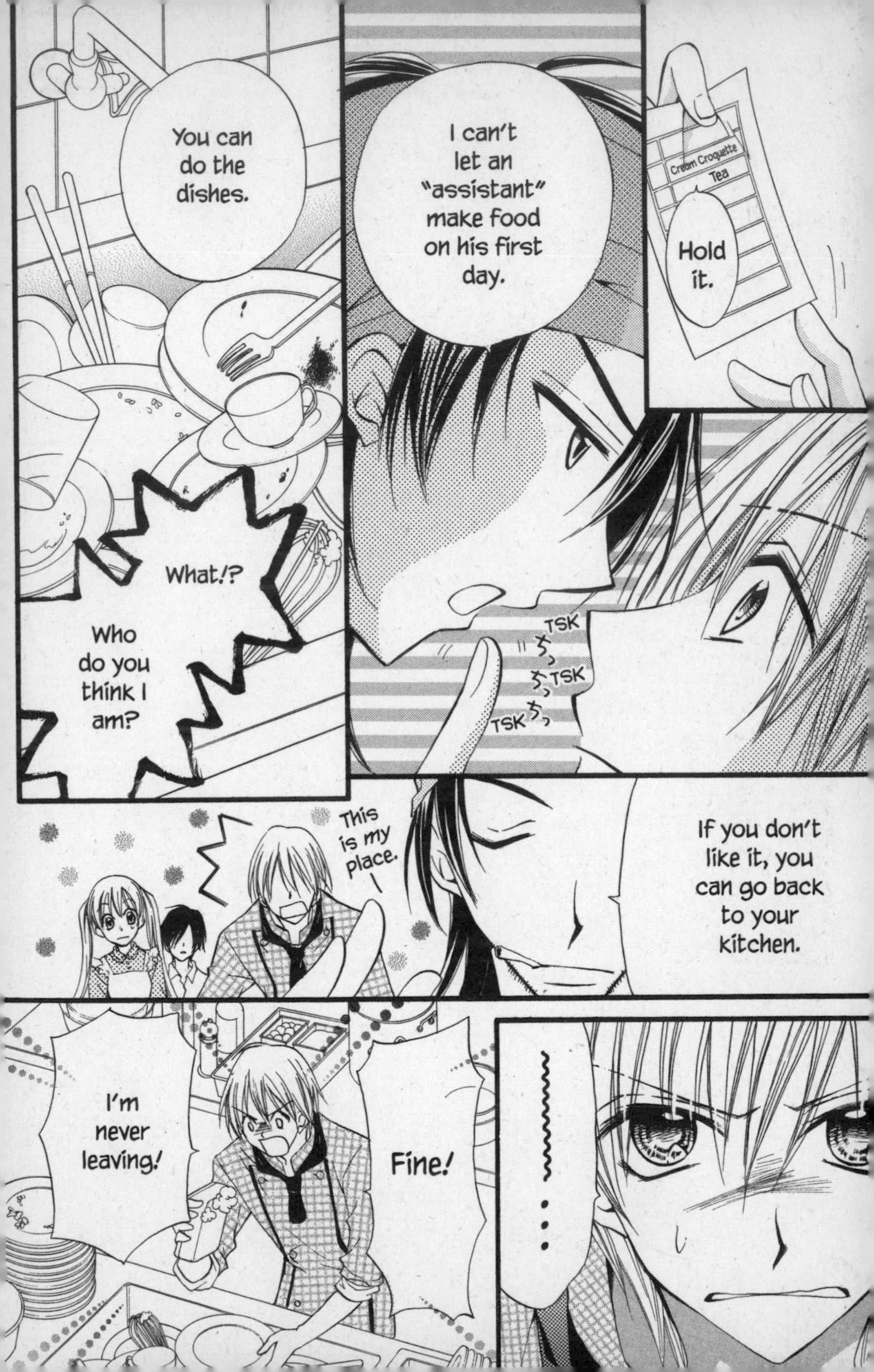
Cream Croquette
Tea
Hold it.
I can't let an "assistant" make food on his first day.
TSK
ちっ
TSK
ちっ
TSK
ちっ
You can do the dishes.
What!?
Who do you think I am?
If you don't like it, you can go back to your kitchen.
This is my place.
......
Fine!
I'm never leaving!

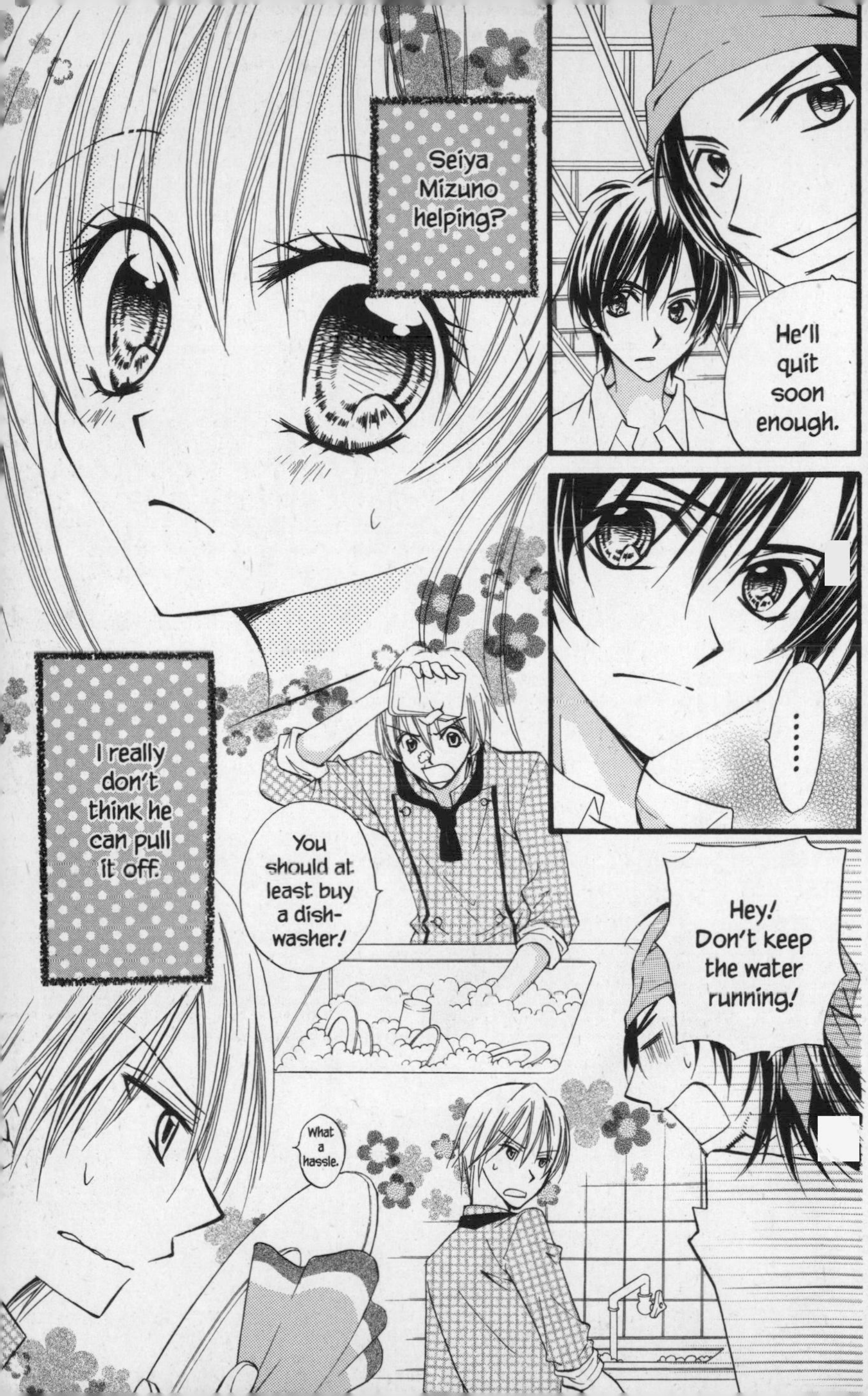
He'll quit soon enough.
......
Seiya Mizuno helping?
I really don't think he can pull it off.
Hey! Don't keep the water running!
You should at least buy a dish-washer!
What a hassle.

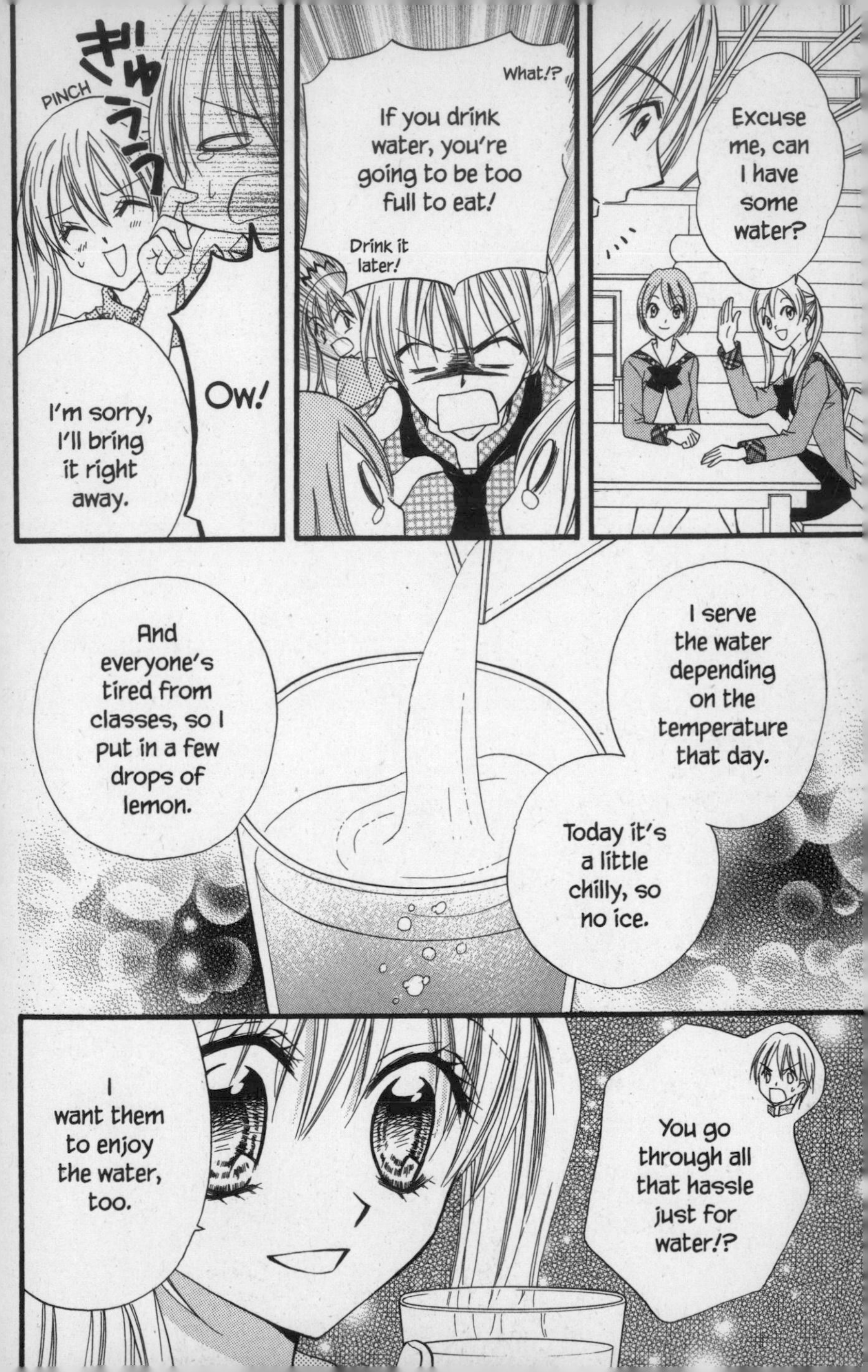
Excuse me, can I have some water?
What!?
If you drink water, you're going to be too full to eat!
Drink it later!
PINCH
Ow!
I'm sorry, I'll bring it right away.
I serve the water depending on the temperature that day.
Today it's a little chilly, so no ice.
And everyone's tired from classes, so I put in a few drops of lemon.
You go through all that hassle just for water!?
I want them to enjoy the water, too.

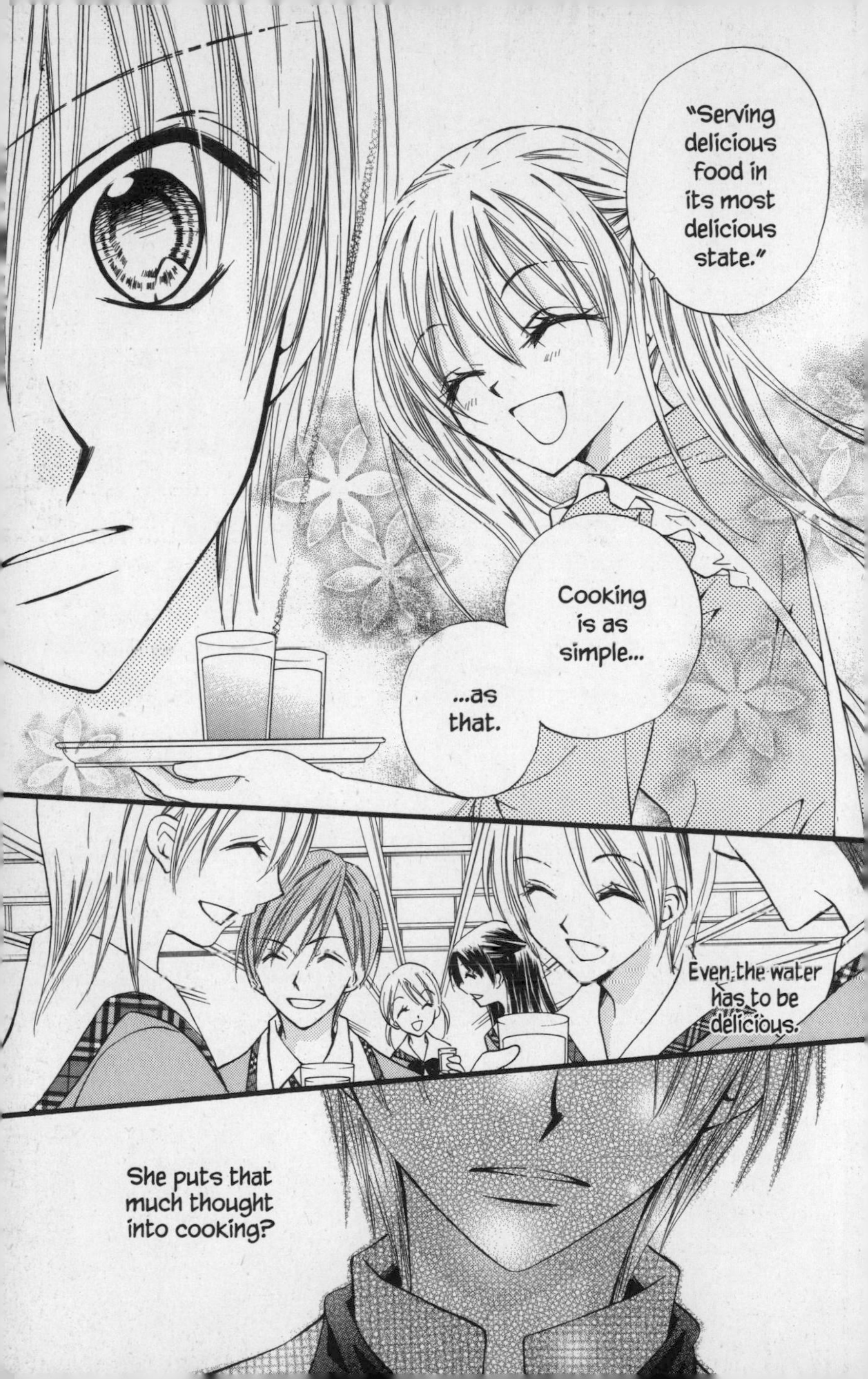
"Serving delicious food in its most delicious state."
Cooking is as simple...
...as that.
Even the water has to be delicious.
She puts that much thought into cooking?

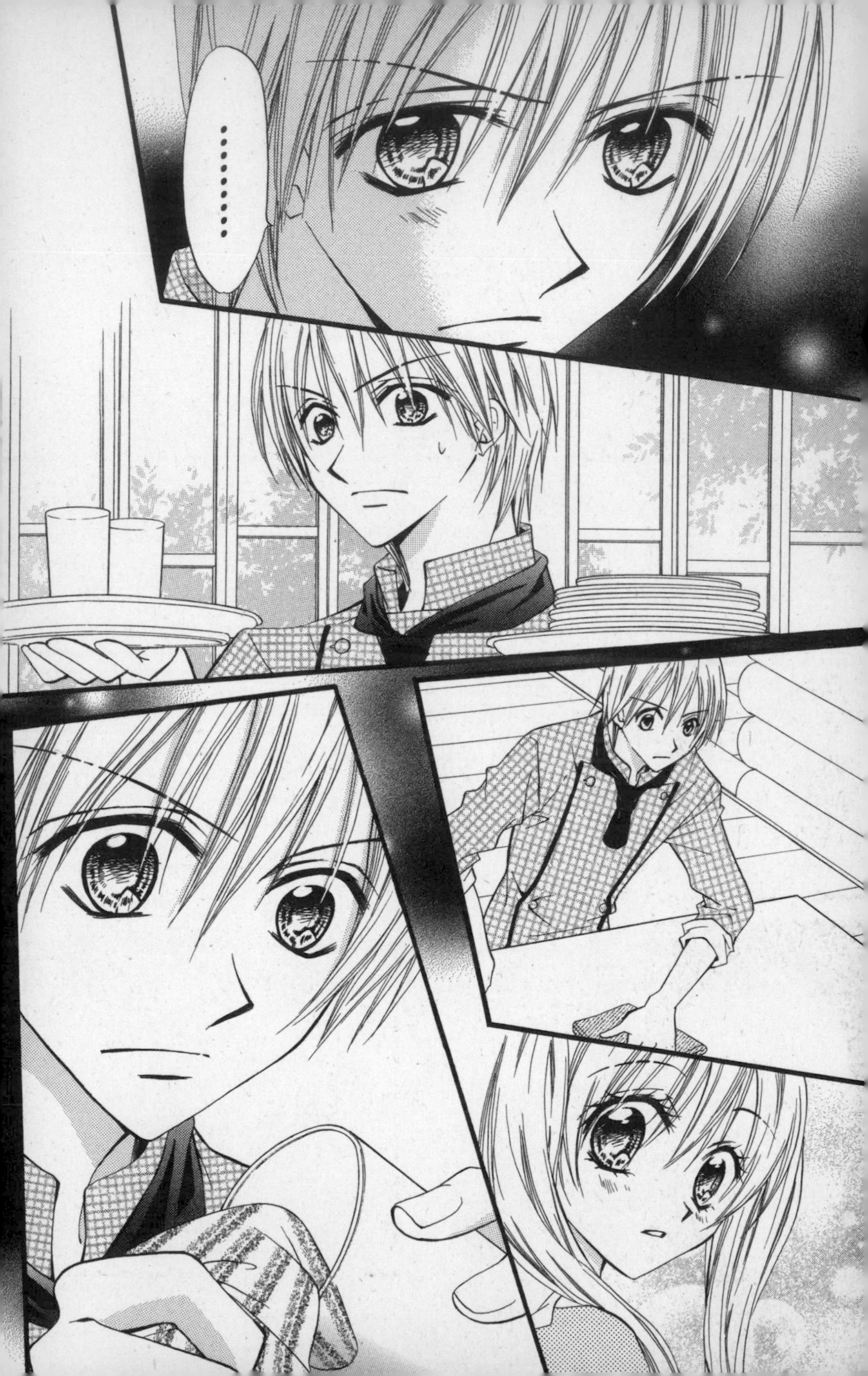
....

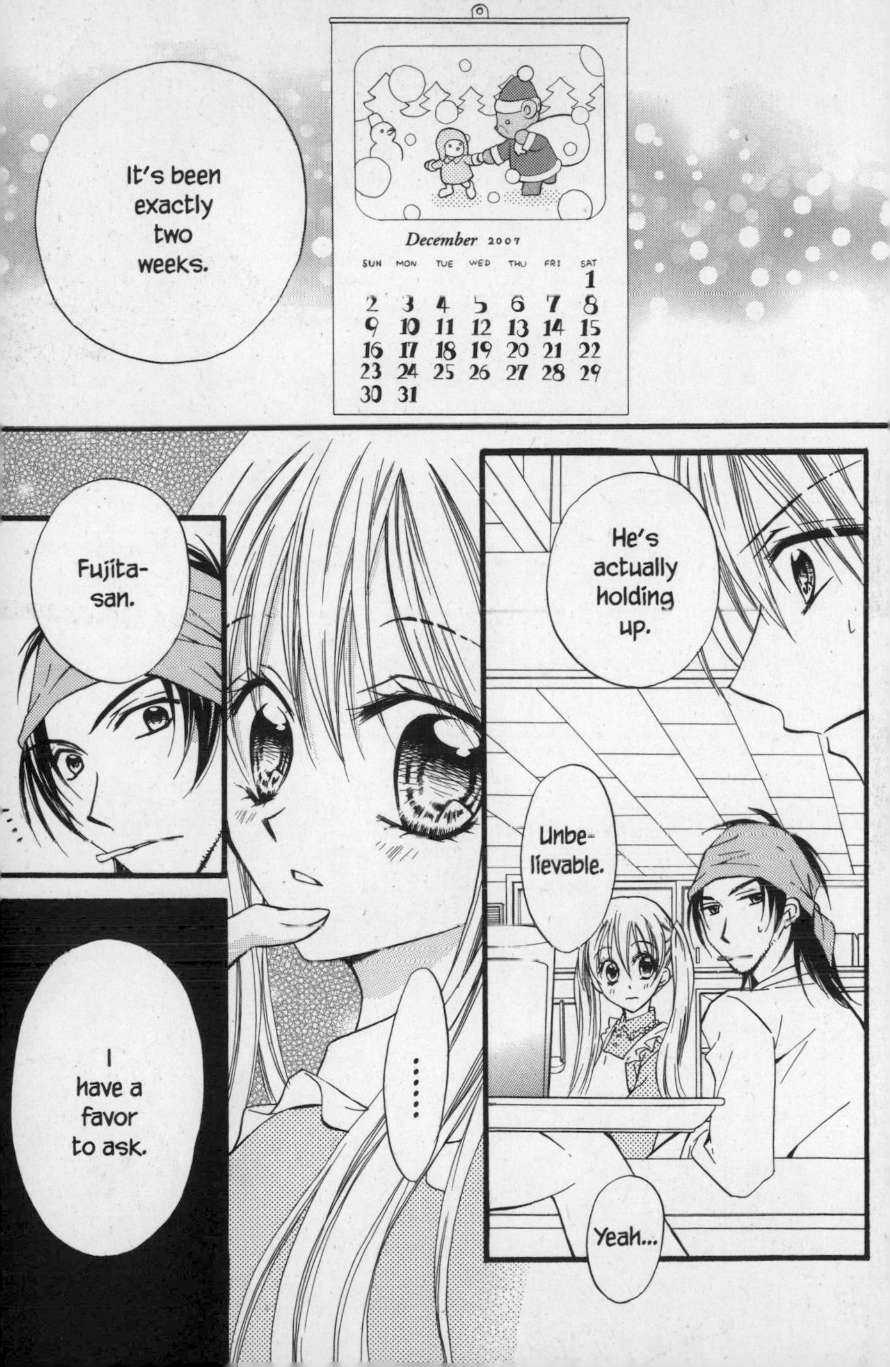
December 2007
SUN MON TUE WED THU FRI SAT
1
2 3 4 5 6 7 8
9 10 11 12 13 14 15
16 17 18 19 20 21 22
23 24 25 26 27 28 29
30 31
It's been exactly two weeks.
He's actually holding up.
Unbelievable.
Yeah...
......
Fujita-san.
I have a favor to ask.

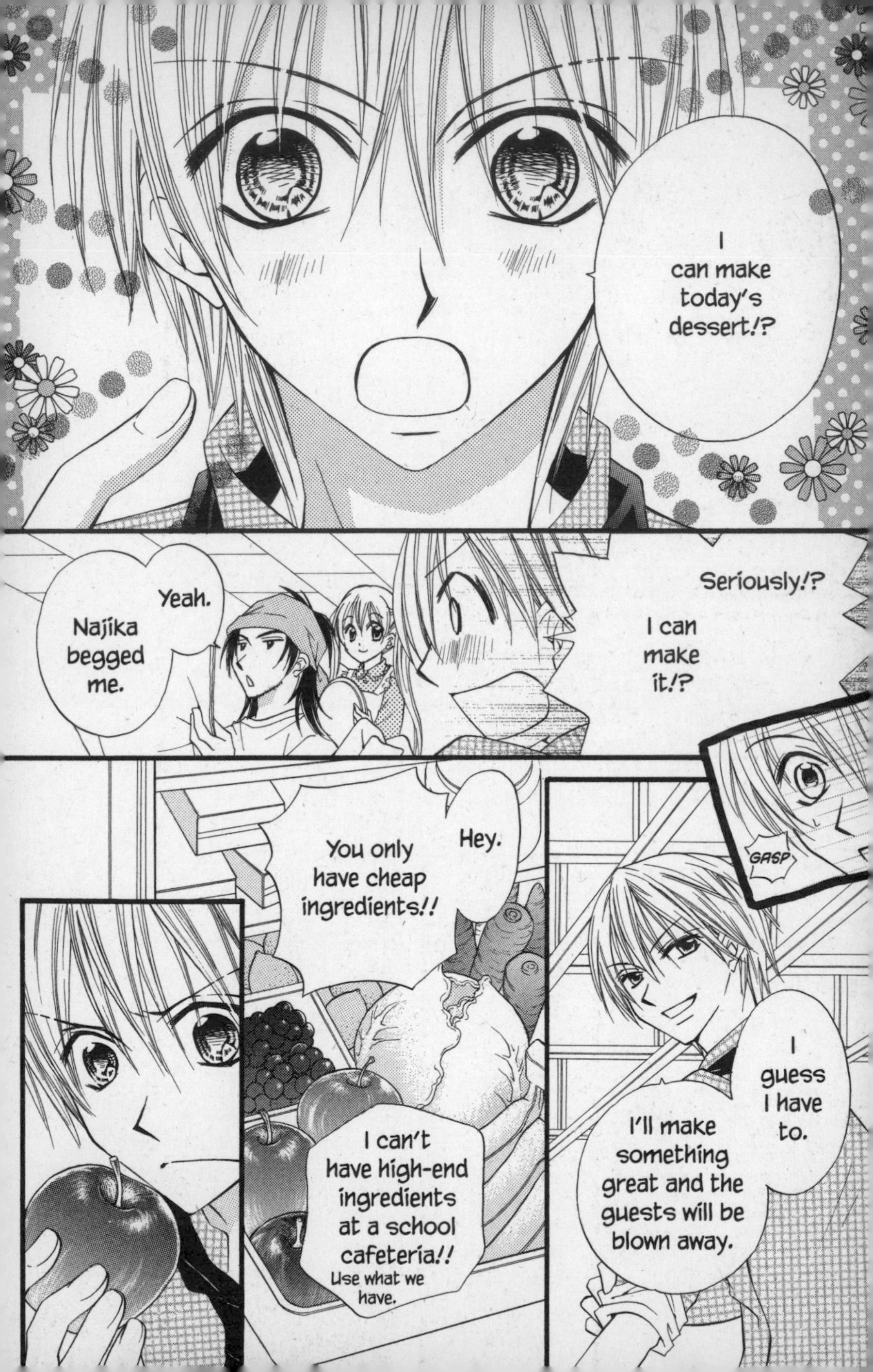
I can make today's dessert!?
Seriously!?
I can make it!?
Yeah.
Najika begged me.
Hey.
You only have cheap ingredients!!
I can't have high-end ingredients at a school cafeteria!!
Use what we have.
GASP
I guess I have to.
I'll make something great and the guests will be blown away.

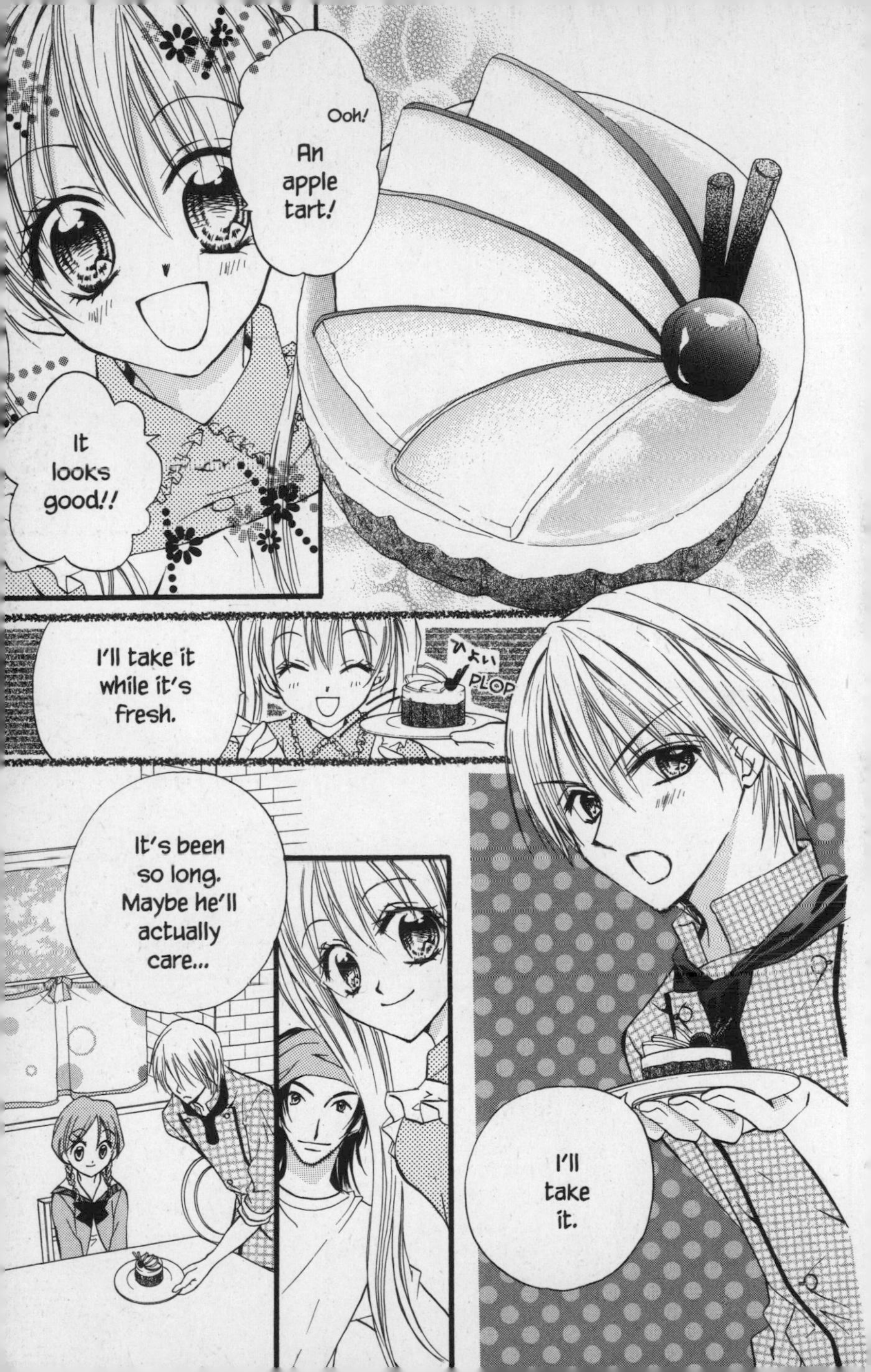
Ooh! An apple tart!
It looks good!!
I'll take it.
I'll take it while it's fresh.
ひょい PLOP
It's been so long. Maybe he'll actually care...

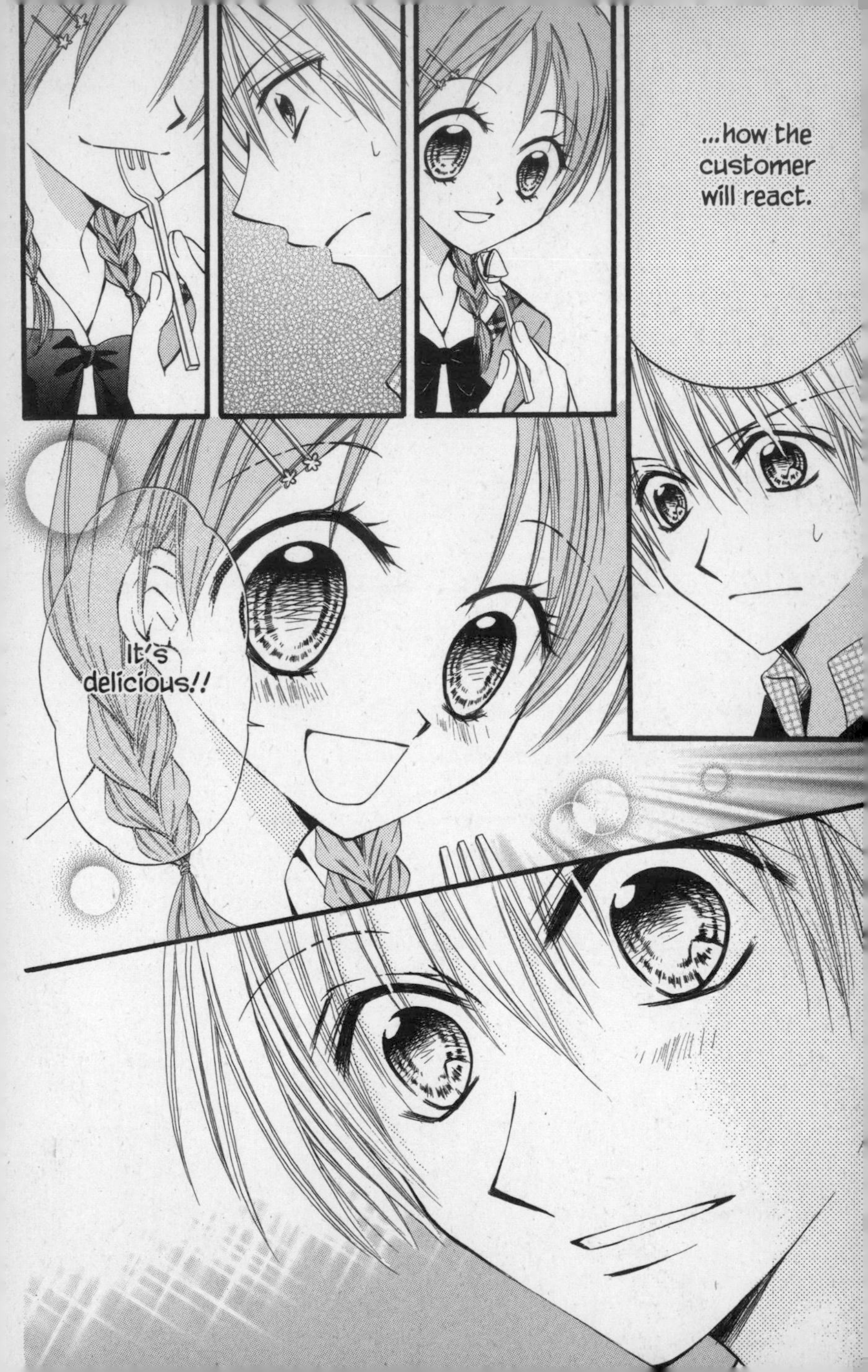
...how the customer will react.
It's delicious!!

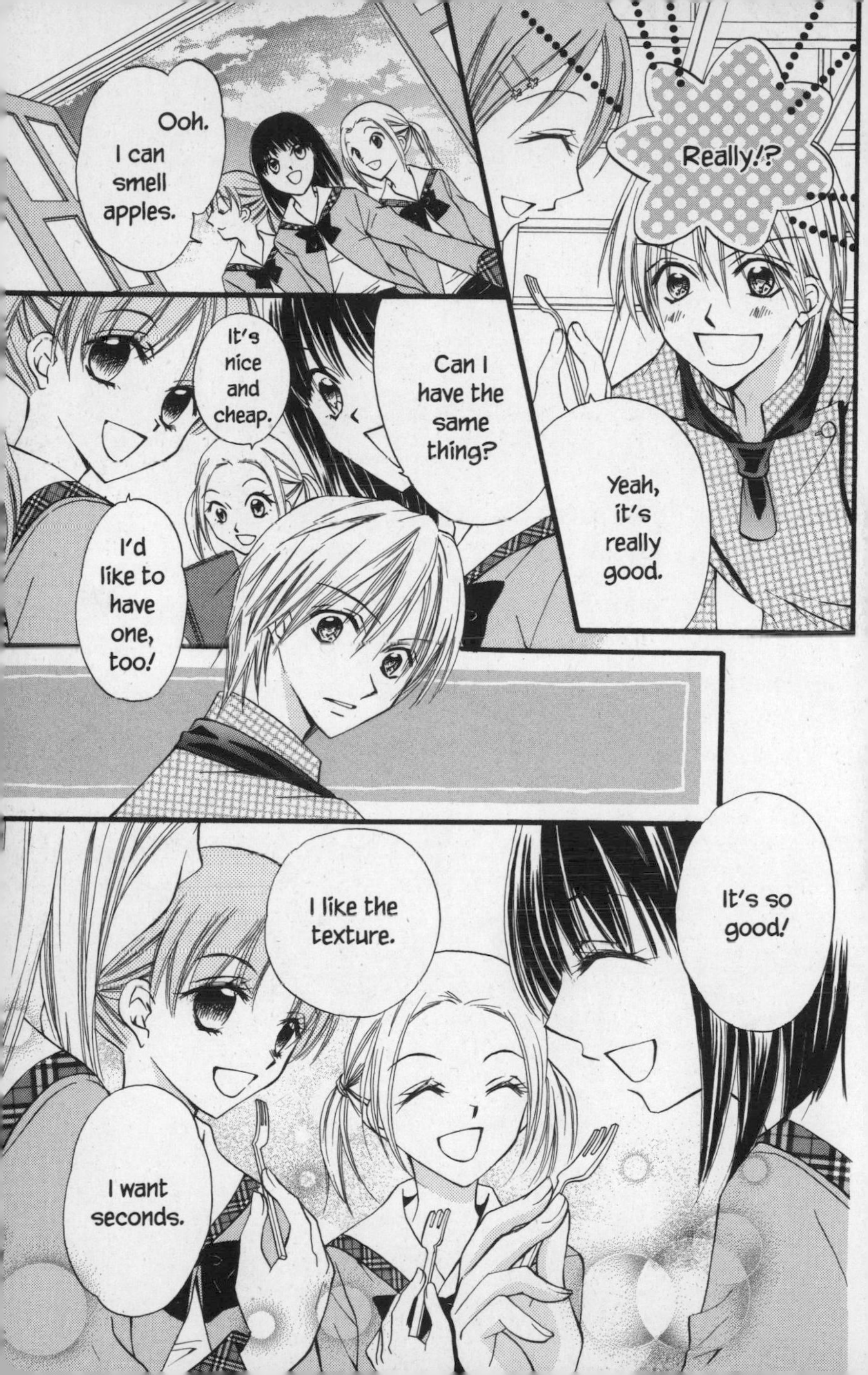
Really!?
Yeah, it's really good.
Ooh. I can smell apples.
Can I have the same thing?
It's nice and cheap.
I'd like to have one, too!
It's so good!
I like the texture.
I want seconds.

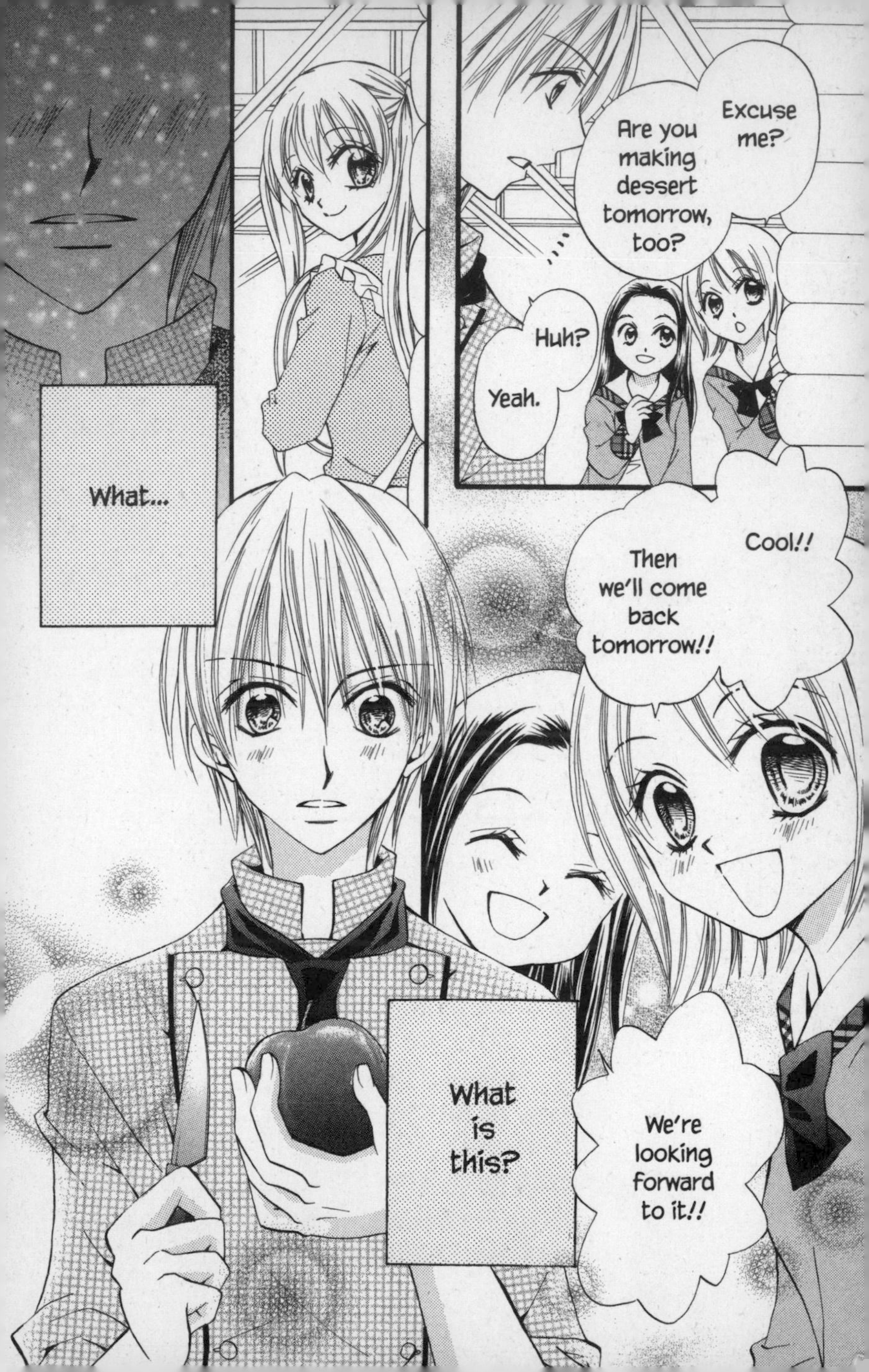
Excuse me?
Are you making dessert tomorrow, too?
...
Huh?
Yeah.
Cool!!
Then we'll come back tomorrow!!
What...
We're looking forward to it!!
What is this?

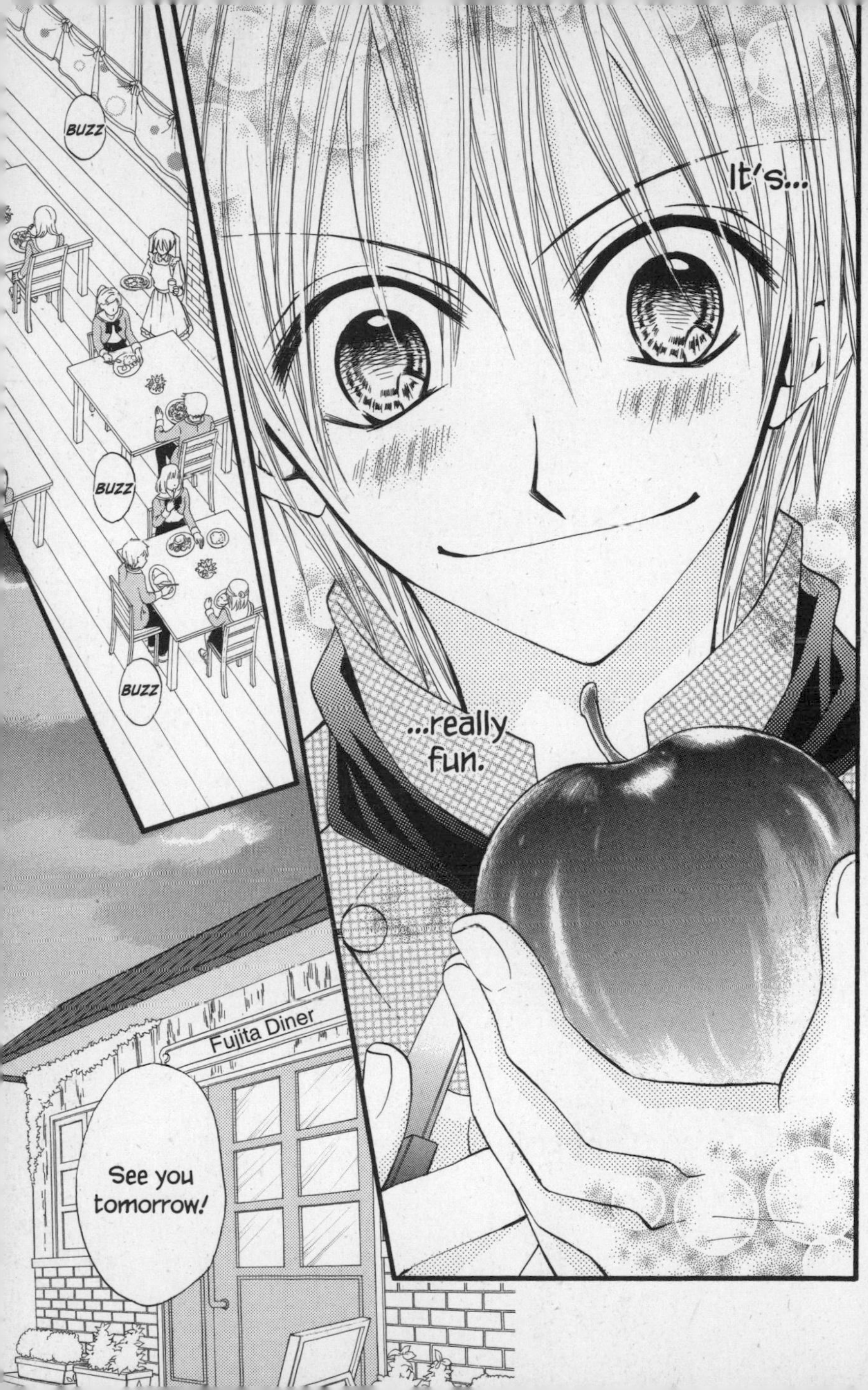
It's...
...really fun.
BUZZ
BUZZ
BUZZ
Fujita Diner
See you tomorrow!

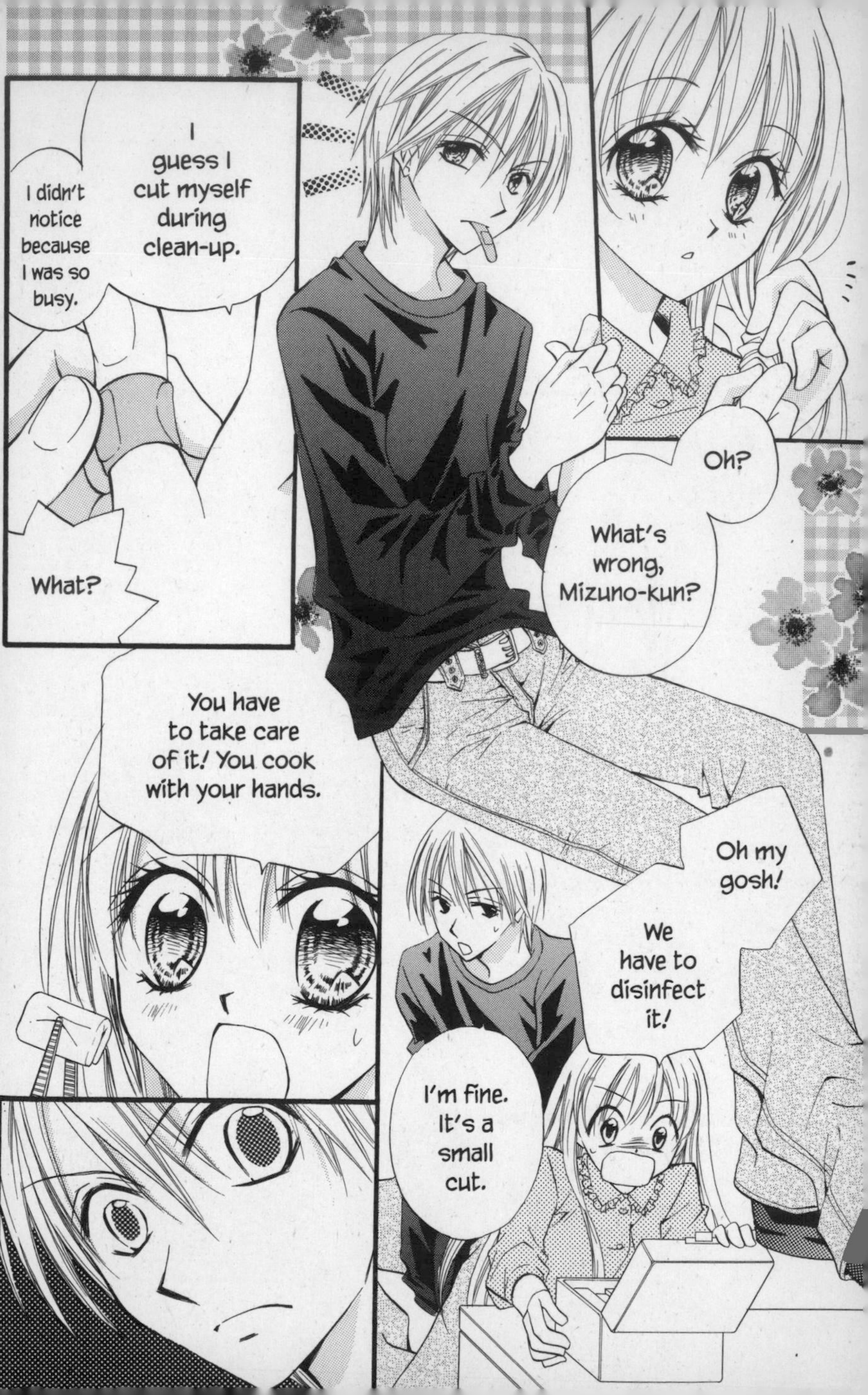
Oh?
What's wrong, Mizuno-kun?
I guess I cut myself during clean-up.
I didn't notice because I was so busy.
What?
Oh my gosh!
We have to disinfect it!
I'm fine. It's a small cut.
You have to take care of it! You cook with your hands.

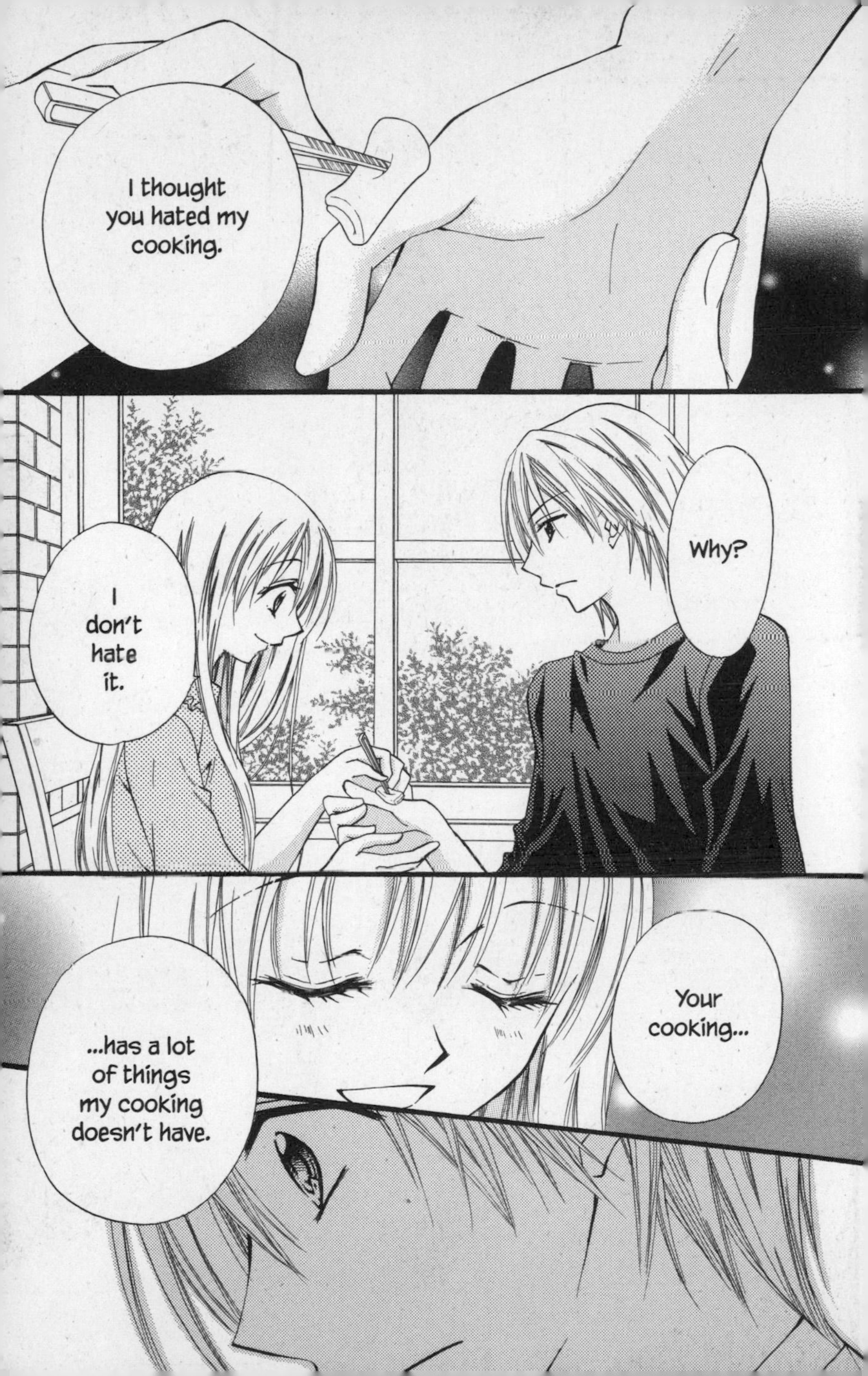
I thought you hated my cooking.
Why?
I don't hate it.
Your cooking...
...has a lot of things my cooking doesn't have.

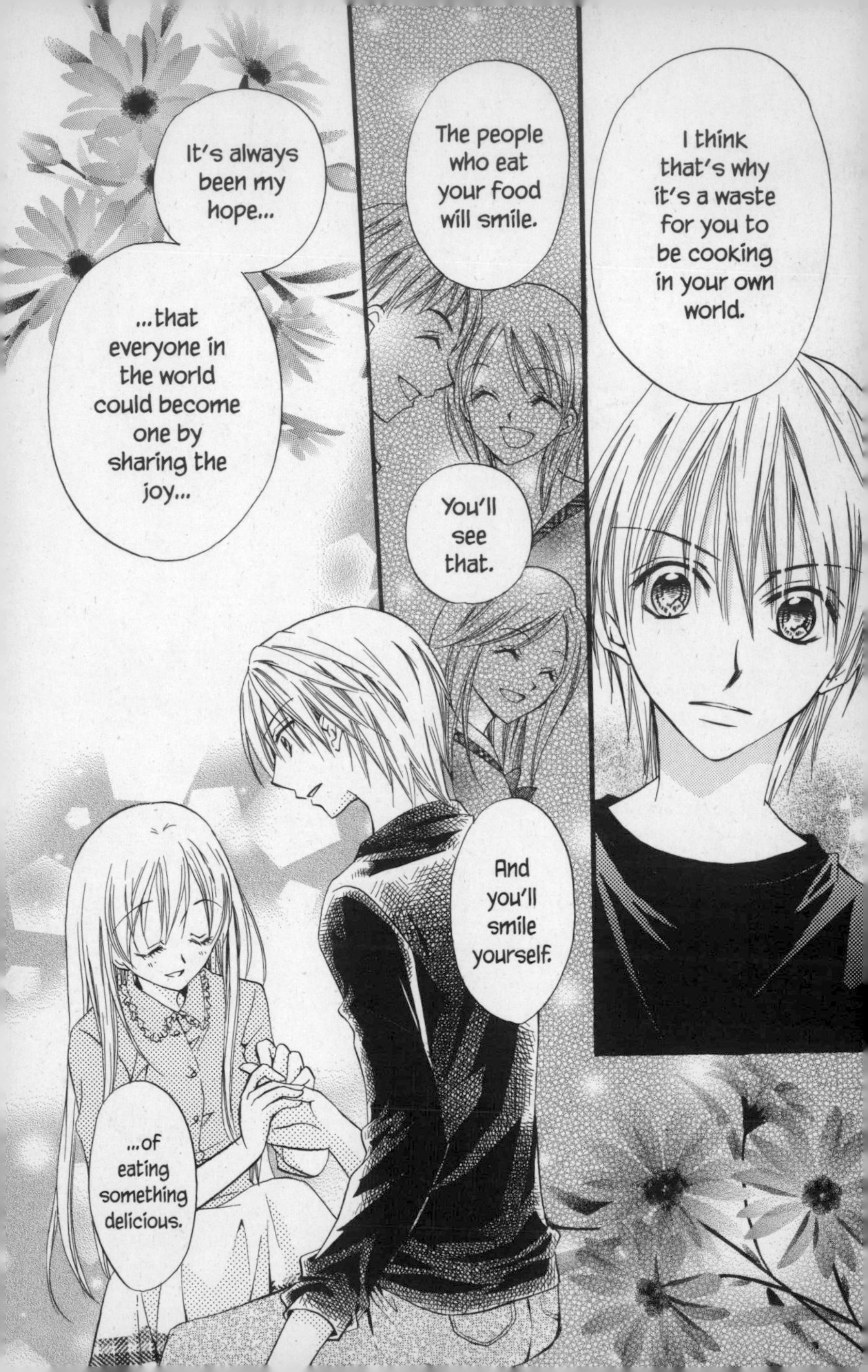
I think that's why it's a waste for you to be cooking in your own world.
The people who eat your food will smile.
You'll see that.
And you'll smile yourself.
It's always been my hope...
...that everyone in the world could become one by sharing the joy...
...of eating something delicious.

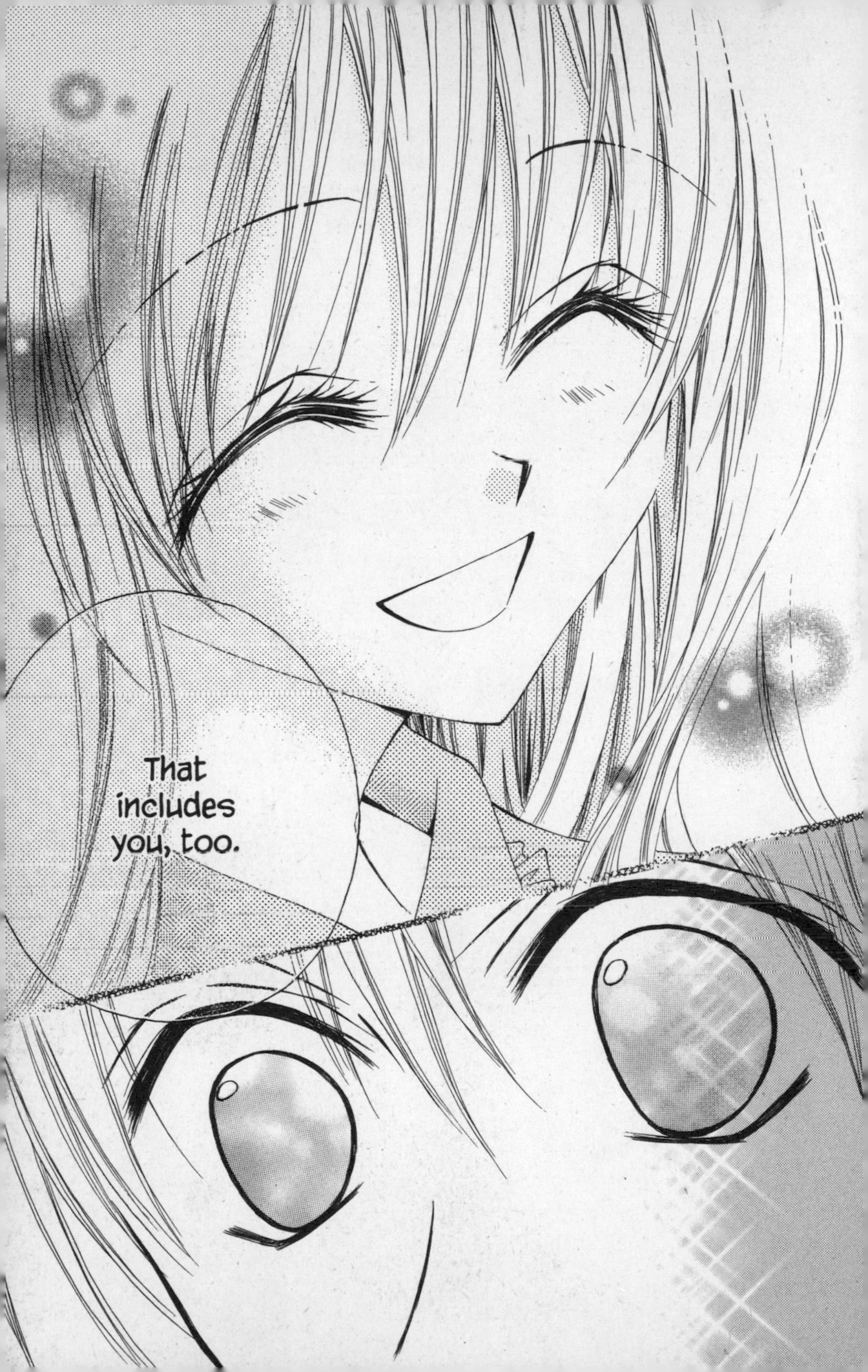
That includes you, too.

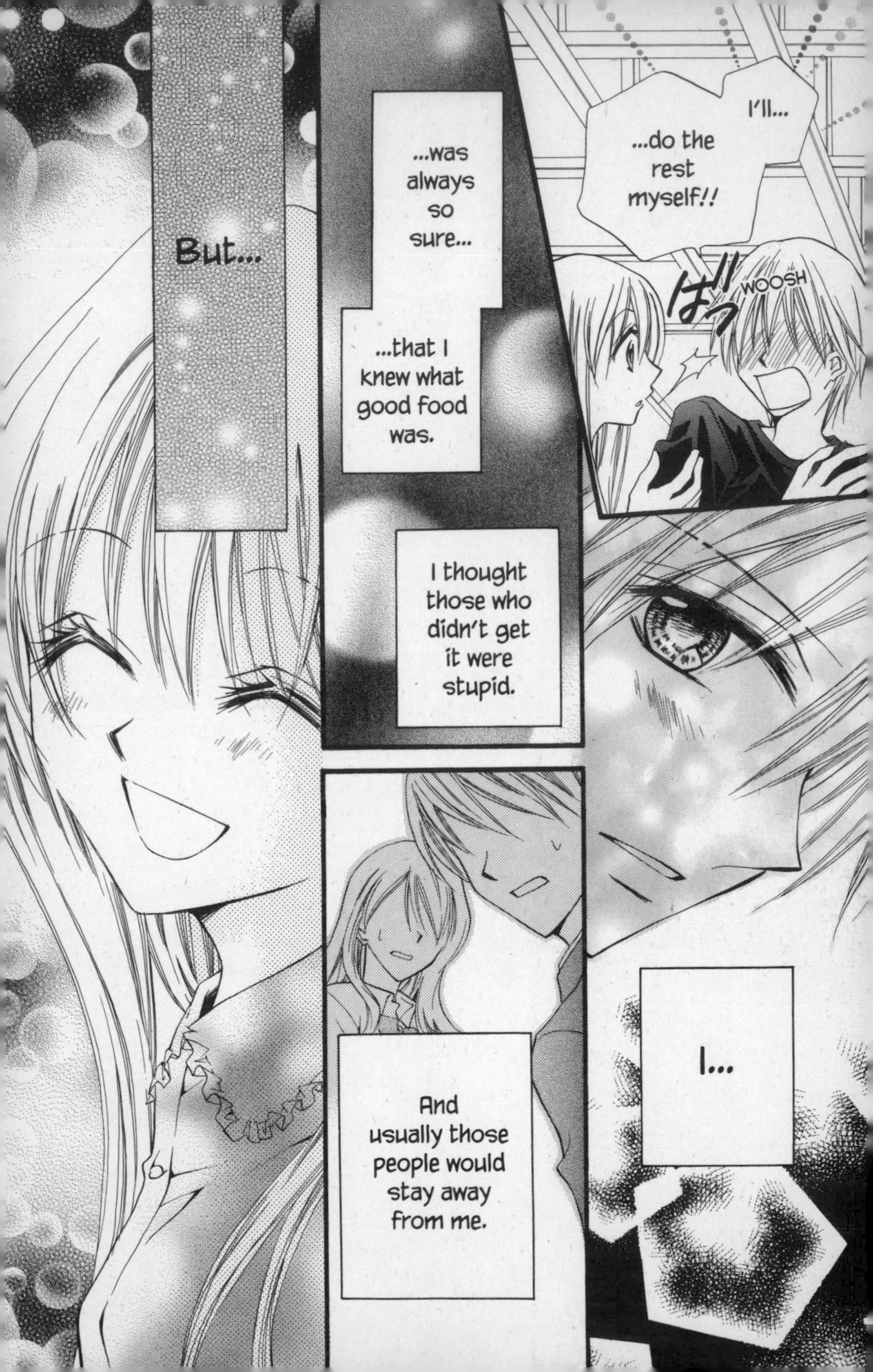
I'll...
...do the rest myself!!
ばっ
WOOSH
I...
...was always so sure...
...that I knew what good food was.
I thought those who didn't get it were stupid.
And usually those people would stay away from me.
But...

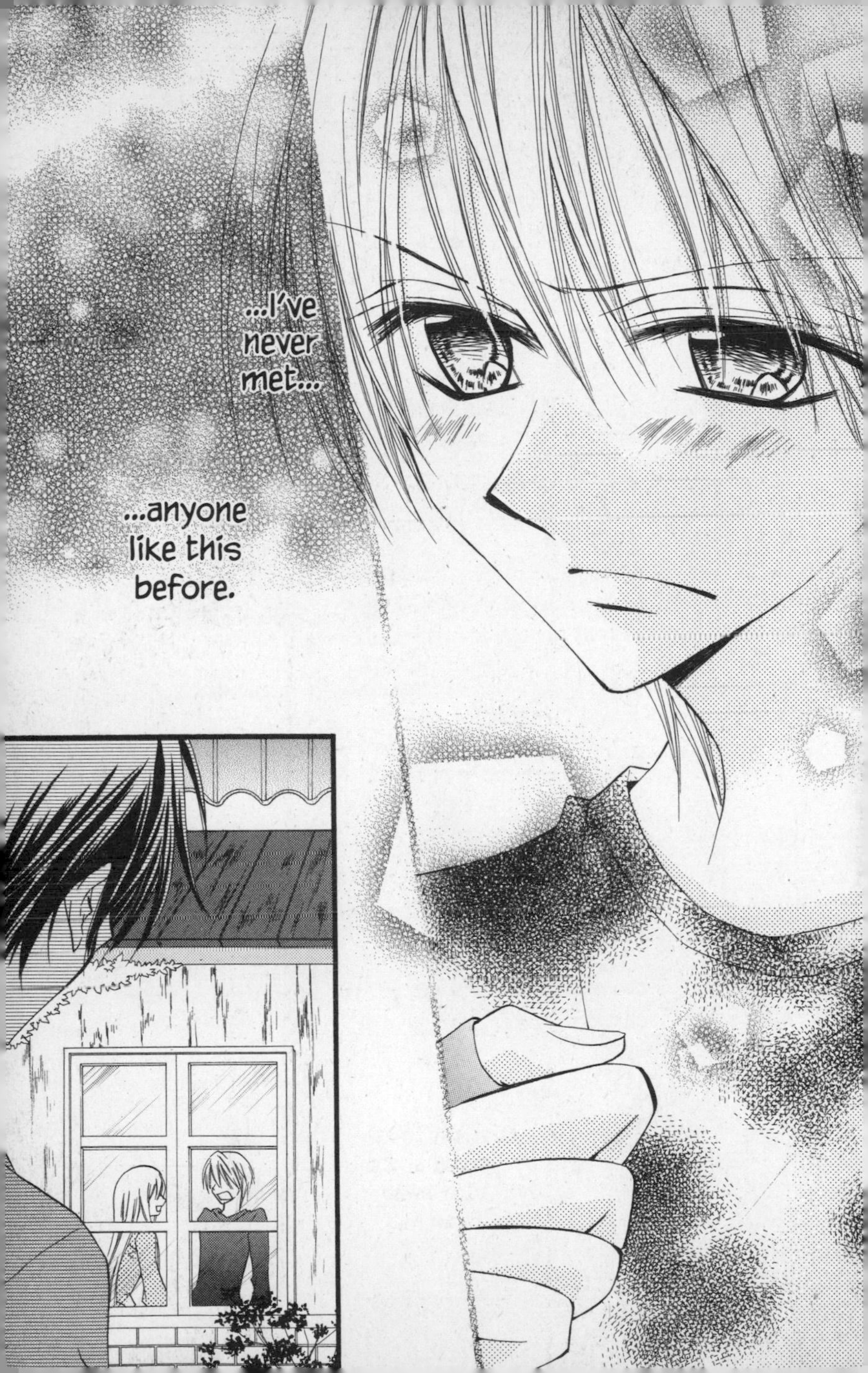
...I've never met...
...anyone like this before.

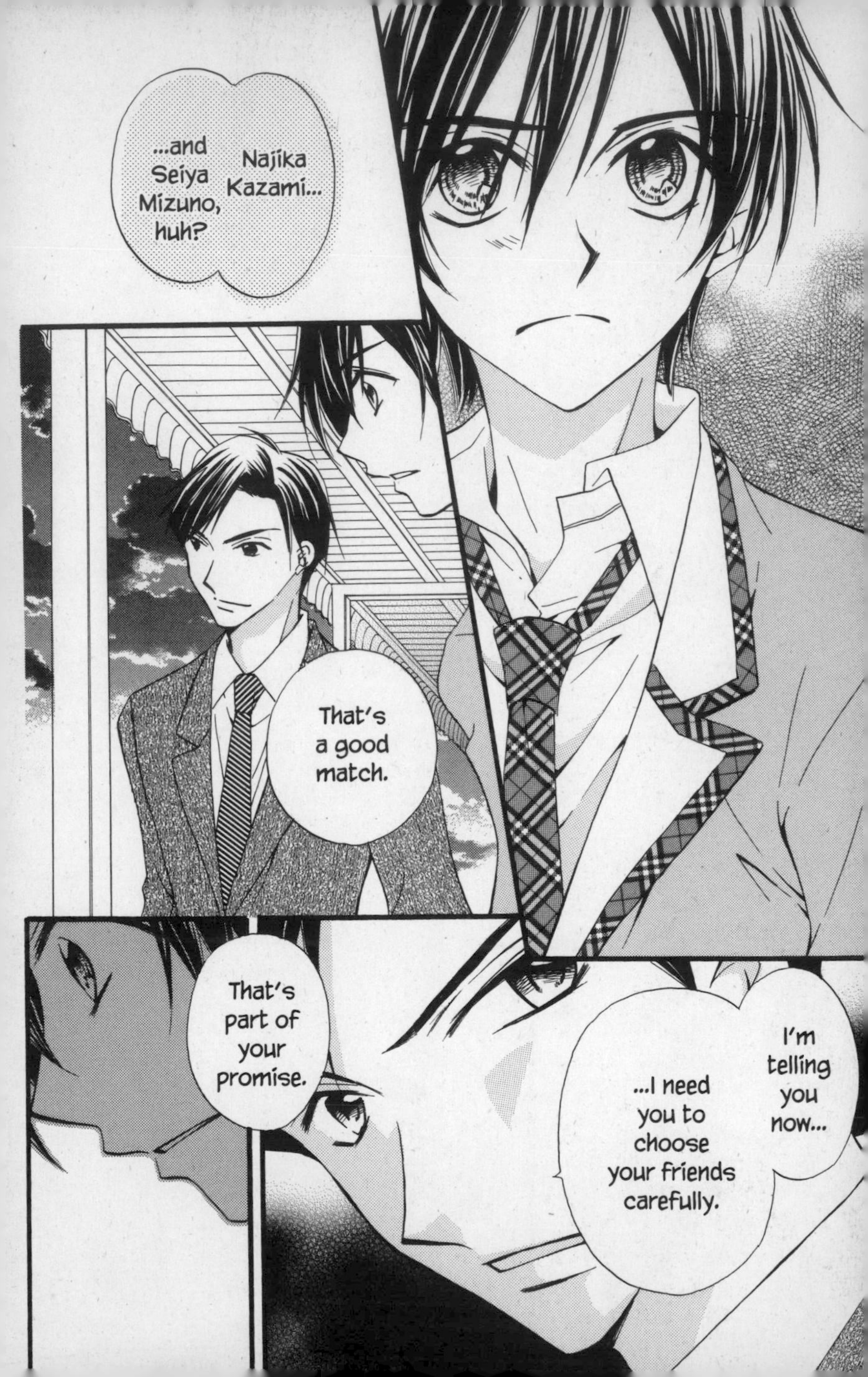
Najika Kazami...
...and Seiya Mizuno, huh?
That's a good match.
I'm telling you now...
...I need you to choose your friends carefully.
That's part of your promise.

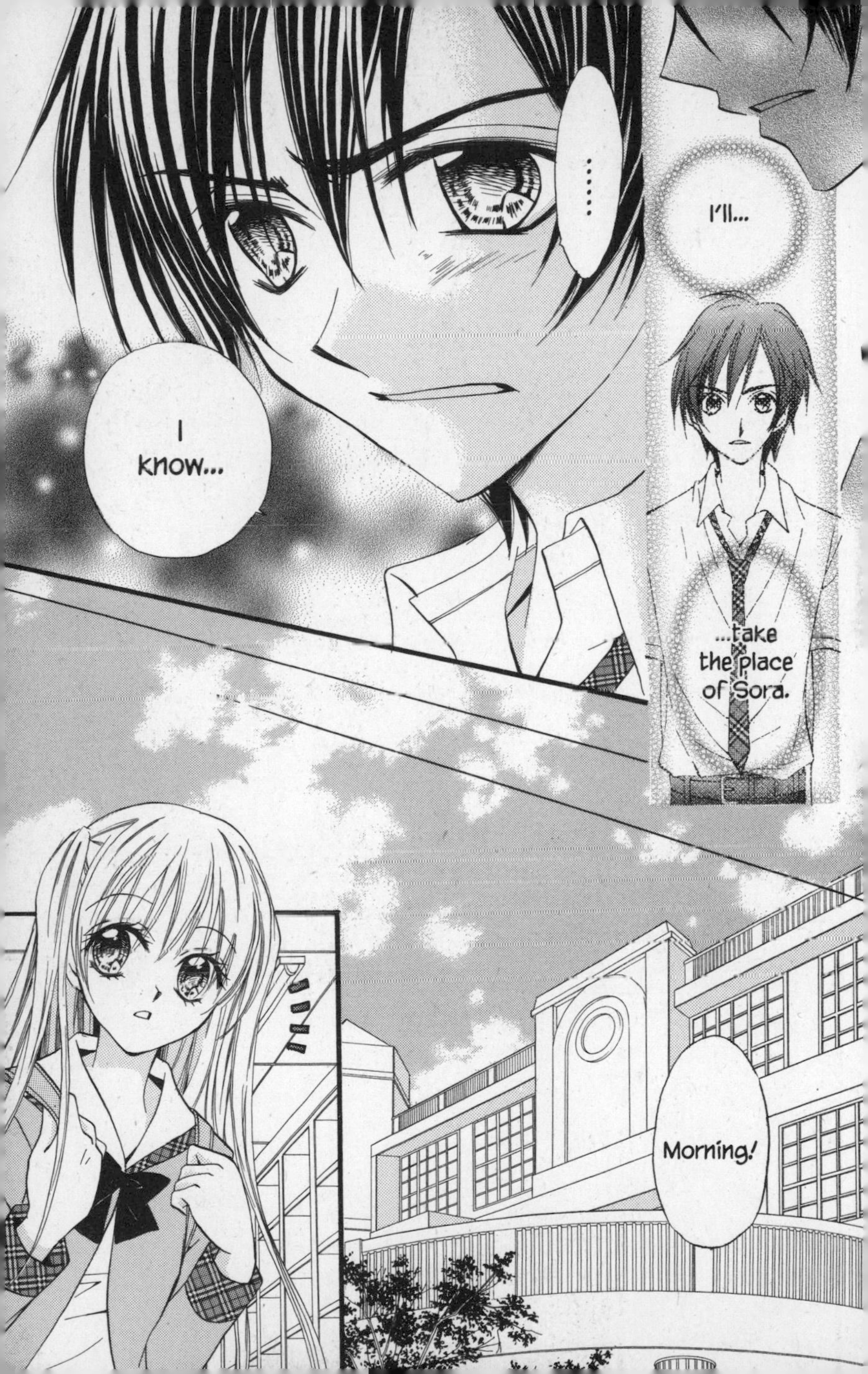
I'll...
...take the place of Sora.
......
I know...
Morning!

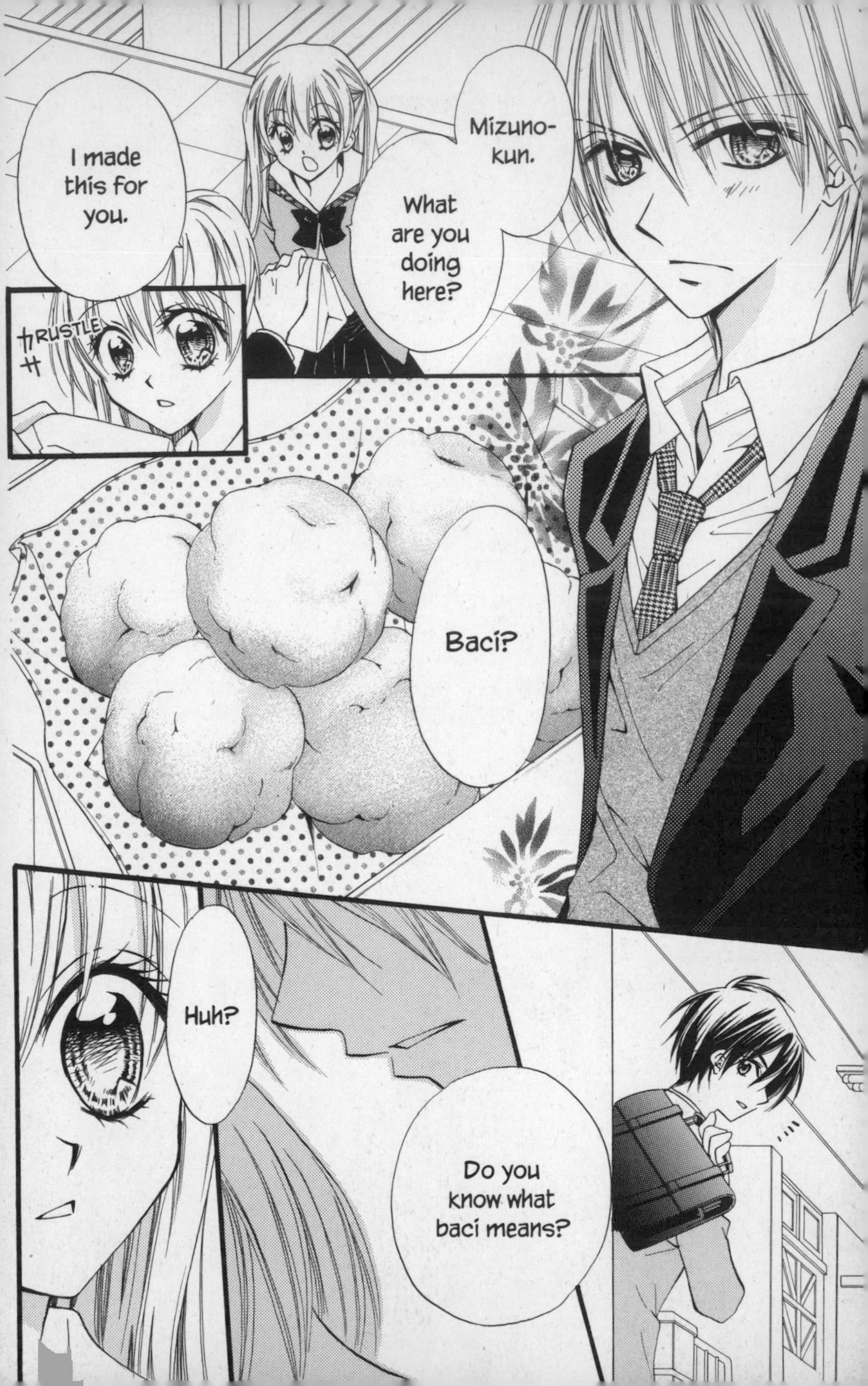
Mizuno-kun.
What are you doing here?
I made this for you.
RUSTLE
Baci?
Do you know what baci means?
Huh?

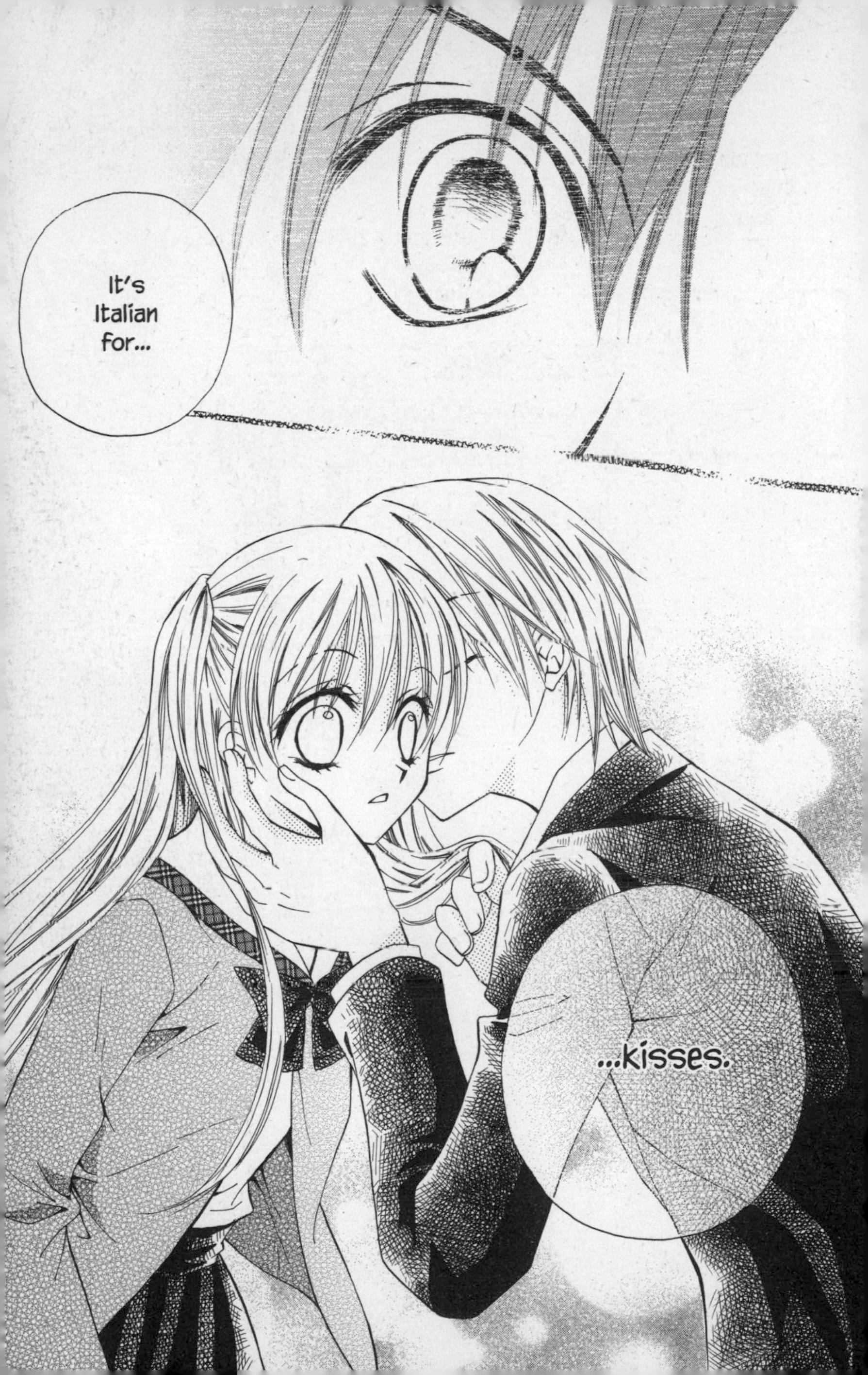
It's Italian for...
...kisses.

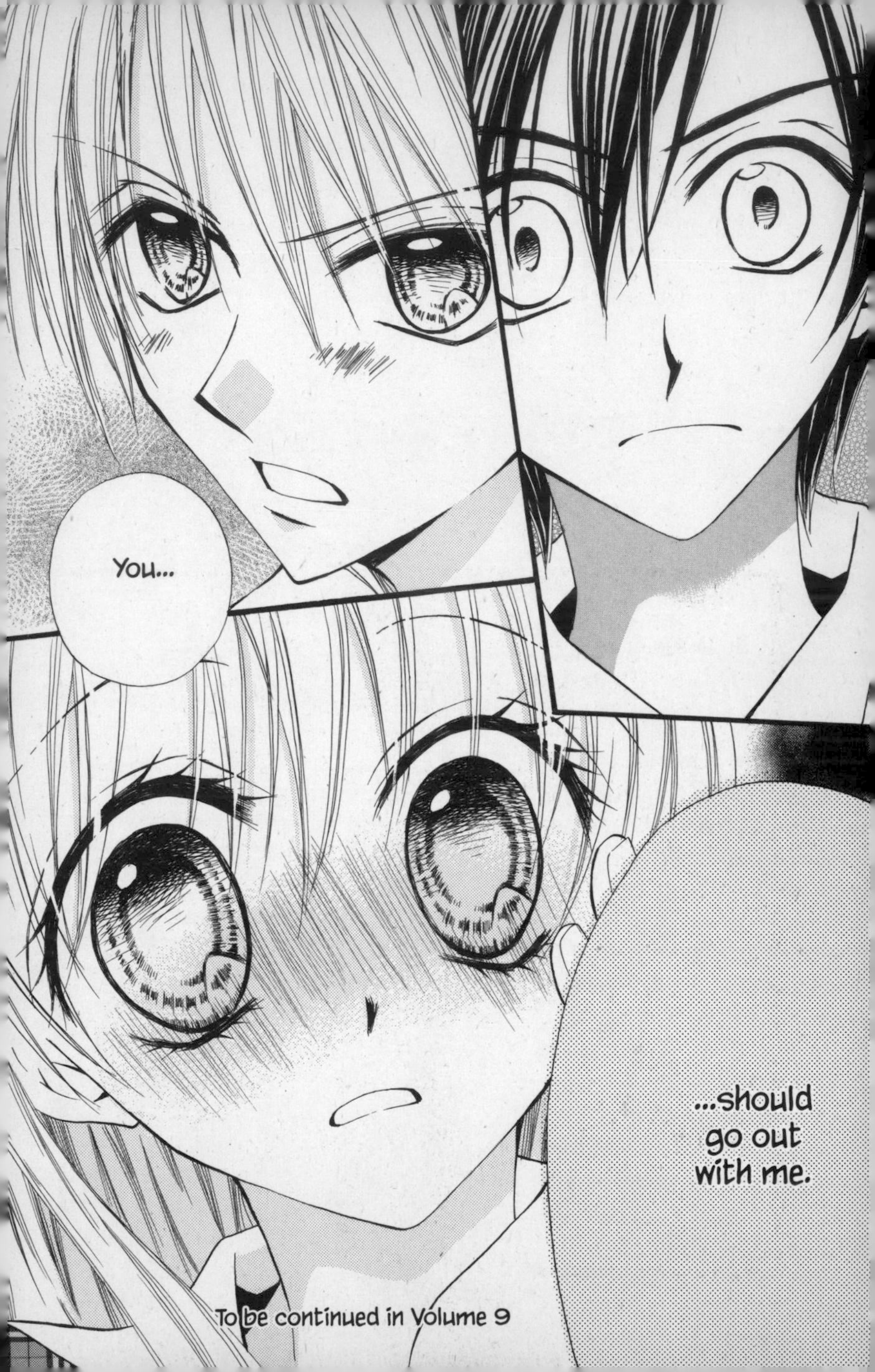

You...
...should go out with me.
To be continued in Volume 9

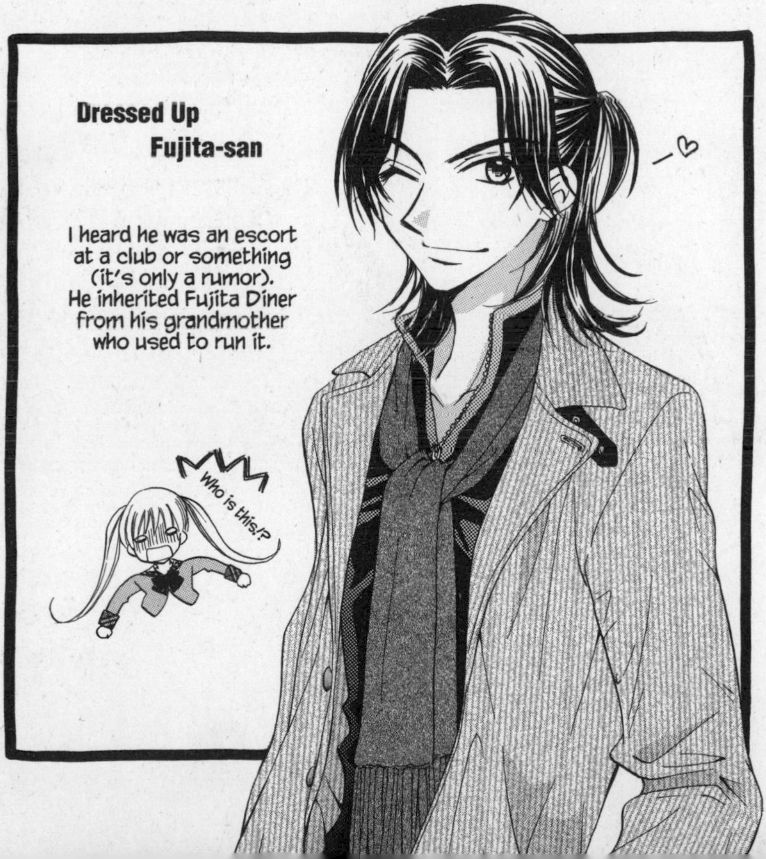
Dressed Up
Fujita-san
I heard he was an escort at a club or something (it's only a rumor). He inherited Fujita Diner from his grandmother who used to run it.
Who is this!?

Afterword

Hello! This is Ando.

It's already Volume 8!! I can't believe how time flew. It seems like the series started yesterday... No wonder I'm getting older.

I had decided to draw Daichi for the back cover, but I couldn't think of a good composition. I drew Seiya just to test him out and I was able to draw him easily.

Next time...next time for sure I will draw Daichi!!

So I will see you in Volume 9 with Daichi on the back cover. ♥

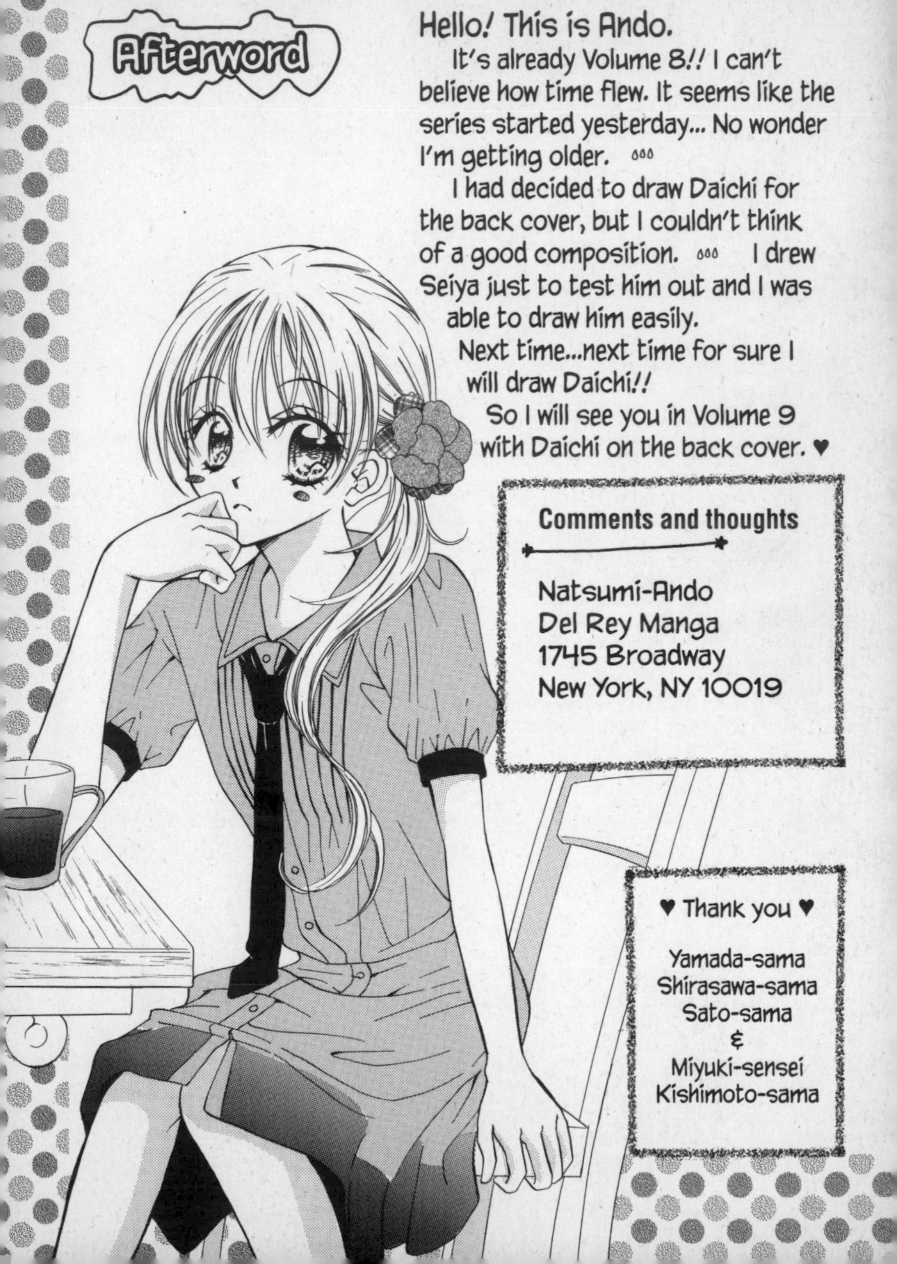

Comments and thoughts

Natsumi-Ando
Del Rey Manga
1745 Broadway
New York, NY 10019

♥ Thank you ♥

Yamada-sama
Shirasawa-sama
Sato-sama
&
Miyuki-sensei
Kishimoto-sama

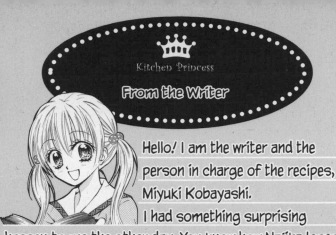

Kitchen Princess

From the Writer

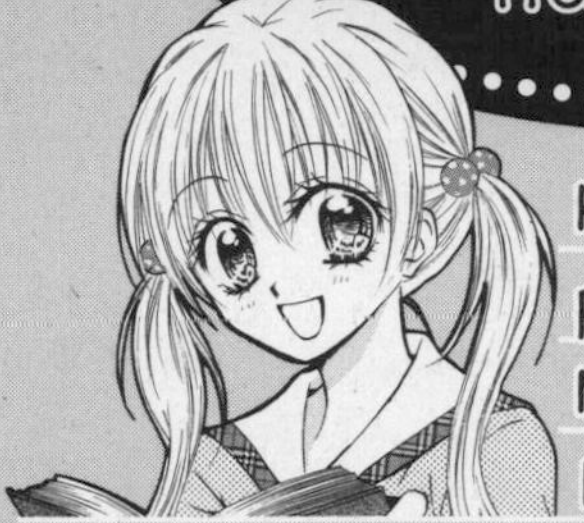

Hello! I am the writer and the person in charge of the recipes, Miyuki Kobayashi.

I had something surprising happen to me the other day. You know how Najika loses her sense of taste in Volume 6? I don't know if it's because I wrote that incident or because I killed off Sora, but my editor lost his sense of taste, too. It was scary!!

When I first heard about it, I thought, "Are you Najika!?" but it was no time to kid around! Lately there are many children who are losing their sense of taste. The main reason is that they don't have a well-balanced diet—and they are especially not getting enough zinc! Zinc is found in oysters, liver, beef, cheese, and milk, among other things. Please try to put some zinc in your diet! My editor is all better now, so there's nothing to worry about anymore!

Kitchen Princess made its debut in the September 2004 issue of *Nakayoshi*. It's been four years already. Thank you to all the readers who support Najika and her friends.

Finally, I would like to thank Natsumi Ando-sensei, my editor Kishimoto-san, and our editor in chief Matsumoto-san.

I'll see you in Volume 9!

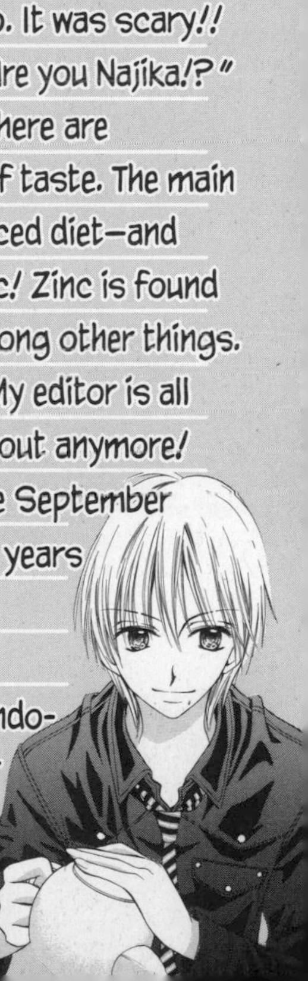

About the Creator

Natsumi Ando

   She was born January 27 in Aichi prefecture. She won the 19th Nakayoshi Rookie Award in 1994 and debuted as a manga artist. The title she drew was "Headstrong Cinderella." Her other known works are "Zodiac P.I.," "Wild Heart," and others. Her hobbies include reading, watching movies, and eating delicious food.

Translation Notes

Japanese is a tricky language for most Westerners, and translation is often more art than science. For your edification and reading pleasure, here are notes on some of the places where we could have gone in a different direction in our translation of the work, or where a Japanese cultural reference is used.

Splash pages, page 5

Kitchen Princess was originally serialized in a magazine *Nakayoshi*. In Japanese manga magazines, the "splash page" is the special, full-page illustration that opens each new installment of a series. In some issues, this splash page appears in color, but is then reproduced in black-and-white when the serialized installments are collected in book form.

Millimeters and meters, page 38

5 millimeters is about ½ centimeter. 5 meters is 500 centimeters—or almost 16 feet. It's a big difference!

Rare Cheese, page 43

When Najika writes "rare cheese," she is referring to the soft, creamy cheese that was used in volume 7's cheesecake recipe.

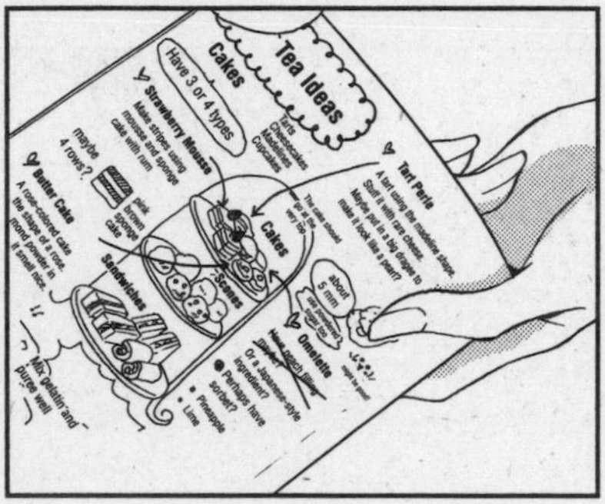
Tea Ideas
Tarts
Cheesecakes
Madelines
Cupcakes
Cakes
Have 3 or 4 types
Strawberry Mousse
Make stripes using mousse and sponge cake with rum
maybe 4 rows?
pink
brown
sponge cake
Butter Cake
Tart Perle
A tart using the madeline shape. Stuff it with rare cheese. Maybe put in a big dragee to make it look like a pearl?
The cake should go at the very top
Cakes
Scones
Sandwiches
about 5 mm
use powdered sugar too
Omelette
Or a Japanese-style ingredient?
Perhaps have sorbet?
Pineapple
Lime
Mix gelatin and puree well

Screentone, page 134

A screentone is a patterned sticker sheet that manga artists use to decorate their art. There are hundreds of patterns, with new ones coming out every so often.

Omrice, page 136

Omrice is a Japanese dish that is similar to an omelette. There is stir-fried rice wrapped inside of eggs. The rice inside has chicken and vegetables, and it is flavored with ketchup. After it is wrapped with a sheet of egg, it is topped again with ketchup.

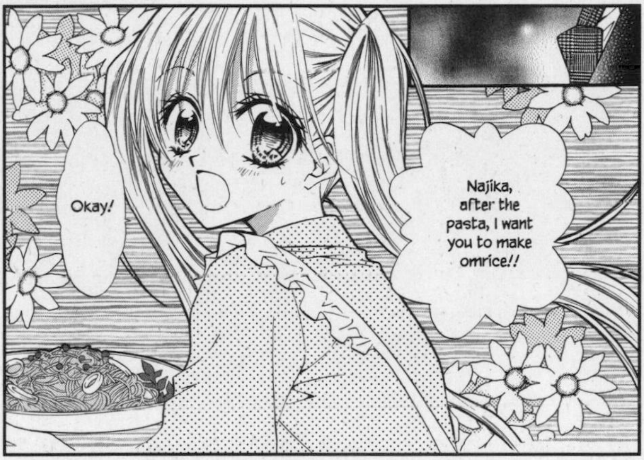
Najika, after the pasta, I want you to make omrice!!
Okay!

Preview of Volume 9

We are pleased to present you a preview from volume 9 of *Kitchen Princess*. Please check our website (www.delreymanga.com) to see when this volume will be available in English. For now you'll have to make do with Japanese!

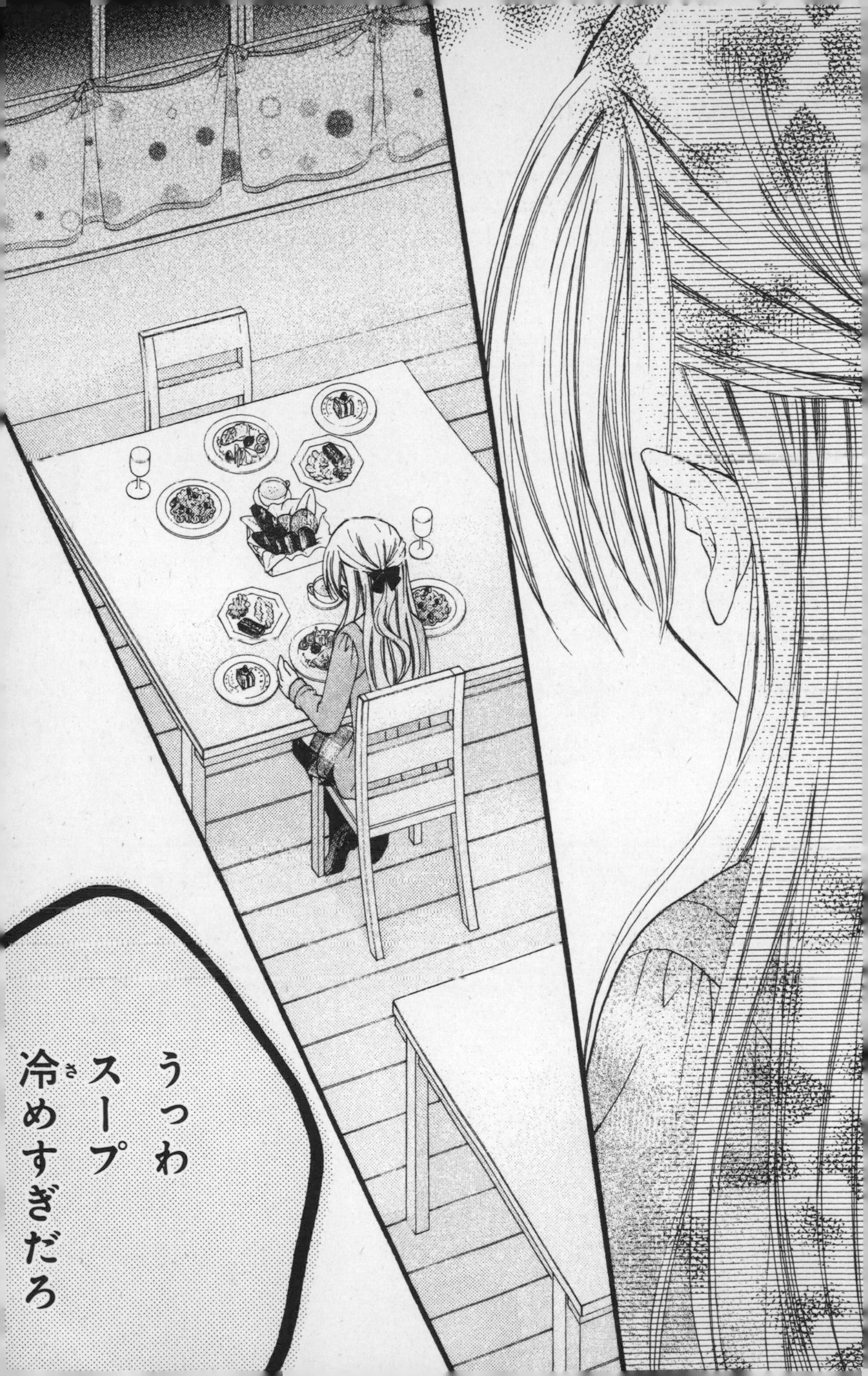
うっわ
スープ
冷(さ)めすぎだろ

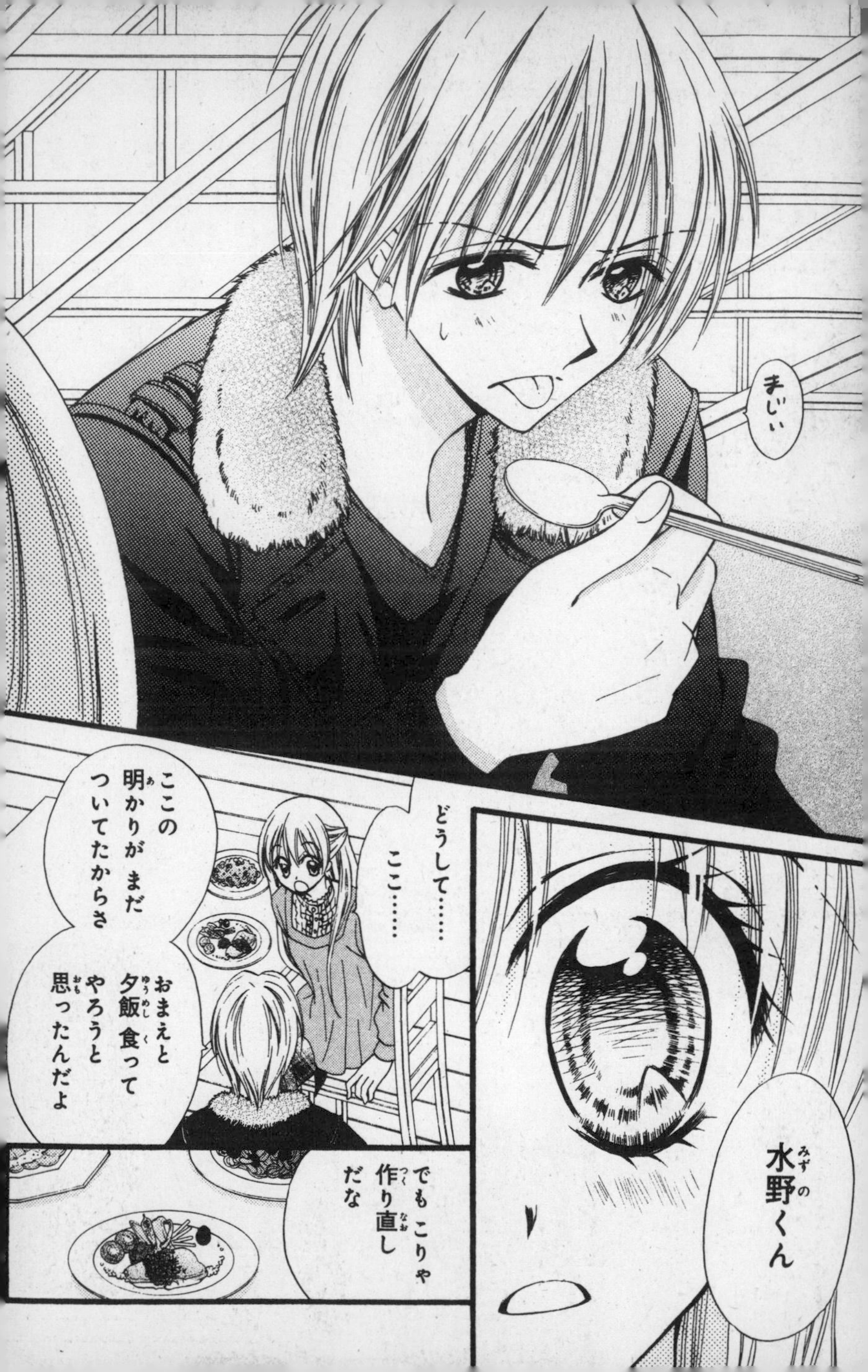
まじぃ
水野くん
どうして ここ……
ここの明かりがまだついてたからさ
おまえと夕飯食ってやろうと思ったんだよ
でもこりゃ作り直しだな

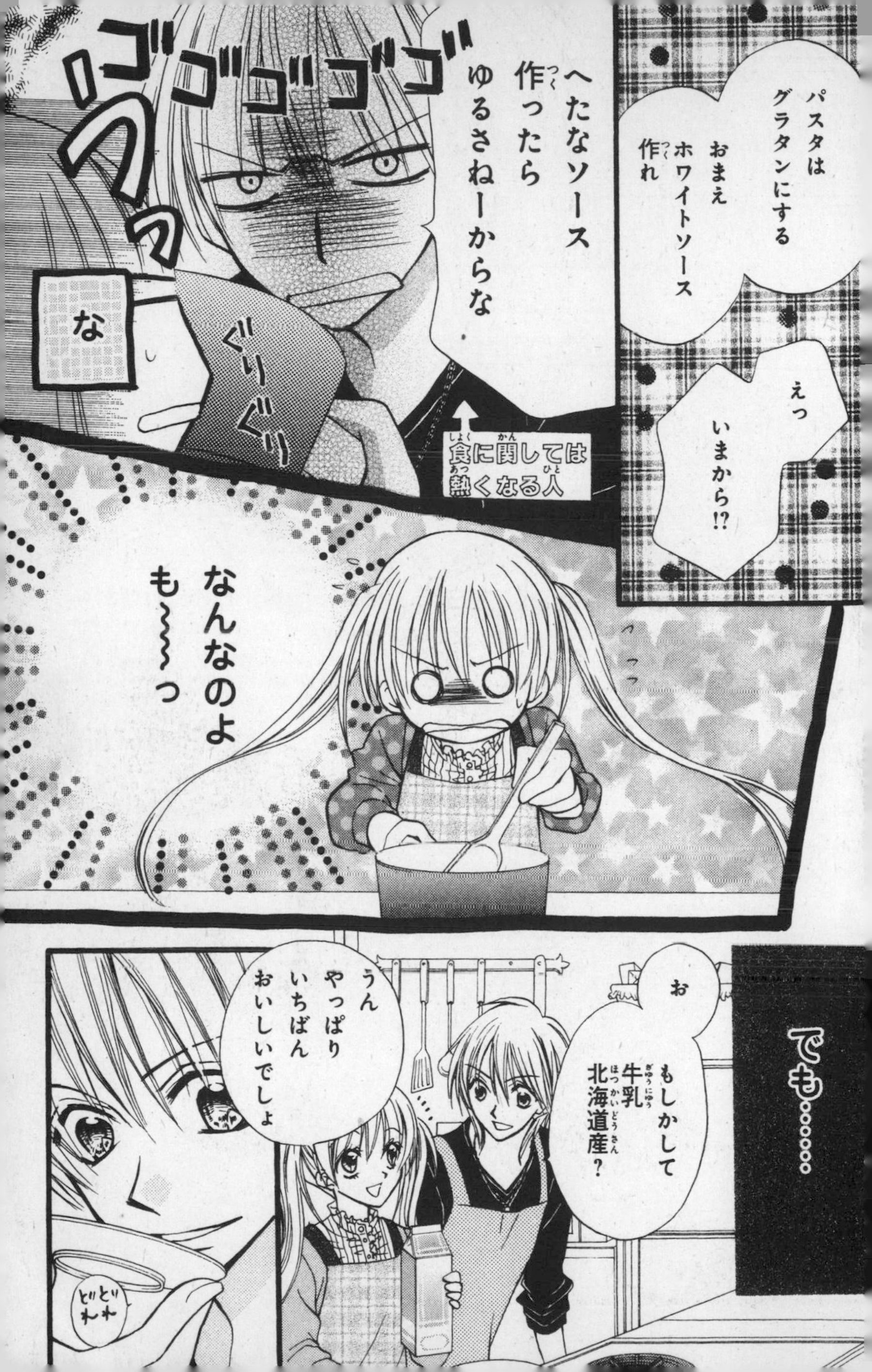
パスタはグラタンにする
おまえホワイトソース作れ
えっ
いまから!?
へたなソース作ったらゆるさねーからな
ゴゴゴゴゴ
うっ
な
ぐりぐり
食に関しては熱くなる人
なんなのよも〜〜〜っ
でも・・・・・・
お
もしかして牛乳北海道産?
うん やっぱりいちばんおいしいでしょ
どれどれ

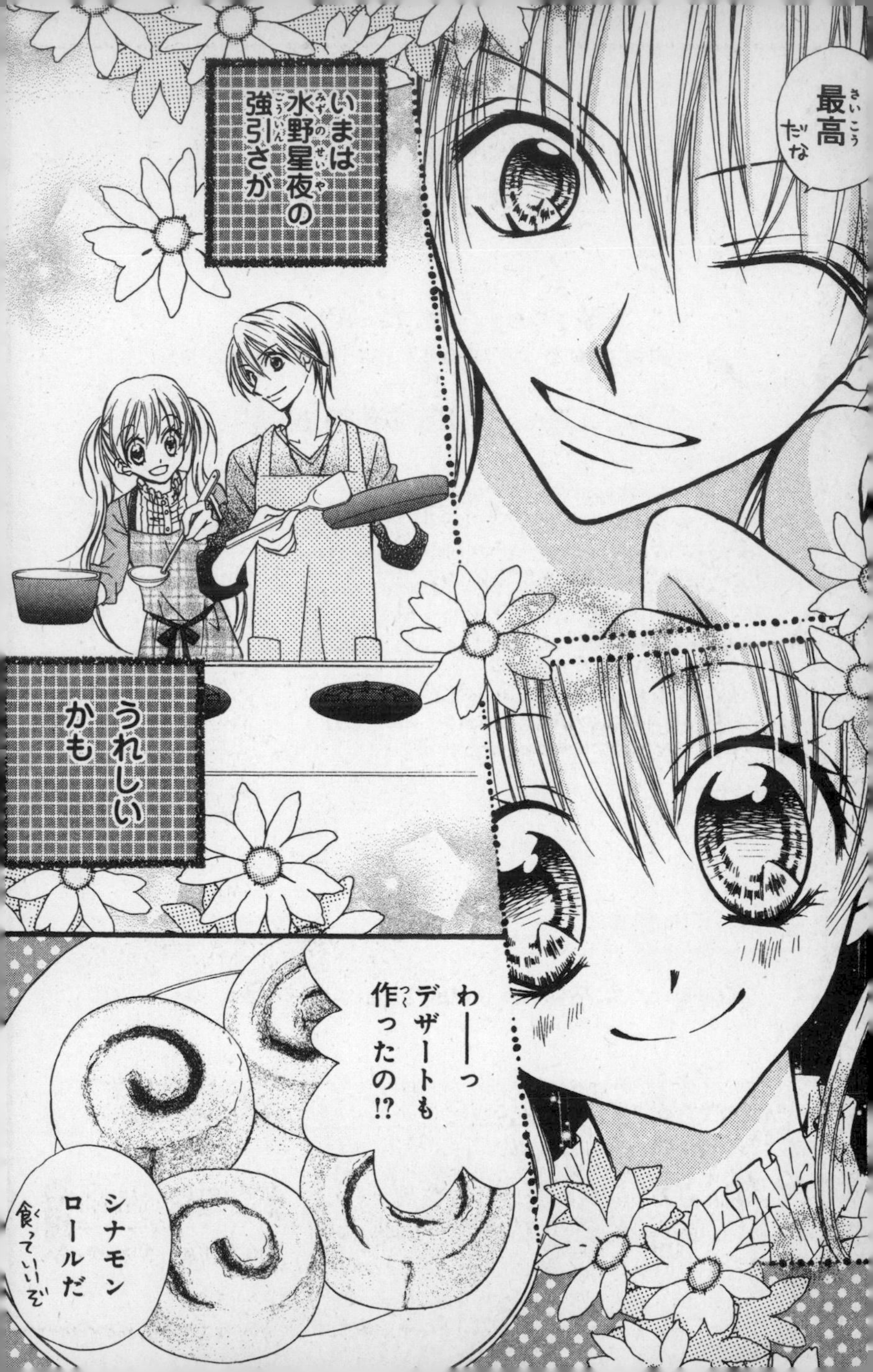

最高だな
いまは水野星夜の強引さが
うれしいかも
わーーっ デザートも作ったの!?
シナモンロールだ 食っていいぞ

KASUMI
かすみ

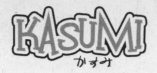

STORY BY SURT LIM
ART BY HIROFUMI SUGIMOTO

A DEL REY MANGA ORIGINAL

Exploring the woods, young Kasumi encounters an ancient tree god, who bestows upon her the power of invisibility. Together with classmates who have had similar experiences, Kasumi forms the Magic Play Club, dedicated to using their powers for good while avoiding sinister forces that would exploit them.

KASUMI
かすみ
volume 1
Story by Surt Lim
Art by Hirofumi Sugimoto

Special extras in each volume! Read them all!

VISIT WWW.DELREYMANGA.COM TO:
- Read sample pages
- View release date calendars for upcoming volumes
- Sign up for Del Rey's free manga e-newsletter
- Find out the latest about new Del Rey Manga series

RATING T AGES 13+

DEL REY MANGA デルレイ
The Otaku's Choice™

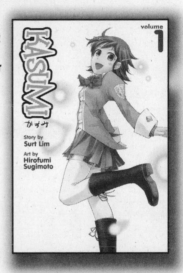

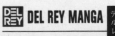

TOMARE!

止まれ

[STOP!]

You're going the wrong way!

Manga is a completely different
type of reading experience.

To start at the *beginning*,
go to the *end*!

That's right! Authentic manga is read the traditional Japanese way—
from right to left. Exactly the *opposite* of how American books are
read. It's easy to follow: Just go to the other end of the book, and read
each page—and each panel—from right side to left side, starting at
the top right. Now you're experiencing manga as it was meant to be!